Books by Walter Piston

HARMONY
COUNTERPOINT
ORCHESTRATION

Harmony

W · W · NORTON & COMPANY

New York · London

Harmony

WALTER PISTON

Fourth Edition

REVISED AND EXPANDED BY

MARK DEVOTO

UNIVERSITY OF NEW HAMPSHIRE

Book Design by Antonina Krass
Layout by Ben Gamit
Text type Linotype Caledonia
Display type Typositor Bauer Bodoni

Music examples engraved by Melvin Wildberger
Type set by Fuller Typesetting of Lancaster
Printing and binding by Haddon Craftsmen

W. W. Norton & Company, Inc., 500 Fifth Avenue, New York, N.Y. 10110

Copyright © 1978, 1962, 1948, 1941 by W. W. Norton & Company, Inc.
Copyright renewed 1969 and 1976 by Walter Piston
Printed in the United States of America.

Fourth Edition

Library of Congress Cataloging in Publication Data

Piston, Walter, 1894–1976.
Harmony.

Includes index.
1. Harmony.   I. DeVoto, Mark.
MT50.P665 1978   781.3   78–2267
7 8 9 0

ISBN 0-393-09034-5

Contents

I
TONAL HARMONY IN COMMON PRACTICE

12. Cadences 184

The Authentic Cadence. Perfect and Imperfect Cadences. The Half Cadence. The Plagal Cadence. The Deceptive Cadence. The Phrygian Cadence. Exceptional Cadential Types.

13. Harmonic Rhythm 199

Definitions. Rhythmic Texture of Music. Melodic Rhythm. Static Harmony. Dissonance and Rhythm. Dynamic Indications. Nonharmonic Chords. Pedals.

14. Modulation 212

Psychological Necessity for Change of Key. Elementary Relationships: Three Stages. Examples of Modulating Phrases. Levels of Tonality: Tonicization and Intermediate Modulation. The Modulation Chain. Related Keys. Interchange of Modes. Exploration of Means. Enharmonic Changes. Abrupt Modulations.

15. The Dominant Seventh Chord 231

Origin of the Harmonic Dissonance. Regular Resolution of the Seventh. Inversions of the Dominant Seventh Chord. The Melodic Tritone.

16. Secondary Dominants 246

Importance and Definition of the Secondary Dominant Function. Resolution. Method of Introduction. Cross-Relation. The Various Secondary Dominant Forms.

17. Irregular Resolutions 261

Definitions of Irregularities. Variety of Chords of Resolution. Irregular Resolutions of the Secondary Dominants.

18. Problems in Harmonic Analysis 275

Purpose of Analysis. Melodic Analysis of Harmony. Extension of the Secondary Dominant Principle: Dual-Function Chords. Violations of Rules of Voice Leading. Harmonic Analysis and Musical Form.

19. The Sequence 294

The Initial Pattern. Harmonic Rhythm. Length of the Sequence. Degree of Transposition. The Nonmodulating Sequence. Secondary Dominants in the Sequence. The Modulating Sequence. Keyboard Practice. The Sequence in Harmonization.

II
AFTER COMMON PRACTICE

Preface to the
Fourth Edition

In the thirty-seven years since its first publication, Walter Piston's *Harmony* has become and remained the most widely-used harmony text in America, and its users now include a third generation. This Fourth Edition, edited and in part written by a second-generation user, is offered as a tribute to the memory of its original author and to the enduring success of the three previous editions.

Piston could well have been content to say his last word about the book in its Third Edition, which was published in 1962, two years after his retirement from teaching. After all, he was first and foremost a composer, and his pen did not retire with him; he was steadily fulfilling commissions even at the age of eighty-two. But in the last year of his life, he was the first to acknowledge the desirability of a further revision, and was willing to interrupt his busy schedule of composing to work on the Fourth Edition.

Piston felt that his years away from the book had put him at a disadvantage; he had not kept up with the evolution of theory teaching since his retirement and had no knowledge of the way his book had been used in the classroom. He was receptive to the publisher's suggestion that he collaborate on the Fourth Edition with someone who had had classroom experience with the Third

Edition. It was thus that I came to work with him on the revision. I had studied composition with Piston during his final year at Harvard, but, more important, I had been trained out of the Second Edition of the book and had used the Third Edition for ten years in my classes at Reed College and the University of New Hampshire. In the course of that decade, I had assembled a detailed list of corrections and suggestions for improvements.

There are many people today who were privileged to have studied with Piston, and who can remember what a revelation and a pleasure his instruction was, and how it continues to shape their musical thinking even years later. When I visited Piston to discuss the book, I was delighted to discover that, although we had only occasionally been in touch during the sixteen years since I had been his pupil, the teacher–student relationship between us had not been impaired by time, and that even as a seasoned harmony instructor I could still learn immensely from him.

Our work together was far from complete at the time of his death in November, 1976. In carrying on alone, I have rewritten the book far more exhaustively than he could have foreseen or approved, to the extent of adding seven new chapters and reworking nearly half of the original material. I could not have done any of this, however, without being sustained by the conviction that I have remained faithful to Piston's central vision. Much of what has been added here, especially in Part II, I received directly from him, some of it in our work in 1976 and some of it from his remarkable seminar on twentieth-century music, of which I kept detailed notes in 1960. I have made a conscious and, I hope, successful effort to integrate my own prose style with Piston's—a difficult enough task when one considers the elegant, economical qualities of his writing, which for the same reasons is no less effective than his music.

Both of us were aware of the need to accommodate changing styles in college-level theory teaching that have become apparent in the past twenty years. The increasing emphasis on the study of melody, line, and level, using the theoretical models of Fux and Schenker, has been felt even in the early stages of theory study, and has resulted in some admirable textbooks. Piston and I both agreed that the melody-linear aspects which formed a considerable part of his book could be strengthened even more; at the same time, we felt that the book should continue to be what it already was, a basic introduction to the principles of harmony. Despite my own experience in teaching the newer methods, I subscribed, as I still do, to Piston's own belief that the essentially vertical approach is still the most valuable introduction to tonal theory for the majority of beginning students. Neither of us questioned the profound pedagogical value of the study of strict counterpoint, no less for its discipline in ear training than for the uncanny enlightenment of tonal music that, through application of Schenker's discoveries, it enables to be revealed; but in our experience such studies are generally too abstract and difficult for most students before the second year. The advantage afforded by the vertical approach still remains the most compelling one: it develops within a relatively short time a set of useful tools for analytical access to a great variety of musical masterworks.

The publisher's request for comments from users of the Third Edition has resulted in a variety of corrections and useful suggestions, and we have incorporated many of them into the new edition. The ordering of the chapters has been slightly changed so as to bring in some basic linear concepts at a somewhat earlier stage than before. The chapter on nonharmonic tones has been much amplified, and a new chapter on melody has been put before it, in the hope that these will prevent the student from falling into the habit of considering harmonic progressions as mere blocklike successions of chords. A separate chapter specifically devoted to the minor mode has been added, so that some of the potentially confusing dissymmetries with the major mode can be more readily understood. For the same reason, the secondary dominant principle is introduced first in Chapter 5, in connection with relative minor and major modes. A new chapter on harmonic analysis (Chapter 18) deals largely with extensions of the secondary dominant principle, incorporating and amplifying Piston's own material from Chapter 26 of the Third Edition. Finally, in response to frequently voiced requests, the scope of the book has been expanded to include tonal harmony in the late nineteenth and early twentieth centuries, covered in the four chapters that constitute Part II.

The Third Edition added seventy-five new examples to those already present in the Second Edition; over three hundred more have been added to this edition, mainly in Part II, while a few have been removed. Although the additions enlarge the book considerably, it was felt that they could only improve it. Like the proverbial picture, one example is worth a thousand words, even when the words are already there, and even though it is in the nature of music that an example may raise as many questions as it resolves. Especially in the earlier chapters, most examples will contain analytical symbols indicating chord types that have not yet been studied by the student. These need not disturb the student's peace of mind if he realizes that sooner or later in the book he will encounter explanations of all these mysterious symbols, which he is free to overlook until the pertinent point arrives. Or, if he is eager and curious, he should read ahead in the book, as Piston often urged his own students to do. To facilitate comparisons among the examples, I have added to this edition several features not present in earlier versions: a separate index of examples, an indication of specific movements where the examples occur, and a thorough system of cross-referencing by means of marginal notes. This last will enable the student to locate instances of a particular phenomenon everywhere in the book, rather than just at the point where the phenomenon is discussed in the text.

The student is encouraged to play all the examples at the piano as well and as frequently as he can, even to the point of memorizing them. For the more complicated examples this will of course not be practical, but we thought it important to strive for accuracy and completeness in the examples, even when this has made some of the orchestral reductions rather detailed. In such cases, students will find it a stimulating classroom exercise to take turns playing examples with four hands at one piano, or even eight hands at two. Outside study of the actual works from which the examples are drawn is also desirable.

The exercises in this book have been given careful consideration. I have relegated many of Piston's longer exercises to Appendix II, replacing them in the chapters with shorter ones of my own. Some of the new exercises differ from the traditional types in that they contain specific suggestions of various kinds, which will make them more comfortable to work out when the more complex chord-types are involved. Another new feature is the group of Special Exercises based on chorales, added to the Supplementary Exercises. These should be taken up not in connection with any particular chapter, but at various times as a parallel activity when the teacher prefers, beginning most likely after Chapter 16 has been studied. As a continuing branch of written study, these Special Exercises can be easily supplemented by comparable exercises devised by the teacher or by the student.

After a year and a half of intense effort, I have ample reason to be grateful to many people who have helped me to complete this book, and I wish to express my thanks to a few of them here. My greatest debt is, of course, to Walter Piston himself. His

guiding spirit in my life as a musician goes far beyond our collaboration on the revision. I have felt his influence at every point in my work on his book, and can only hope that my second-hand skills are equal to what he would have desired.

I am grateful in various ways to several of my colleagues at the University of New Hampshire for valuable discussion and advice. John Rogers, John D. Wicks, Niel Sir, Philip Batstone, and the late Howard Williams have all added to my knowledge. Paul Verrette read the manuscript with great care and made a number of very useful suggestions. In addition, I have profited from the advice and discussion freely given by a number of other workers in the field and would like to single out George Nelson, Wayne Shirley, and Laurence Berman for special thanks.

Victor Yellin most graciously shared with me his work on the omnibus progression (Chapter 28) even before publishing it. He is not to be held to account for my superficial treatment of the omnibus; his own definitive study will probably have appeared by the time this book is ready.

I am ever aware of the role played by my own students in the genesis of this edition. In particular, I wish to thank Elizabeth Robinson, Brian Rolland, and Michael Annicchiarico for reading the revised chapters and making useful comments.

I have benefited profoundly from the advice of Lois Grossman, an amateur musician who is a professor of literature. Her judgement on questions of style has helped me to keep in mind that this book is, after all, for the average music student and not the professional theorist.

The many harmony teachers who responded to the publisher's request for criticisms have added greatly to the improvements in this edition. Most of their suggestions have been employed advantageously and many small errors have been corrected. My thanks and the publisher's are extended to these thoughtful people for their time and concern.

I have been most fortunate in having expert editorial advice at every stage in the preparation of this book. My lasting gratitude goes to Claire Brook and Hinda Keller Farber of W. W. Norton & Company and to Leo Kraft of the City University of New York for their skill, patience, and wisdom.

Mark DeVoto
Durham, New Hampshire
November 1977

Introduction to the
First Edition (1941)

The first important step in the study of harmony is that of clarifying the purpose of such study. Much confusion exists today as to why we study musical theory and what we should expect to learn from it. In the present writer's teaching experience this confusion of outlook furnishes the commonest and most serious obstacle to progress in all branches of musical theory.

There are those who consider that studies in harmony, counterpoint, and fugue are the exclusive province of the intended composer. But if we reflect that theory must follow practice, rarely preceding it except by chance, we must realize that musical theory is not a set of directions for composing music. It is rather the collected and systematized deductions gathered by observing the practice of composers over a long time, and it attempts to set forth what is or has been their common practice. It tells not how music will be written in the future, but how music has been written in the past.

The results of such a definition of the true nature of musical theory are many and important. First of all, it is clear that this knowledge is indispensable to musicians in all fields of the art, whether they be composers, performers, conductors, critics, teachers, or musicologists. Indeed, a secure grounding in theory is even more a necessity to the musical scholar than to the composer, since it forms the basis for any intelligent appraisal of individual styles of the past or present.

On the other hand, the person gifted for creative musical composition is taking a serious risk in assuming that his genius is great enough to get along without a deep knowledge of the common practice of composers. Mastery of the technical or theoretical aspects of music should be carried out by him as a life's work, running parallel to his creative activity but quite separate from it. In the one he is following common practice, while in the other he is responsible solely to the dictates of his own personal tastes and urge for expression.

In the specific field of harmony we must first seek the answer to two questions: what are the harmonic materials commonly used by composers, and how have these materials been used? We cannot afford in the first stages of our study to become interested in the individual composer at the expense of concentration on establishing the norm of common practice. With such a norm firmly in mind, the way will be clear to the investigation of the individual harmonic practices of composers of all periods, and especially to the scientific examination of the divergent practices noticeable in the twentieth century.

Historically, the period in which this common practice may be detected includes roughly the eighteenth and nineteenth centuries. During that time there is surprisingly little change in the harmonic materials used and in the manner of their use. The experimental period of the early twentieth century will appear far less revolutionary when the lines of development from the practice of older composers become clearer by familiarity with the music. As yet, however, one cannot define a twentieth-century common practice.

Hence the aim of this book is to present as concisely as possible the harmonic common practice of composers of the eighteenth and nineteenth centuries. Rules are announced as observations reported, without attempt at their justification on aesthetic grounds or as laws of nature. The written exercises should be performed as exemplifications of the common practice of composers and not as efforts in creative composition. The author believes that through these principles a prompt and logical grasp of the subject will be achieved.

Tonal Harmony in
Common Practice

CHAPTER 1

Scales and Intervals

CHROMATIC AND DIATONIC SCALES

Most music is made up of *tones,* defined as sounds having specific frequencies or pitch. The pitches used in Western music have become standardized over the centuries into the family known as the *chromatic scale.* When considered as a whole, the tones of the chromatic scale are customarily represented in ascending or descending order, as shown by this portion of the chromatic scale beginning on middle C:

EXAMPLE 1–1

distance of one octave

C C♯ D D♯ E F F♯ G G♯ A A♯ B C B B♭ A A♭ G G♭ F E E♭ D D♭ C

Since the middle of the eighteenth century, the standard chromatic scale has been the tempered scale of twelve tones. *Tempered* means that successive tones in the scale differ in frequency by a fixed ratio. If any tone in the chromatic scale is arbitrarily numbered 1, then the thirteenth tone above it in succession will have exactly twice its frequency. Two tones thus differing are said to be an *octave* apart.

1

In the notation commonly used, the tempered scale is divided into octave groupings whose constituent pitches are designated by the ordinary letter-names. In the tempered system there is no audible difference between, for instance, F sharp and G flat; the different symbols arise in our system of notation, which in turn was developed to meet the needs of tonal music, the chief concern of this book.

(The term *note* has historically been used interchangeably with *tone*. Many writers now prefer to reserve the word *tone* to mean an actual sound, and to use *note* to mean a symbol written on music paper as the representation of a sound. In the same way, the word *pitch* may also be employed, as it is here, to mean "a sound having a particular pitch." This book will not always be so fastidious about these distinctions, but it is nevertheless a good idea to be aware of the definitions in use today.)

Tonal music is based on, but not restricted to, the scale of seven pitches called the *diatonic scale*. The major and minor scales are different types of diatonic scale. The seven pitches are called *degrees* of the scale and are customarily numbered with roman numerals I through VII, regardless of key. The scale of a particular key is determined by the pitch of its first degree, the *key-note* or *tonic*. The type of scale is determined by the distribution of half-tone and whole-tone steps above the first degree. In any particular scale, the seven pitches are defined as equivalent to the pitches of the same letter-names, regardless of the octave in which they may be found.

Here are the fundamental diatonic scales having C as the key-note, together with the related A minor scale:

EXAMPLE 1–2

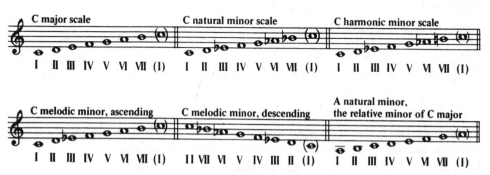

The following example shows representative scales on other key-notes. A knowledge of all the scales on the twelve possible key-notes, together with their appropriate key signatures, will have already been acquired by most readers of this book.

EXAMPLE 1–3

The scale degrees are referred to not only by roman numerals, but by the following names as well:

I. *Tonic* (the key-note)

II. *Supertonic* (the next step above the tonic);

III. *Mediant* (halfway up from tonic to dominant);

IV. *Subdominant* (as far below the tonic as the dominant is above it);

V. *Dominant* (actually a dominant element in the key);

VI. *Submediant* (halfway down from tonic to subdominant);

VII. When the distance from the seventh degree up to the tonic is a half-tone step, this degree is called the *leading-tone*, because of its melodic tendency toward the tonic. When the distance is a whole-tone step, as in the descending melodic minor scale, it is not a leading-tone and is thus called the *minor seventh degree*, though the term *subtonic* has also been used.

Roman-numeral designations and the names just given are also used for triads built on the scale degrees. These will be discussed in the next chapter.

The chromatic scale, which in tonal music originates in the semitonal alteration of the diatonic scale degrees, is most conveniently considered as an expansion of the other scales. The appropriate notation of this scale (for instance, whether one should write A sharp or B flat) is determined by melodic and harmonic circumstances to be considered later.

The different usages of the minor scales will also be the subject of extensive treatment in this book. For the present, it will be sufficient to recognize that it is the natural minor scale that determines the key signature.

3

The term *interval* refers to the scalar distance between the two
tones, measured by their difference in pitch, although it is more
accurately used to describe the sonority resulting from the simultaneous sounding of two tones. If the two tones are not heard at
the same time, but are consecutive tones of one melodic line, the
interval is called a *melodic interval,* as distinguished from the
harmonic interval, in which the two tones are sounded together.

EXAMPLE 1–4

harmonic interval   melodic interval

The general name of an interval is found by counting the lines
and spaces included by the two notes.

EXAMPLE 1–5

unison   second   third   fourth   fifth   sixth   seventh   octave   ninth

The specific name of an interval (the kind of 3rd, 7th, etc.)
may be found by various methods, a simple one being to compare
the interval to a major scale constructed upon the lower of the
two notes as a tonic. If the upper note coincides with a note of
the scale, the interval is *major,* except in the case of octaves, fifths,
fourths, and unisons, for which the term *perfect* is used.

EXAMPLE 1–6

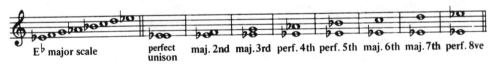

Eᵇ major scale   perfect   maj. 2nd maj.3rd perf. 4th perf. 5th maj. 6th maj.7th perf. 8ve
                        unison

If the upper note does not coincide with a note of the scale, the
following considerations are to be applied:

    a. A major interval made a half tone smaller, by chromatically
       lowering its upper note or raising its lower note, becomes
       minor. Conversely, a minor interval made chromatically a
       half tone larger becomes *major.*

    b. A major interval, or a perfect interval, made chromatically
       a half tone larger becomes *augmented.*

    c. A minor interval, or a perfect interval, made chromatically
       a half tone smaller becomes *diminished.*

4

EXAMPLE 1–7

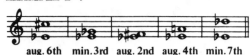

aug. 6th   min. 3rd   aug. 2nd   aug. 4th   min. 7th

In the example above, consider the interval of a sixth, E flat to C sharp. If the C had been natural it would have fallen in the scale of E-flat major and the interval would have been a major sixth. The sharp, by raising the top note, has the effect of making a major interval a half tone larger. Therefore, statement *b* in the paragraph above is applied, and the interval is called an "augmented sixth."

When the lower note is preceded by a sharp or flat, the interval may be analyzed first without the sharp or flat, and the result compared with the original interval by reference to the rules above. For example, suppose the interval to be from D sharp up to C. The scale of D-sharp major, with nine sharps, is not convenient as a measuring device. Taking the scale of D major, we find that C is half tone short of the seventh degree. The interval D to C is therefore a minor seventh. The restoration of the sharp to the D makes the interval a half tone smaller, by raising the lower note; hence it is a diminished seventh.

The major second and the minor second are identical with the whole-tone step and half-tone step respectively, and thus correspond to the two ordinary types of scale-degree contiguities. The names *whole step* and *half step* (or *semitone*) are also in common use.

It is also sometimes convenient to classify intervals by their semitone measurement, that is, using the chromatic scale as the measuring device. This measurement, which does not take into account enharmonic differences (see below, page 8), is especially useful in discussing atonal music, but has little application in tonal music. The semitonal classification of intervals is given in the table below.

ORDINARY INTERVAL-TYPE OR ENHARMONIC EQUIVALENT	SEMITONAL INTERVAL
Unison or dim. 2nd	0
Min. 2nd, aug. unison	1
Maj. 2nd, dim. 3rd	2
Min. 3rd, aug. 2nd	3
Maj. 3rd, dim. 4th	4
Perf. 4th, aug. 3rd	5

Aug. 4th, dim. 5th (*tritone*)	6
Perf. 5th, dim. 6th	7
Min. 6th, aug. 5th	8
Maj. 6th, dim. 7th	9
Min. 7th, aug. 6th	10
Maj. 7th, dim. octave	11
Perf. octave, aug. 7th	12

The student is urged to perfect himself, by exercises in dictation or other processes of ear training, in the ability to recognize the intervals by ear when they are played or sung, and to hear mentally intervals written or printed.

COMPOUND INTERVALS

An interval greater than an octave may be reckoned by subtracting the octave. (The interval number is obtained by subtracting 7, e.g., 7 subtracted from a twelfth leaves a fifth.) Such intervals are called *compound intervals*. Some of these, however, the ninth, for example, are characteristic features of certain chord structures and are usually called by the larger number.

EXAMPLE 1–8

perf. 5th   maj. 9th   min. 3rd   maj. 3rd (10th)

CONSONANT AND DISSONANT INTERVALS

A *consonant interval* is one which sounds stable and complete, whereas the characteristic of the *dissonant interval* is its restlessness and its need for resolution into a consonant interval. These qualities are admittedly open to subjective, personal, and evolutionary interpretation, but it is clear that in the common practice of composers the following classification holds true:

Consonant: the perfect intervals and the major and minor thirds and sixths;

Dissonant: the augmented and diminished intervals and the major and minor seconds, sevenths, and ninths;

Exception: the perfect fourth is dissonant when there is no tone below its lower tone. It is consonant when there is a third or perfect fifth below it.

EXAMPLE 1–9

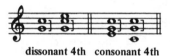

dissonant 4th consonant 4th

The major and minor thirds and sixths are frequently set apart from the perfect intervals and termed *imperfect consonances*. This distinction has little significance for the harmonic style of the eighteenth and nineteenth centuries. Only the sixth, when in certain tonal relationships with the bass, seems to lack the stability of the perfect consonances and to need resolution to the fifth.

EXAMPLE 1–10

Music without dissonant intervals is often lifeless and negative, since it is the dissonant element which furnishes much of the sense of movement and rhythmic energy. The history of musical style has been largely occupied with the important subject of dissonance and its treatment by composers. It cannot be too strongly emphasized that the essential quality of dissonance is its sense of movement and not, as is sometimes erroneously assumed, its degree of unpleasantness to the ear.

HARMONIC INVERSION

The term *inversion* is applied to a variety of procedures in music. In harmonic inversion of intervals equal to or smaller than a perfect octave, the lower pitch is moved up an octave, or the upper pitch is moved down an octave, thus:

EXAMPLE 1–11

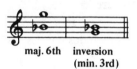

maj. 6th   inversion
(min. 3rd)

7

Under the operation of inversion:

Unisons become octaves, and vice versa;
Seconds become sevenths, and vice versa;
Thirds become sixths, and vice versa;
Fourths become fifths, and vice versa;
Major intervals become minor, and vice versa;
Augmented intervals become diminished, and vice versa;
Perfect intervals remain perfect.

The term *complementation,* borrowed from geometry, has also been applied to the procedure. A major sixth and a minor third are thus said to be complementary intervals, or simply complements.

ENHARMONIC INTERVALS

In our tempered scale system it often happens that two or more intervals sound alike when played on the piano, even though they are widely different in their meaning. A good example is the augmented second, which cannot be distinguished from the minor third without further evidence than the sound of the two tones. One interval is called the *enharmonic equivalent* of the other.

EXAMPLE 1–12

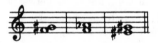

When these intervals are heard in their harmonic context, however, their difference becomes clearly audible.

EXAMPLE 1–13

Notes which are enharmonically equivalent are said to belong to the same pitch-class, as are pitches which are related as perfect octaves. The pitch-class C, for instance, includes all Cs, B sharps, and D double-flats.

8

THE CIRCLE OF FIFTHS

*See also
Appendix I*

The relationship of keys in the familiar circle of fifths is one of the bases of our notational system. The circle of fifths is arranged clockwise by successive ascending dominants, and counterclockwise by successive descending subdominants. Adjacent keys in the clockwise direction differ by the addition of a sharp or the subtraction of a flat, the note affected being the fourth degree of the old scale or the seventh degree of the new scale; in the counterclockwise direction, adjacent keys differ by the subtraction of a sharp or the addition of a flat, the note affected being the seventh degree of the old scale or the fourth degree of the new scale. Keys near each other along the circle are said to be closely related, such as A major and E major or D major; those far apart are distantly related, such as A major and E-flat major or B-flat major.

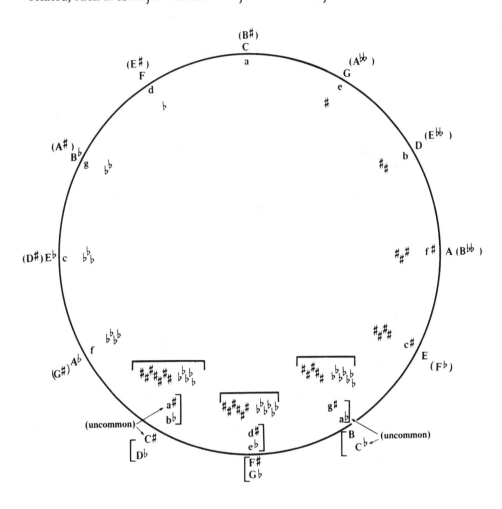

In the diagram, major keys are listed in capital letters outside the circle, their corresponding relative minors in lower-case letters inside; the associated key signature, of course, applies to both. Enharmonically equivalent keys are shown coupled together with square brackets. Key designations in parentheses are also enharmonic equivalents which are sometimes encountered; such instances are notated only by direct use of accidental signs, never with double sharps or double flats in the key signature.

EXAMPLE 1–14: Chopin, *Piano Concerto in E minor*, II

D♯ major (equivalent of ⁀)

E♭ major

EXERCISES

The exercises offered in this book are intended as specimens or suggestions for further exercises to be invented by the teacher or by the student himself. They do not pretend to supply adequate practice or training. It goes without saying that the material in each chapter must be thoroughly assimilated before proceeding to the next. The exercises must be multiplied until that end is achieved.

1. Name the following intervals:

2. With F sharp as the lower tone, construct these intervals: min. 3rd; aug. 6th; dim. 5th; perf. 4th; aug. 2nd; maj. 7th; min. 9th; aug. 5th.

3. With D flat as the upper tone, construct these intervals: dim. 5th; maj. 9th; dim. 7th; min. 2nd; aug. 4th; perf. 5th; min. 6th; dim. 3rd.

4. Write enharmonic equivalents of the intervals in Ex. 3.

5. From what scales may the following fragments have been taken?

6. Construct a major scale in which C sharp is the sixth degree.

7. Construct a descending melodic minor scale with D as the tonic.

8. Name the interval from supertonic up to submediant in the harmonic minor scale.

9. Write and name the dissonant intervals which may be formed between the tonic and other tones of the scale of E major.

10. Write and name the consonant intervals which may be formed between the third degree and other tones of the natural minor scale of B flat.

Supplementary exercises for this chapter and for the succeeding chapters will be found at the conclusion of the text, commencing on page 544.

CHAPTER 2

Triads

CHORD FACTORS

The combination of two or more harmonic intervals makes a *chord*. The simplest chord is the *triad,* a chord of three tones obtained by superposition of two thirds. The triad may be said to be the basis of our harmonic system, a place it still holds despite numerous radical developments in tonal music.

The names *root, third,* and *fifth* are given to the three factors of the triad. These terms are retained to identify the factors of the triad in whatever order they may be arranged.

EXAMPLE 2–1

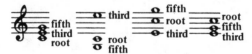

INVERSIONS

A triad with its root as its lowest tone is said to be in *root position.*

A triad with its third as its lowest tone is said to be in the *first inversion.*

A triad with its fifth as its lowest tone is said to be in the *second inversion.*

EXAMPLE 2-2 · · · TRIADS

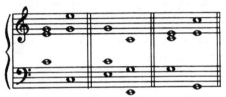

root position   first inversion   second inversion

Taking the major scale of the tonic C, and using only the notes of this scale, superposition of thirds gives the following triads:

EXAMPLE 2-3

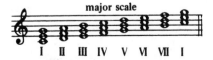

major scale

I   II   III   IV   V   VI   VII   I

Triads of the minor scales will be considered in Chapter 4.

KINDS OF TRIADS

The triads formed on a given scale differ not only in pitch, but also, depending on the intervals in their makeup, in the quality of their sound. There are four kinds of triads, classified according to the nature of the intervals formed between the root and the other two tones.

A *major triad* is composed of major third and perfect fifth.

A *minor triad* is composed of minor third and perfect fifth.

An *augmented triad* is composed of major third and augmented fifth.

A *diminished triad* is composed of minor third and diminished fifth.

The student should learn by practice to distinguish by ear the four types of triads.

EXAMPLE 2-4

maj.   min.   aug.   dim.

The major and minor triads are consonant chords because they contain only consonant intervals. The diminished and augmented   13 triads, on the other hand, are dissonant because of the presence of the dissonant intervals, diminished fifth and augmented fifth.

Roman numerals identify not only the scale degree, but also the chord constructed upon that scale degree as a root, whether the chord is in root position or in an inversion.

EXAMPLE 2–5

C: V   V   II   II   IV   IV

In the major mode, three triads are major—I, IV, and V; three are minor—II, III, and VI; and one is diminished—VII. A useful convention of harmonic analysis is to write the Roman numerals of major and augmented triads in capital letters, and those of minor and diminished triads in lower case. (Some writers prefer in addition to add the superscript symbols $+$ and $°$, to indicate augmented and diminished, respectively, but we will have other uses for these symbols in this book and will not follow that practice.)

Most music of the eighteenth and nineteenth centuries is conceived on a harmonic basis of four-part writing. This means vertically four tones in each chord, and horizontally four different melodic parts. The three-part writing often observed in the classics frequently suggests four parts, whereas larger numbers of apparent parts, as for instance in an orchestral score, are usually the result of the duplication of one or more parts in a basically four-part texture.

The study of harmony is concerned with the principles underlying the construction of this common basis of four-part writing. The exercises are ordinarily worked out in four parts or voices. The term *voices* does not necessarily mean that the parts are to be sung. It does suggest, however, that the separate parts proceed with a certain ideal vocal quality which is possessed by all good melodic music, whether intended for human voices or for instruments.

In order to define these four voices, we shall follow the usual custom of naming them for the four classes of singing voices—soprano, alto, tenor, and bass—somewhat arbitrarily restricting their ranges to an approximation of the ranges of human voices.

14

EXAMPLE 2–6

soprano   alto   tenor   bass

There is no harm in exceeding these limits occasionally, as long as the balance or "center of gravity" of each voice remains well within its normal range, and extreme notes are sparingly employed.

DOUBLING

Since the triad contains but three constituent tones (factors), it is evident that another is needed for four-part harmony. With triads in root position, the fourth tone is customarily a duplication of the root an octave or two higher, or even at the unison. This duplication is called *doubling*.

THE LEADING-TONE TRIAD

Though of common occurrence in the first or second inversion, the triad on the leading-tone is rarely found in root position and will be omitted from the earliest chapters of this book. It contains a dissonant interval, a diminished fifth, the lower tone of which is the leading-tone itself, with its strong tendency toward the tonic. In later chapters, we will learn how the leading-tone triad substitutes for the dominant triad or dominant seventh chord.

Whatever the position of the leading-tone triad, doubling of its root is avoided. Doubling of the leading-tone as the third of V is likewise avoided; occasionally, however, one finds the doubled leading-tone as the fifth of III.

SPACING

One rarely hears music that is purely harmonic, in which the vertical effect is free from modifications due to horizontal, or melodic, influences. The principles of voice leading always take precedence   15 over considerations of the chord as such, since chords themselves have their origin in the coincidence of melodic movement. At the same time, the harmonic sense demands an arrangement of the vertical sonority which will give clarity and balance, and even on occasion such subjective qualities as beauty, brilliance, or somberness.

The commonest arrangement of a chord places the wider intervals at the bottom, with the smaller intervals at the top. This bears a resemblance, as has often been pointed out, to the distribution of overtones in the harmonic series, but it must be admitted that the parallel between the usage of composers and the "chord of nature" stops there. Compare, for instance, a triad in first inversion with the series of overtones generated by its lowest tone.

Overtones: see Appendix I

EXAMPLE 2–7

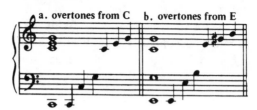

In four-part texture, intervals wider than the octave are usually avoided between soprano and alto, and between alto and tenor, but are considered quite satisfactory between tenor and bass.

EXAMPLE 2–8

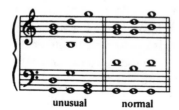

CLOSE AND OPEN POSITION

When the three upper voices are as close together as possible, the spacing is described as *close position.* Otherwise the chord is in *open position,* provided all three factors are present. It will be noticed that in close position the three upper voices are all within the range of a single octave, whereas in open position there is a distance of more than an octave between soprano and tenor. In arranging a root-position triad in close position, having a given soprano note, the alto will take the next immediately available chord note below the soprano. If open position is desired, the alto will not take this first available note, but will take the next below. The tenor will fall into place with the only note left, as the bass will of course take the root, in whatever octave is convenient.

EXAMPLE 2–9

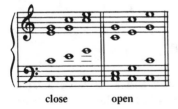

close   open

Close and open position are of equally common use. The choice of one or the other is subject to various conditions, among which melodic progress of the parts is perhaps the most important. Another is the question of ranges. If the soprano voice is in a high register, for example, close position may result in placing the other voices too high. The ideal of balance in a single chord would. be to have all voices in corresponding registers—all high, all medium, or all low—but this achievement is seldom possible, because of melodic direction and other influential considerations.

One should listen carefully to the relative effect of various spacings of the same chord and notice the kind of spacing used in music heard. The intervals between the voices are an important factor in the texture and actual sound of the music. In the common-practice period of harmonic usage this has been largely a matter of effective distribution of given chord tones, but, with the twentieth century, composers have become much more preoccupied with specific intervals and their combination into individual sonorities.

NOTATION

In writing exercises in four parts, the student should use the conventional four-part choral layout on two staves such as is found in hymn books and Bach's 371 chorale harmonizations. The soprano and alto are always on the upper staff; the tenor and bass, on the lower. The soprano and tenor stems always point up; the alto and bass stems, down.

A different convention is sometimes to be seen in older harmony treatises, with soprano, alto, and tenor together on the upper staff, often sharing a single stem per chord. This arrangement makes it more difficult to examine the motion of the individual voices, particularly when these do not all move together. The three-on-one arrangement is, however, useful in keyboard exercises, particularly in the realization of figured bass, when the upper three parts will be taken by the right hand.

EXERCISES

1. The teacher will play a major scale and afterwards a triad derived from that scale. The student will tell the kind of triad and the scale degree which is its root.

One cannot overestimate the value of this type of ear-training exercise. Facility can be gained only through regular practice, with the aid of another person to do the playing. The most satisfactory and feasible method is to get together a small group of students and let each take a turn at the piano.

2. Identify the following triads as to kind (major, minor, or diminished), and indicate by roman numerals and key their possible derivations as to major scale and degree. (For example, the first triad given is major, IV of B major, or I or E major; etc.)

3. Write three different spacings in a standard four-voice arrangement of each of the following triads. Use root position only, doubling the root.

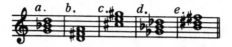

4. Write in four parts, in both close and open position, the following triads, using root position with the root doubled:

   a. IV in B-flat major
   b. V in C-sharp major
   c. VI in E major
   d. III in D major
   e. II in F major

f. IV in A major

g. I in E-flat minor

h. VI in E major

i. VII in G major

j. II in A-flat major

5. By the use of accidentals only (sharps, flats, or naturals), write each of the following triads in three additional ways, altering them so as to illustrate in each case the four types—major, minor, augmented, and diminished:

CHAPTER 3

Harmonic Progression in the Major Mode: Rules of Voice Leading

H*armonic progression* is one of the principal resources of co-herence in tonal music. The term implies not just that one chord is followed by another, but that the succession is controlled and orderly. The common practice of composers has added some definition to these implications: certain harmonic successions are more commonly utilized than others, and the ways in which the successive harmonies are connected are ordinarily restricted to certain procedures.

Although the two questions are in a sense inseparable, the matter of succession can be regarded as independent of the forms of the chords themselves. As more of these forms are studied, it will become more apparent that the individual sonority of the two chords is of less importance than the relation of the two roots to each other and to the scale from which they are drawn. Chords are identified primarily by their situation in the tonality or, in other words, by the scale degree serving as root. Hence, chord succession can be reduced to root succession (or root progression), which in turn can be translated into roman numerals representing a succession of scale degrees. The variety of chords built upon these roots cannot alter this relationship, and no change in the makeup of the chords can remedy an inappropriate root progression. These principles lie at the foundation of the theory of harmonic structure.

TABLE OF USUAL ROOT PROGRESSIONS

The following generalizations are based on observation of usage, with no attempt at justification by suggesting reasons of an acoustical nature (although such physical hypotheses have from time to time been devised). They are not proposed as a set of strict rules to be rigidly adhered to.

> I is followed by IV or V, sometimes VI, less often II or III.
> II is followed by V, sometimes IV or VI, less often I or III.
> III is followed by VI, sometimes IV, less often I, II, or V.
> IV is followed by V, sometimes I or II, less often III or VI.
> V is followed by I, sometimes IV or VI, less often II or III.
> VI is followed by II or V, sometimes III or IV, less often I.
> VII is followed by III, sometimes I.

It is important to form an appreciation of the qualities of these progressions, qualities which do not readily lend themselves to description by words. As a first step in comparing root progressions, one can place them into three categories:

> a. Root motion by a fourth or fifth;
> b. Root motion by a third (or sixth);
> c. Root motion by a step (or seventh).

Triads with roots a fourth or fifth apart will have one note in common. By far the most important such relationship is the V–I progression, which is generally considered the strongest harmonic relationship in tonal music. One can easily sense the strength of this progression by playing the bass alone.

EXAMPLE 3–1

Other progressions with root moving down a fifth (or up a fourth) seem to have an analogous effect, although in less marked degree.

21

EXAMPLE 3–2

Root movement down a fourth (or up a fifth) gives the reverse of those above. Comparison shows the effect to be distinctly different. The IV–I progression is the most important of these; it has the effect of acting as a contrast, or counterbalance, to the V–I relationship.

EXAMPLE 3–3

Triads with roots a third apart will have two notes in common; in other words, they will differ by only a single note. Such progressions are considered weak, because they involve such relatively slight change in the makeup of their notes. In the major mode, a root progression of a third will mean a change from a major triad to a minor, or vice versa. When the root moves up a third, the root of the second chord has just been heard as the third of the first chord; when the root descends a third, the root of the second chord comes as a new note.

EXAMPLE 3–4

When the root proceeds by step, the second chord will consist of a completely new set of notes, and hence will have the effect of introducing a new harmonic color. Stepwise root progressions are considered strong, although not equally; IV–V, for example, is frequently encountered, whereas II–I is relatively rare in root position.

EXAMPLE 3–5

MAJOR
MODE

Root motion by seventh can ordinarily be considered as root motion by the complementary interval, the step, in the opposite direction; likewise, root motion by a sixth is comparable to root motion by a third. Intervals wider than a fifth are not often used in root-position root successions, except the octave, which is sometimes used to help obtain a new spacing.

The above comparative description of root motions should not be considered as either prescriptive or exhaustive. Nor should "weak" progressions be equated with "undesirable," because they form an important resource of contrast.

The differences between all these progressions are best appreciated by repeated listening, by trying them out in variety of spacings, and, later in this book, by incorporating them in different combinations into the exercises. We will next consider them in Chapter 6.

CONNECTION OF CHORDS:
TWO RULES OF THUMB

The smooth connection of chords is more than anything else a linear or melodic process, in which the structure of chords as simultaneously-sounding different horizontal parts must continually be appreciated. Even the most obviously homophonic music of the common-practice era shows that composers were always attentive to linear considerations, and it is not too much to say that the balance between vertical and horizontal aspects is the most strikingly constant characteristic of the period.

Our study of the connection of chords will necessarily begin in a reductive and rudimentary way, using root-position triads in four parts moving note against note. The restrictiveness of these conditions is likely to be considered frustrating at first, and the results of their application only remotely related to actual music. What is important to remember, however, is that different kinds 23 of music apply these principles broadly in different ways. The limitations of the early harmony exercises are designed to provide intensive exposure to essential principles of part writing. If the rest of this chapter seems to be forbiddingly hedged with rules and prohibitions, the student may take comfort that nowhere else in this book will nearly so many of these be found. Above all, he should remember, both in his original exercises and in his analyses of masterworks, that music is the result of composition, not of the application of rules.

The following Rules of Thumb describe the simplest procedures to follow in connecting two triads in root position. What is particularly sought is contiguity, or smoothness of linear movement from chord to chord. For this reason, augmented and diminished intervals, and any intervals wider than a sixth (the octave sometimes excepted), are generally avoided in melodic progression as being somewhat awkward.

Rule of Thumb 1. If the two triads have one or more notes in common, these are usually repeated in the same voice, the remaining voice or voices moving to the nearest available position.

EXAMPLE 3–6

C: I   V

In the example, G is a common tone of both triads, so it is repeated in the same voice, the alto. The other two voices move to the nearest position available—C down to B, E to D. (The notes of the second chord are G, B, D, G. The two Gs have been used, one by the bass since that is the root, and the other by the repeated alto. Therefore, B and D are the only available tones.) If C had gone to D, E would have been forced to take B, the only note left, and this would not have been to the nearest position.

Exception: In the progression II–V, when the fourth degree is in the soprano of II, it is customary not to repeat the common tone, but to move the three upper voices down to the next available position. (This exception does not apply if the fourth degree is in the alto or tenor.)

24

EXAMPLE 3–7

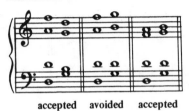

accepted   avoided   accepted

Rule of Thumb 2. If the two triads have no tones in common, the upper three voices proceed in opposite direction to the bass, always to the nearest available position.

EXAMPLE 3–8

IV V   II III   III IV

Exception: In the progression V–VI, the leading-tone moves up one degree to the tonic, while the other two voices descend to the nearest position in the chord, doubling the third, instead of the root, in the triad on VI. This exception always holds true when the leading-tone is in the soprano of V; when it is in an inner voice, Rule of Thumb 2 may sometimes apply.

EXAMPLE 3–9

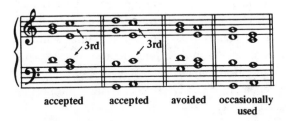

accepted   accepted   avoided   occasionally
                                    used

If the Rules of Thumb are followed strictly, the connection be-tween the chords will be correct according to the practice of voice leading in harmonic progression. The purpose of this procedure is to ensure the smoothest possible connection of two chords, so that one seems to flow into the next. Continued application of the process, however, will result in rather dull music.

EXAMPLE 3–10

The example above is in close position. Application of the Rules of Thumb to the same root succession, but beginning in open position, yields no less dull results.

EXAMPLE 3–11

Comparison of the two versions shows that the voice leading is identical in both; the soprano and alto of the second version are in fact a mere harmonic inversion of the same voices in the first version.

The above solutions, which are correct but hardly more than that, are a good demonstration of both the usefulness and the limitations of the Rules of Thumb. One should therefore try to discover what additional musical interest may be gained by departing from the Rules of Thumb from time to time. In such departures, the first place to consider is the soprano line, which is instinctively heard as a melody and so must receive more care in its construction than the inside voices.

When the root is repeated, it is advisable to change the position of the other voices, for variety.

EXAMPLE 3–12

A change from open to close position, or vice versa, whether the roots are different or not, is often a good way to obtain a new soprano note.

EXAMPLE 3-13

I   VI

The occasional use of a triad without fifth, usually composed of three roots and one third, may help to free the soprano line. It is not advisable to omit the third, as that leaves the empty sound of the open fifth.

EXAMPLE 3-14

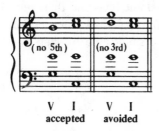

V   I   V   I
accepted   avoided

Doubling of the third or fifth instead of the root is another means of making more notes available for the soprano part. A chord composed of root, fifth, and doubled third is generally preferred to one of doubled root and doubled third. The leading-tone should not be doubled when it is the third of V; it may be doubled when it is the fifth of III.

EXAMPLE 3-15

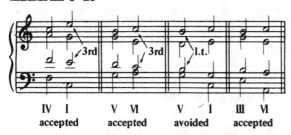

IV   I   V   VI   V   I   III   VI
accepted   accepted   avoided   accepted

Rhythmic division of some notes of the soprano into smaller time values is a frequent resource in the making of a melody, as is like-   27 wise the tying over of possible repeated notes to make notes of larger time values. The student is advised to use this device sparingly at first, in order to gain experience in the vertical arrangement of the chords before adding rhythmic complications.

EXAMPLE 3–16

I   VI   IV   V   I   V

All of these suggested departures from the Rules of Thumb entail the risk of violating one or more of the Rules of Motion, to be discussed in the next section of this chapter.

As by various means the voices are given more freedom of movement, attention must be given to the ways in which they may move, both as regards their individual melodic lines and their relative melodic progression. The terms *conjunct* and *disjunct* motion are used to describe the movement of a single line by step and by skip respectively.

EXAMPLE 3–17

conjunct   disjunct

A good melodic line contains mostly conjunct motion, with the disjunct motion used judiciously for variety. Too many skips make for angularity, rather than for the desired flowing quality. It will be noticed that the bass is likely to contain more skips than the other parts, while the alto and tenor as a rule have few, if any, large disjunct intervals. In using only triads in root position, the bass will necessarily be more disjunct than is ordinarily desirable.

More will be said on the subject of melody in Chapter 7.

RULES OF MOTION

Unlike the Rules of Thumb, which are general guidelines, the rules of this section are more or less rigorous, not to be departed from except in certain special circumstances.

Two voices may move relatively in three ways: in contrary motion, in oblique motion, or in similar motion.

In *contrary motion*, the voices move in opposite directions:

EXAMPLE 3–18

In *oblique motion*, one voice remains stationary while the other moves:

EXAMPLE 3–19

In *similar motion*, both voices move in the same direction:

EXAMPLE 3–20

In similar motion, if the two voices keep the same distance apart, they are said to be in *parallel motion*. (A major third followed by a minor third is still a succession of parallel thirds, even though the thirds are unequal in size.)

EXAMPLE 3–21

parallel sixths

Two voices moving in parallel motion are melodically less independent than otherwise, and may be looked upon as a single voice with duplication. Parallel intervals of the unison, octave, and perfect fifth have been systematically avoided by composers of the eighteenth and nineteenth centuries, whenever it has been their intention to write a texture of independent voices. This prohibition originally stems from the contrapuntal practice of the fifteenth century.

29

EXAMPLE 3–22: Avoided Parallels

unisons   octaves   perfect fifths

Parallel perfect fifths and octaves are avoided between all pairs of voices, but are considered especially objectionable between soprano and bass. Nonparallel consecutive motions such as fifth to twelfth, unison to octave, and vice versa, are also generally avoided.

EXAMPLE 3–23

Parallel thirds and sixths are common. Parallel fourths are used if supported by parallel thirds below.

EXAMPLE 3–24

See Ex. 6–11

avoided   accepted

Parallel dissonant intervals occur in certain circumstances arising from the use of contrapuntal nonharmonic tones and irregular resolutions of dissonant chords.

The relative motion of the voices is planned to preserve their independence as separate parts. The maximum of independence is furnished by contrary motion, but it is obviously not possible for four parts to move in four different directions. Oblique motion is useful to contrast a moving voice with one that is standing still. In similar motion care must be taken that the movement is not so consistently similar that one part is merely a companion to the other, without individuality of its own.

THE DIRECT OCTAVE AND FIFTH

Composers seem to have been careful about any approach by similar motion to the intervals of octave and perfect fifth. While such matters belong to the domain of the study of counterpoint, the prominence of these intervals when between the outside voices, bass and soprano, necessitates recognition of the practice.

An octave or a perfect fifth is not usually approached by similar motion with skips in both voices. This combination is often referred to as *hidden octaves,* or *hidden fifths,* but the terms *direct octave* and *direct fifth* will be employed here.

EXAMPLE 3–25

I   V⁶

Exception 1: In changing the spacing of the same harmony, direct fifths by skip may be freely used.

EXAMPLE 3–26

always permitted

(The example above, consisting of a single harmony, does not constitute harmonic progression.)

Exception 2: In the V–I progression, particularly in a final cadence, the direct fifth may be used when the leading-tone skips down to the fifth degree, but only when the leading-tone is in an inner voice (alto or tenor).

EXAMPLE 3–27

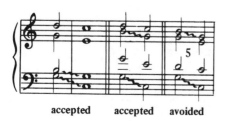

accepted   accepted   avoided

31

Similar voice leading in comparable progressions, having the same intervallic relationship but on other scale degrees, such as III–VI or I–IV, is occasionally found.

The direct octave and direct fifth are permitted between soprano and bass when the soprano moves by step and the bass by skip, but not the other way around. In upward movement, the preferred motion to a direct octave is with the soprano moving by a minor second, acting as a leading-tone, although some whole-step motions are quite acceptable.

EXAMPLE 3–28

II	V	II	V	V of V	V	IV	II	IV	II	III	VI	III	VI	VI	II
unusual		preferred (cf. Ex. 3–7)		usual		possible		much better		unusual		preferred		acceptable	

Direct octaves or fifths with skip in one voice and step in the other are freely used between any other two voices. (Of course, direct octaves or fifths with steps in both voices constitute parallel octaves or fifths.)

TREATMENT OF THE LEADING-TONE

The leading-tone is unlike any other degree of the diatonic scale in its feeling of a melodic need to rise. This property necessitates special treatment for the leading-tone when it is in the soprano voice. (In root-position progression, the leading-tone triad is not used and thus does not appear in the bass.) In V–I and V–VI, if the leading-tone is in the soprano of V, it will, as a rule, ascend to the tonic note in the second chord. If the leading-tone is in an inner voice, it may ascend to the tonic or it may descend.

EXAMPLE 3–29

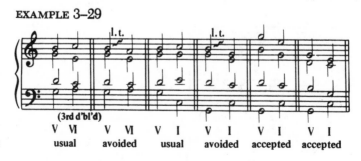

(3rd d'bl'd)											
V	VI	V	VI	V	I	V	I	V	I	V	I
usual		avoided		usual		avoided		accepted		accepted	

The interval formed by the leading-tone and the fourth degree below (augmented fourth) or the fourth degree above (diminished fifth) is called the *tritone*, i.e., three whole-tone steps. It has a peculiar kind of sound and was looked on with disfavor in the era of strict counterpoint, when it was referred to as *diabolus in musica* (devil in music). The roughness of its effect was softened or avoided with consistent skill. In the period of common harmonic practice, there seems to be only one form of the tritone that was nearly always shunned by composers. This is in the progression V–IV in root position. The leading-tone in V and the bass of IV are in relation of a tritone, and the term *false relation* is used to express this relationship between two successive tones which do not occur melodically in the same voice. The false relation of the tritone is easily heard in V–IV when the leading-tone proceeds to the tonic in the soprano voice, but is constantly used when the leading-tone is in either alto or tenor. The reverse progression, IV–V, does not show the false relation even when the leading-tone is in the soprano voice, and may be used in any position.

More on this subject in Chapter 15

Exception: Ex. 17–11

EXAMPLE 3–30

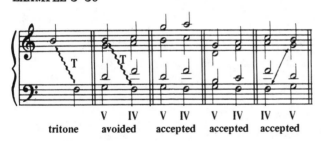

OVERLAPPING AND CROSSING

When two voices move upward in similar motion, the lower voice is not usually allowed to move to a position higher than that just left by the upper voice. This avoids ambiguity to the ear, which might follow an apparent melodic progression between the two voices. The corresponding rule holds for descending movement.

EXAMPLE 3–31

33

It is apparent that direct motion to or from a unison is prohibited by this rule. One special case, however, is commonly accepted. This is when the leading-tone in the tenor rises to the tonic with the dominant bass also ascending; the situation is seen to be little different from the comparable progression in contrary motion.

E.g., Ex. 6–37

EXAMPLE 3–32

V   I   V   I

The movement of one voice from a position below another voice to one above it, or vice versa, is called *crossing*. It is of common occurrence in instrumental music, but it also occurs occasionally in contrapuntal vocal music, including Bach's chorales. Because it is sometimes confusing to the ear, crossing should be avoided at this stage in our study.

E.g., Ex. 6–36

EXAMPLE 3–33

SIMILAR MOTION OF FOUR VOICES

As a general rule, all four parts should not move in the same direction when the triads are in root position. This rule is relaxed in the case of final cadences, as when a particular soprano note is desired (such as in Example 3–27, page 31). In such cases, at least one part must move by step.

PROCEDURES OF WORK

Exercises written at this early stage in the study of harmony will not have much resemblance to most actual music. Questions of style, therefore, will have little bearing at first. One does not expect fine four-part contrapuntal writing in the first studies of root-position triads. Moreover, the emphasis in harmonic study will, of necessity, be mostly directed to the chords. Nevertheless, it is never too early to try to discern, even in one's primitive efforts, those qualities which are musically desirable, even when much of the time one solution to a particular problem may sound as good as another, or better than another, for no immediately identifiable reason.

Nor is it too early to apply one's experience in the exercises to analysis of actual examples. The most suitable examples at this stage will be found in the predominantly homophonic styles of nineteenth-century hymns and part-songs. Such music may be studied a phrase at a time, the more complex chords and contrapuntal writing being ignored for the present, while attention is given to the choice of triads, the shape of melody and bass, and the structure of the phrase. All of these topics will be discussed further in later chapters.

At least two versions should be made of exercises which call for a considerable number of chords. The first version should follow closely the Rules of Thumb given above, even though the result may be poor melodically, as in Examples 3–10 and 3–11. This will help to familiarize the student with the principles of connection of triads and will then serve as a basis for the departures necessary to obtain a better soprano line. These departures need not be numerous or radical.

EXAMPLE 3–34

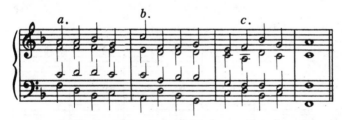

a. Starting with the third in the soprano raises the voices to a middle position in their range and gives them a little more space in which to move.

b. The doubling of the third in III avoids the repetition of the note A on the first beats of two successive measures. The three upper voices then move down, treating the III–VI progression as analogous to II–V.

c. The chord VI has its third doubled, as is usual in the progression V–VI. This gives a choice of repeating the common tone F in either tenor or soprano, as well as offering an opportunity of changing from close to open position.

The following is a third version of the same series of triads. The departures from the basic procedure should be determined and analyzed by the student.

EXAMPLE 3–35

Here are two fine examples of root-position writing. They should be studied carefully, with attention to unity, variety, smooth connection, and melodic shape.

EXAMPLE 3–36: Chopin, *Nocturne*, Op. 37, No. 1

EXAMPLE 3–37: Brahms, *Ich schell mein Horn ins Jammertal*, Op. 43, No. 3

It has been thought useful to include symbols of harmonic analysis with the examples, even though some of these symbols may not be immediately understood by the reader. All such indications will be clarified in subsequent chapters. Some writers use upper-case roman numerals for major and augmented triads, and lower-case for minor and diminished, a procedure which is not followed in this book but which may be helpful to some students.

EXERCISES

1. Write, in four parts, three different arrangements of each of the following harmonic progressions, in root position:

    a. V–VI in E major
    b. IV–V in D major
    c. I–VI in F-sharp major
    d. VI–V in C major
    e. V–I in A major
    f. II–V in E-flat major
    g. VI–IV in B-flat major
    h. II–V in G major
    i. III–VI in C-sharp major
    j. V–VI in A-flat major

2. Add soprano, alto, and tenor parts to the following basses, using triads in root position. Make two versions of each, the first version complying strictly with the Rules of Thumb for connecting triads, the second version containing departures from the Rules of Thumb so as to ensure a good melodic soprano part.

In this type of exercise, as in all the harmonization exercises in this book, it is essential to provide a root analysis shown by roman numerals, as in the examples.

d.

e.

f.

g.

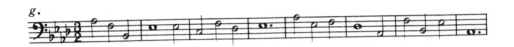

h.

3. Locate the violation (overlapping voices) which occurs in Example 3–10. How could it be avoided? This violation remained unnoticed in the first three editions of this book. There is a lesson to be learned from this: violations may escape even careful searching, especially when they do not sound obtrusive. This does not mean that it is pointless to avoid violations of the rules. It does mean that the rules are not so rigorous and hard-edged that the occasional inadvertent violation inevitably leads to a poor musical result.

CHAPTER 4

The Minor Mode

SCALE DIFFERENCES

Study of the minor mode creates some special difficulties for the beginner. The main obstacle is that whereas the major mode is defined by a standard set of triads, the minor mode is not. In the minor mode, several types of triads and scales are used, the usage depending on different conditions and contexts. Repeated observation shows that in the period of common harmonic practice, music in the minor mode is only very rarely limited to one type of minor scale.

The distinguishing characteristic of music in the minor mode is that the tonic triad is always minor. Beyond this, one sees that other triads are defined flexibly. The dominant triad appearing before minor I, for example, is nearly always major, with the leading-tone rising to the tonic; but under other conditions, it may be a minor triad, without the leading-tone expectation. The seventh degree as the third of V is thus usually major; but the seventh degree as the fifth of III is regularly minor. It is the differences among the usages of the scale degrees in the minor mode that accounts for some of the quirks in ordinary musical notation. The three flats of the key signature of C minor, for instance, indicate that the third, sixth, and seventh degrees of the scale are inflected with flat signs, in contrast to the same degrees in the scale of the parallel mode, C major. But in all our ordinary ex-

39

perience of music in C minor, having the key signature of three flats, miscellaneous B naturals are nearly always to be found, and often A naturals as well, even when no change of key has taken place.

The relationships between the scale degrees are summarized in the three traditional minor-scale forms:

EXAMPLE 4–1

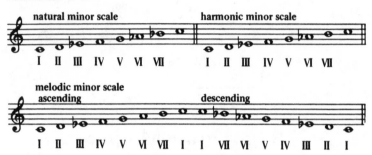

The *natural minor scale* corresponds to the key signature, as was mentioned in Chapter 1, and is equivalent to the descending form of the melodic minor. It has the same notes as the relative major scale (E-flat major), of course, but these correspond to different degrees of that scale.

The *harmonic minor scale* includes the major seventh degree, or leading-tone. The distance between sixth and seventh degrees is an augmented second; this interval is more often than not avoided in melodic motion. Why the scale is called "harmonic" will be discussed shortly.

The *melodic minor scale* is so called because the melodic motion of minor-mode music is often matched to its interval pattern. The scale includes the major sixth and seventh degrees in ascending motion, the minor sixth and seventh degrees in descending motion. Stepwise melodic progression from the fifth degree upward to the tonic will usually proceed along the major sixth and seventh degrees; descending motion from the tonic down to the dominant will often include the minor seventh and sixth degrees.

EXAMPLE 4–2: Beethoven, *Piano Concerto No. 3*, I

Allegro con brio

EXAMPLE 4–3: Bach, *Well-Tempered Clavier, II*, Prelude No. 6

These examples show the use of the complete scale in a melody, a common occurrence in the eighteenth and nineteenth centuries. Throughout the period, examples may be found of the major sixth and seventh being used in descending order.

EXAMPLE 4–4: Bach, *French Suite No. 1*, Minuet II

The opposite case—the minor sixth and seventh used in ascending order up to the tonic—is, however, rare until after common practice. The semitonal ascent of leading-tone to tonic was such a strong convention that composers were reluctant to alter it. Most apparent instances of such melodic progression during the common-practice period will be seen to involve triads other than V and I.

The descending melodic minor corresponds to the natural minor scale; the ascending melodic minor is identical with the major scale except for the third degree. The harmonic minor scale is a sort of hybrid of the two melodic forms; it is called "harmonic" because much, though not all, of the harmony regularly used in the minor mode is made up of triads based on this scale, the remainder deriving from the melodic minor forms.

TRIADS IN THE MINOR MODE

Because the sixth and seventh degrees vary according to use and context in the minor mode, it follows that there will be different kinds of triads containing one or the other of these degrees. The chart below gives all the possibilities.

41

EXAMPLE 4–5

Some elementary observations are: the tonic triad is the only triad that does not contain either the sixth or the seventh degree, and that therefore remains unchanged regardless of the type of minor scale used; four triads in the ascending melodic minor, II, IV, V, and VII, are identical with those of the major mode; the whole collection includes three diminished triads, II, VI, and VII, and one augmented triad, III. In the example, we have employed the acute (✓) and grave (✖) accents, preferred by some authors to show the linkage of the triad with the ascending and descending melodic minor scales, respectively; beyond mentioning them here, however, we shall mostly avoid these symbols in this book.

The following diagram separates the various triads into groups according to the harmonic minor scale and those triads that differ from it in the melodic minor forms.

EXAMPLE 4–6

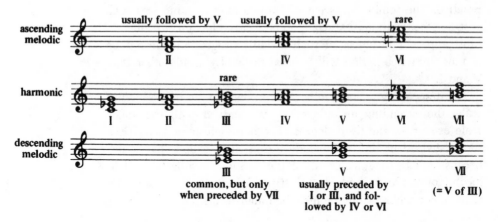

The harmonic minor scale was formerly used in several texts, including earlier editions of this one, as the one scale by which all seven triads of "the minor mode" were defined. That view now seems overly simple on the one hand, and confusing on the other. The three-staff diagram above is a more accurate accounting of the triads as actually employed by composers, but it requires some explanation.

MINOR
MODE

The mediant triad in the harmonic minor creates the most important difficulty in the traditional point of view; this augmented triad is only infrequently encountered in common practice. We can safely omit discussing it here; a few examples will be shown in later chapters. By far the commonest form of III associated with the minor mode is the III major triad, whose fifth is the minor seventh degree of the scale. This triad, formed from the descending melodic minor scale, is identical with the tonic triad of the relative major scale and tends to be heard that way; its function will be discussed at the end of Chapter 5.

See Exx. 6–22, 8–31, 11–23

As a general rule, the ascending melodic minor forms of II and IV (minor and major triads respectively) are used only in conjunction with the ascending melodic minor scale, when that scale is used in a clear melodic succession in one voice, from the sixth degree to the seventh degree to the tonic, usually with the fifth degree preceding as well.

EXAMPLE 4–7

c: II   V   I

EXAMPLE 4–8: Bach, Chorale No. 105, *Herzliebster Jesu*

See also Exx.
5–33, 7–6, 18–11

b: V$_5^6$ of IV IV V$_9^o$ of V V IV$^\varepsilon$ V$_5^6$ I V$_9^o$ I V

The ascending melodic minor form of VI, a diminished triad, is rarely used.

In like manner, the descending melodic minor V is generally used in conjunction with a downward scale progression beginning with the minor tonic.

43

EXAMPLE 4–9: Bach, Chorale No. 47, *Vater unser im Himmelreich*

See also Exx.
14–3, 26–13

d: I V⁶ I VII⁶ I⁶ I⁶₄ V I V⁶ IV⁶ V (V of III) III VI IV⁶ V

See Chapter 30:
The Decline of
Dominant
Harmony

The minor V was almost never used before the tonic triad until late in the nineteenth century; such a usage is not considered common practice.

The diminished triad on the supertonic, though a dissonant triad, is used fairly freely in common practice in root position, and abundantly in the other positions; its root or third may be doubled, but doubling of the fifth is avoided.

The diminished triad on the leading-tone is of course identical with the leading-tone triad of the major mode. Its use and function in the minor mode are the same as in the major: it is seldom used in root position, and it functions like an incomplete dominant seventh chord. We will learn more about it in Chapters 6, 15, and 21.

The major triad in the minor seventh degree (subtonic) is associated with major III in the great majority of cases, acting as its dominant.

HARMONIC PROGRESSION

The Table of Usual Root Progressions in the Major Mode, given in Chapter 3, applies also to the minor mode, with these differences:

III (major) is also often followed by VII (major).
VII (major) is followed by III, sometimes VI, less often IV.
VII (diminished) is followed by I.

VOICE LEADING

All of the rules and procedures of motion and voice leading discussed in Chapter 3 apply with equal validity to the minor mode.

The differences in scale structure in the minor mode, however, will ordinarily entail some further restrictions, for instance where motion by an augmented second must be avoided.

A good illustration is the progression II–V, which can move in only two ways when the root of II is doubled; all other motions lead to the motion of an augmented second or a tritone in one of the parts, or to forbidden parallels. When the third is doubled there is no possible motion without violations.

EXAMPLE 4–10

Occasionally the progression I–II is encountered in root position in the minor mode, perhaps a little more frequently than in the major mode. When the fifth of the tonic chord is doubled it then becomes possible to move in parallel motion from a perfect fifth to a diminished fifth. This special kind of parallel-fifth motion has always been accepted between any pair of voices. It is more frequently met with in connection with the dominant seventh chord. The reverse motion—diminished to perfect fifth—is also permitted, except between the outer voices.

EXAMPLE 4–11

EXERCISES

1. Write out the progressions given in Chapter 3, Examples 3–2 through 3–5, but incorporating the various degrees of the minor scales, and comparing the results with the major-mode forms by careful listening.

2. Write out the progressions listed in Chapter 3, Exercise 1, according to the instructions given, but using the minor scales instead of the major.

45

3. Add soprano, alto, and tenor parts to the following basses. These harmonizations are to be worked out like those in Chapter 3. To avoid confusion, triads on III and VII have not been called for. Two versions of each bass should be written, as before. Brackets indicate places where the harmony should employ the ascending or descending melodic minor scale form in one of the versions; where brackets are not given, the dominant will of course be the major form.

CHAPTER 5

Tonality and Modality

MODAL SCALES

Tonality is the organized relationship of tones in music. This relationship, as far as the common practice of composers in the eighteenth and nineteenth centuries is concerned, implies a central tone with all other tones supporting it or tending toward it, in one way or another.

Modality refers to the choice of the tones between which this relationship exists. Tonality is synonymous with key, modality with scale. In addition to the major, minor, and chromatic scales, a large number of special scales called *modal* scales can be constructed in any given tonality. Several of these scales are central to the pretonal music of the fifteenth and sixteenth centuries; we will study them in detail in Part Two of this book, in connection with their reappearance in nineteenth-century music. As illustration, a few are given here on the key-note C.

EXAMPLE 5-1

The Aeolian mode is identical with the natural minor scale; the older name, like the term *Ionian mode* for the major scale, was employed until the seventeenth century.

These modes may be transposed into all tonalities, simply by changing the pitch of the tonic note and preserving the interval relationships.

EXAMPLE 5–2

E: Dorian   G: Phrygian

B♭ : Lydian   F♯ : Mixolydian

Many modes taken from folk songs and even oriental scales have been used occasionally by composers. Artificial scales have been invented, containing a distribution of intervals not known before. But all of these must await investigation until the first task in the study of harmony is accomplished, namely the clear and firm establishment of the norm of common practice by reference to which these extraordinary resources are to be appreciated. We limit ourselves, therefore, to the three modes or scales described in Chapter 1—major, minor, and chromatic, the last considered as an expansion of the other two.

The acknowledged authority of the major and minor modes over a period of some three hundred years has given rise to the expression *major-minor system* often applied to our music. We are so imbued with this tradition that we tend to interpret music based on other modes as being in either major or minor, usually with somewhat unsatisfactory results. How often it is that the ear accepts the impression of C major at the opening of the second movement of Brahms's *Fourth Symphony*, only to find soon afterward that E is the tonal center.

EXAMPLE 5–3: Brahms, *Symphony No. 4*, II

E: Phrygian

Instances like the above, of the use of modes other than major and minor, are fairly numerous during the harmonic period but are by no means frequent enough to be called common practice.

TONAL FUNCTIONS OF THE SCALE DEGREES

Tonality, then, is not merely a matter of using just the tones of a particular scale. It is more a process of setting forth the organized relationship of these tones to one among them which is to be the tonal center. Each scale degree has its part in the scheme of tonality, its tonal function.

It is not the place here to attempt to outline the acoustic and psychological origins of these tonal functions. Let it suffice to report their existence as shown by the usage of composers.

Dominant and subdominant seem to give an impression of balanced support of the tonic, like two equidistant weights on either side of a fulcrum.

EXAMPLE 5–4

I V I IV I

The above could represent the scheme of harmonic progress of many a short piece of music, the first objective being the dominant, followed by return to the tonic, and then introduction of the subdominant to make the last tonic more satisfying and final. Other degrees are used to amplify and decorate this design.

Tonic, dominant, and subdominant are called the *tonal degrees,* since they are the mainstay of the tonality. In a given tonality these degrees remain the same for both modes.

EXAMPLE 5–5

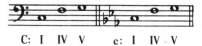

C: I IV V   c: I IV - V

49

Mediant and submediant are called the *modal degrees*. They have very little effect on the tonality but suggest the mode, since they are generally different in major and minor.

EXAMPLE 5–6

C: III VI   c: III VI

The supertonic is most often treated as dominant of the dominant.

EXAMPLE 5–7

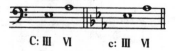

II V I
(V of V)

Harmonically, however, the supertonic often tends to become absorbed into the subdominant chord, especially in certain positions, when it can be called an actual, modified subdominant.

EXAMPLE 5–8

II I
(IV)

The supertonic should, therefore, be included in the list of tonal degrees, since it partakes of both dominant and subdominant characteristics, but should be distinguished from I, IV, and V, as having much less tonal strength.

The seventh degree, leading-tone, for all its importance as an indicator of the tonic through its melodic tendency, has not been treated as a basic structural factor in tonality. It remains a significant melodic tone, common to both modes. It is seldom regarded as a generator of harmony, but is usually absorbed into the dominant chord. The progression leading-tone to tonic may be described as melodically VII–I and harmonically V–I.

In terms of harmonic roots, overemphasis on the modal degrees tends to give the effect of a mode, and tonality, other than that intended. The modal degrees, by their insistence, are accepted by the ear as tonal degrees of another scale.

EXAMPLE 5–9

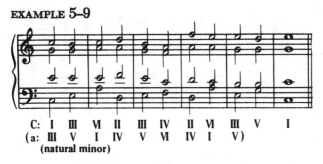

C: I III VI II III IV II VI III V   I
(a: III V   I   IV V   VI IV I   V)
(natural minor)

It follows that the tonal structure of music consists mainly of
harmonies with tonal degrees as roots (I, IV, V, and II), with the
modal-degree chords (III and VI) used for variety. It is interesting to note how in a single tonic chord one third degree is sufficient to "color" any number of doublings of the two tonal degrees
and to define the mode.

EXAMPLE 5–10

DOMINANT HARMONY

The strongest tonal factor in music is the dominant effect. Standing alone, it determines the key much more decisively than the
tonic chord itself. This fact is perhaps not apparent with simple
triads, but should be borne in mind throughout the study of harmony. The addition of dissonances, especially the seventh above
the dominant root, creates tendency tones which serve to aug-
ment the feeling of tonality inherent in the combination of leading-tone and dominant root. Establishment of a key or confirmation of it, by reinforcing the tonic by means of one of the many
forms of dominant harmony, is an everyday occurrence.

EXAMPLE 5–11: Beethoven, *Symphony No. 3* ("Eroica"), IV

Allegro molto

E♭: V of III   III   VI ?   II   V

EXAMPLE 5–12: Chopin, *Prelude*, Op. 28, No. 16

EXAMPLE 5–13: Schubert, *Mass No. 5 in A flat*, Gloria

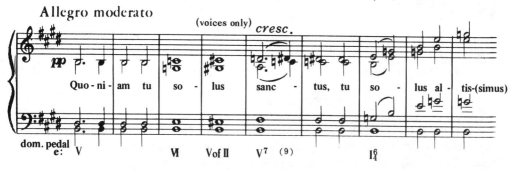

The use of dominant harmony before the tonic is by no means confined to the establishment of a key. The progression may occur anywhere, but is particularly to be found at the end of a phrase, where it is called the *authentic cadence*. The authentic cadence as the final progression of a movement is vastly more frequent than any other type; virtually any work will furnish an example.

EXAMPLE 5–14: Bach, Chorale No. 350, *Werde munter,
mein Gemüte*

EXAMPLE 5–15: Beethoven, *Symphony No. 5*, I

Allegro con brio

c: V I V I V I V I V I V I V I V I

The alternation of tonic and dominant for long stretches at a time, with no other harmony, is of common occurrence in music throughout the Classical and Romantic periods, particularly in dance forms.

EXAMPLE 5–16: Schubert, *Ländler for the Fair Ladies of Vienna*, Op. 67, No. 2

D: V⁷ (9) I V⁷ (9) I V I

EXAMPLE 5–17: Beethoven, *Symphony No. 5*, IV   *See also Ex. 9–14*

Allegro

C: I V I V⁷ I V⁷ I V I

EXAMPLE 5–18: Chabrier, *España*

Allegro con fuoco

F: I V i

It will be noted that the minor triad on the dominant root is almost never used for these purposes. Without the leading-tone, the dominant effect is drastically weakened, as the alternate   53 analysis in Example 5–9 shows. The minor dominant commonly occurs as companion to the descending melodic minor scale, but only exceptionally does the tonic triad follow it.

TONAL STRENGTH OF CHORDS

A single chord heard by itself is capable of a number of interpretations as to its tonality.

EXAMPLE 5–19

F: I	E: I
Bb: V	G: VI
C: IV	C: III
A: VI	B: IV

This ambiguity, which will later prove advantageous to the process of modulation, is greatly lessened when two chords are heard in a harmonic progression. The progressions have in themselves implications of tonality, although in varying degrees.

EXAMPLE 5–20

C: V I	C: I IV	C: VI III	C: VI II	C: IV II
G: I IV	F: V I	e: IV I	a: I IV	Bb: V III

The greatest tonal strength in harmonic progressions involving only triads results from contrasting dominant harmony with subdominant harmony, including the possibility of the supertonic as sharing some of the qualities of both. The presence of the tonic chord itself is not necessary to the establishment of a key. More important is the dominant. The progressions IV–V and II–V cannot be interpreted in more than one tonality, without chromatic alteration; hence they do not need the tonic chord to show the key. The progression V–VI, although possible to hear as the relatively uncommon progression I–II in the dominant key, is strongly indicative of a single tonality.

It may be necessary for a third chord to be heard if the harmonic progression is to define the tonality. By adding another chord to the successions in the above example, they can be rendered almost unmistakably in C.

EXAMPLE 5–21

C: IV V I   I IV V   V VI III   VI II V   IV II V

Similarly, a third chord could be selected which would confirm
the alternative tonalities given in Example 5–20.

EXAMPLE 5–22

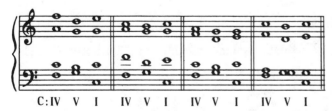

G: I IV V   F: IV V I   e: IV I V   a: I IV V   Bb: V III II

These elementary tonal units, groups of two or three chords
with distinct meaning as to key, might be regarded as musical
"words." The student is advised to write as many of these formulae as possible in a notebook where they will be available for
consultation, beginning with the commonest, like IV–V–I, I–IV–V,
etc., and even including some that he may invent. They should
then be studied for their individual qualities, their strength of
tonality and rhythmic feeling, and notice should be taken of their
frequency of use in music and of the varied forms in which they
may appear.

Variations of the formulae by differences in doubling, spacing,
and choice of soprano note are resources already available to the
student.

EXAMPLE 5–23

C: IV V I   IV V I   IV V I   IV V I

Change of mode from major to minor, or vice versa, does not
affect the tonality of the formula, and it is one of the important
means of variation. Ex. 5–22 could be written as follows, the
only change being in the modes. The last measure shows that the   55

results of the mode change may not always be as satisfactory as the original.

EXAMPLE 5–24

g: I IV V   f: IV   V I   E: IV I   V   A: I IV V   bᵇ: V III II

The study of harmony deals with the variants of these fundamental formulae, or "words." It will be found that they exist in the most complex texture, and from the very beginning much attention should be given to harmonic analysis of standard works, to bring out the endless capacity for varied treatment of these harmonic structural elements. Compare these three presentations of the formula II–V–I:

EXAMPLE 5–25: Mozart, *Sonata*, K. 330, III

*See also Exx.
6–13, 8–7, 8–28,
8–57, 9–10,
9–15, 12–5, 15–9,
18–8, 19–10,
20–17, 22–8,
24–25, 24–27,
and even 31–19*

C: II⁶   V⁷   I

EXAMPLE 5–26: Chopin, *Etude*, Op. 10, No. 6

eᵇ: ⁻II⁶   V⁷   I

EXAMPLE 5–27: Beethoven, *Sonata*, Op. 13 ("Pathétique"), II

56

Aᵇ: II   V   V/I   I

The modal implications of the chord progressions have less basic significance than their tonal implications. Major and minor modes are not as distinct in usage as their two scales would seem to indicate, and it is sometimes uncertain which is intended by the composer.

Fluctuation between major and minor has always been common. In this example, the progression I–V is repeated with change of mode, a change involving but one note—the third degree. The mode change is thus brought about within the tonic chord, the dominant proceeding to the major or minor tonic with equal ease.

EXAMPLE 5–28: Beethoven, *Sonata,* Op. 53 ("Waldstein"), III

The following example shows the mode change following a chord whose third is a modal degree of the other mode. This type of change is necessarily more abrupt and consequently more unusual.

EXAMPLE 5–29: Haydn, *Sonata No. 8,* II

57

The harmonic progression may itself contain chords from both modes.

EXAMPLE 5–30: Mendelssohn, *Song without Words,* Op. 102: No. 2, *Retrospection*

This use of the sixth degree of the minor mode in the midst of chords in the major mode adds the interest of color and is of frequent occurrence. Both the subdominant and supertonic with minor sixth degree are freely used when the prevailing mode is major. The submediant major triad (on the minor sixth degree) can occasionally be found. Because this triad includes the minor third degree, it implies an actual change of mode when used in conjunction with the major tonic; this relationship is characteristic of the late part of the period of common practice.

See also Exx. 12–16, 12–18, 18–7

But see also Ex. 12–29

EXAMPLE 5–31: Wagner, *Tristan und Isolde,* Act II, Scene 2

The reverse of the above situation, on the other hand, is quite different and restricted. The major-mode forms of II and IV (with major sixth degree) are normally used in connection with the minor mode only when the sixth degree ascends to the seventh, according to the melodic minor scale, as was shown in Chapter 4.

Minor-mode use of these chords without this melodic condition seldom occurs in common practice (see Example 5–29).

THE PICARDY THIRD

In the eighteenth century it was almost a mannerism to end on a major tonic triad even though the movement had been unmistakably in minor throughout. This major third was called the *tierce de Picardie* or *Picardy third*.

EXAMPLE 5–32: Bach, *Well-Tempered Clavier*, I, Prelude No. 4

See also Ex. 14–4

RELATIONSHIP OF RELATIVE MAJOR AND MINOR: THE SECONDARY DOMINANT PRINCIPLE

The keys of C major and A minor, to take the simplest example, are called *relative major and minor* because they have the same key signature, and for the most part use the same set of notes. The distinction between the two keys is defined, in the theoretical sense, by the key-note, the tonic. But in actual music, what mostly defines the key is not just the scale used, but the way the tonic triad is used—where it appears, and how often, and with what kind of preparation and emphasis. As was shown earlier, the tonal strength of the tonic is greatly enhanced by a dominant preceding it. Thus, one might expect to be able to determine whether a given phrase, or group of phrases, or even a whole piece, is in C major or A minor by several tests: by examining initial and final chords, by comparing the relative abundances of C major and A minor triads, and by looking for the presence of G sharps, which would ordinarily suggest the leading-tone, the third of V, in A minor.

EXAMPLE 5–33: Bach, Chorale No. 48, *Ach wie flüchtig,*
ach wie nichtig

It is plain that the example above begins and ends in A minor, the beginning and ending both being clearly marked by V–I progressions. The second measure, however, would seem to be in C major, especially if one imagines a V–I construction in that key comparable to the first measure. The second measure could be interpreted as I–VII–III in A minor, but this does not account for the strong dominant feeling in C major; on the other hand, it does not seem right to say that after hearing a piece in A minor for one measure one suddenly hears it in C major for the next, forgetting all about A minor, until just as abruptly one hears the next two measures in A minor again.

A compromise between these two interpretations allows the entire phrase to be analyzed in A minor. The second chord in the second measure is certainly the dominant of C, and C is III in A minor; therefore, the dominant will be called V of III. The V of III is said to *tonicize* III, to make it momentarily heard as a tonic even while memory allows one to be aware that A minor is the real tonic of the phrase as a whole. This interpretation is an application of what is called the *secondary dominant principle.*

The secondary dominant principle will be discussed thoroughly in later chapters, but it is important that the student be introduced to it early. The use of secondary dominant harmony everywhere throughout the common-practice period is one more confirmation of the importance of the dominant–tonic relationship. Since the concept of "V of . . ." can be applied to any degree of the scale, it points to the possibility of a greatly magnified vocabulary of chords available in any one key.

Returning to the example, one should consider the A minor and C major triads and their respective dominants. As far as their different factors are concerned, the only discrepancy is between G sharp and G, the difference between leading-tone and minor-seventh degree in the A minor scales. The different applications of G sharp and G depend on the relative tonal stress on A, by means of its dominant with leading-tone G sharp, and on C, by means of its dominant with root G. What is suggested by the example is that relative minor and major are closely associated, not just by their scalar similarities, but in their actual musical usages that take advantage of those similarities.

It is this strong association between relative minor and major that accounts for a great deal of the different triadic and scalar types that are so often found in music written in the minor mode. The major triad on III in the minor mode, without the leading-tone, is much the commonest form of mediant harmony in the minor, and its dominant, the major triad on the minor seventh degree, is seldom found other than before III. This association has a direct formal consequence on a larger scale as well; examination of numerous examples from common practice, especially works of the Classical period, shows that pieces of all types (fugues excepted) beginning in the minor mode will first modulate to the relative major more often than to any other key.

The reverse of this association is not borne out in practice. Most music whose principal tonality is major tends to be not nearly as closely involved with the relative minor as the other way around, the commonest modulation being to the key of the dominant.

Here is a somewhat longer illustration of the procedure shown in Example 5–33. The student should analyze it and then compare the two.

See also Exx.
7–23, 8–31

EXAMPLE 5–34: Schubert, *Symphony No. 9*, II

With such a large number of triadic possibilities relative to those of the major mode, one might be led to think that composers would prefer the minor mode for its potential harmonic richness. History shows the opposite, however, to be true. Throughout the common-practice period, but particularly after the Baroque era the major mode seems to have interested composers more than the minor.

The Baroque era contains the most numerous examples of extended forms using minor keys as principal tonalities. But the ritornello form of the Baroque concerto, as well as the aria da capo form, regularly uses major keys for contrasting episodes when the main key is minor. The practice carried over into the classical sonata form, where a first theme in the minor mode is almost invariably succeeded by a second theme in the relative major. At the same time, there was a decline in the use of a minor key for the main tonality of a large work; only two of Mozart's forty-one symphonies, for instance, have this property. Nor were minor keys generally favored as subsidiary tonalities in movements whose main tonality is major, though there are some notable exceptions to this.

All this is not to say that composers came to shun the minor mode. A four-movement symphony with an allegro first movement in the major mode would often have a slow movement in the relative minor key (Beethoven, *Symphony No. 3*; Schubert, *Symphony No. 9*) or the parallel minor (Beethoven, *Symphony No. 7*; Schumann, *Symphony No. 2*), or the first movement itself might start with a slow introduction in the parallel minor (Beethoven, *Symphony No. 4*). On balance, it seems fair to say that even while composers generally preferred the major as the stronger mode, they regarded the minor as an indispensable resource of contrast.

In a work with the first movement in minor, more often than not there would be a change to the parallel major for part or all of the final movement (Beethoven, *Symphony No. 5*; Brahms, *Symphony No. 1*). A work like Chopin's *Second Piano Sonata*, with all four movements in minor, must be regarded as unusual, though the first three movements all have extensive sections in the relative major.

CHROMATICISM AND TONALITY

Chromaticism is the name given to the use of tones from outside the major or minor scales. Chromatic tones began to appear
in music long before the common-practice period, and by the
beginning of the period formed an important part of its harmonic resources. Chromatic tones arise in music partly by the use
of modal mixture which permits us to include both A flat and A
natural in C major, partly by means of secondary dominant harmony, partly by the use of a special vocabulary of altered chords,
and partly in certain nonharmonic tones. The extension of these
resources in the nineteenth century emphasized the tendency of
the major and minor modes to merge into what one is finally
tempted to call a chromatic mode.

It is apparent that establishment and maintenance of a key may
be a complicated procedure, especially in a long symphonic
movement when the key may change many times before returning
to the original. We have seen how tonality may be defined within
short phrases, and we know from experience that, for instance,
Beethoven's *Symphony No. 1 in C major* is fundamentally "in C
major" even though many other tonalities may be found in it.
Our study of harmony will eventually shed much light on how one
key may change to another, and how composers have considered
tonal design in both small and large contexts.

The understanding of these complexities belongs naturally to a
more advanced stage in the study of harmony, but there are two
points of which the student should be made aware from the
start. The first is that the parallel and relative modes, major and
minor, tend to become interchangeable, even when only triads are
used. Examples from musical literature should be noted and the
formulae added to the collection of progressions. In the exercises
of the present stage, II and IV can be used with either major or
minor sixth degree in the major mode, and the final tonic chord of
the minor mode may have a major third. It is understood that
these are effects of variety, not to be too regularly introduced.

The second important point is that notes outside the scale do not
usually affect the tonality. This principle may cause difficulty at
first, but it should be announced early, if only to emphasize the
fact that tonality is established by the progression of roots and
the tonal functions of the chords, even though the superstructure
of the music may contain all the tones of the chromatic scale.

63

Writing some of the exercises without key signature, using accidentals when needed, is helpful for showing the differences in mode and tonality. The traditional signatures of major and minor modes on the same tonic are misleading in that they suggest much more difference than actually exists.

1. Write the modal degrees of the following scales:

    a. A-flat minor
    b. C-sharp major
    c. D-flat major
    d. G-sharp minor
    e. E-flat minor

2. Give the tonalities and modes (major or minor) of the following progressions:

3. Write each of the following harmonic formulae in four different versions, using only triads in root position. Each version should have a different spacing, and, where possible, should make use of chords from the parallel mode or a different minor-scale form.

    a. C minor: VI–II–V
    b. E major: II–V–VI
    c. D-flat major: V–VI–IV
    d. A minor: IV–V–I
    e. F major: V–IV–I

4. Harmonize the following basses in four parts, root position only:

a.

b.

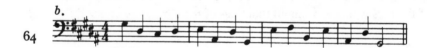

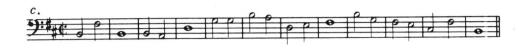

c.

d.

5. Write three different four-part harmonizations in root position for each of the following basses, one version as given, one version in the parallel mode (changing the key signature from major to minor or vice versa), and the third version in the major mode using II, IV, or VI from the minor mode at suitable places.

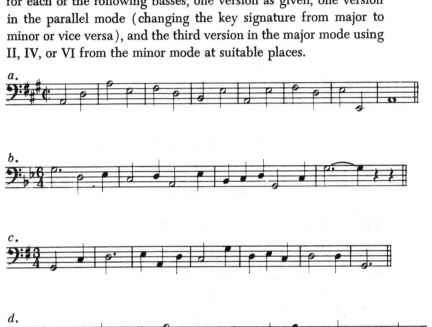

a.

b.

c.

d.

6. Write two different versions in four parts of the following successions of chords, using no key signature (root position only). Invent a different meter and rhythm for each version.

    a. Key of G: VI–IV–II–V–VI–IV–I–V–I
    b. Key of E flat: V–I–IV–V–VI–IV–II–V–I–IV–V–I

7. Construct an original chord succession, starting with a series of roman numerals, arranged with attention to the proper distribution of modal and tonal degrees, and to the quality of the harmonic progressions involved. The series should finally be worked out in four parts, with suitable meter and rhythm.

65

CHAPTER 6

The First Inversion—
The Figured Bass

ARABIC-NUMERAL NOTATION

If the third of a triad is in the bass, the triad is said to be in *first inversion,* regardless of where the root may appear above it. Triads in the first inversion are also called *chords of the sixth,* the characteristic interval being the sixth caused by the inversion of the third.

Adopting the method of musical shorthand developed by composers in the Baroque era, most theorists designate inversions of chords by arabic numerals showing the intervals between bass and upper voices. Thus, a triad in first inversion is represented by the figures $^6_3$, or simply ^{6}, the third being understood. With roman numerals identifying the roots, any chord in any inversion can be shown symbolically by this method.

Spacing and doubling are not prescribed by the figures. A $^6_3$ chord will of course have the third in the bass, but the root and fifth may be placed above it in any order or octave.

Though we will not discuss the dominant seventh chord, the most important of the seventh chords, until a later chapter, it is shown in Example 6–2 in all of its positions to illustrate the figuring used for such chords. The backward sequence (7, 6–5, 4–3, 2) of the abbreviated figuring forms a convenient memory device.

EXAMPLE 6–1

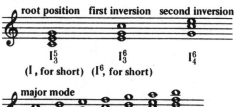

root position   first inversion   second inversion

I_3^5 I_3^6 I_4^6

(I, for short) (I^6, for short)

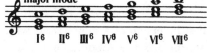

major mode

I^6 II^6 III^6 IV^6 V^6 VI^6 VII^6

minor mode

I^6 II^6 III^6 IV^6 V^6 VI^6 VII^6

EXAMPLE 6–2

root position   first inversion   second inversion   third inversion

complete figuring:	V_5^7 $_3$	V_5^6 $_3$	V_4^6 $_3$	V_4^6 $_2$
for short:	V^7	V_5^6	V_3^4	V^2 (or V_2^4)

DOUBLING

In triads in root position, the general rule is to double the root, to obtain a fourth tone for four-part writing. This is less generally the rule with triads in first inversion.

The choice of a tone to double is not dependent on whether the triad is major, minor, augmented, or diminished. Nor does it appear to have been, throughout this period of common practice, a question of effective sonority to the ear. The deciding factor is almost invariably the position of the doubled tone in the tonality. In other words, tones are doubled which are important to solidity of the key.

Customary procedure in doubling in triads in the first inversion can be stated in these two rules:

a. If the bass (not root) of the first-inversion triad is a tonal degree, it is doubled.

b. If the bass of the triad is not a tonal degree, it is not doubled, but a tonal degree in the chord is chosen for doubling.

EXAMPLE 6–3

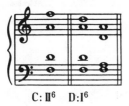

C: II⁶   D: I⁶

In the above example of the first inversion of a minor triad with D as a root, the F in the first instance is the subdominant, since the key is C. In the second case, the same chord is regarded from the point of view of D minor, in which F is a modal degree, so that either the D, tonic, or A, dominant, is doubled by preference.

Regardless of what tone is chosen for doubling, all three normal factors—root, third, and fifth—should be present in any inversion of a triad. This is because ambiguity may result if one of them is omitted. If the root is omitted in a triad in first inversion, it will most likely be heard as a root-position triad, without fifth, on the tone a third above the intended root. If the fifth is omitted, the chord might be interpreted as a second-inversion triad with missing root.

EXAMPLE 6–4

C: I⁶ or III? I⁶ or VI⁶₄?

Voice-leading considerations may occasionally dictate the use of such incomplete chords in passing; nevertheless, it remains a good rule that inverted triads in harmonically strong situations should not omit any factors.

GENERAL EFFECT OF THE FIRST INVERSION

Harmonically, considered vertically as a sonority, the triad in its first inversion is lighter, less ponderous, less blocklike, than the same triad in root position. It is therefore of value as an element of variety when used with root-position chords. Compare the individual sound of the triads in the two versions of a series of triads given below.

EXAMPLE 6–5

Melodically, the use of first-inversion triads permits the bass to move by step in progressions in which the roots would move by skip. It is difficult to arrange a smooth melodic line for the bass when the chords are all in root position. The bass will also possess that advantage hitherto allowed only the upper voices, of moving from root to third, and vice versa, in the same harmony.

EXAMPLE 6–6

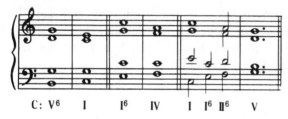

Rhythmically, the triad in first inversion is of less weight than one in root position. In the example above, the progressions V⁶–I, I⁶–IV, and II⁶–V are felt as weak-to-strong rhythms, and the I–I⁶ as strong-to-weak. The student is reminded, however, that the almost inevitable presence of other factors influencing the rhythm makes it unwise to draw conclusions from a single criterion. In the following example, there can be no doubt that the rhythmic stress is on the first beat of the second measure.

EXAMPLE 6–7: Brahms, *Symphony No. 1*, II

Andante sostenuto

There are no new principles of voice leading or of harmonic progression involved in the use of triads in first inversion. The objective of smooth connection of the chords is ever to be kept in
mind, the normal progression of the voices being always to the
nearest available position. It remains a true principle of contrapuntal practice that doubling and spacing are less important than
melodic movement.

EXAMPLE 6–8

See also Ex. 11–6

G: II I⁶ II⁶   V

Here the stepwise contrary motion in soprano and bass is
thought desirable enough to permit the doubling of the modal
degree B in the second chord, I⁶, even though that note has the
prominence of being in the outside voices.

CONSECUTIVE FIRST-INVERSION TRIADS

When several first-inversion triads occur in succession, there is a
tendency for the parts to move in similar motion. Many examples
of the following manner of voice leading may be found.

EXAMPLE 6–9

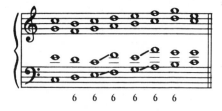

6   6   6   6   6   6

The direct octaves between tenor and bass can, however, be
avoided, and a more balanced arrangement made:

70

EXAMPLE 6–10

6   6   6   6   6   6

In fast tempo, a succession of parallel first-inversion triads may sound more like a triadic doubling or thickening of a single melodic line than a succession of actual harmonic progressions.

EXAMPLE 6–11: Beethoven, *Sonata*, Op. 2, No. 3, IV

In the example above, the first two measures are perceived as a single tonic harmony whose motion is entirely melodic, proceeding to IV in the third measure. Passages in slow tempo comparable to the above offer the ear more of an opportunity to fix on the individual root motions, but they rarely contain so many consecutive first-inversion triads.

Usage of the Various Triads

The first inversion of the tonic triad is one of the most useful chords, and at the same time one of the inversions most neglected by the beginner. It serves as a useful alternative where the root-position tonic triad might sound too strong, and often provides the necessary variety when a chord is needed to follow the dominant. I⁶ is also a natural harmony to support a melody moving from tonic to dominant by skip.

Some common formulae containing I⁶:

71

EXAMPLE 6–12

$$\text{I}^6 \quad \text{II}^6 \quad \text{V} \qquad \text{I} \quad \text{I}^6 \quad \text{IV} \qquad \text{V} \quad \text{I}^6 \quad \text{IV} \qquad \text{IV} \quad \text{I}^6 \quad \text{V}$$

EXAMPLE 6–13: Beethoven, *Piano Concerto No. 1*, I

Allegro con brio

$$\text{C: I} \qquad \text{I}^6 \qquad \text{II}^6 \qquad \text{V}^7 \qquad \text{I}$$

EXAMPLE 6–14: Schumann, *Carnaval*, Op. 9: I, *Préambule*

Quasi maestoso

$$\text{A}^\flat\text{: IV} \quad (\text{I}^6)\text{IV} \quad \text{V}^2 \qquad \text{I}^6 \qquad \text{V}^4_3 \quad \text{I} \qquad \text{V}^4_3 \text{ of V} \quad \text{V}$$

EXAMPLE 6–15: Mozart, *Sonata*, K. 332, I

Allegro

$$\text{d: V}^{\,\circ\,6}_{5} \qquad\qquad \text{I}^6$$

The supertonic triad in first inversion is very common in cadences, where it precedes and introduces a dominant effect. It is
strongly subdominant in feeling, the subdominant being the bass
tone and usually doubled. II⁶ often follows I, whereas II in root
position is generally considered an awkward progression from I in
root position. In minor, the first inversion is preferred to the root-
position diminished triad. This minor form is not unusual in com-
72 binations with the major tonic triad.

Common formulae:

EXAMPLE 6–16

II⁶ V I   II⁶ V I   I II⁶ V VI II⁶ I

EXAMPLE 6–17: Haydn, *String Quartet*, Op. 76, No. 4, II

Adagio

E♭: II   V of II II⁶ II   I⁶₄ V   I

EXAMPLE 6–18: Brahms, *Symphony No. 4*, IV

Allegro energico e passionato

e: IV⁶   II⁶   I   IV⁶   V⁷of V   I⁶   V⁴₃   I

III₆ is not usually an independent chord; it is a good example of the kind of chord made by temporary displacement of one or more tones of some other chord, in this case nearly always the dominant. For this reason, it is considered harmonically weaker than the first-inversion triads of the tonal degrees, and must be employed judiciously.

EXAMPLE 6–19

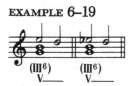

(III⁶)   (III⁶)
V___   V___

The augmented triad on III in the harmonic minor mode, mentioned in Chapter 4 as an uncommon chord in any case, is probably more often found in the first inversion than in root position.   73

Example 6–22 shows this chord actually substituting for a dominant.

Like all other chords of the sixth, it may be found in scalewise passages of weak rhythmic value.

When it proceeds to VI, the third degree may be doubled and regarded temporarily as a dominant of the sixth degree.

Common formulae:

EXAMPLE 6–20

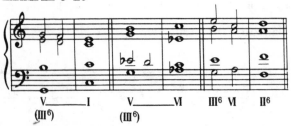

V——I   V——VI   III⁶ VI   II⁶
(III⁶)   (III⁶)

EXAMPLE 6–21: Brahms, *Violin Sonata,* Op. 108, II

Adagio

D: I   III⁶   VI   I⁶

EXAMPLE 6–22: Wagner, *Die Walküre,* Act II, Scene 1

Heftig

E: III⁶   I

EXAMPLE 6–23: Chopin, *Polonaise,* Op. 40, No. 1

Allegro con fuoco

A: III   II⁶   III⁶ IV⁶   V   I

sion of the subdominant triad is often used after
welcome change from VI when the bass moves
also avoids the false relation of the tritone be-
soprano, likely to occur in the progression V–IV
e in the upper voice.

of course valuable for relieving the weight of the
root position, retaining the strength of the root
progression and at the same time imparting lightness and a melodic quality to the bass.

Common formulae:

EXAMPLE 6–24

EXAMPLE 6–25: Schumann, *Piano Concerto*, Op. 54, I

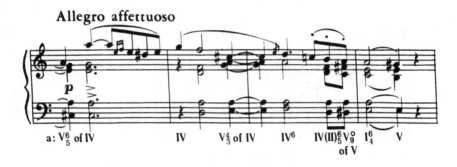

EXAMPLE 6–26: Brahms, *Schicksalslied*, Op. 54

75

EXAMPLE 6–27: Beethoven, *Symphony No. 2*, III

The third of the dominant is the leading-tone, and the placing of that degree in the bass gives the bass strong melodic significance in addition to lessening the harmonic rigidity of the progression. The bass as leading-tone usually moves to the tonic, so that the next chord will probably be I, as in Examples 6–29 and 6–30.

At times the bass may proceed downward, as in a descending scale. In the minor mode, this would be the occasion for the use of the descending melodic minor scale in the bass, as in Example 6–37.

Formulae:

EXAMPLE 6–28

EXAMPLE 6–29: Beethoven, *Symphony No. 9*, III

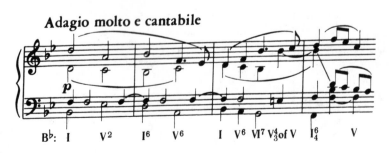

EXAMPLE 6–30: Mozart, Overture to *Don Giovanni*, K. 527

d: I   V⁶   I

EXAMPLE 6–31: Chopin, *Prelude*, Op. 28, No. 20

c: I   VI⁶   V‿‿   IV⁶ Fr. V‿‿

The VI⁶ chord is similar to III⁶ in its incapacity to stand as an independent chord. It is nearly always the tonic chord, with the sixth degree as a melodic tone resolving down to the fifth. Usual exceptions to this are found in scalewise progressions of successive chords of the sixth.

Formulae:

EXAMPLE 6–32

See also Ex. 13–9

I   V   VI⁶ V⁶   I   I   IV⁶

EXAMPLE 6–33: Franck, *Symphony,* I

See also Ex. 21–2

D: I‿‿‿‿‿‿‿‿‿

EXAMPLE 6–34: Chopin, *Waltz in E minor* (op. posth.)

e: V   I   VI⁶   V⁶

The leading-tone triad in first inversion is commonly used as a passing chord between the tonic chord in root position and its first inversion. In this case it is rhythmically weak, hardly disturbing the effect of tonic harmony, and it may be analyzed as a grouping of melodic tones above the tonic root. On the other hand, if dwelt upon or otherwise given any prominence, it may be felt as a true dominant harmony, the root V being understood.

In VII⁶ the second degree is most often doubled in preference to the more strongly tonal fourth degree, but instances in which the fourth degree is doubled are numerous (Example 6–37).

Formulae:

EXAMPLE 6–35

See also Exx.
4–9, 12–7, 23–15

I   VII⁶   I⁶   IV   VII⁶   I⁶   II⁶   V   I⁶   VII⁶   I
(I————————IV)

EXAMPLE 6–36: Bach, Chorale No. 20, *Ein' feste Burg*

D: I   VI   I   VII⁶   I   V of V   V   VI   VII⁶of VI   VI⁶   III   IV   VII⁶   I   V   I

EXAMPLE 6–37: Bach, Chorale No. 16, *Es woll'*
uns Gott genädig sein

78

b: V   I   V⁶   IV⁶   V   IV   I⁶   VII⁶   I   V

EXAMPLE 6–38: Mozart, *Piano Concerto*, K. 488, III

A: I   VII⁶   I⁶   Vof V⁶₄ I   V

Keyboard Harmony and the Figured Bass

It is assumed that the student will devote a certain portion of time, preferably every day, to the practice and eventual memorization of the harmonic formulae given in each chapter, learning them in various spacings and in all keys. Additional constraints may be introduced, such as playing the parts with crossed hands, or not playing one of the inner parts and singing it instead. With such practice the progressions and their voice leading will become instinctive.

The advantages afforded by proficiency in keyboard harmony are considerable. The applications in improvisation are obvious, but the main value of keyboard skills is that they accustom the ear to instantaneous solutions to standard harmonic problems. Beyond the formulae, one should apply one's technique to the realization of figured bass at the keyboard.

The figured bass had a practical use in the days of Bach and Handel, when the ever-present harpsichord or organ required a guide to the harmonic background of the music in order to fill in missing parts or to reinforce weak ones. The *basso continuo* was prescribed in scores up into Mozart's time, but fell out of use thereafter as the orchestra became standardized in its instrumental makeup and as the art of conducting developed. Today, specialists in Baroque performance often train themselves in rapid figured-bass reading, but even this is no longer regarded as a necessary skill when so many works are published with the figured bass already realized.

Although in general use in the study of harmony, the figured bass is of somewhat limited value as a written exercise. It is a good shorthand method of designating chords, but the working-out of figured basses entails no problem of choosing the appropriate harmony. The problem is solely one of distribution of given materials, correct voice leading, and construction of a smooth so- 79 prano melody. There is some usefulness in this as a written exercise, particularly in the early stages of study, but much more benefit will be obtained from working out figured basses at the keyboard. They should be played anew each time, taking different soprano notes to start. It is extremely important that they be played rhythmically, even if very slowly.

The principle of denoting upper voices by arabic numerals permits all kinds of melodic tones to be prescribed in addition to the chords. The proper method of reading the figures consists of finding the notes by interval and afterwards identifying the resulting chord. The combinations of figures, with practice, get to be as familiar as the chords themselves.

Accidentals are shown by placing the desired signs next to the numerals representing the notes to be affected. An accidental sign standing alone, or under a number, signifies that the third above the bass is to receive that sign. The leading-tone sharp or natural in the minor mode is indicated that way. A line drawn through the numeral has the same effect of chromatically raising the note to which the numeral refers. A straight horizontal line placed after a figure means that the note represented by the figure is maintained in the harmony to the end of the line, regardless of the change of bass; this sign will be encountered in connection with nonharmonic tones.

EXAMPLE 6–39

The full figuring for a triad in root position would be $\frac{8}{5}$, but $\frac{}{3}$ this is used only to prescribe the exact doubling. The order of voices from the top down need not follow that of the numerals; the figuring is the same whether root, third, or fifth is in the soprano voice. Root-position triads are so common that it is assumed that one is meant when no figure appears. Sometimes just a 5 or a 3 is given to make sure that a triad in root position will be used, or that the factor indicated will be the soprano note of the root-position triad. For the first inversion, a 6 is sufficient indication, the third being thereby understood, as shown in Example 6–1.

The student should be aware that not all published figured basses conform rigorously to these symbol rules. The Bach Gesellschaft Edition scores, for instance, sometimes use the sharp sign for chromatically raising a tone even where only a natural sign would be called for,

EXAMPLE 6–40

6♯ = 6♮

and frequently does without the straight horizontal lines mentioned above, assuming that in ordinary situations the static harmony will be understood.

EXERCISES

1. Write in four parts the following series of chords indicated by symbols:

    a. C minor: III⁶–I–IV
    b. G major: I–I⁶–IV
    c. A♭ major: III⁶–VI–II⁶
    d. A minor: V–I⁶–IV
    e. B♭ major: I–VII⁶–I⁶
    f. E♭ major: I⁶–II⁶–V
    g. D minor: VI⁶–V⁶–I
    h. B minor: II⁶–V–I
    i. F major: I–V–IV⁶
    j. D major: II⁶–V–I

2. Write out the four-part harmony indicated by the following figured basses:

a.

b.

c.

66 6   6   6 66 5

d.

6 6 # 6 # 6   6   6 6 6 6 # #
         #

e.

6   6 6   6 5 6 6   6

f.

6♮ 6 6 ♮——   6 6   ♮ 6   6 6 6 ♮__

3. Harmonize the following basses, using root-position triads and, where appropriate, first-inversion triads.

a.

b.

c.

d.

e.

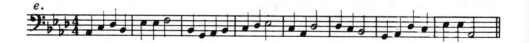

CHAPTER 7

Function and
Structure of Melody

In the most basic sense, a melody is any group of tones meant to be heard as a succession, the succession being organized in some way. Successive statement of the tones by a monophonic instrument ("melody instrument"), or by a singer, is of course a basic kind of melodic organization. More usually, however, when one thinks of melody it is a particular melody: one which has an identity, and an organization that is intended to be perceived.

That melody is so intrinsic to music is shown by the way we identify individual pieces. We recognize pieces by their themes or tunes, not by their harmony or particular form, nor by whether or not they are sung by a chorus or played by a string quartet. When we hum or whistle to ourselves, it is melody that we hum or whistle, our recollection of the melody serving at all times to guide and recreate in our mind's ear as much of the totality of the piece as we can remember. Just a few notes may be all that is needed to identify unmistakably a particular melody. The melodic progress of a piece of music may contain thousands of notes, but the melodies using those notes are defined by their own identities and character.

Though the art of music throughout history has produced melodies of every conceivable variety, it has also used these melodies   83 to impart order and meaning to compositions large and small. The structure of melody and the melodic functions of music constitute an enormous and complex subject that this chapter cannot hope to cover more than very superficially. Rather, it is hoped that some of the ideas developed here will enable the student to begin to approach the subject in several ways.

USES OF MELODY

Melody has many different functions in music, and melodic character and structure often depend on the uses to which melodies are put. The most important melodic function is that of the *theme,* a melody which recurs in a composition and which forms part of its larger organization. Not all melodies, of course, are themes; and some themes are not melodies.

In polyphonic music, the thematic character of a melody often determines, or is determined by, the way it will be used, and this in turn will have an effect on the character of the other parts in the polyphony. An interior or accompanimental part, for instance, may be very plainly melodic, even though one does not normally listen to it for its melodic individuality.

EXAMPLE 7–1: Beethoven, *Symphony No. 5,* IV

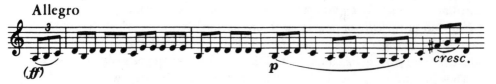

This is even more likely to be true of bass lines, when these are so frequently written to assure a maximum of contrapuntal opposition to melodies placed in the upper voice.

EXAMPLE 7–2: Bach, Cantata No. 140, *Wachet auf,* No. 4

A principal melody may be exposed against any type of accompaniment, whether entirely chordal or busily contrapuntal or anything in between. Other things being equal, a melody that

84 is the top voice of a texture is likely to be automatically heard as

the principal voice. If a middle or lower voice is to be given melodic prominence, it will normally be stressed dynamically, by reinforcement of its instrumentation, or by lessening the activity of the surrounding accompaniment.

EXAMPLE 7–3: Beethoven, *String Quartet,* Op. 59, No. 1, I

A *countermelody* is deliberately contrasted with a principal melody both rhythmically and contrapuntally, especially when there is little or no additional melodic activity. The main countermelody in the example below is the part moving in steady sixteenth notes; the principal melody, in the upper voice, has already been heard earlier in the movement; a subsidiary countermelody is heard on the offbeats of the principal melody.

EXAMPLE 7–4: Schubert, *Symphony No. 9,* II

An instrumental solo used this way in combination with a solo singer and additional harmonic accompaniment is called an *obbligato;* many examples appear in opera and in sacred music with orchestral accompaniment.

A *collateral part* is a part that does not double a melody at the unison or octave but follows along with it, often in thirds or sixths, with minimal rhythmic or contour differentiation from the principal melody.

85

EXAMPLE 7–5: Bach, *Magnificat:* No. 8, *Esurientes*

*See also Exx.
8–30, 8–45*

E: I   V (7) I   V (7) I   V$_9^o$ of II   II   V of II

Other melodic types and usages which may be distinguished in various kinds of music are:

1. *Cantus firmus.* Generally associated with sacred music of the Baroque era and earlier, this term implies a theme of regularly spaced notes without much rhythmic differentiation, usually as part of a contrapuntal composition with a faster-moving texture surrounding it. In Protestant sacred music of the Baroque era, the most familiar cantus firmi are hymns, usually called *chorales;* in Catholic sacred music of the Renaissance and earlier, cantus firmi are derived from chant, sometimes from popular tunes.

Cf. Ex. 4–9

EXAMPLE 7–6: Bach, *Orgelbüchlein:* No. 37, *Vater unser im Himmelreich*

d: V   I   IV^6 V   I   IV(II)$_5^6$ V$^{(7)}$ I

2. *Tune.* This term is useful for designating melodies with regular periods (such as four-bar phrase groups), strong tonic and dominant cadences, and often an internal structuring within and between phrases, such as organization into rhythmic or intervallic motives. Tunes have a "closed" structure; they do not imply any continuation beyond the final phrase. Two broad categories of tunes are songs and dances. Song tunes are usually conceived as matched syllabically to a text in rhymed verse. They are characterized by a relatively small range (usually not more than a tenth), a quality of singability, and a lack of wide intervals or complex rhythms. Dance tunes are similarly structured but not necessarily so restricted; wide skips and lively rhythms frequently suggest an instrumental character.

3. *Symphonic melody*, one designed to be used as a theme in a larger work. Such a melody is shorter than a tune, and usually avoids a strong cadence on the tonic; without such a conclusive ending, it thus implies that a continuation is possible or even necessary, that something else must happen. In their use, melodies of this type are ordinarily subject to changes during the course of the composition, changes which achieve thematic variety while at the same time ensuring that the original thematic identity is not lost from memory. They may be used in every type of contrapuntal combination with or without motivic fragmentation, as in fugal writing; they may be fragmented and the fragments repeated with seemingly endless variety, as in Beethoven's technique; they may be continued and extended with new phrases, as in Mozart's; they may be transformed rhythmically and metrically into new and independent guises, as in Liszt's; they may be repeated in toto without change but in a variety of keys, as in the ritornello forms of the Baroque. In large compositions of the Classical era and after, the variety of manifestations of a theme, and the variety of formal purposes it serves, are often more important considerations than the intrinsic properties of the theme itself.

4. *Ostinato*. This term (Italian for "obstinate") refers to a melody, usually short and in the bass, that repeats over and over again. Some formal types, such as the passacaglia and chaconne, use the ostinato bass continuously throughout. A few particular ostinato melodies, called *grounds* or *ground basses*, were in widespread use in the works of many different sixteenth-century composers; twentieth-century popular music has seen a revival of this technique.

5. *Connective or decorative melodies.* These are plainly not themes, but they serve to connect phrases, or even prominent tones within a phrase, in a smooth, flowing way.

EXAMPLE 7–7: Beethoven, *Sonata*, Op. 13 ("Pathétique"), I

Allegro molto e con brio

EXAMPLE 7–8: Chopin, *Piano Concerto in F minor*, II

The type of melody in the Chopin example above, with its free, undivided, almost blurred succession, at lightning speed, is called a *roulade*. The roulade is most characteristic of the virtuoso piano styles of the nineteenth century, but it may be found occasionally in earlier music, including in vocal cadenzas of opera arias, where it probably originated.

6. *Figurational melody*. The successive tones in a repeated pattern are melodic just as in any other melody, but nevertheless figuration is usually employed to project harmony more than melody. Some figurations depend on characteristic usages of instruments; the example below could not easily be imagined played on anything other than a piano.

EXAMPLE 7–9: Chopin, *Etude*, Op. 25, No. 12

It is important to remember that the melodic characteristics noted here are seldom displayed to the exclusion of all else in the melodies of actual music. Some symphonies have songlike or cantus-firmus–like themes; others have themes that are transformed into accompanimental figures; many songs have melodies that are dancelike and vice versa. But that such distinctions can be made at all attests to the richness of melodic variety that musical tradition affords.

SHAPE

The distribution of tones in a melody is marked by changes of direction, by range, by various high and low points, and by the variability of all of these as to where they occur in the phrase. Together all of these aspects constitute the contour of the melody, an important determinant of its character.

A good melody will usually have a restricted range within which most of its tones will occur, with a high point or a low point which may be anywhere in the phrase. Secondary high points or low points are common, but do not usually repeat the primary high or low point. The majority of melodies seems to favor a rising–falling curve over a falling–rising curve, but there are many examples of the latter, as well as of mixed types of curves.

EXAMPLE 7–10: Mozart, *Piano Concerto*, K. 467, II

EXAMPLE 7–11: Beethoven, *Sonata*, Op. 28, I

EXAMPLE 7–12: Bach, *St. Matthew Passion*, No. 27

Where the melody begins or ends may not be as important for defining the contour as it is for anchoring the tonality. But in general, a melody will return in the phrase to approximately the same point where it began, within a fourth or fifth at most. Melodies that start high and end low, or vice versa, are less common.

EXAMPLE 7–13: Schubert, *Nähe des Geliebten,* Op. 5, No. 2

Langsam, feierlich, mit Anmut

From the metric standpoint, the beginning of a melodic phrase is measured by the appearance of a downbeat, which may or may not be preceded by an upbeat. The upbeat, also called the *anacrusis,* is analogous to a weak syllable that begins a line of verse; it may include the entire beat preceding the downbeat, or just a portion of it, as in the example above.

THE MOTIVE

The name *motive* is given to a short thematic unit, melodic or rhythmic or both, which is subject to repetition and transformation. A motive is thematic because it is recurrent and recognizable; at the same time, it is not usually an independent melody because its characteristic appearance is as a constituent part of a melody.

EXAMPLE 7–14: Bach, *Clavier Concerto in D minor,* III

The motive in the example above has the rhythmic pattern of two sixteenth notes followed by an eighth note, repeated regularly, and thus it is a rhythmic motive; but it is also a melodic motive, because its melodic pattern, a principal tone with lower neighbor note, is the same throughout.

In all applications of a motive one expects to find variety as much as unity, and transformations as much as literal restate-

90

ments. Yet the degree of resemblance, not the degree of variation, should be the criterion of whether or not a particular
configuration of notes is motivic. If the transformation of the motive is so extensive that it is no longer recognizable as resembling
the original, then it is no longer the motive but something else,
perhaps a new motive; on the other hand, any resemblances
among transformed motives will enable them to be considered as
related.

EXAMPLE 7–15: Mozart, *Symphony No. 38*, K. 504, I

The lengthy theme above shows five different versions of a
motive, labeled a^1, a^2, a^3, a^4, a^5, all differing by their exact note
content or duration and by their intervallic content (a major
sixth between the first and second notes in a^1 and a^2, a minor
seventh in a^3 and a^4, an octave in a^5). But the resemblance of
contour among all of these different versions is considered greater
than their intervallic, durational, or pitch differences, and thus
they are all considered related versions of one motivic shape a.
Another aspect is the location of these motivic statements in the
measure with respect to the barline; when this is considered, the
various a's fall into two exactly comparable two-measure patterns,
which we have labeled A^1 and A^2 as representing a classification
of a's on a slightly higher level than that of the individual a's. The
second half of the melody shows no resemblance to the a motive
at all, other than the elementary relationship of four successive
eighth notes; instead, a new motive (b^1, b^2, b^3) appears.

Motives can be as short as two notes or even a single note,
though when they are longer than seven or eight notes they cannot
be used as frequently or as flexibly because they occupy a comparatively larger amount of musical space. This is admittedly a
matter of definition that depends on the hearer's ability to retain patterns, and on the consideration of where one thematic
or formal level ends and another begins. It is most convenient to
regard a motive as a unit that allows at least two statements within
a phrase.

Motives are mainly an aspect of melody, and thus far they have been discussed in connection with leading melodies, but any part of a musical texture may be motivic, whether the principal melody, secondary melody, or accompaniment. The term *figuration* is used to denote a repeated melodic pattern that is accompanimental or subsidiary to a principal melody.

EXAMPLE 7–16: Chopin, *Prelude*, Op. 28, No. 8

The example above shows an interior melody using a single rhythmic motive, in the middle of a texture of two figurations, one in the right hand, the other in the left.

The contrapuntal style of the late Baroque often included a pervasive use of short motives in any or all melodic parts, as a means of continuity in the individual melodic lines (Example 7–6). At the opposite extreme was a favorite technique of Beethoven, which was marked by the relentless repetition of motives as a means of extending musical time and action. The following example shows an opening melody made up of two different motives which then become separated; in conjunction, transformation, and repetition, the two motives account for forty-two of the forty-six measures of the example.

EXAMPLE 7–17: Beethoven, *Leonore Overture No. 3*

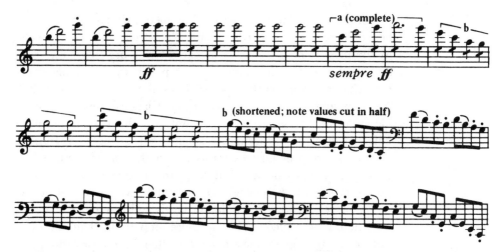

All of the above is melodic, because it has note-to-note melodic
continuity, and except for the four measures of sustained high G
it is all thematic, because it is made up of motivic fragments of
the opening theme. Yet the entire passage has melodic importance
only at the points where the complete theme is stated, at the beginning and again at *sempre ff;* the rest of it is connective, a way
of extending the psychological action of the theme through many
measures. Even when the complete theme is not present, we know
that the musical space around it somehow belongs to it because
its motivic fragments mark the space. (The tonality marks the
space, too, by providing a single key framework in which the theme
can operate, but that is a different consideration.)

The Phrase

What a musical phrase is can perhaps best be defined by analogy:
the phrase in music is comparable to the line in rhymed verse.
The phrase shows a certain regularity in its number of measures,
which is usually four or eight. It ends with a cadence, which is not
a pause but something more like a breath that does not interrupt
the flow of one phrase into the next. Most important, the phrase
is perceived as a unit of musical thought, like a sentence or
clause, and it generally implies that another phrase is to follow
unless it shows a certain amount of finality. The phrase is what
measures the beginning and ending of a melodic unit, as well as
the point of departure for the next.

Phrase structure is one of the most important regulators of
musical time. At the most immediate level, we perceive tones   93

organized by rhythm and measured by meter, which is the perception of a regularly occurring pattern of strong and weak beats. At the most remote level, we perceive music organized into separate movements of different formal types, with a sectional structure characterizing each type, such as the exposition, development, recapitulation, and coda of the Classical sonata form. A hierarchy of phrase structure accounts for the various levels in between these time extremes. A small group of measures forms a phrase; a group of phrases forms a period or a subsection; half of a phrase may be a subphrase. An enormous variability in phrase types is to be encountered in music, which is why not all writers agree on what the different levels and categories of phrasing should be called. What is more important than an exact nomenclature is an appreciation of the different interpretations that may be made from different viewpoints.

When phrases or subphrases occur together in balanced or matched pairs, that is, when the second phrases seems to complement or answer the first, the two phrases are called *antecedent* and *consequent*. The antecedent–consequent relationship is found everywhere in music, especially in dance forms and songs, but in many other types as well. The paired relationship of phrases is so common as to suggest that it fills a deeply felt instinctive need, both in the metric and formal sense, like rhyme in poetry.

The following theme by Mozart is analyzed from the standpoint of motive and phrase on several levels.

EXAMPLE 7–18: Mozart, *Sonata*, K. 331, I

The overall form is simple: eight measures balanced by eight measures, with a two-measure extension at the end. Furthermore, one notices that measures 5–8 are very similar to 1–4, with 5–6 exactly like 1–2, and 13–16 are closer still to 5–8, again with 13–14 exactly like 1–2. Only 9–12 show significant departure from the patterns of the others, and even measure 9 shows a kinship of rhythm and shape with measure 1. The example is a simple illustration of the skillful balance between association of similar ideas and contrast of dissimilar ideas that is characteristic of musical form as practiced by the masters.

HARMONY IN MELODY

It is apparent that not all melodic successions are purely melodic, just as not all chords consist of notes attacked simultaneously. Most kinds of music, particularly instrumental music, will show on nearly every page examples of chords stated to some extent in arpeggiated form, that is, with the factors of the chord stated in melodic succession. There is no doubt that a succession of tones such as in the right- or left-hand part of the example below is by definition melodic, because one note follows another; at the same time it is plain that we do not hear it as a note-to-note melodic succession, for the melodic motion of these notes is subsidiary to the harmonic element when we consider the total succession of forty-eight notes.

EXAMPLE 7–19: Chopin, *Etude*, Op. 25, No. 1
("Aeolian Harp Etude")

We can see more clearly what the real harmonic and melodic elements are by making a reduction which removes repeated successions of triadic factors by notating them as a single simultaneous chord. This leaves as the principal melodic element the succession of tones given in large notes by Chopin. The rest is all harmonic support, the progression moving smoothly with only steps and common tones except in the bass.

95

EXAMPLE 7–20

A melody may imply a polyphony of distinct melodic lines rather than just one line and chordal support. The melody given below suggests what has been called a *compound line,* two parts merged into one. One possible way of hearing the separate lines is shown.

Cf. Ex. 7–12

EXAMPLE 7–21: Bach, *Well-Tempered Clavier, II,* Prelude No. 1

The preceding examples of melodies in keyboard music depend at least theoretically on the harmonic support of a left-hand part, even though in the Chopin example the left hand does little more than duplicate the tones of the right and provide a bass, while the left hand of the Bach consists of nothing but two measures of a sustained C pedal point. Music for an unaccompanied monophonic instrument, on the other hand, can rely on no simultaneities at all. All harmony in such music, including bass support or at least the appearance of one, must be provided internally, within the melody itself. For this reason, monophonic music is very useful for harmonic study, even though it constitutes but a very small part of the common-practice repertory. The best examples are found in the sonatas and partitas for solo violin and the suites for solo cello by J. S. Bach; all of these works also contain passages of multiple stops which contrast with the extensive monophonic writing. The following example is from an entirely monophonic work.

EXAMPLE 7–22: Bach, *Sonata for Unaccompanied Flute:* I, Allemande

a: I V_9^o I V^7 I V_9^o I V^7

I   IV⁶   I$^6_4$ IV⁷   V⁷   (^9_o)   (7)   I   V⁷ of VI

VI
C: IV   II   V   III   VI   IV   V   I

Internal harmony is one of the most important aspects that must be considered when a melody is to be analyzed, but it must not be supposed that all melodies will show an obvious internal harmony. Many melodies do not suggest just one harmonic interpretation, but rather a choice of interpretations; many others will hardly suggest any harmony at all except in a very rudimentary way, such as tonic harmony suggested by repetition of the tonic note. Most types of cantus firmus, which are mostly very conjunct, nonrhythmic, and slow-moving, implying a change of harmony with nearly every note, will fall into these categories.

Most melodies of the common-practice period will probably be included in the broad middle category, in which conjunct motion will be contrasted with arpeggiation of triadic factors, and, somewhat less often, disjunct motion that does not imply a triadic stabilization of the disjunct interval. Ordinarily such melodies will require at least part of their harmonic interpretation to be supplied externally, by the accompaniment. For instance, the triadic portions of the initial measures of the following example are easy enough to follow in the melody alone, but the last three measures might be variously interpreted if the actual accompaniment were not present.

EXAMPLE 7–23: Beethoven, *Violin Sonata*, Op. 47 ("Kreutzer"), I

It often happens, even in the course of a mostly polyphonic piece, that a melody is stated alone, without any supporting harmony. If such a melody does not clearly imply a harmonic background, then the ear is left to imagine one, which may not be easy to do unambiguously. Such ambiguities may of course be resolved at a later point in the piece. The following example shows a four-measure melody with octave doubling, its altered restatement, and the harmonized versions of both from later in the movement, each excerpt followed by two measures of continuation to show some of the harmonic context. What is interesting is that the harmonizations are probably not exactly what might have been predicted on the basis of the unharmonized melodies. Nevertheless, there is nothing implausible about the harmonizations; they are entirely satisfactory both in their immediate context and as resolution of expectations of the original statements. Composers constantly have to deal with problems like these, though they think of them not as problems but as opportunities for expression and invention.

EXAMPLE 7–24: Schubert, *Symphony No. 9*, III

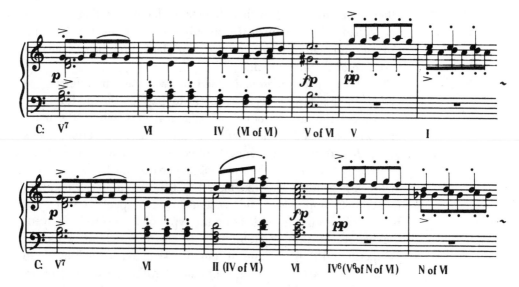

C: V⁷   VI   IV (VI of VI)   V of VI   V   I

C: V⁷   VI   II (IV of VI)   VI   IV⁶(V⁶ of N of VI)   N of VI

To summarize, we should observe that just as the faculty of musical memory enables us to assimilate all the notes of a melody as a single idea, rather than just as a succession of tones, so does memory enable us to hear the harmonic relationship between arpeggiated tones in a melody, even when this relationship is hidden by stepwise motion. The ear searches a melody for such a harmonic basis, instinctively fixing upon whatever triadic configuration is most prominent at a given time, and relating it to the next configuration that appears. It is plain, however, that the sense of internal harmony in a melody is affected by any amount of stepwise motion, because adjacent steps in conjunct melody are dissonant with respect to each other. When a melodic succession is conjunct—which is to say, most of the time—the perception of harmony within the melody will depend to an all-important extent on the shape of the melody, on the location of its notes with respect to the barline, on the rhythmic relationship of the tones to each other, and on the repetition of whatever motives there may be. All of these factors will be involved in determining which of the tones will reinforce or weaken any underlying harmony.

MELODIC VARIATION

The idea of introducing changes in a melody when it is restated is certainly one of the most important principles of musical form; its most systematic manifestation, the technique of theme and variations, has existed in music for nearly four centuries. Like the other topics discussed in this chapter, melodic variation is a vast and varied subject, which will be only summarily dealt with here. For the moment, we will confine our discussion to ornamental variation of the melodic line.

The term *ornamentation* is used in two ways in referring to music. In the narrow sense it refers to part of the performance practice of the late Baroque and Classical eras, where the notes of a written melodic line would be "adorned" with various kinds of rapidly-executed grace notes and combinations of short melodic figures. The French composers of keyboard music in the mid-eighteenth century had the most highly evolved usage of ornaments, both improvised and written down. A special set of symbols came into use for indicating the types of figures to be played; the variety of these can be seen in the harpsichord works of Couperin and Rameau, and in some works of Bach, such as No. 5 of his *Three-Part Inventions* (*Sinfonias*). Although the use of ornaments was at times so profuse as to be a stylistic mannerism, there is no doubt that they constituted a valuable adjunct to melodic variety when skillfully employed. Beginning in the later part of the eighteenth century, the use of ornamental symbols declined in favor of the practice of writing out the actual notes with their appropriate time values, although some symbols such as the grace-note sign, the turn (∾), and the trill sign continued in common use, in some cases even into the present day.

In the broader sense, ornamentation of a melodic line involves adding tones to it in such a way that its original form or profile can still be discerned. A simple instance is given below, showing the original statement of a theme and the somewhat boisterously ornamented version that immediately follows it.

EXAMPLE 7–25: Beethoven, *Trio*, Op. 97 ("Archduke"), IV

The melody by Mozart given above in Example 7–18 is the theme of a variation set. The beginning of the first variation is shown in Example 8–13, showing adjacent tones added to the rhythmically stronger notes of the theme, as was mostly the case in the Beethoven example just shown. The beginnings of some of the other variations are shown below.

EXAMPLE 7–26: Mozart, *Sonata*, K. 331, I

Var. 2

Var. 5   Adagio

Var. 6   Allegro

There is some bias in the preceding example, in that the complete melodies are not given, nor are the more divergent variations shown (nos. 3 and 4). The student should examine the entire movement to obtain a balanced view. Nevertheless, the example illustrates a valuable point: that the theme and the variation beginnings cited are different mainly in rhythm and in the occasional addition of a decorative tone, and, in the sixth variation, in meter as well. What are more striking than the differences, however, are the similarities. So similar, indeed, are the above variations to the original theme that they give the impression of being ornamentations not just of the theme itself but of an even simpler melodic outline, of which Mozart's original theme is perhaps itself an ornamentation.

One might, for instance, look for such a background line by a process of reducing the melody by successive elimination of details. The analysis then becomes a question of what is detail as opposed to what is central, a question whose answer is by no means always instantly apparent. The following example, using only the first half of the theme, shows one way such a reduction might be accomplished.

101

EXAMPLE 7–27

In *a* above, the first stage of reduction, repeated notes are merged into single notes. In *b*, neighbor notes are deleted, and the tones to which they were neighbors likewise merged into single notes. In the third reductive stage, *c*, barlines and durational values are eliminated, but a notational hierarchy has been constructed which to an extent takes account of the metric values of the notes in the melody. The downbeat tones seem in this case to be the more important, and they are shown in white notes beamed together with solid lines; the dashed beam points up an apparent connection between tones that are the same pitch. The remaining notes, given as stemless black notes, are either arpeggiations to the main notes (because of their parallel relationship) or passing tones or neighbor notes, these last two being indicated by slurs connecting their surrounding principals. In stage *d*, passing tones and neighbor notes are deleted, repeated tones that remain are condensed, and the arpeggiations placed together with their principals. In the final stage, the arpeggiations are removed, leaving only the three scale degrees C sharp, B, and A as the basic foundation of Mozart's melody. This type of analysis has been variously called *reduction technique, level analysis,* or *layer analysis.*

One might well apply the same kinds of reduction procedures to an entirely different melody, systematically deleting ninety percent of its notes, and come up with an identical final reductive stage. What this means, of course, is that there can be family resemblances among different melodies. But one should not make the mistake of thinking that the family resemblance is the same thing as the essence. It is not possible that the underlying three-step melodic progression shown in the reduction in any way implies or generates the finished theme. Mozart himself may well have been aware that his theme was supported by or based on the three-note succession, but even the certainty of that awareness would really mean next to nothing; what is meaningful for the piece, and hence for the listener, is the actual theme as the composer wrote it, with all its individuality.

On the other hand, the student should recognize that the search for a possible reduction of a melody, along the lines just shown, can be a valuable exercise in mental hearing. Such a reduction can bring to light important structural relationships in a melody, especially when the reduction is carried to a middle level, with most of the details remaining; more than that, reduction shows that levels of perception may exist in a melody itself, just as they exist on the larger scale of motives, phrases, and groups of phrases, as well as in larger formal units. For the most part, however, melodic investigations of this kind are a part of advanced musical study and should be undertaken cautiously at this stage, without trying to put too fine a point on detailed interpretation.

MELODY IN VARIATION FORMS

The Mozart variations, though well suited to the demonstration just given, are actually a less than typical example of the theme-and-variation form, because for the most part they stay very close to the theme. A more usual procedure, in Mozart's time and after, would be to retain the original theme literally in only one or two variations as a secondary voice, with different countermelodies superimposed; the other variations would vary the melody more substantially, and vary in addition the supporting harmony, the meter, the mode, even the key. Viewed as a whole in the common-practice period, the best works using the theme-and-variation form are marked by extreme departures from the melodic outline of the theme. One would probably find it difficult, for instance, to perceive the melodic relationship between the theme and the melody of the third variation of Brahms's famous Haydn set, on first hearing.

EXAMPLE 7–28: Brahms, *Variations on a Theme of Haydn,* Op. 56

The variation sets of Bach, Mozart, and later composers show that where the variations depart significantly from the melody, the element of unity among the variations is provided principally by the supporting harmony and the phrase structure, though these too may be subjected to variation. The most famous examples of this type are Bach's *Aria with 30 Variations* (the "Goldberg Variations"), which are variations on a 32-measure ground bass, and Beethoven's *33 Variations on a Waltz by Diabelli,* Op. 120.

APPROACH TO MELODIC ANALYSIS

Analysis of a melody should begin with the determination of its phrase and subphrase boundaries, including cadence and subcadence, and where the first downbeat occurs. Motivic subunits of rhythm or interval pattern may then be considered, and their possible correlation with changes of harmony. Melodic climaxes, as well as rhythmic stresses, are often to be related to important harmonic changes.

An attempt should be made to determine the harmonic structure of the melody from the melodic characteristics alone, where a harmonic structure is apparent. The reduction through successive levels to uncover the fundamental underlying motion of the melody is also useful, though many melodies will prove to be not readily susceptible to this kind of analysis. The student is advised not to attempt it in any case until he has completed Chapter 8, Nonharmonic Tones.

When a melody is considered as an element of a complete texture in a given passage, its internal structure can be seen more clearly in relation to the whole. It is important, however, to appreciate the qualities of structure that may be discerned by studying melodies in isolation. Melody is, to a greater extent than any other aspect, the wellspring of the compositional process, in which the individualities of the composer's inspiration are often most apparent.

The student should not be daunted by the unforeseen appearance of subtle or difficult questions that may arise in the course of analysis. Certainly he should guard against being too easily satisfied with a simple analysis, but he should also be aware that a too-rigorous analytical approach may do little to increase the understanding. The subtleties of great music are always worth revealing; nevertheless, one does not uncover them in a single effort, but rather over a lifetime of study, and with a variety of analytical methods, no one of which can be comprehensive. The accumulation of experience in analysis leads one to develop formal and logical procedures for understanding music, which is all to the good; at the same time, experience increases the keenness of one's musical intuition, which often turns out to guide comprehension in ways that are beyond formalism and logic. With both of these awarenesses in mind, the analyst realizes that his own efforts to an extent mirror the composer's.

EXERCISES

1. Analyze the following melodies from the standpoint of shape, phrase, rhythm, motive structure, and internal harmony. Summarize your findings about each melody in a paragraph of not more than 100 words, accompanied by not more than two examples or diagrams.

a. **Presto** (J. S. Bach)

etc. 105

2. Examine a work or movement in theme-and-variation form. Choose three variations and compare their uses of the theme with the theme as originally stated. What are the differences? What are the similarities?

3. Compose melodic fragments so as to appropriately fill the blanks in the following melodies.

a. Tempo di menuetto (Schubert)

b. Allegro (adapted from Haydn)

c. (Andante) (J. S. Bach)

d. (Schumann)

4. Construct melodies using the indicated rhythms, and using only notes which are factors of the indicated triads.

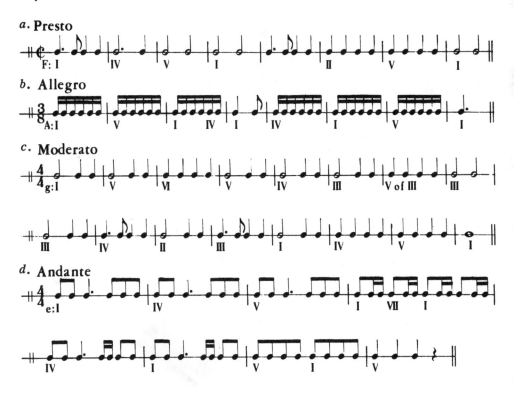

a. Presto

F: I   IV   V   I   II   V   I

b. Allegro

A: I   V   I   IV   I   IV   I   V   I

c. Moderato

g: I   V   VI   V   IV   III   V of III   III

III   IV   II   III   I   IV   V   I

d. Andante

e: I   IV   V   I   VII   I

IV   I   V   I   V

e. **Menuetto**

D:I V I V VI II V

I IV II V I IV I V I

f. **Mazurka**

c: I V I V IV I II V I

108

CHAPTER 8

Nonharmonic Tones

It is noticeable that the texture of music contains melodic tones which are not members of the chord against which they are sounded. Literally, there is no such thing as a nonharmonic tone, since tones sounding together create harmony. We know this process to be the very origin of chords. But the language of music has grown like any other language. Certain forms become established through usage. We sense a harmonic background capable of reduction to a comparatively small number of chords which we call the harmonic material of music. These chords make up the harmonic scheme we have been drawing up to represent the skeleton, or framework, upon which the more complex melodic structure rests. As we have seen, they contribute their own underlying rhythmic life to the whole.

MELODIC DISSONANCE

We have remarked before that the principle of polyphony is two-dimensional, that is, vertical and horizontal. Its assumptions are that the ear can perceive a harmonic relationship between two   109

tones sounded simultaneously, and a melodic relationship between two tones sounded in succession. The combination of these
two relationships is the contrapuntal relationship, and the ear's
perception of counterpoint is simultaneously harmonic and melodic. All polyphonic music involves all three of these elements,
though to different extents in different kinds of music. The most
plainly chordal music will have melodic relationships in its successive tones, and a contrapuntal relationship between its melodic relationships; the most elaborately linear polyphony will
have contrapuntal relationships between its melodic lines, and
harmonic relationships between its simultaneous tones.

In the previous chapter we saw that melodic relationships can
imply harmony, the simplest case being when successive melodic
tones are factors of a chord. The triadic arpeggiation of melodic
tones necessarily means disjunct motion, because the factors of a
triad are not adjacent tones in the scale. (The converse of this is
not necessarily true, because a melodic skip, for example a seventh, can occur between two tones which are not factors of a
triad.)

Conjunct or stepwise motion implies the dissonant relationship
of adjacent tones, by definition, because the major second and the
minor second are defined to be dissonances. The other side of
this coin is the fact that any dissonant interval may be converted
into a consonant interval by the stepwise displacement (by either
a major or a minor second) of one of its factors; in other words,
any dissonance has a possible stepwise resolution to a consonance.
These empirical facts are the basis of the theory and practice of
counterpoint. On the one hand they permit stepwise melodic
motion, while on the other hand they make it harmonically necessary.

Taking the opposite approach, we can easily ascertain by experiment that any consonance may be converted to a dissonance
by the stepwise displacement of one of its factors. With somewhat
more effort we can determine that a consonance may undergo
stepwise displacement of one of its factors within the scale, and the
resulting interval may still be consonant; this happens only when
the perfect fifth moves to a sixth, or vice versa, by oblique motion,
the so-called 6–5 motion. When the perfect fourth is supported by
a third below it, it is consonant and its upper tone may descend
to form a third; but this motion will then necessarily form a 6–5

110 relationship with the tone underneath.

EXAMPLE 8–1

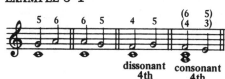

Up to now we have considered triads as fixed entities in musical texture, their factors not being allowed to move except to change the spacing or when the entire chord moves to a new harmony. Melodic motion that produces dissonant intervals has thus been excluded from our consideration. In this chapter we will investigate dissonances arising in melodic motion. These dissonances are called *nonharmonic tones*. The discussion above has been aimed at showing that stepwise melodic motion, which is after all the most basic type of melodic motion, can both generate and resolve dissonances. Our purpose here will be to discover how these occur and how they fit into the structure of melody and harmony.

It is important to understand that the nonharmonic tones do not derive their melodic and rhythmic characteristics from the fact that they are foreign to the harmony. Their true nature is inherently melodic and can be discovered by study of the melodic line alone. The purely melodic quality is emphasized by their not agreeing with the chord tones, but it frequently happens that one of these tones is identical with a chord tone.

One exception: the pedal (see Exx. 8–52— 8–56)

EXAMPLE 8–2

The E in the tenor is a chord tone, while that in the soprano is a melodic decoration of the resolution to C of the suspended D.

The implied anachronism in the accepted term *nonharmonic tones* may be explained on the ground that during the period of harmonic common practice, which we are studying, the composers were so chord-minded that it may be assumed that they created melody with reference to harmony. In this way the tones would be more readily divided into those which are chord tones and those which are not. This is the point of view recommended 111 in the study of harmony, leaving the other more linear aspects to the study of counterpoint and melodic analysis. This pedagogical conceit, however, is simultaneously a warning. Neither harmony nor counterpoint is complete in itself as a description of or justification for the practice of composers.

THE PASSING TONE

A melodic skip may be filled in with tones on all intervening steps, either diatonic or chromatic. These are called *passing tones*.

EXAMPLE 8–3

In our examples, passing tones will be indicated with the abbreviation "p.t.", or, where too many of these abbreviations would crowd the example, by a cross mark (+).

The interval filled in by passing tones is not necessarily an interval between two members of the same chord.

EXAMPLE 8–4

I   IV   I   VI

Passing tones are rhythmically weak, and may occur on any beat or fraction of the measure. They are not accented. The "accented passing tone", that is, on the strong beat or the strong portion of a weak beat, is really an appoggiatura, discussed later in this chapter. In the example below, it is obvious that the passing tones are unaccented even though taking place on the beat.

EXAMPLE 8–5: Beethoven, *Sonata*, Op. 10, No. 3, IV

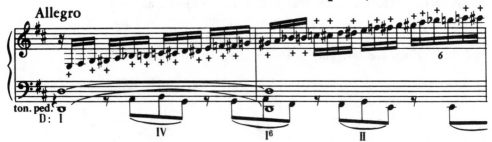

The composer may cause a passing tone to be accented by the use of dynamic signs, calling for an accentuation which otherwise would not occur.

EXAMPLE 8–6: Mozart, *String Quartet*, K. 387, II

Passing tones are employed in all voices, and when used simultaneously in different voices they may result in a degree of complexity. Too many such tones tend to obscure the underlying framework and weaken the effect of the music. The student is advised to study the works of Johann Sebastian Bach as models of balance in the use of all nonharmonic tones. In applying these resources in exercises it is recommended that they be sparingly used at first, emphasizing the clarity of harmonic structure.

EXAMPLE 8–7: Bach, Chorale No. 369, *Jesu, der du meine Seele*

EXAMPLE 8–8: Bach, *Well-Tempered Clavier, II*, Fugue No. 17

In the minor mode, the sixth and seventh degrees, when they are used as passing tones, will be derived from the melodic scale, ascending or descending.

113

EXAMPLE 8–9

C: I.   V   +   I

THE NEIGHBOR NOTE

The *neighbor note* (the commonly-used synonym *auxiliary tone*, or simply *auxiliary*, will also be employed in this book) is a tone of weak rhythmic value which serves to ornament a stationary tone. It is approached by either a half step or a whole step from the tone it ornaments, and it returns to that tone.

EXAMPLE 8–10

EXAMPLE 8–11: Bach, *Brandenburg Concerto No. 3*, I

A change of harmony may take place as the neighbor returns to the main tone.

EXAMPLE 8–12: Brahms, Chorale Prelude, *Es ist ein Ros' entsprungen*, Op. 122, No. 8

114

The neighbor note is not always a scale degree of the key, but is frequently altered chromatically to bring it a half tone closer to the main tone. When it is below, it has the character of a temporary leading-tone of the scale degree it attends.

EXAMPLE 8–13: Mozart, *Sonata*, K. 331, I

The upper and lower neighbors combine to form a melodic turn of five notes around a central tone.

EXAMPLE 8–14: Schumann, *Carnaval*, Op. 9: No. 5, *Eusebius*

The melodic figure shown in the example above is often found with the third note omitted. Such a grouping is called the *double neighbor note*, implying that it is a single tone ornamented by two neighbor notes.

EXAMPLE 8–15: Berlioz, *Symphonie fantastique*, II: *A Ball*

EXAMPLE 8–16: Liszt, *Sonata*

Two or three neighbor notes occurring at the same time in similar motion make a chord which might be termed a *neighbor chord* or an *auxiliary chord*.

EXAMPLE 8–17: Liszt, *Les Préludes*

The *incomplete neighbor note* (labeled IN) is the result of omission of either the initiating or the returning principal tone. It is a component of the escape-tone and reaching-tone formulae, discussed below, but it is also seen independently from them. In the following example, the incomplete neighbors are analogous to appoggiature, but are rhythmically weak.

EXAMPLE 8–18: Beethoven, *Sonata*, Op. 31, No. 1, II

Many instances of grace notes are incomplete neighbor notes of the leading-tone type, comparable to the above example.

Like the passing tone, the neighbor note is not invariably a dissonant tone; it is consonant when it is a component of a fifth moving to a sixth and back again. When neighbor to the fifth of a triad in root position, it remains consonant with the third of the triad, becoming itself the root of a triad in first inversion; the harmonic progression resulting is ordinarily considered to be very weak if it has taken place at all, thus underscoring the nature of the consonant neighbor note as a melodic tone.

EXAMPLE 8–19

The neighbor note differs from the passing tone in that it inhibits melodic progression; it prevents a melody from moving from one point to another. For this reason its melodic usefulness is more limited. In common practice the neighbor note is not usually found in rhythmic isolation, apart from adjacent figures of the same time value. More generally, it is found repeated, or in combination with other nonharmonic tones in the same voice or other voices, or as part of a recurring motive repeated several times (Example 8–11). By itself, in the absence of motivic, ornamental, or contrapuntal considerations, the neighbor note may give the impression of being unnecessary to the texture or to the progress of the melody, and in such a case it might be better omitted.

The restricted usage of the neighbor note, as contrasted with the passing tone, is in part a survival from the contrapuntal practice of the sixteenth century, where the dissonant neighbor note was employed in third-species motion (four notes against one) but not in second-species motion (two notes against one).

THE ANTICIPATION

As its name implies, the *anticipation* is a kind of advance sounding of a note. It is rhythmically like an upbeat to the tone anticipated, to which it is usually not tied.

See also Ex. 9–14

EXAMPLE 8–20: Mozart, *Symphony No. 34*, K. 338, I

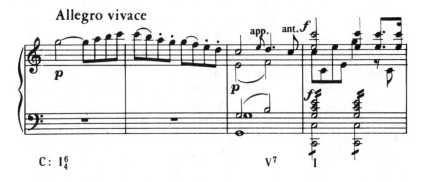

The anticipation is ordinarily shorter in time value than the principal tone, as in the preceding example. The following example of figurational anticipations shows them of equal time value.

117

EXAMPLE 8–21: Bach, *St. Matthew Passion*, No. 36

The anticipation in the cadence shown below, with the tonic sounding simultaneously with its own leading-tone, is an example of the so-called *Corelli clash*.

EXAMPLE 8–22: Handel, *Concerto Grosso*, Op. 6, No. 5, IV

THE APPOGGIATURA

All nonharmonic tones are rhythmically weak, with the single exception of the *appoggiatura* (pl. *appoggiature*). The derivation of the term (from the Italian verb *appoggiare*, "to lean") gives the best clue to its character. It gives the impression of leaning heavily on the tone into which it finally resolves, by half or whole step. The rhythm of the appoggiatura followed by its note of resolution is invariably strong-to-weak.

The force of the appoggiatura depends on the way in which the ear perceives it as relating to the surrounding harmony. Ordinarily the appoggiatura will resolve to a consonant factor of the chord. An additional consideration is the question of preparation. The appoggiatura is a smoother, less obtrusive component of the melodic line when it is self-prepared, the same pitch appearing before it either as a factor of the preceding harmony (*a* in the example below) or as a nonharmonic tone (*b*). The next smoothest preparation of the appoggiatura is by step from above or below (*c*, *d*).

118

It is not prepared if it enters by skip *(e)*. This type of appoggiatura is necessarily more abrupt melodically.

EXAMPLE 8–23

The appoggiatura is special among the nonharmonic tones in being characterized by different types of preparation. In general, the other nonharmonic tones are intrinsically prepared, like the passing tone and the suspension, and the quality of their dissonance cannot be expected to vary except insofar as they are used in combination in different voices at the same time. The preparation or nonpreparation of dissonance is less a rule of counterpoint than a detail of style, and may be inconsistent in different works by the same composer.

EXAMPLE 8–24: Bach, *Well-Tempered Clavier, I,*
Prelude No. 24

EXAMPLE 8–25: Bach, *Well-Tempered Clavier, I,* Fugue No. 24

In arranging an appoggiatura with a four-part chord, it is customary to avoid doubling the note of resolution, especially when the appoggiatura is not in the upper voice. The note of resolution is doubled in the bass in chords in root position, the appoggiatura being far enough above to be clearly followed melodically.

119

EXAMPLE 8–26

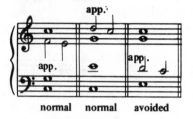

normal   normal   avoided

EXAMPLE 8–27: Beethoven, *Sonata*, Op. 7, IV

Allegretto

E♭: II   V⁷   I   V

The appoggiatura may be below the note toward which it is
tending. Commonest of this type is the leading-tone appoggiatura
to the tonic.

EXAMPLE 8–28: Chopin, *Prelude*, Op. 28, No. 8

(Molto agitato)

f♯: III   –II⁶   V⁷   I

The preceding example is a nineteenth-century survivor of
eighteenth-century notational convention, which employed a special ornamental symbol resembling the grace note but lacking the
diagonal cross-stroke. To avoid confusion, most modern editions
write out the appoggiatura and resolution with their proper note-
values.

EXAMPLE 8–29: Beethoven, *Sonata*, Op. 2, No. 1, III

execution:

Like the neighbor note, the appoggiatura is often found as a chromatically altered scale degree. The alteration gives it an added tendency toward its destination similar to the tendency of a leading-tone.

EXAMPLE 8–30: Brahms, *Piano Concerto No. 2*, IV

The rarely used augmented triad on III in the minor mode contains a built-in appoggiatura.

EXAMPLE 8–31: Schubert, *Andantino varié for Piano Four Hands*, Op. 84, No. 1

A most pungent form of appoggiatura is that of the lowered seventh degree, descending minor, standing for the sixth degree and sounding against the leading-tone in dominant harmony. This creates the somewhat unusual interval of the diminished octave in what is called a *simultaneous cross-relation*.

EXAMPLE 8–32: Bizet, *l'Arlésienne*, Suite No. 1: No. 4, *Carillon*

See also Exx. 5–27, 8–12, 12–12, as well as 28–31 and 31–60

Several appoggiature sounding together make an appoggiatura chord. The most familiar such chord is the dominant chord sounded over a tonic bass, usually as a delayed resolution of a dominant harmony earlier in the phrase. This so-called *five over one* is common in cadences (Example 8–18). The dominant appoggiatura may also be used in a deceptive cadence, for instance to VI.

EXAMPLE 8–33: Haydn, *Sonata No. 11*, II

THE SUSPENSION

The *suspension* is a tone whose natural progression has been rhythmically delayed.

EXAMPLE 8–34

The suspension occurs on the strong beat or on the strong portion of a weak beat, but is rhythmically weak with respect to the tone which prepares it, because of the tie. In this way it differs from the prepared appoggiatura. (It is worth noting that this difference was considered especially important in the strict counterpoint of the sixteenth century, which permitted the suspension but not the appoggiatura.) The characteristic tied note serves to delay the melodic motion while the harmony moves under it, and it also weakens the appoggiatura effect created by the simultaneous attack on the two notes that make up the dissonant interval.

EXAMPLE 8–35: Couperin, *Harpsichord Pieces, Book II:*
Sixth Order; *Les Barricades mystérieuses*

In many situations, however, the distinction between suspension and prepared appoggiatura is not possible to make, nor is it of any consequence. In the following example, the repeated notes in the second violins are clearly not tied over the barline, and the preparation of each suspension is equal to half the length of the measure; the first bassoon, not shown in the example, doubles an octave below the second violins, in sustained notes tied over the barline.

EXAMPLE 8–36: Mozart, *Piano Concerto*, K. 467, II

If the first of the two tied notes is shorter than the second, the effect is rather of an appoggiatura anticipated, or arriving too early.

EXAMPLE 8–37: Bach, *Christmas Oratorio*, Part II: Sinfonia

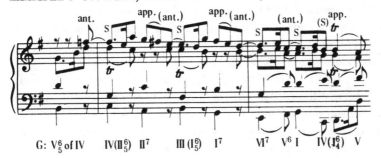

The resolution of the suspension is usually to the scale step below, but the upward resolution is not infrequent. If the suspended note is a leading-tone, or a chromatically raised tone, it will have a natural resolution to the note above.

EXAMPLE 8–38: Beethoven, *String Trio*, Op. 3, VI

When several tones are suspended at once, they constitute a suspended chord, so that there may be two harmonies heard at the same time, a familiar effect in cadences of slow movements.

EXAMPLE 8–39: Brahms, *Intermezzo*, Op. 117, No. 2

SUCCESSIVE NONHARMONIC TONES

Nonharmonic tones may occur in succession, their normal resolutions being overlapped with or interrupted by the next tone, or the resolution may be postponed by the interpolation of a harmonic note that is not the note of resolution. Such linear combinations of nonharmonic tones are called *ornamental resolutions*. The principle of nonimmediate resolution of nonharmonic tones is a resource of melodic vitality, particularly in music with prominent contrapuntal elements.

The suspension does not usually resolve on a fraction of a beat, particularly the second half of the first beat. In normal rhythmic movement the amount of time a note is suspended is at least the value of one whole beat or pulse. There are, however, a number of ornamental resolutions of the suspension which may provide melodic activity before the actual note of resolution arrives. These ornamental resolutions may occur in the form of neighbor note, escape tone (E), reaching tone (R), or anticipation, or there may be a chord tone interpolated between the suspension and its resolution.

EXAMPLE 8–40

EXAMPLE 8–41: Handel, *Suite No. 3:* II, Fugue

d: IV⁶   I⁶   V⁶₄   V of V   V   IV⁶   I   V⁶

EXAMPLE 8–42: Bach, *Well-Tempered Clavier, II,* Fugue No. 5

D: I   II ⁽⁷⁾   V   I (V⁶of IV)(IV) VII⁶ I V

ESCAPE TONE AND REACHING TONE

The escape tone and reaching tone, in their most characteristic
forms, are interpolations between suspensions and their resolutions, as shown in Example 8–40*b* and *c,* and in comparable
resolutions of appoggiature. Their essential shape consists respectively of step followed by skip and vice versa, the second motion
always in opposite direction to the first. The *escape tone* is like a
note escaping from the direction of the melodic movement and
having to return by skip, that is, by an interval larger than a
second. On the other hand, the *reaching tone* is the result of
having gone too far, so that it is necessary to turn back by step
to the note of destination.

EXAMPLE 8–43

melodic movement   melodic movement

EXAMPLE 8–44: Haydn, *String Quartet*, Op. 76, No. 3, III

C : I   V⁷   I

EXAMPLE 8–45: Brahms, *Variations on a Theme by Haydn*, Op. 56

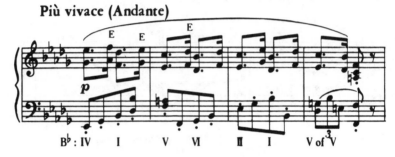

Bᵇ : IV   I   V   VI   II   I   V of V

EXAMPLE 8–46: Mozart, *Sonata*, K. 533, II

bᵇ: I   II   VII⁶   I⁶

EXAMPLE 8–47: Chopin, *Mazurka*, Op. 59, No. 2

Aᵇ: I   VI⁶₅   V⁷ of V   V⁹

    The French equivalent *échappée* is used in many books instead of *escape tone*. What we call the *reaching tone* was formerly called 126 *cambiata* (Italian for "exchanged") because of its supposed resemblance to the *nota cambiata* of sixteenth-century counterpoint, but this term is now obsolete.

The escape-tone and reaching-tone patterns may be used to bridge any melodic progression of a second, up or down. It is not necessary that the initiating tone be a dissonance. When the escape tone proceeds from a chord tone, it will of course be dissonant with the chord; the reaching tone will be dissonant with the chord of destination.

The pattern of step and skip in opposite directions may be applied to wider intervals as well. In such cases, the escape tone or reaching tone is more obviously an incomplete neighbor note.

EXAMPLE 8–48: Schubert, *Rondo in A major for Piano Four Hands,* Op. 107

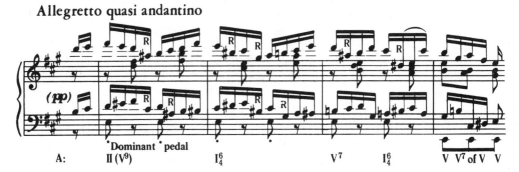

"FREE" TONES

All the nonharmonic tones thus far discussed have an explicit or implicit linear connection with their surrounding harmony. The passing tone is between two harmonic tones; the neighbor note ornaments a single tone; the appoggiatura, suspension, and reaching tone have stepwise resolutions; the escape tone is initiated by stepwise motion, and the anticipation is itself a harmony note temporarily displaced. We have also seen that nonharmonic tones may be combined in linear succession so as to merge or connect their melodic tendencies and to postpone their resolution. It would seem, then, that the practice of composers shows the possibility of immense variety in the treatment of nonharmonic tones, but that the basic assumption of linear connection to the harmonic background is never absent, even though this connection may sometimes be difficult to find.

127

If one could conceive of a "free" tone without any such connection to the harmony, then such a tone would have to be a
dissonance approached by skip and quitted by skip. Such tones
can be found, but analysis almost invariably shows them to be lin-
early comprehensible, even if not at the most immediate level.
Some of them will be types of harmonic dissonance, a concept discussed later in connection with the dominant seventh chord.
Others can be explained as extensions of the various nonharmonic-
tone types.

EXAMPLE 8–49: Bach, *Well-Tempered Clavier, II,*
Prelude No. 1

C: I   V⁷of IV   IV⁷   II⁶

In the example above, the A in the bass marked with the
arrow appears at first sight to be a dangling tone interposed in
a C-major triad; but without much effort one can hear it as an
anticipation, not directly but as the third of the IV which follows
it, as though by octave transfer to the alto voice. The following,
similar example of an interrupted anticipation is simpler, though
it sounds rather more strained.

EXAMPLE 8–50: Bach, *Christmas Oratorio,* Part I, No. 9

D: I⁶₄   V

Comparable problems of hearing arise in conjunction with irregular successions of nonharmonic tones, when the preparation or
resolution is not readily apparent. The possible interpretation will
often depend on the intuition of the listener and may or may
not be supported by evidence in the score.

EXAMPLE 8–51: Beethoven, *String Quartet*, Op. 59, No. 1, III

Adagio molto e mesto

In the preceding example, the E flat is an apparent appoggiatura to the D flat, which is itself a dissonant tone resolving to the F, another appoggiatura, over the wide skip of a sixth. Without the E flat, the D flat would be an escape tone of very short duration, and this makes it an unsatisfactory tone for an appoggiatura to lean on. One possible way of hearing the melodic connections in this passage would be to imagine the upper melody to be part of a compound line, forming a five-part texture with the lower voices, as the reconstruction shows. Parenthetical notes are imagined by the ear to be part of the lines. Dotted straight lines show the melodic connections within the lines; ties show the apparent sustaining of the C between the lines. Such a reconstruction simplifies the melodic relationships of the example, but it has the obvious disadvantage of depending on the perception of tones which are not present in the actual music. It is one thing for the listener to imagine, by means of memory, the continuation of a tone already sounded; it is quite another to imagine the implied existence of a tone not sounded at all. Moreover, one may object quite legitimately that the reconstruction destroys the strange and beautiful individuality of Beethoven's melody as he wrote it. Nevertheless, such reconstructions may be a valuable aid in understanding complex melodic motion, provided that their limitations are clearly perceived; at the same time that they may reveal structural coherence, they should remind us that art dwells in subtle details.

THE PEDAL

The name *pedal* (sometimes *pedal point* or *organ point*) is applied to a tone that persists in one voice throughout several changes of harmony. The pedal is the one exception among the   129 nonharmonic tones in that it is not melodic. It tends to render the harmonic rhythm static, and this effect is usully offset by the use of chords dissonant both in themselves and with the pedal. A typical pedal will be at some moment foreign to the harmony with which it sounds, though it customarily begins and ends as a member of the harmony. Thus the pedal effect is distinct from the related phenomenon of static harmony (Chapters 9 and 13).

There are almost no restrictions as to the use of the pedal. It may appear in the bass, as the upper voice, or as an inner part. It may be on any degree of the scale, although by far the commonest pedals are on the tonic or dominant, most often in the bass.

The term *pedal* originated as descriptive of the natural procedure of holding down an organ pedal key while improvising on the manuals above. As subsequently developed by composers, however, the device seems far from the implications of its name. It is often broken into rhythmic patterns and decorated by other tones, even attaining thematic significance in ostinato figurations.

The strength of tonality inherent in the pedal makes it a very effective device for establishing or maintaining a key, even though the accompanying harmony may go far afield. As such, it has been too often relied on by inferior composers, but it is also found frequently and to excellent effect in the works of the masters. One of the commonest usages of the dominant pedal is as a preparation for the recapitulation section of a movement in sonata form, or in a slow introduction just before the exposition; similarly, the tonic pedal appears frequently in the coda section to reinforce the finality of the key.

The following example shows the variety of harmonies arranged by Verdi to underscore the tolling of a midnight bell.

EXAMPLE 8–52: Verdi, *Falstaff*, Act III, Scene 2

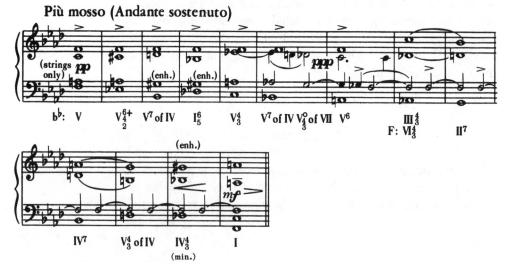

When the pedal is of short duration, with only one or two dissonant harmonies, it may be possible to regard it as the prolongation of a single chord at a more remote time level, the intervening harmony appearing as a chord of nonharmonic tones.

EXAMPLE 8–53: Clementi, *Sonatina*, Op. 36, No. 4, I

On the other hand, the following example allows an opposite kind of interpretation: the harmonic progressions are stronger than the pedal, because the harmonies are central to the tonality rather than remote from it, because the pedal is not in the bass, and because only one harmony is dissonant with it. In this case, the pedal is more like a suspension resolving irregularly, the harmony moving to absorb it, rather than the pedal itself moving to meet the harmony. Such suspension-pedals are not uncommon in the nineteenth century.

EXAMPLE 8–54: Schumann, *Piano Quintet*, Op. 44, II

Though the pedal may be of no more than a measure's duration, it may extend much longer, even through an entire piece. Examples of such lengthy pedals should be analyzed for the effect of the pedal on the harmonic rhythm and the general tonal scheme. Pedal-point pieces can be short and relatively simple harmonically, like Schubert's song *Die liebe Farbe* (*Die Schöne Müllerin*, No. 16) or the musettes of the French Baroque, or of considerable length with much contrapuntal activity, like the fugue that concludes Part III of Brahms's *German Requiem*, thirty-six measures of $\frac{4}{2}$ time in moderate tempo.

A double pedal is sometimes used, tonic and dominant usually in the form of a drone bass, making the key even more secure. 131

The drone of the following example is maintained through the entire piece.

EXAMPLE 8–55: Tchaikovsky, *The Nutcracker, Arabian Dance*

The pedal is considered, at least theoretically, as one of the origins of twentieth-century polyharmony. It is certain that when one key is represented by a pedal, perhaps a double or triple pedal, one can hear suggestions of a second key simultaneously sounded by dissonant harmony above, as in Examples 8–52 and 8–55. The following example may also be cited as an ancestral type.

EXAMPLE 8–56: Saint-Saëns, *Piano Concerto No. 4*, II

COMPLEXITIES

The application of nonharmonic tones simultaneously and successively in different voices can result in considerable complexity of texture and sound. The student should early become accustomed to searching for a multiple nonharmonic explanation when confronted by a chord containing more than one apparently dissonant element and to seeing whether the nonharmonic elements can be considered part of a larger line.

EXAMPLE 8–57: Chopin, *Etude*, Op. 25, No. 8

D♭: II (IV)$^6_5$ V^7 I

EXAMPLE 8–58: Lalo, *Namouna*, Prelude

G: I$^6_4$ V$^8_3$of V/V   V^7 I$^6_4$ V^7/I?

APPLICATION

The practical application of the principles of nonharmonic tones
will involve two different processes, one analytical and one constructive. The first will be called into play in the practice of
harmonizing a given part. It will be necessary to devote much
thought in the melodic analysis to deciding which are essential
notes and which are nonharmonic tones. The experience of harmonic analysis of compositions will prove helpful in this respect.

It is recommended that the constructive process be based on the
hypothesis of the harmonic background as the origin of melodic
parts. The steps would be as follows:

1. Choose a key and a succession of roots as the basis of a
phrase. Let us take, for example: A major, I–IV–II–V–I.

2. Construct a bass melody accommodating these roots, allowing the possibility that the third of the triad may appear for
greater melodic flexibility and smoothness.

EXAMPLE 8–59

A: I   (6) IV II   V^6 (5)   I

3. Add three upper voices in a simple harmonization of the indicated scheme.

EXAMPLE 8–60

A: I (6) IV II V⁶ (5) I

4. Consider the various possibilities of nonharmonic tones that may be applied, beginning with the simplest. It may be convenient or even necessary to rearrange the spacing and distribution of chord factors that were arrived at in the previous step.

EXAMPLE 8–61

A: I (6) IV II V⁶ + (5) I

5. After the simpler amplifications of the basic texture have been decided upon, more advanced ornamentations may be added to any or all parts. This step is practically without limit as to possible variants, although it is pointless to strive for complexity.

EXAMPLE 8–62

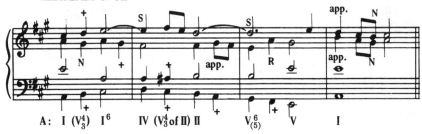

A: I (V₃⁴) I⁶ IV (V₃⁴ of II) II V⁽⁵⁾⁶ V I

EXERCISES

1. Apply the five-step process given above to the following root successions, using each as the basis of a four-bar phrase. Give careful consideration to the rhythm of the root changes.

    a. B-flat major: I–VI–II–V–VI–V–I
    b. C-sharp minor: I–V–I–IV–II–V–VI
    c. G major: I–V–I–IV–I–V–III–VI–II–V–I

In addition to these and the Supplementary Exercises for this chapter, many of the bass exercises of the previous chapters may be adapted to the conditions given above.

2. Realize the following figured basses in four parts, incorporating nonharmonic tones into the added parts where appropriate.

a.

b. **Andante**

3. Harmonize the following bass in four parts, observing the nonharmonic tones indicated, but otherwise using only triads in root position and first inversion, and introducing other nonharmonic tones in the added parts.

Maestoso

4. Harmonize the following unfigured basses, employing various nonharmonic tones in the added parts.

a.

5. Construct a bass for the following melody according to the rhythm and nonharmonic tones indicated.

6. Systematically examine ten examples from earlier chapters in this book and identify their nonharmonic tones.

distribution of chord
...ce in the structure.
...sive research during
...t diversity of effect

...vals, like a rhyth-
...he eighteenth and

following two examples,
...e of dignity and sturdiness

...onic Etudes, Op. 13

...e Young,

CHAPTER 9

The Harmonic Structure
of the Phrase

NUMBER OF MEASURES IN THE PHRASE

A phrase of music seldom contains as many changes of harmony as the average harmony exercise. It may be argued
that the purpose of the harmony exercise is to teach the manipulation of chords, and that the more chords it is made to contain
the more practice the student will have. But here, as in all other
stages of our study, we must continually recall the objective of harmonic theory, namely the clarification of the practice of composers in the use of chords. Harmonized chorales and hymn-
tunes, with harmony changing more or less regularly on every
beat, represent a very small part of the literature of music in the
eighteenth and nineteenth centuries and, however admirable and
appropriate to their purpose they may be, they are only partially
representative of the common practice of the period.

Just as regularity and symmetry seem to have been sought in
rhythm, those qualities are found to be much in evidence when we
consider phrase structure. The great majority of phrases, when
they have not undergone extension or development, are of four
and eight measures. In very slow movement a phrase may contain
only two measures and in a fast tempo it may contain sixteen.

Since we are concerned primarily with norms, we shall deal at
first with four- and eight-measure phrases. The student will no-

tice, however, the added musical interest of the phr[ase]
which do not agree with the standard. These irregula[r]
fall into two categories. For the most part they [will be]
which were originally four or eight measures lon[g]
but have been made longer by one or more te[chnical devices]
such as the sequence or the deceptive cade[nce, de-]
vices to be examined later in this book. Many [examples]
can be found where the phrase is actually co[mposed of an odd]
number of measures.

EXAMPLE 9–1: Brahms, *Ballade*, Op. 118, No. 3

Allegro energico

g: V⁷ I   IV⁷ V   III⁷ VI   II V(min.) I   IV   V of V   V

EXAMPLE 9–2: Dvořák, *Slavonic Dance*, Op. 72, No. 3

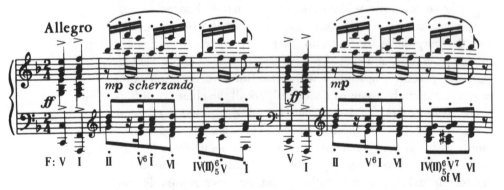

Allegro

mp scherzando   *mp*

F: V I   II V⁶ I VI   IV(II)⁶₅ V   I   V I   II V⁶ I VI   IV(II)⁶₅ V⁷ VI
of VI

The student may speculate as to how these phrases might be
recomposed so as to have four and eight measures respectively,
and judge the results against the original versions.

NUMBER OF HARMONIC CHANGES

It is possible that the phrase be constructed on a static harmony,
although there is usually some particular reason for this. Below is
an example of a phrase which serves as introduction to the main

PHRASE
STRUCTURE

DISTRIBUTION OF CHO[RDS]

The harmonic rhythm, that is to say, the [distribution of]
changes in the phrase, is of great importa[nce.]
This principle should be the subject of exten[ded study, and]
the study of harmony, to bring out the grea[t variety that can be]
achieved by harmonic means.

Changes of harmony occurring at regular int[ervals, like a rhyth-]
mic pulse, are characteristic of much music of t[he eighteenth and]
nineteenth centuries.

EXAMPLE 9–6: Brahms, *Waltz*, Op. 39, No. 1

Andante sostenuto

p

E: I   V⁷   I   V₃⁴   I   III⁶₄(V)   V⁹

Usually, however, the root changes will form a pa[ttern, the har-]
monic rhythm made up of short and long time va[lues, or groups]
of weak and strong harmonic progressions.

EXAMPLE 9–7: Beethoven, *Sonata*, O[p.]

Andante

p

g: V I V I V

The Harmonic Structure
of the Phrase

NUMBER OF MEASURES IN THE PHRASE

A phrase of music seldom contains as many changes of harmony as the average harmony exercise. It may be argued that the purpose of the harmony exercise is to teach the manipulation of chords, and that the more chords it is made to contain the more practice the student will have. But here, as in all other stages of our study, we must continually recall the objective of harmonic theory, namely the clarification of the practice of composers in the use of chords. Harmonized chorales and hymn-tunes, with harmony changing more or less regularly on every beat, represent a very small part of the literature of music in the eighteenth and nineteenth centuries and, however admirable and appropriate to their purpose they may be, they are only partially representative of the common practice of the period.

Just as regularity and symmetry seem to have been sought in rhythm, those qualities are found to be much in evidence when we consider phrase structure. The great majority of phrases, when they have not undergone extension or development, are of four and eight measures. In very slow movement a phrase may contain only two measures and in a fast tempo it may contain sixteen.

Since we are concerned primarily with norms, we shall deal at first with four- and eight-measure phrases. The student will no- 137

tice, however, the added musical interest of the phrases he finds
which do not agree with the standard. These irregular phrases will
fall into two categories. For the most part they will be phrases
which were originally four or eight measures long in conception,
but have been made longer by one or more technical processes,
such as the sequence or the deceptive cadence, harmonic devices to be examined later in this book. Many instances, however,
can be found where the phrase is actually conceived with an odd
number of measures.

EXAMPLE 9–1: Brahms, *Ballade,* Op. 118, No. 3

EXAMPLE 9–2: Dvořák, *Slavonic Dance,* Op. 72, No. 3

The student may speculate as to how these phrases might be
recomposed so as to have four and eight measures respectively,
and judge the results against the original versions.

NUMBER OF HARMONIC CHANGES

It is possible that the phrase be constructed on a static harmony,
although there is usually some particular reason for this. Below is
an example of a phrase which serves as introduction to the main

body of the piece, setting the stage for what is to come. The same phrase is used to close the piece.

EXAMPLE 9–3: Mendelssohn, *Song without Words,*
        Op. 62: No. 4, *Morning Song*

The other extreme, represented by the following two examples, is very restless in fast tempo but capable of dignity and sturdiness when the movement is rather slow.

EXAMPLE 9–4: Schumann, *Symphonic Etudes,* Op. 13

EXAMPLE 9–5: Schumann, *Album for the Young,*
        Op. 68: No. 41, *Northern Song*

Most phrases will show a more balanced harmonic activity. The chord changes are designed to lend life and movement without drawing too much attention to themselves. No rule can be given, as all degrees of variation in the amount of harmonic change can be found between the two extremes.

139

The harmonic rhythm, that is to say, the distribution of chord
changes in the phrase, is of great importance in the structure.
This principle should be the subject of extensive research during
the study of harmony, to bring out the great diversity of effect
achieved by harmonic means.

Changes of harmony occurring at regular intervals, like a rhythmic pulse, are characteristic of much music of the eighteenth and
nineteenth centuries.

EXAMPLE 9–6: Brahms, *Waltz*, Op. 39, No. 1

Usually, however, the root changes will form a pattern of harmonic rhythm made up of short and long time values, as well as
of weak and strong harmonic progressions.

EXAMPLE 9–7: Beethoven, *Sonata*, Op. 49, No. 1, I

THE PHRASE BEGINNING

Phrases do not necessarily begin with the tonic chord, nor do they
necessarily begin on the first beat of a measure. Rhythmically, the
start may be either *anacrusis* (upbeat) or *thesis* (downbeat).
Harmonically, it is customary in the first two or three chords,
the first harmonic formula, to make clear the tonality. As has been
pointed out, this does not require the presence of the tonic chord.

EXAMPLE 9-8: Mozart, *Sonata*, K. 281, III

Here the first chord is actually the dominant of C, but, since the key is B flat and C is the second degree, the chord is properly called V of II.

THE PHRASE ENDING

The end of the phrase is called the *cadence*. The origin of this word (from the Latin *cadere*, "to fall") suggests its significance in the phrase, as a kind of metrical punctuation mark. Like the final syllable of a line of metrical verse, the cadence is metrical in function; at the same time, to continue the analogy, the cadence is always marked by a certain conventional harmonic formula, just as metrical verse is ordinarily marked by rhyme. It will suffice here to indicate the essential features of two types of cadence, as these will be the object of detailed study in a later chapter.

The *authentic cadence* is comparable to the full stop or period in punctuation, and consists of the progression V–I.

The *half cadence* or *semicadence* is like a comma, indicating a partial stop in an unfinished statement. It ends with the chord V, however approached.

The following example shows two phrases, the first ending with a half cadence and the second with an authentic cadence.

EXAMPLE 9-9: Mozart, *Sonata*, K. 333, III

II   V   I⁶   II⁶   I⁶₄   V   I

authentic cadence

Exx. 7–15, 7–18

The terms *antecedent* and *consequent* were introduced in
Chapter 7 to designate respectively the first and second members of a matched pair of phrases, or the first and second halves
of a single phrase. What is implied by these two terms is the idea
of a beginning followed by a result, a balanced "before" and "after," the musical action of the second phrase complementing that
of the first phrase as though by necessity. Not all phrases will
show an antecedent–consequent structure, for many can be found
that show an essentially unitary organization, or that appear to be
made up of several segments of different lengths.

Where a balanced division can be felt, the antecedent–consequent relationship preserves the metric unity of the phrase or the
phrase pair. In most cases, it will be apparent first of all in the or-

*Compare the
cadences of this
example and Ex.
7–15*

ganization of the principal melody. Where there are motives in
the melody, the commonest procedure will be to organize the
harmonic changes to coincide with them, especially when they are
metrically regular.

EXAMPLE 9–10: Mozart, *Piano Concerto*, K. 488, I

A: I   V⁶   VI⁷   V⁶₅ of V   V²

I⁶   VI⁷   II⁷   V⁷   I   I   V

Phrase endings are differentiated in harmonic rhythm as to whether they present their final chord as a downbeat or as an upbeat. A cadence having its final chord as a downbeat, usually shown by placing the barline just before the final chord, is called a *masculine cadence*. The example below shows a masculine cadence.

*See also Exx.
6–37, 7–6, 8–20,
8–50*

EXAMPLE 9–11: Beethoven, *Violin Concerto*, Op. 61, I

A cadence in which the two final chords give the strong-to-weak, down–up, rhythmic progression is called a *feminine cadence,* or feminine ending, as in the example below.

*See also Exx.
8–18, 8–31,
8–45, 9–10*

EXAMPLE 9–12: Schumann, *Album for the Young,*
Op. 68: No. 24, *Harvest Song*

SEQUENCE

When a harmonic progression is restated in succession, the restatement being transposed to another degree of the scale, the result is a *harmonic sequence*. This very common procedure is an important means of obtaining harmonic variety and extension. Many different sequential types can be found in music even into the twentieth century, and the most important of these will be

143

discussed in Chapter 19. For the present, the student should learn to recognize the characteristic features of the sequence: systematic transposition of a harmonic pattern and its concomitant melodic and rhythmic patterns.

EXAMPLE 9–13: Schubert, *Waltz*, Op. 9, No. 3

In the preceding example, the harmonic progression of the third and fourth measures, II–V, is in the same intervallic relationship to that of the first and second measures, I–IV. The interval of progression is up a perfect fourth, tonic to subdominant; the interval of sequentiation, that is, between the progressions, is a step (I–II). The only differences between the patterns is that some melodic or harmonic intervals are changed from minor to major or vice versa; these adjustments keep both patterns within the A-flat major scale, and no accidentals are involved. (Had the transposition been kept exact, the third measure would have required D natural instead of D flat.)

It is apparent that the sequential procedure means that the harmonic progression itself is motivic, and . therefore is an organizer of musical time. This is especially true when, as is most often the case, the sequence is a *regular sequence*, that is, when not just the root succession, but all of the harmonic factors and their associated melodic motion and rhythm, are transposed without substantive change. Example 9–8 above shows how one progression and its sequential restatement account for the entire antecedent of the phrase.

UNITY AND VARIETY

The principles governing the selection and distribution of chords within the phrase are those of unity and variety, conditioned by any special purpose for which the phrase is constructed. Such a special purpose is illustrated by Example 9–3, in which the static harmony was appropriate for the introductory function of the phrase. Another special purpose would be that of transition, in which the phrase would be in a state of moving from one place to another, tonally speaking. Another would be the presentation of a phrase previously heard but in a new form, with varied harmony, or with developments and extensions.

Before such aspects are investigated, it is important to know what the harmonic structure consists of in normal phrases having no extraordinary functions, but whose role is simply that of presentation or exposition of the musical thought without development or manipulation.

Harmonically, a phrase consists of a series of harmonic progressions or formulae designed to make clear and maintain the tonality, and to confirm and enhance the harmonic implications in the melodic line. These are principles of unity. The harmony alone will often seem to possess too much unity, with many repetitions of the same root progressions. This is balanced by other significant features in the phrase.

EXAMPLE 9–14: Beethoven, *Sonata*, Op. 49, No. 2, II

(See also Example 9–6.)

Ordinarily, however, it will be found that a great deal of attention has been paid to the matter of balance between unity and variety, both in the choice of roots and in their rhythmic distribution. Investigation of this practice in the works of various composers is extremely profitable.

The more obvious principles of harmonic variety, such as change
of key (modulation), use of secondary dominants, and chromatic
alteration of chords, will all be extensively treated later in this
book. At this point we will concentrate on the different kinds of
musical variety that may be obtained by variation of melody and
texture. Our basic procedure will consist of the following steps:

    a. Analysis of a given phrase, deriving a rhythmic pattern
       of root progressions, shown by roman numerals.

    b. Construction of a four-part harmonic scheme showing the
       reduction of the original texture to these terms.

    c. Using as a basis the root successions obtained in the first
       step, together with their rhythmic pattern, composition of
       several original phrases unlike the given phrase.

There follows here an illustration of the application of these
steps.

EXAMPLE 9–15: Mozart, *Violin Concerto*, K. 268, II

a. The pattern of root changes is as follows:

EXAMPLE 9–16

The initial upbeat is so comparatively short as to give the impression of anticipating the downbeat with I on the first beat of
the first full measure. The I occupies the whole measure. In the
second full measure the harmonic rhythm of V–I is a short-long,
down-up, whereas measure three gives II–V as long-short, proceeding to I on the next downbeat, making a masculine authentic
cadence.

    b. The original texture can be reduced to the following four-
146   part harmonic scheme:

EXAMPLE 9–17

c. Taking advantage of the slow tempo to gain variety in the melodic lines by moving about among the chord tones, a version like the one below can be made, using triads in root position and chords of the sixth. Note also the organization of the melodic rhythms.

EXAMPLE 9–18

Next, a version may be written introducing one more elaborating element, such as the use of passing tones. At this stage, it is best to avoid complex melodic writing using the full range of non-harmonic tones, until more fluency is acquired in their use. For the same reason, the student is advised to write not more than two notes against one in the basic pulse, unless they are chord tones or passing tones. Rhythmic motives and patterns may be introduced as an element of variety.

EXAMPLE 9–19

Alla marcia

It is also instructive to write versions in three parts or even two, so as to gain experience in melodic writing. At first, a version using only chord tones should be made, with the bass adhering fairly closely to the basic root succession.

EXAMPLE 9–20

Tempo di menuetto

Passing tones and neighbor notes may then be permitted, which will increase the flexibility of the melodic line.

EXAMPLE 9–21

Composition of more elaborate versions may be attempted as available time and skills allow. In versions that involve counterpoint of any complexity, it is extremely important that every note be carefully evaluated for its melodic effect; such evaluation naturally belongs much more to the study of counterpoint than to harmony, and the student's attention ought not to be widely diverted from the subjects at hand. Other elements of variation that may be introduced are change of mode, change of meter, or substitution of one or two different harmonies for chords of comparable tonal strength (IV substituted for II[6], for example).

EXERCISES

1. Treat the phrases given below, following the three steps as in the example above.

    a. Derive the rhythmic pattern of the roots of the harmony.
    b. Construct the four-part harmonic scheme.
    c. Construct new phrases from the derived harmonic basis.

Beethoven, *Variations on a Theme by Salieri*, WoO 73, Theme

Couperin, *Harpsichord Pieces, Book III:* Sixteenth Order,
L'Hymen-Amour

Majestueusement

Other phrases, chosen from among the examples in this book,
may be used additionally.

2. Construct original phrases, four measures in length:

    a. Starting with anacrusis and ending with feminine cadence;

    b. Starting on thesis and ending with masculine cadence;

    c. With minimum of harmonic activity balanced by melodic
       movement;

    d. With maximum of harmonic activity and little melodic
       movement.

3. Construct phrases according to the following patterns:

    a. A-flat major, two-four time, slow:

       |I   V |I   V |I   V   VI II|V |

       (*Cf.* Beethoven, *Sonata,* Op. 13, II.)

    b. D major, three-four time, fast:

       V|I | V |I |I |V |I II |V |

       (*Cf.* Beethoven, *Sonata,* Op. 10, No. 3, III.)   149

c. A major, two-four time, slow:

V|I   II |V |I   IV II |V

(*Cf.* Schumann, *Album for the Young*, Op. 68, No. 28, *Remembrance.*)

d. A-flat minor, six-eight time, moderately fast:

|I |I |V |V |III |V of III|III   I|V   I|

(*Cf.* Schubert, *Auf dem Wasser zu singen*, Op. 72.)

CHAPTER 10

Harmonization
of a Given Part

PURPOSE

I t must not be thought that the ultimate objective of the study of harmony is the acquisition of the ability to harmonize melodies. That is an accomplishment which ought naturally to come as a by-product of the proper scientific study of harmonic usage, but an accomplishment for which there is a singular lack of opportunity or necessity. Except in restricted, specialized fields, such as piano improvisation in popular music, a musician is seldom called upon to furnish harmony for a melody. Nor does even the composer think of a melody and its harmonization as the result of separate processes; the invention of melody and harmony, in all essentials, proceed simultaneously and together in the mind's ear.

The mental steps involved in the process of harmonization make it, however, one of the most valuable exercises in the study of harmony, and it should be regarded always as a means rather than an end. The function of a harmony exercise is to clarify principles by practical experience with the material. The attempt to go over the same ground, to solve some of the same problems as the composer, will afford, as no purely analytical process can, an insight into the nature and details of these problems and into the manner and variation of their solution.

During the period we are taking as that of harmonic common 151 practice, nearly all the melodies are of harmonic origin. They were either evolved from chord tones, with the addition of nonharmonic melodic tones, or they were conceived as having harmonic meaning, expressed or implied. So the process of harmonization does not mean invention, but in a sense rediscovery of elements already in existence.

Nevertheless, one should discourage the ambition to discover the "author's harmony," especially in academic, manufactured, textbook exercises. There is nothing more depressing than the perusal of the "key to the exercises." Even if the given soprano is a melody by Mozart, no premium should be placed on guessing the exact chords and their arrangement as used by the composer. The profit for the student lies in the intelligent comparison of his own version with that by Mozart.

It is characteristic of the nature of music that any melody is capable of suggesting more than one choice of chords, to say nothing of the numerous possibilities of arranging them. True harmonization, then, means a consideration of the alternatives in available chords, the reasoned selection of one of these alternatives, and the tasteful arrangement of the texture of the added parts with due regard for consistency of style.

At first, we shall consider the harmonization process using only triads, leaving for later in this chapter the incorporation of nonharmonic tones.

Analysis of the Melody

In order to find the available chords for consideration, one should strive to make as complete a harmonic analysis of the melody as possible, in as many versions as seem to present themselves. The first question is, of course, the tonality. Some melodies of restricted range may offer several possibilities of key and mode, even if we limit ourselves to the use of triads in root position.

EXAMPLE 10–1

C: V   I   IV VI   III IV   V   G: I   IV VI   V IV   I V   I

e: I   VI I   IV II   V (VII)   I

The possibilities for different interpretations as to tonality and
mode of a melodic phrase will increase with the student's further
acquaintance with harmonic resources.

Determination of the key will depend upon the diagnosis of the
cadence. At present there are but two cadences to be considered,
one ending on the dominant chord, and one ending with the
progression V–I. In the example above, the final note was interpreted in turn as dominant of C, tonic of G, and mediant of E.
Tonalities containing one flat or more were not acceptable because
of the B natural in the melody. Likewise, keys of two sharps or
more were not good since C natural was present. The absence
of the F made it possible to choose keys containing either F sharp
or F natural. In the E minor version, the leading-tone triad in
root position was used for the soprano note A, and is here clearly
a form of dominant harmony, although not the most satisfactory
dominant chord that could be used.

Having decided on the key and having marked the Roman
numerals of the last two chords, one should next consider the
frequency of change of the harmony. With triads in root position
there will not be a great deal of flexibility in this, but two opportunities may be offered for departure from the monotonous
regularity of one chord for each soprano note.

MELODIC SKIPS

When a melody moves by skip, it is likely that the best procedure
will be to use the same harmony for both notes.

EXAMPLE 10–2

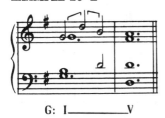

G: I_____V

153

Exceptions to this will usually arise from questions of harmonic rhythm. If the two notes involved in the skip occur at a point where the harmonic rhythm would appropriately move from weak to strong, then the harmonic roots will probably be different.

EXAMPLE 10–3

G: I V VI IV I V

Such a rhythmic effect is generally placed so that the second chord falls on the first beat of a measure, giving rise to the often-stated rule that it is better to change root over a barline. The weak-to-strong rhythm may, however, be found within the measure, just as the first beat, as we have seen, is sometimes not the strongest.

EXAMPLE 10–4

G: I V VI IV I V

SUSTAINED TONES

If the harmonic rhythm seems to demand frequent chord changes, it may happen that a tone of the melody will hold through as a tone common to two or more different chords.

EXAMPLE 10–5

G: I VI IV V III VI V

It is, of course, possible that melodic movement in the other voices, without change of root, may be more desirable.

154

EXAMPLE 10–6

G: IV   V   I   V

Available Chords

After having decided on the tonality and having made a prelim-
inary decision as to the general harmonic activity, or frequency of
chords, each note of the given part should be examined for its
possibilities as a chord tone. These should actually be written,
as roman numerals, in order that all the mental steps may be
clearly seen.

In working with a given bass only one chord was available for
each tone, since the given bass notes were at the same time the
roots of the triads. When an upper voice is given, each tone furnishes a choice of three triads. A given tone can be the root, the
third, or the fifth.

EXAMPLE 10–7

This step is shown applied to a short melodic soprano part:

EXAMPLE 10–8

Selection of Chords

In determining the possible choices of chords, it may be helpful
to review the Table of Usual Root Progressions in Chapter 3.

Let us first consider only root-position triads. In the last measure
of the preceding example we can at once eliminate the VI and

the IV, as we wish to end the phrase with either V or I. Since I remains, the cadence will be an authentic cadence, so we choose V to precede the I. The VII would not be a good substitute for V here because it would give a doubled leading-tone. In measure 4 we can also eliminate the VII in favor of the stronger IV or II. In measure 3 either I or VI could serve for the whole measure. In measure 2 the VIIs can be struck out, since they would lose their identity if associated with the V. Also the II will prove a trouble-some choice for the second beat as it would make parallel octaves if followed by I, and would not give a very satisfactory bass inter-val if followed by VI. So we conclude that measure 2 had better contain either IV–V or II–V. These eliminations leave the follow-ing alternatives:

EXAMPLE 10–9

Considering what we now have from the standpoint of unity and variety, and harmonic rhythm, we see that the only chance to use VI is in measure 3, and that the progression V–VI would be good here as a variation to the V–I which must come at the end. So we eliminate the I, and in consequence decide that we had better use I in the first measure for unity. In measure 4 both IV and II could be included under the same soprano note, adding variety of melodic and harmonic rhythm, in which case we would not use II in measure 5, but keep V for the whole measure.

The above reasoning brings us to the conclusion below, with the resultant bass part. It is obviously not the only conclusion possible, but the bass appears to be a good one. Comparison of the two melodic curves shows a good amount of contrary motion, a qual-ity to be sought between soprano and bass.

EXAMPLE 10–10

Writing the inside parts will often require irregularities of doubling and changes of position. Care should be taken to make the connections as smooth as possible and to avoid parallel octaves and fifths.

EXAMPLE 10–11

The above are mental steps in the reconstruction of the harmonic background of a given melodic part. It is inadvisable to hurry over them or to omit them in favor of a harmonization which happens to present itself spontaneously, especially in the first stages of study. The weighing of the pros and cons, so to speak, of each problem of detail and of the whole constitutes a profitable experience and practice which even the person gifted with a flair for improvisatory harmonization cannot afford to miss.

CONTRAPUNTAL APPROACH:
MELODY AND BASS

In the method of harmonization just described, the final choice of chords was determined by a process of selection of individual chord progressions, chiefly on the basis of their mutual connectibility from chord to chord. The bass line appeared as a result of this selection process; even though some of the details of the bass line, such as beginning and ending on the tonic note, may have been kept in mind from the start, we were concerned with the bass primarily as a succession of roots, and not as an independently conceived melody with its own melodic shape.

The shape and individuality of the bass line will inevitably become more important to the harmonization when first-inversion triads are included in the allowable chords. Let us then try to see what possibilities are made available when we plan the harmonization by first considering only the melody and a bass line together.

First of all, since we are using only triads in root position and first inversion, there will be only four possible intervals between 157

soprano and bass: octaves, perfect fifths, thirds, and sixths, including their compounds. Dissonant intervals are necessarily excluded. (The two exceptions, the augmented fifth and the diminished fifth, will occur relatively seldom, when III or II in the
minor mode, or VII in either mode, is used in root position.)
These intervals can be classified by their possible application
under our restricted conditions:

a. A fifth (or twelfth, etc.) between soprano and bass means
   that the complete chord will be a root-position triad.
b. A sixth (or thirteenth) between soprano and bass means
   that the complete chord will be a first-inversion triad.
c. An octave (or double octave) between soprano and bass
   will mean either a root-position triad or a first-inversion
   triad; if the latter, the triad will have its third doubled.
d. A third between soprano and bass will mean either a root-
   position or a first-inversion triad, with no specifications as
   to doubling.

Having in mind the above repertory of possible intervals, let
us now attempt to construct a bass line against a given melody,
not ignoring root considerations, but focusing our attention principally on the melodic characteristics of the bass and only secondarily considering what the roots of the resulting chords will be. We
choose here a four-measure phrase ending with a half cadence.
The cadential bass note, therefore, will preferably be the dominant note F, though we may also consider the leading-tone, the
bass of the dominant triad in first inversion, as a somewhat weaker
alternative.

EXAMPLE 10–12

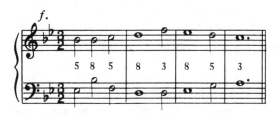

In *a* we see the possibility of harmonization entirely in root-position triads, any first-inversion triads being more or less weak. The bass is melodically dull; it is made up entirely of skips, the tonic note appearing five times, and it sounds like nothing so much as an "elementary exercise bass" similar to those used first in Chapter 3. This is precisely what we are trying to avoid in the two-part approach.

Solution *b* is a definite improvement. The tonic appears three times, but only near the beginning of the phrase, where it may be strongly asserted to contrast with the dominant harmony at the end. Following the third tonic note, the bass moves smoothly. Three parallel sixths in a row is not too many, though four

159

might be; it is desirable to keep soprano and bass independent in their motion most of the time. The repetition of the F at the end of the bass descent is a melodic weakness, and its harmonization, which must be III⁶–V, is also weak.

Solution *c* is better still. There is a good deal of contrary motion between the two parts, though not so much as to seem automatic and slavish. The G in the first measure helps the bass to get away from the tonic, making the return of the tonic in the second measure somewhat less repetitive than in *b*. The skip down to D and the answering step to E flat gives the bass already a wider range than in *b*, the return to E flat helping to maintain the balance of the curve. The B flat in the third measure makes a strong approach to the cadential F, although it might be considered to contribute too much additional tonic to what has gone before, especially if the D in the second measure were to be harmonized as a first-inversion I.

Solution *d* shows an even more imaginative beginning. The tonic note does not appear until the second measure, but it is the clear goal of the bass line and thus is all the stronger when it does appear. The second and third measures duplicate the last three notes, D–C–B flat, of the beginning, an undesirable repetition somewhat offset by the different rhythm. In addition, these measures show four thirds in succession. These could not be harmonized with all root-position triads without an excessive amount of manipulation of the inner parts in order to avoid parallel fifths and octaves; on the other hand, all first-inversion triads would not be very suitable, since VI⁶, with B flat in the bass, is weak before V at the end. The likely harmonization for these two measures would be I–I⁶–VII⁶–I, which eliminates the excess of parallel motion but also employs too much tonic harmony.

Another nontonic beginning appears in solution *e*. With a bass-line tonic goal comparable to that of *d*, two skips in a row without returning is not a fault here. But the remainder of the bass melody is too disjunct without more conjunct motion to offset the skips, and the direct octave on D in the third measure, implying either a weak III or a I⁶ with doubled third, is not the best.

In *f* the oblique motion of fifth to octave is natural enough, but its implication of IV–I with the tonic note in the soprano sounds like a plagal cadence at the wrong point in the phrase. The re-

*Plagal cadence:
see Chapter 12*

peated D in the second measure affords less contrast than in the second measure of *a*, *b*. or *c*, and would probably best be given the same harmony for both notes, so as to avoid the weak I–III

relationship; for this purpose I⁶ with doubled third is not as strong as root-position I would be, and the only other alternative, III, is more static than I⁶ and somewhat weak after V: The ending, VI–V⁶ or VI–VII, is inevitably less satisfactory, as is the implied melodic tritone on successive downbeats of the last two measures.

By choosing and combining the best motions from these six solutions, selecting appropriate harmonies where a choice exists, and constructing suitable inner parts, we might arrive at a harmonization like the following:

EXAMPLE 10–13

B♭: IV I⁶ VII⁶ I I⁶ IV I V

It should be borne in mind, however, that other equally satisfactory or even better solutions might be devised, since the six bass lines we examined in detail obviously do not exhaust all possibilities, even within the restrictions of note-against-note triads in root position and first inversion.

The above comparisons will give some idea of the different criteria of evaluation that must be applied simultaneously in the construction of a good bass line. These criteria are both melodic and contrapuntal, as well as harmonic; one must consider not only melodic shape but the intervallic and motional relationship with another part, at the same time that one considers the root both in itself and in relation to roots preceding and following, whether in the bass or in some other part. To have all these things in mind sounds like a difficult task, but it is apparent that the possibilities are limited enough to permit thorough searching, while at the same time they are broad enough to permit a good deal of variety. The assiduous and sensitive musician will always be aware that different good possibilities exist and can be discovered, and that the development of constructive and evaluative skills through repeated exercises of this kind is of central importance to his musicianship.

USE OF FORMULAE

It was advocated in the course of the discussion of tonality (Chapter 5) that groups of two or three chords might be learned as commonly recurring formulae or harmonic words. A vocabulary of such words is extremely useful in the planning of a harmonization. One recognizes an upper voice of one of the formulae as part of the melody and the stage of considering alternate chords becomes a stage of considering alternate formulae.

EXAMPLE 10–14

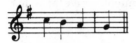

This group of notes, or motive, instead of being regarded as four isolated chord tones to be related, could be remembered as the familiar upper voice of a number of formulae, such as these:

EXAMPLE 10–15

Or, if chords in first inversion are included:

EXAMPLE 10–16

The principles of unity and variety are noticeable in a good harmonization. The harmony does not go so far afield as to be irrelevant to the intentions of the melody, but it is desirable that it should at some moment present some aspect which is not entirely commonplace and expected. The bass should be a good contrapuntal line in comparison with the given part. The harmonic rhythm should be planned to corroborate the fundamental pulse implied by the melody and to add rhythmic interest at points where this is not contributed by the given voice. The rhythmic and melodic style of all the added parts should be in accord with the style of the given part.

Analysis of the given melody alone will ordinarily suggest the character of the harmonization to be made, and will permit decisions about the kind of harmonic rhythm as well as possibilities of the use of nonharmonic tones. A melody of pronounced rhythmic and motivic construction, for instance, will usually be best accommodated by changes of harmony with either the basic length of the motive or the basic pulse of the measure, or occasionally twice that long; less often will it be found that such a melody is suited for note-against-note harmonization. On the other hand, melodies of slow or moderate tempo, moving for the most part in equal time values, are well adapted to note-against-note harmonization, the harmonic rhythm matching the melodic rhythm for the most part. The student should study a melody carefully before proceeding to its actual harmonization, in order to understand its phrase structure and to be able to estimate the range of possible harmonic rhythms best suited to it. The ideal to be kept in mind is a maximum of textural consistency of phrase, motion in the given part being balanced at different times by motion in the other parts. There is nothing duller than a pedestrian harmonization that is correct in all details of voice leading but that adds nothing of interest to support the given melody.

The following example illustrates a common fault of beginners' exercises.

EXAMPLE 10–17

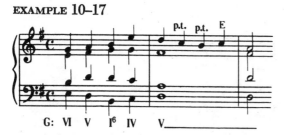

G: VI V I⁶ IV V_____

The first measure shows a harmonic rhythm of steady quarter notes, but the second and third measures have a harmonic duration of six full quarters, and the melody notes on the second, third, and fourth quarters of the second measure are given as nonharmonic tones. As such these are rhythmically weak with respect to the measure, even though they have the same duration as the previously established harmony changes, and the static harmony underneath sounds insipid by comparison.

A partial repair of this measure might be effected thus:

EXAMPLE 10–18

G: VI V I⁶ IV V____I V

The first two beats of the second measure still have the same harmony, and the C on the second beat is still a passing tone, but the position of the other three voices changes, giving motion to the texture. The new harmony on the third beat is welcome, but the fourth beat of the melody is still decidedly dull as an escape tone. What is obviously called for, then, is another harmony change on the fourth beat.

EXAMPLE 10–19

G: VI V I⁶ IV V____I II⁶ V.

Some nonharmonic tones might now be added, for increased melodic and rhythmic interest in the harmonizing parts.

EXAMPLE 10–20

The general principle to be kept in mind is that melodic non-harmonic tones must be faster than the harmonic rhythm; otherwise, they will sound like dangling harmony notes.

THE CHORALE: INTRODUCTION

It was remarked in Chapter 8 that the works of J. S. Bach serve
as supreme models in the application of nonharmonic tones. With

respect to the problem of matching voices to given melodies, no-where is this more true than in the 371 chorale harmonizations, four-part settings of hymn tunes from the Protestant and Catholic rites of nearly two centuries, only a handful of the tunes being by Bach himself. The student will find it profitable to examine these chorales frequently, especially during the first year of harmony study. A number of the chorales appear in several harmonizations, which are well worth comparing. Some of the chorales present special problems in analysis that will cause difficulties and should be avoided at the present stage; these include chorales on modal melodies (Nos. 15, 34, 160, etc.), and some chorales of exceptional length (Nos. 132, 133, etc.). Many of the chorales contain at least one modulation, those in the minor mode often have diminished seventh chords, and nearly all the chorales make use of secondary dominants and nondominant sevenths. The student may confine his analytical exercises to individual phrases of reasonably restricted tonality, skipping the more complicated chords; or he may read ahead in the appropriate chapters of this book so as to gain some familiarity with the more advanced harmonic resources of the chorales.

It is also instructive, and at this point not too early, for the student to try his hand at chorale harmonization, using selected isolated phrases showing a clear authentic cadence or half cadence. Harmonization of complete chorale melodies should await a later stage. Preferably at least two or three different versions should be made for each phrase, including one version using only triads in root position and first inversion without nonharmonic tones.

EXERCISES

1. Harmonize the following soprano melodies, using triads in root position and first inversion. Write two versions of each, the first without any nonharmonic tones, the other using them in the added parts.

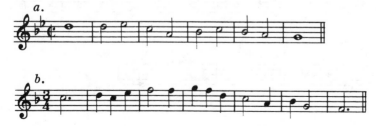

2. Harmonize the following soprano parts, observing the nonharmonic tones indicated. Other nonharmonic tones may be introduced in the added voices.

166

3. Harmonize the following soprano parts, first making a careful melodic analysis to determine the nonharmonic tones present.

a. **Andante**

b. **Moderato**

c. **Allegro**

4. Add three upper voices to the following basses, forming triads in root position and first inversion.

a.

b.

c.

d.

5. Harmonize the following phrases drawn from chorale melodies.

a. *Valet will ich dir geben*

b. *Alle Menschen müssen sterben*

c. **Jesu, meine Freude**

d. **Ach Gott vom Himmel, sieh darein**

e. **Nun danket alle Gott**

f. **O Gott, du frommer Gott**

168

CHAPTER 11

The Six-Four Chord

When a triad is so arranged that its original fifth is the lowest tone (second inversion), the resulting combination is known as the *six-four chord*, the intervals between bass and upper voices being sixth and fourth.

EXAMPLE 11–1

Since the fourth is a dissonant interval when its lowest tone is the bass, and the sixth but an imperfect consonance, the six-four chord is an unstable chord. It is normally the product of vertical coincidence of moving voices. In its characteristic usages it can be analyzed as a grouping of nonharmonic tones.

THE CADENTIAL SIX-FOUR CHORD

By far the most prominent of the chords in this category is the familiar tonic six-four found in cadences. It has the cadential ef-   169 fect of a dominant chord in which the sixth and the fourth above the bass form appoggiature to the fifth and third respectively, while at the same time it draws the ear's attention to the tonic note as a moving tone. Thus the tonic six-four used in this way shares tonic and dominant properties simultaneously, and for this reason it is a harmonically strong chord even though it must be resolved.

EXAMPLE 11–2

In four-part writing the bass of the cadential six-four chord is doubled, since it is the inactive tone, and also since it is the real root of a dominant chord in root position.

It will be profitable to compare the above formula with the following closely related effects.

EXAMPLE 11–3

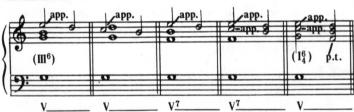

The cadential six-four chord, with its resolution to the dominant chord, has the rhythmic value of strong-to-weak. In its most characteristic form it marks a strong downbeat, and the barline is most often placed just before it. The harmony preceding the cadential six-four chord is one that would introduce the dominant by means of a weak-to-strong progression, for example, IV–V, II–V, or even I–V.

See also Exx.
5–29, 21–8

EXAMPLE 11–4

EXAMPLE 11–5: Wagner, *Die Meistersinger*, Act I, Scene 1

It must be remembered, however, that the placing of the bar-lines, representing the meter, may be often at variance with the harmonic and melodic rhythms. The six-four chords in the two examples below occur on what are felt to be strong beats, not necessarily first beats of the measures. Not only does the longer time value of the dominant harmony give it rhythmic weight, but the downbeat feeling of the two appoggiature, the sixth and the fourth, contributes melodically to the effect. But this effect of strong–weak, down–up, concerns only the I_4^6–V cadential progression itself. In terms of the rhythmic sense of the whole phrase, the dominant harmony, represented by I_4^6–V, gives, in these two excerpts, a good example of a strong upbeat to the tonic harmony of the following downbeat.

EXAMPLE 11–6: Beethoven, *Sonata*, Op. 2, No. 2, II

EXAMPLE 11–7: Mozart, *Sonata*, K. 331, I

171

When the chord before the cadential six-four chord is tonic, the progression is nevertheless felt as weak-to-strong, since the root change is actually I–V.

EXAMPLE 11–8: Beethoven, *String Quartet*, Op. 18, No. 2, II

Adagio cantabile

Chords on V and III are less appropriate to introduce the cadential six-four chord, as the resulting harmonic rhythm is either strong-to-weak or static.

EXAMPLE 11–9

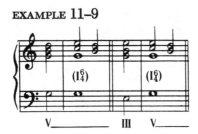

The sixth or the fourth, or both, may occur as suspensions, tied over from the previous beat, instead of as appoggiature. In this case the harmonic rhythm remains weak-to-strong, while the melodic rhythm of the two voices involved becomes strong-to-weak.

EXAMPLE 11–10

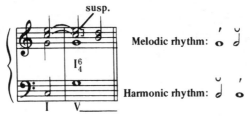

In the next example, the chord on the first beat of the second measure could be described as a supertonic six-four chord, but the sixth is a suspension and the fourth an appoggiatura, so that the basic harmony of the first two beats is really VI.

EXAMPLE 11–11: Mozart, *Piano Quartet,* K. 478, II

B♭:   I   V⁰₉ of VI   (II⁶₄) VI   V⁶ of V   I⁶₄   V⁷   I

The sixth and fourth, although they are by origin nonharmonic tones, may function as principal melodic tones with further embellishment. Thus the E in the second measure of the example below, the sixth of the chord, is decorated by the appoggiatura F sharp and the auxiliary D sharp.

EXAMPLE 11–12: Brahms, *Intermezzo,* Op. 117, No. 3

c♯: II⁷   I⁶₄   V⁷   I

In keeping with the contrapuntal character of the sixth and fourth, care is taken, as a rule, to observe their natural resolution to the step below. The following resolutions represent exceptions to this rule, although they are not infrequently encountered. Their use is justified by melodic considerations, as when a particular soprano note is desired.

EXAMPLE 11–13

I⁶₄ V   I⁶₄ V   I⁶₄ V

EXAMPLE 11–14: Mozart, *String Quartet*, K. 421, II

F: I   II⁶   I⁶₄   V   I

EXAMPLE 11–15: Bizet, *Jeux d'enfants:* No. 3,
La Poupée: Berceuse

B : I⁶   V⁶₄ I⁶   I⁶₄ V⁷ I

Other harmonies may be interpolated between the six-four
chord and its resolution to the dominant. The quality of suspense
inherent in the cadential six-four chord is retained by the ear until the dominant is reached.

EXAMPLE 11–16: Bach, Chorale No. 252, *Jesu, nun sei gepreiset*

B♭: VI   II⁶   II⁷   I⁶₄ II⁶ V   I
aux,
chord

EXAMPLE 11–17: Chopin, *Mazurka*, Op. 50, No. 3

c♯: V°⁶₅   It.   I⁶₄   V⁴₂   I⁶   V⁴₃   I⁶₄

$$V^7 \quad I$$

This effect of suspense is carried to the extreme in long, developed, concerto cadenzas, which are inserted between the cadential six-four chord and the expected dominant. In such cadenzas, which typically last for several minutes, the six-four suspense is chiefly symbolic; it is usually entirely forgotten by the time the dominant finally arrives.

THE APPOGGIATURA SIX-FOUR CHORD—
NONCADENTIAL

Although found chiefly in cadences, the six-four chord formed from the notes of the tonic triad may be used as a strong rhythmic effect elsewhere in the phrase. The cadential impression will not be likely if such a chord occurs early in the phrase and it may be avoided by melodic continuity in the voices.

EXAMPLE 11–18

$$E^\flat: \quad I\text{——}IV \quad I^6_4 \quad V \quad \quad V \text{ of } VI \quad VI$$

Analogous chords are used on other degrees of the scale, the combination IV^6_4–I being fairly common.

EXAMPLE 11–19: Clementi, *Sonatina*, Op. 36, No. 6, II   *Cf. Ex. 18–14*

Allegretto spiritoso

$$D: \quad IV^6_4 \quad I \quad \quad V/I \quad I$$
$$(I\text{——})$$

If the root of a triad remains stationary while its third and fifth rise one degree and return, a six-four chord is formed. This type differs from the appoggiatura type in that it is weak rhythmically and the sixth and fourth must enter from below in the manner of neighbor notes. A simple analysis of one root for all three chords is always possible, the sixth and fourth being nonharmonic tones.

EXAMPLE 11–20

$$I \quad (IV_4^6) \quad I$$

EXAMPLE 11–21: Chopin, *Etude*, Op. 10, No. 5

$$G\flat: I \quad (IV_4^6) \quad I \qquad i \quad (IV_4^6) \quad I$$

EXAMPLE 11–22: Wolf, *Spanish Song Book, II:* No. 5,
Auf dem grünen Balkon

$$A: \quad I \qquad\qquad IV_4^6 \qquad\qquad I$$

The six-four in Example 11–19 has the melodic form of an auxiliary six-four, but differs rhythmically. The following example shows a different type of auxiliary six-four, resulting from the neighbor-note motion of the root of the triad. This unusual use of the augmented-triad form of III in the minor mode might also be regarded as a substitute for V⁶, the fifth of the chord, E, being replaced by the suspended F from the surrounding tonic. The interesting enharmonic ambiguity with the chord on the fourth beat of the next measure should be noted.

EXAMPLE 11–23: Schubert, *Sonata in B flat,* Op. posth., I

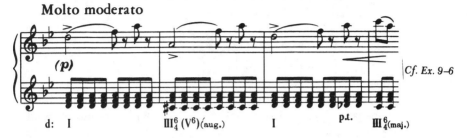

THE PASSING SIX-FOUR CHORD

It is the bass, rather than the upper voices, that gives its name to the passing six-four chord. Here the bass is a passing tone between two tones a third apart, usually of the same harmony. The rhythmic value of the passing six-four chord is therefore weak. Its upper voices enter and leave by step, so that they may be explained contrapuntally in relation to the surrounding harmony, the sixth as neighbor, the fourth as harmony note, and the octave of the bass as passing tone. The passing V_4^6 between I and I^6 is identical in function to the passing VII^6 used in the same way (compare Example 6–35).

EXAMPLE 11–24

EXAMPLE 11–25: Mozart, *Sonata,* K. 330, II

177

EXAMPLE 11–26: Brahms, *Piano Concerto No. 2*, I

Allegro non troppo

Bb: I6   V   I   VII6   IV64 VII   IV6   V7   I6

In the following example of the passing six-four chord, the two inner parts remain stationary while bass and soprano proceed as passing tones.

EXAMPLE 11–27: Mendelssohn, *Song without Words*, Op. 85: No. 4, *Elegy*

Andante sostenuto

D: I   Fr. of VI   VI64 II7 I64 V7   I

THE ARPEGGIATING SIX-FOUR CHORD AND OTHER FORMS

The bass may touch upon the fifth in the course of its melodic movement among the tones of the chord, without producing the dissonant effect of a six-four chord. It must be decided on rhythmic grounds whether or not the fifth is the real harmonic bass. Certainly in the example below, the fifth in the bass is unimportant contrapuntally and is merely a tone in a broken chord.

See also Exx.
9–14, 11–8

EXAMPLE 11–28: Mozart, *String Quartet*, K. 465, I

Allegro

178

C: I   V/I   I_____

The most frequently encountered usage of this type is the arpeggiating six-four, in which the fifth alternates with the root in the bass of tonic harmony, the tonic six-four substituting for the dominant. The fifth gives a suggestion of dominant feeling without an actual harmonic change, at the same time providing an alternate form of the tonic. The arpeggiating six-four is often seen in keyboard music as part of figurations such as Alberti basses, and in "vamp" accompaniments in waltzes and marches. In orchestral music the bass of the arpeggiating six-four is a favorite ostinato role for the kettledrums, which are most often tuned to tonic and dominant.

See also Ex. 5–18

EXAMPLE 11–29: Schubert, *Ecossaise No. 1,* from Op. 18

In the following example the dominant pedal underlying the entire phrase is like a large anacrusis to the root-position tonic at the end. The same phrase begins and ends the song.

EXAMPLE 11–30: Schubert, *Nachtviolen*

Six-four chords of contrapuntal origin are frequent and can be understood as groupings of any of the nonharmonic tones. They are usually not of sufficient rhythmic importance to be looked upon as chords, but rather should be regarded as combinations of melodic factors.

EXAMPLE 11–31

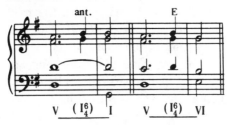

Composers have occasionally been attracted by the feeling of suspense in the six-four chord and have specifically exploited the effect by means of uncharacteristic resolution. The following example is comparable in its voice leading to the nondissonant arpeggiating six-four of the type just shown, but its rhythmic placement shows it to be strongly cadential. The lack of the expected intervening dominant chord is dramatic; the appoggiatura leading-tone on the downbeat of the third measure is the only dominant element present.

EXAMPLE 11–32: Beethoven, *Symphony No. 9*, I

Allegro ma non troppo, un poco maestoso

The following example shows an authentic cadence on the lowered supertonic (Neapolitan) used as a temporary tonic, but atypically in the six-four position, which resolves contrapuntally later in the measure.

EXAMPLE 11–33: Schubert, *Sonata*, Op. 42, II

Andante poco moto

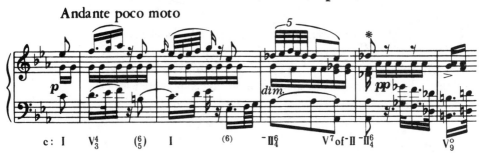

Schumann preferred to end the Romance in F sharp with what seems like a dangling six-four, with only the faintest suggestion of a root-position tonic chord. Of course, this is partly a pianistic effect.

SIX-FOUR CHORD

EXAMPLE 11–34: Schumann, *Romance*, Op. 28, No. 2

Cf. Ex. 23–27

Common formulae including six-four chords, to be played in all keys, and in as many suitable arrangements as possible:

EXAMPLE 11–35

EXERCISES

1. Write in four parts the following series of chords indicated by the symbols, choosing in each case an appropriate meter and rhythm:

    a. A minor: VI–II⁶–I⁶₄–V

    b. B♭ major: II–I⁶₄–V–I

    c. G minor: V–VI–I⁶₄–V

    d. E major: V–I⁶₄–V–VI

181

e. C minor: I–V$_4^6$–I^6–V
f. D major: IV$_4^6$–I–I$_4^6$–V
g. B minor: I–I$_4^6$–II^6–V
h. F major: I$_4^6$–III^6–IV–I

2. Work out the following figured basses in four parts:

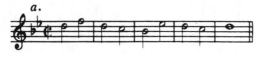

3. Harmonize the following soprano parts, introducing six-four chords where appropriate:

c. Moderato

d. Andante

4. Harmonize the following basses:

a. Allegro

b. Adagio

CHAPTER 12

Cadences

There are no more important formulae than those used for
phrase endings. They mark the breathing places in the
music, establish the tonality, and render coherent the formal structure.

It is remarkable that the convention of the cadential formulae
could hold its validity and meaning throughout the entire period
of common harmonic practice. The changes that took place in ex-
ternal manner, in harmonic color, did not disturb the fundamental cadence types, but seemed only to serve to confirm their acceptance.

THE AUTHENTIC CADENCE

The harmonic formula V–I, the authentic cadence, can be extended to include the II or IV which customarily precedes. In
addition, we now have the cadential six-four chord, whose natural
function is to announce the cadence. The tonic six-four is, of
course, the double appoggiatura on the dominant root. Thus a

final cadence incorporating these preparatory elements in order, as II⁶–I⁶₄–V–I or IV–I⁶₄–V–I, will be harmonically very strong.

EXAMPLE 12–1: Bach, *Well-Tempered Clavier, II,* Fugue no. 9

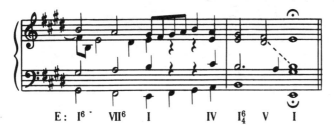

*"Rule,
Britannia"?*

The example above shows the strength and finality of this cadence in simple form. There are many ways of varying the arrangement of the formula. In the example below, II is replaced by its close relative, V of V, and instead of the tonic six-four, the fourth alone above the bass appears as a suspension.

EXAMPLE 12–2: Handel, *Suite No. 6,* Fugue

The final tonic chord may receive some ornamentation, such as a suspension or an appoggiatura.

EXAMPLE 12–3: Tchaikovsky, *Romance,* Op. 5

The dominant chord may continue to sound over the final tonic in the bass, later resolving, or it may act as an appoggiatura chord to the tonic in a feminine cadence.

185

EXAMPLE 12–4: Franck, *Violin Sonata*, I

Cf. Exx. 8–18, 8–39

A: V   I   V of V   V_____   I_____

PERFECT AND IMPERFECT CADENCES

The use of the authentic cadence is not restricted to final phrases. It is often employed elsewhere, but with less emphasis on its finality. The most conclusive arrangement, with dominant and tonic chords in root position and the tonic note in the soprano at the end, is generally called the *perfect cadence*, all other forms of the authentic cadence being termed *imperfect*, meaning less final.

A hard and fast distinction between what are perfect and what are imperfect cadences is not possible, nor is it important. The degree of finality is dependent upon many contributing factors and each case should be judged on its own merits.

The approach to the tonic by means of the first inversion of the dominant chord is generally considered a less conclusive cadential effect.

EXAMPLE 12–5: Mendelssohn, *Prelude*, Op. 25, No. 6

B♭: II⁶   V⁷   V⁶₅   I

If the tonic chord itself is inverted the phrase will probably be extended so that the real cadence comes later. Placing the third in the soprano usually gives less feeling of finality than having the tonic in both outside voices. The following example by Beethoven shows an imperfect authentic cadence, with third in soprano and feminine ending, balanced by a perfect cadence with masculine ending and tonic in soprano and bass.

EXAMPLE 12–6: Beethoven, *Symphony No. 8*, I

THE HALF CADENCE

EXAMPLE 12–7: Bach, Chorale No. 1, *Aus meines Herzens Grunde*

The cadential six-four chord is also employed to accentuate the half cadence, common formulae being IV–I$_4^6$–V, II–I$_4^6$–V, VI–I$_4^6$–V, I–I$_4^6$–V.

EXAMPLE 12–8

187

EXAMPLE 12–9: Mozart, *Sonata*, K. 576, II

Adagio

A: I   V$\frac{6}{5}$ I   IV   II^6 I$\frac{6}{4}$ V

The tonic may be suspended into the dominant chord, without six-four, or may appear as appoggiatura to the leading-tone.

EXAMPLE 12–10: Brahms, *Intermezzo*, Op. 117, No. 2

Andante non troppo

b♭: VI   IV$\frac{6}{5}$ Fr.   V

In many cases the chord before the dominant will contain a chromatically raised fourth degree, making a leading-tone to the dominant. This has more melodic than harmonic significance, as illustrated by the reaching tone G sharp in the example below.

EXAMPLE 12–11: Beethoven, *Sonata*, Op. 2, No. 2, II

Largo

D: V$\frac{6}{5}$ I   V

This temporary leading-tone may, however, be of sufficient harmonic strength to give the chord the character of dominant of the dominant (V of V), thus tonicizing the dominant which follows. The example below shows the V of V as an appoggiatura chord over the dominant root.

EXAMPLE 12–12: Schubert, *String Quintet*, Op. 163, I

It is not always a straightforward matter, nor is it necessarily essential, to differentiate between a half cadence containing the tonicizing V of V and an authentic cadence in the key of the dominant. When the subsequent phrase is still in the tonic key it seems unnecessary to declare that there is a modulation just on account of one chord. On the other hand, if there is a strong series of chords in the dominant key leading up to the cadence, it would appear more logical to recognize an intermediate modulation in the analysis. This distinction will be explored more fully in Chapter 14.

THE PLAGAL CADENCE

The *plagal cadence* (IV–I) is most often used after an authentic cadence, as a sort of added close to a movement. The subdominant chord seems tonally very satisfactory after the emphasis on dominant and tonic.

EXAMPLE 12–13: Chopin, *Etude*, Op. 25, No. 8

For a modern example, see Ex. 31–73

There are many instances of the plagal cadence as a phrase ending, without a preceding authentic cadence.

EXAMPLE 12–14: Handel, *Messiah*, Hallelujah Chorus

EXAMPLE 12–15: Schumann, *Symphonic Etudes*, Op. 13

The minor form of subdominant harmony is frequently used in the plagal cadence at the end of a movement in the major mode. It gives a particularly colorful ending.

EXAMPLE 12–16: Mendelssohn, Overture to *A Midsummer Night's Dream*

The supertonic may be added to the subdominant chord without impairing the effect of plagal cadence. It may appear as a passing tone or it may be a chord tone in a seventh chord in first inversion. Used in this way, the II_5^6 is regarded as a substitute for IV.

More on this in Chapter 23; see also Ex. 20–25

EXAMPLE 12–17

190

IV   I   IV(II)$_5^6$ I

EXAMPLE 12–18: Brahms, *Symphony No. 1*, II

CADENCES

Andante sostenuto

E : V⁰₉ of IV   IV⁶   II⁶₅   I

THE DECEPTIVE CADENCE

There remains the fourth general type of cadential formula, the *deceptive cadence*. It is similar to the authentic cadence except that some other chord is substituted for the final tonic. There are as many deceptive cadences as there are chords to which the dominant may progress, plus the variations in arrangement which composers have devised. Needless to say, some are more "deceptive" than others and some will seem overworked.

The deceptive cadence is quite as good an indicator of the tonality as the other cadences—often even better. It is generally true that the key is established more strongly by the firm appearance of the dominant than by the chord to which the dominant ultimately resolves. Furthermore, as we saw in Chapter 5, some progressions involving the dominant, such as V–IV, can be heard unambiguously in only one key.

By far the most frequent alternative to V–I is V–VI. In the example below, the dominant chord appears as appoggiatura chord over the sixth degree.

EXAMPLE 12–19: Schubert, *Sonata*, Op. 120, I

Allegro moderato

See also Exx.
8–33, 14–7

A :   V⁰₉ of II   II   I⁶₄   V⁷   VI

If the minor sixth degree is used for the submediant chord, in a phrase which has been predominantly major, there is more of the element of surprise in the resolution. Composers sometimes accentuate this effect, as in other deceptive cadences, by a sudden change of nuance or of orchestration.

EXAMPLE 12–20: Schubert, *String Quartet*, Op. 29, I

Between the V and the VI, the dominant harmony of the sixth degree may be used as a passing chord. This does not change the main outline of the cadence or the tonality.

EXAMPLE 12–21: Beethoven, *Sonata*, Op. 101, I

Upon the same bass as the V–VI cadence, the chord of resolution may be the subdominant in first inversion.

EXAMPLE 12–22: Schumann, *Wer machte dich so krank?*, Op. 35, No. 11

In the following example the appoggiatura B flat adds to the effectiveness of the deceptive cadence, which is here especially strong as it has been led up to with every musical and psychological appearance of a conclusive ending of the entire prelude.

EXAMPLE 12–23: Bach, *Well-Tempered Clavier, I,*
Prelude No. 8

Bach introduced still another deceptive cadence in the same piece, after that shown above. This time the dominant resolves to a tonic chord which has been altered to make it a dominant of the subdominant.

EXAMPLE 12–24: Bach, *Well-Tempered Clavier, I,*
Prelude No. 8

Dominants of other degrees of the scale, as well as various types of chromatically altered chords, may be found in the deceptive cadence. These are principally used in modulation and will be illustrated in several later chapters.

As can be seen in several of these examples, the deceptive cadence often serves as a joint between two overlapping phrases. Phrases are overlapping when the second phrase begins simultaneously with the arrival of the last chord of the first phrase. Overlapping phrases are to be seen in Examples 12–20, 12–23, and 12–24.

Phrases which are not overlapping may seem so on first sight, owing to melodic continuity in the final measure of the first phrase. In this case the melodic movement over the last chord in the cadence is in the form of anacrusis to the first downbeat in the second phrase. This frequently happens in the half cadence.

EXAMPLE 12–25: Mozart, *Rondo*, K. 485

The use of a deceptive cadence near the end of a piece helps to sustain the musical interest at the moment when the final authentic cadence is expected. It also provides the composer with an opportunity to add another phrase or two in conclusion.

Cadences are sometimes extended by repetition of the cadential formula, or by lengthening the time values of the harmonic rhythm while continuing the melodic activity above.

EXAMPLE 12–26: Bach, *Well-Tempered Clavier, I,* Fugue No. 4

THE PHRYGIAN CADENCE

The so-called Phrygian cadence is a Baroque mannerism consisting of a IV⁶–V final cadence in the minor mode at the end of a slow movement or slow introduction. It implies that a fast movement is to follow without pause, generally in the same key. The Phrygian cadence is so called, not very accurately, because of the half-step relationship in the bass, supposedly a late survivor from the II–I cadence of the fifteenth century. The following example of Phrygian cadence precedes a final movement in G major.

EXAMPLE 12–27: Bach, *Brandenburg Concerto No. 4,* II

The reader is invited to examine the unusual Phrygian cadence in Bach's *Third Brandenburg Concerto*. It occupies a single Adagio measure of IV⁶–V in E minor between two fast movements in G major, and thus serves as the entire slow movement! Perhaps in Bach's time it was meant as a cue for keyboard improvisation, like a cadenza.

EXCEPTIONAL CADENTIAL TYPES

In the nineteenth century composers began to search for new harmonic bases for cadential formulae as a way of varying the forms that had by then been established for the better part of two centuries. The results of the search often appear most dramatically in the final cadence of a movement or a work, where the harmony is especially noticeable as being set off from what has preceded it. Below are two examples from Chopin, one of the earliest and boldest experimenters with cadential harmony.

EXAMPLE 12–28: Chopin, *Etude,* Op. 25, No. 4

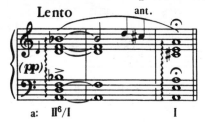

EXAMPLE 12–29: Chopin, *Sonata,* Op. 58, III

Both of these examples can be considered as variants of the plagal formula; in each case the chord used has two factors in common with the IV for which it substitutes.

The following celebrated example is an early instance of a dissonant harmony serving as the final chord of a piece. Some writers have justified it as summarizing the rather uncertain tonality of the entire song; in any case, the chord is generally held

195

to have an implied resolution, though an irregular one, in the beginning of the next song. This explanation is somewhat easier to accept if one thinks of the end of the first song as a contrapuntally modified Phrygian cadence.

EXAMPLE 12–30: Schumann, *Dichterliebe*, Op. 48: No. 1, *Im wunderschönen Monat Mai*, and No. 2, *Aus meinen Tränen spriessen*

Cadential formulae, to be played in all keys:

EXAMPLE 12–31

EXERCISES

1. Write in four parts of the following series of chords indicated by symbols. Each short phrase should be given rhythmic organization, with barlines showing the meter chosen. Introduce nonharmonic tones.

196

a. E♭ major: VII⁶–I–I⁶–IV–I⁶₄–V–I
b. D minor: I–VI–IV–II–V–I
c. G major: I⁶–IV–V–VI–II–I⁶₄–V
d. A minor: V⁶–I–IV–II–I⁶₄–V–VI
e. D major: I–VII⁶–I⁶–IV–I⁶₄–V–I
f. F♯ minor: II–V–VI–II–V–I–IV–I

2. Work out the following figured basses in four parts:

a.

b.

c.

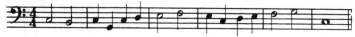

3. Harmonize the following unfigured basses:

a. **Moderato**

b. **Andante**

c. **Moderato**

4. Harmonize the following soprano parts:

a. **Andante**

CHAPTER 13

Harmonic Rhythm

DEFINITIONS

It is assumed that the conceptions *meter* and *rhythm* are understood. Meter is simply measure. Meter has no rhythm. But music so often has a rhythmic pulse with which the meter coincides at important points that we think the meter is rhythmic. We then speak of strong and weak beats of the measures, forgetting that the rhythm of the music came first, and that afterwards came the effort to place the barline at points of rhythmic stress. Obviously, the first beat of a measure should receive rhythmic stress only when the music calls for it, and not because it happens to be the first beat.

The action of many influences, important among them dance music and dance forms, combined in the eighteenth and nineteenth centuries to instill the idea of regular pulse (undifferentiated recurring beats) into all music. The period of harmonic practice which we are studying is at the same time the period in which there held sway the greatest "tyranny of the barline." Composers of earlier centuries worked with free and flexible rhythms like those of fine prose, and in the twentieth century there has been an attempt to recapture the principle of that higher organization of rhythm; but from Bach to Debussy it cannot be denied that the rule is regularity of beats and of measures.

That we' are still far from an appreciation of the subtleties and mastery of rhythm even under our conventionalized system, shown in the works of the best composers, is largely due to our 199 acceptance of the doctrine of strong and weak beats as a substitute for the open-minded appraisal of the rhythmic values of each individual musical phrase. The study of rhythm is rendered more complex by the phenomenon of up and down beats. Either of these may be strong or weak, which is to say that rhythmic stress may possess the feeling of up or down. We try to place the barlines so that strong downbeats come as first beats of the measures, but musical notation provides no way of indicating when this is not so.

It is difficult to reconcile the rhythms of the following examples with the familiar classification of beats of the measure into strong, weak, and weaker.

EXAMPLE 13–1: Bach, *English Suite No. 2:* III, Sarabande

Here, as we know by tradition to be characteristic of the sarabande, the stress is on the second beat of the measure. The third beat is entirely without accent, the effect of the measure being that of a short first beat followed by a heavy second beat lasting twice as long.

EXAMPLE 13–2: Mozart, Overture to *The Magic Flute,* K. 620

Here the only accent is on the fourth quarter, the six eighth notes being all of equal rhythmic value. Mozart has underlined the natural rhythm by marking the accented sixteenth note group *forte.* To suggest that the barline should be located before this accent, which is clearly a strong upbeat, would be unthinkable.

EXAMPLE 13–3: Brahms, *Capriccio,* Op. 116, No. 3

In this example, the second beat of the first measure is at least
as strongly accented as the first beat. There is no stress at all on the
first beat of the second measure, the downbeat, and the ensuing
three quarters serve as upbeat (anacrusis) to the third measure.
Thus the second measure begins with a weak downbeat.

RHYTHMIC TEXTURE OF MUSIC

In its total effect on the listener, the rhythm of music derives from
two main sources, melodic and harmonic. We omit from this discussion the percussive resource, exemplified by the bass-drum
stroke, not because it has not been significantly employed, but because its habitual role has been to heighten or underline either
melodic or harmonic rhythms.

Examination of the following example will show these two kinds
of rhythm.

EXAMPLE 13–4: Beethoven, *Sonata,* Op. 31, No. 3, III

The melodic rhythms here combined may be indicated thus:

EXAMPLE 13–5

The four patterns are clearly not in agreement as to accents or
points of rhythmic stress.

Taking the roman numerals of the harmonic analysis as indicating the distribution of the root changes in the phrase, we can
write the pattern of the harmonic rhythm thus:

EXAMPLE 13–6

Admitting the inadequacy of this merely quantitative notation of rhythm, there are nevertheless two significant observations to be made:

a. The pattern of harmonic rhythm, although differing from each of the patterns of melodic rhythm, is the product of the combination of these. This is an excellent corroboration of the often-repeated statement that chords are made by moving voices. On the other hand, it is entirely feasible to reverse the process. The composer may have started with the harmonic pattern and have derived from it the melodic lines.

b. The root changes, which give the rhythmic pattern of the harmony, are not regular in time, like a regular pulse, nor are they of equal rhythmic value, quite apart from the unequal time values they possess. Both of these aspects of harmonic rhythm, frequency of change of root and the quality of that change, must receive attention in a study of harmony as used by composers.

MELODIC RHYTHM

There need not be as much diversity in patterns as found in the Beethoven example. It is true that rhythmic independence of melodic lines is the test of good counterpoint, but music is not always contrapuntal and the complexity of its texture varies between wide limits.

The rhythmic outline of all the voices may coincide, in which case the resultant harmonic rhythm will be in agreement with the melodic rhythm, although not necessarily with the meter.

EXAMPLE 13–7: Beethoven, *Sonata*, Op. 53 ("Waldstein"), I

Allegro con brio

EXAMPLE 13–8: Schumann, *Symphony No. 1* ("Spring"), I

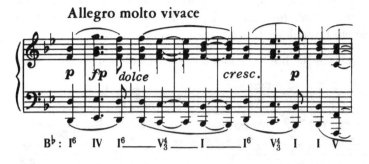

Allegro molto vivace

Bᵇ: I⁶   IV   I⁶____V⁴₃____I____I⁶   V⁴₃ I   I V

harmonic rhythm:

In the above examples the top voice is heard as a melody. This is called homophonic music, as distinguished from polyphonic music, in which two or more independent melodic lines are heard in combination.

When all else is subordinated to one melodic line we have melody and accompaniment. The accompaniment is frequently lacking in rhythmic interest, to avoid lessening the prominence of the melody. The following is an example of flexibility in melodic rhythm combined with regularity in the root changes of the harmonic rhythm.

EXAMPLE 13–9: Chopin, *Nocturne*, Op. 48, No. 1

Lento

C: I   VI⁶   V⁶₅   I   VI   IV(II)⁶₅

harmonic rhythm:

E.g., Exx. 32–4,
32–5

In the latter part of the nineteenth century some composers became interested in complicated part writing of a chromatic nature, and, in their efforts to conceal the underlying harmony   203 and increase the contrapuntal interest, obscured and even obliterated the feeling of harmonic progression. Whether deliberate or inadvertent, this amounted to an impoverishment of the rhythmic life of the music, though much else was gained instead.

For vitality of contrapuntal texture over a clear harmonic rhythmic background, the works of J. S. Bach remain the models of perfection throughout the period.

EXAMPLE 13–10: Bach, *Well-Tempered Clavier, I,* Fugue No. 1

C: V VI V⁶ I V⁶ III VI II   V⁶₅ I II VII of IV II⁶V² I⁶ VI II V
                    IV

harmonic rhythm:

Frequency of root change and rhythmic quality of the changes are, then, the two main features of harmonic rhythm. When the harmony changes with much frequency the effect is apt to be one of restlessness.

See also Ex. 9–4

EXAMPLE 13–11: Beethoven, *33 Variations on a Waltz by Diabelli,* Op. 120, No. 28

Allegro

sf (stacc.) *sf* *sf* *sf* *sim.*

C: V°₉ of IV IV V°₆ of IV IV⁶ V°₄ of V V⁶ V°₉ of V V V°₉ of VI VI V°₄ of VI VI⁶
        ⁵   ³   ³ G: II⁶ V°₄ of II II⁶
                                      ³

(G:) V°₉ of II II V°₆ of II II⁶ IV I⁶₄ V°₆ of V V°₉ I V⁷(°₄) II⁶₄+   V⁷ I
      ⁵   ⁵   ₂ (B♭ ³=A♯) I⁶₄
                              (D♭ =C♯)

harmonic rhythm:

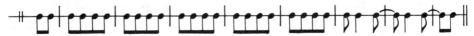

Widely spaced changes of harmony give the impression of breadth and relaxation.

EXAMPLE 13–12: Mozart, *Symphony No. 40*, K. 550, I

harmonic rhythm:

STATIC HARMONY

There are instances of complete absence of harmonic rhythm throughout whole sections of a composition. One of the most famous examples of this effect of static harmony is the prelude to Wagner's music-drama *Das Rheingold,* where the chord of E-flat major serves as the unchanging background of the entire prelude, one hundred and thirty-six measures in moderate tempo.

Static harmony, or absence of harmonic rhythm, is more often felt as a defect in music by composers of inferior gifts. Like all other technical resources, it is bound to be ineffective when the result of indifference or unawareness on the part of the composer. *Cf. Ex. 9–3* On the other hand, it is successful when appropriately used. Often it arises from the elaboration of a single chord, as in the following example.

EXAMPLE 13–13: Beethoven, *Sonata,* Op. 106 ("Hammerklavier"), I

The rhythmic quality of the harmonic change is influenced by a number of factors, often of no little subtlety and open to differences of opinion as to their values, but it is of prime importance to the student if he aspires to an insight into the function of harmony as a musical means.

DISSONANCE AND RHYTHM

Dissonance is contrapuntal in principle, and it is an important element in motion. The dissonant chord and its resolution may compose either an up–down or a down–up progression. The harmonic rhythm is concerned with root movement and is either confirmed or contradicted by the polyphonic superstructure.

EXAMPLE 13–14

Nonharmonic tones have their own rhythmic values of strong and weak. It is axiomatic that these values have meaning only when their pace is equal to or shorter than that of the harmonic rhythm.

DYNAMIC INDICATIONS

Directions for nuances of loud and soft, *crescendi* and *diminuendi*, accents, *sforzandi*, and the like, are of course not elements of harmonic rhythm. Their use is ordinarily to confirm and accentuate the natural rhythmic feeling already present in the music, although sometimes for a particular expressive purpose the composer may employ them in a contrary sense.

EXAMPLE 13–15: Beethoven, *Sonata*, Op. 31, No. 3, II

Cf. Ex. 6–27

In the example above, the second chord, although a dominant seventh chord, is in a position and inversion which would allow of its complete absorption into the tonic chord, the soprano and bass being passing tones and the alto a neighbor note. The accent indicated by Beethoven would probably never have occurred to the player if no dynamic signs had been given.

NONHARMONIC CHORDS

The question raised by the Beethoven example, of whether a vertical combination of tones is an independent chord, or just some melodic tones which happen to harmonize at the moment, depends upon various considerations and is often open to differing interpretations. It will have to be decided mainly on rhythmic grounds, but one should take into consideration the general pace and musical intent of the piece.

In a slow tempo the ear has time to fix on every chord change and hear it for its harmonic value, even in a passage like the following, where the parallel writing and the absence of root position give the impression of passing motion.

EXAMPLE 13–16: Haydn, *Sonata No. 29*, II

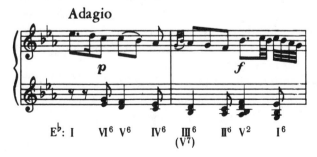

The above example is comparable in construction, but completely opposite in effective hearing, to Example 6–11, from Beethoven's *Piano Sonata,* Op. 2, No. 3. In that example the first-inversion chords between I and IV were momentary and melodic, not harmonic. The difference between the two examples is in their harmonic perception, which in turn is due entirely to the great difference in tempo.

In the following example the speed of the music justifies a broader view of the harmony than would be indicated merely by the root changes.

EXAMPLE 13–17: Mozart, *Piano Concerto,* K. 271, III

In the example above, although the dominant harmonies in the first three measures are all in root position, they are rhythmically weak with respect to the tonic; moreover, the upper part of the dominant harmony forms a double neighbor surrounding the tonic note. In the last four measures tonic and dominant functions are the reverse of what they were in the first four. Thus with these considerations it seems reasonable to invoke a harmonic meter of one chord per four measures.

Here is another example, from a work written over a century later by a composer whose style is entirely different from Mozart's, that shows a comparable underlying harmonic basis.

208

EXAMPLE 13–18: Lalo, *Namouna*, Thème varié

The way we have interpreted these examples suggests that just as there are nonharmonic tones there may also be nonharmonic chords, triadic sonorities which arise from combinations of non-harmonic-tone motions in simultaneous voices. We have already seen that it was possible to interpret certain dissonant chords in this way, such as VII^6 and the passing and auxiliary six-four chords. In those cases, the dissonant chords were assessed as having weak rhythmic value, and now we have done the same for consonant triads, even those in root position. In the Mozart example above, the root of the root-position V is not considered as a nonharmonic tone like a passing tone or neighbor note, but rather as an arpeggiated tone extending or anticipating the tonic harmony.

PEDALS

The pedal effect, in which a tone, usually the bass, is held through harmonies which are foreign to it, is rhythmically static, since it tends to deprive the harmonic progressions above of their basses and to cause them to be heard as melodic tones over a single root. However, the changes of harmony in the upper voices may succeed in offsetting the static feeling of the pedal by asserting their independent harmonic rhythm.

EXAMPLE 13–19: Chopin, *Mazurka*, Op. 6, No. 4

209

EXERCISES

1. Construct phrases in four parts, having the following patterns of harmonic rhythm and employing the harmonies suggested by the given numerals, using root position or first inversion except where otherwise specified. Write two versions of each pattern, one in moderate tempo with no note-values shorter than an eighth note in the added parts, and the other in slow tempo, including sixteenth notes in the added parts.

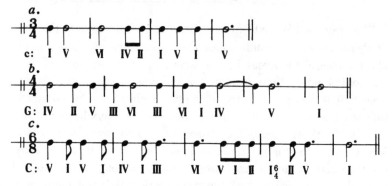

2. Write phrases in four parts, having the following patterns of harmonic rhythm and employing optional harmonies:

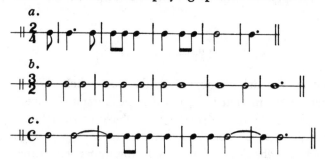

3. Work out the following figured basses in four parts:

c.

4. Harmonize the following unfigured basses:

a.

b.

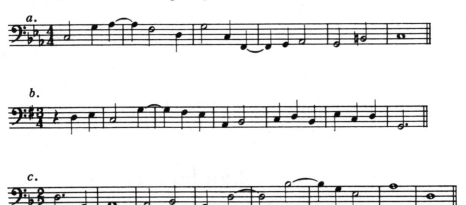

c.

5. Harmonize the following soprano parts:

a.

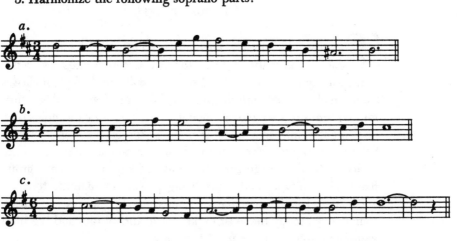

b.

c.

CHAPTER 14

Modulation

PSYCHOLOGICAL NECESSITY FOR
CHANGE OF KEY

Tonality, like physics, encompasses both static and dynamic states. The static state of tonality is represented by music that never departs from a fixed diatonic collection of pitch-classes from which its notes are drawn. A good deal of sixteenth-century music sounds this way to our modern ears, and more examples than one might think exist in later periods, for example in many of Schubert's waltzes. Even where chromatic nonharmonic tones are added to a diatonic texture, the sense of key may remain firmly fixed. The unifying and centralizing powers of diatonic tonality, as defined by the practice of composers for several centuries, remain even today the most important historical fact and the most valuable resource of the art of harmony.

At the same time that the concept of a single tonality using a single scale is a fundamental basis of the music we know best, it is not the only defining condition, nor can it be a sufficient condition except in limited cases. In the common-practice era, single-scale pieces are invariably short. The preference of composers has decreed that compositions of any substantial length must involve the incorporation of tones from outside the underlying diatonic scale and, in the vast majority of cases, a change of key, the adoption of a different tonal center to which all the other tones are to be related.

The process involved in changing from one tonal center to another is called *modulation*. Modulation represents the dynamic state of tonality. The word implies that there is a key in which a piece of music begins, a key into which it progresses, and a process of progressing.

Modulation also implies the practical basis by means of which tonalities themselves can be said to possess tonal functions in relation to one another. Modulation is an element of variety, but also of unity, when the balance of the keys in support of a main tonality is used to advantage. The key scheme, or pattern of keys, is therefore one of the most significant ingredients of form. Beethoven's *Third Symphony* is said to be "in E-flat major," and while it is obvious that the first movement begins and ends on the E-flat major triad and maintains the three-flat key-signature throughout its nearly 700 measures, it is also obvious that a large part of this twenty-minute-long movement is occupied with music *E.g., Ex. 26–27* that does not use the E-flat major scale at all. Thus in some sense E-flat major is a defining background of the tonality of the movement, a sort of basic state, within which all of the other keys that appear in the movement are somehow embraced, be they closely related keys like B-flat major or A-flat major or relatively remote keys like E minor. The listener perceives that these different keys are related compositionally, because they are part of a unified composition; the analyst can establish the relationships of the keys according to their intrinsic properties as well as according to Beethoven's intentional use of them.

Modulation is therefore part of the philosophy of musical form; it implies the composer's drawing of a distinction between one key and another. The comprehension of modulation is also an aspect of hearing and of analysis, and thus it is the hearer who must also draw the distinction. We can illuminate this task by constructing some definitions and limitations.

Elementary Relationships:
Three Stages

There are three stages in the mental process of effecting a modulation within a phrase. First, a tonality has to be made clear to the hearer. Second, the composer at some point changes his tonal center. Third, the hearer is made aware of the change, and the new tonal center is made clear to him.

In the first stage, the establishment of the first key, the principles described in Chapter 5 on tonality should be observed. It is not essential that the tonic chord should appear, but the dominant must be made to sound as such. Indecision due to overuse of modal degrees and their harmonies may result in the whole phrase being heard as in the second key, especially if the second key is strongly established.

The second stage of the modulation involves the choice of a chord which will be conveniently susceptible to the change of tonal viewpoint. In other words, it will be a chord common to both keys, which we will call the *pivot chord,* and to which we will give a double analysis.

For example, the C major triad could be employed as a pivot chord in a modulation from C to G, indicated thus:

EXAMPLE 14–1

{C: I
{G: IV

The pivot chord selected is preferably not the dominant of the second key, because under most circumstances such a chord will not be a fundamental chord in the first key. In the second stage we are still at the point where only the composer is aware that a modulation is to take place. The sounding of the dominant chord of the new key belongs to a later stage, when the hearer is made to realize that a new tonal center is being felt. To put it a little more technically, the pivot chord should be placed in advance of the appearance of the dominant chord of the new key.

The following scheme represents a modulation effected by means of the pivot chord shown above:

EXAMPLE 14–2

$$C:\ IV\ II\ V \begin{cases} C:\ I \\ G:\ IV\ II\ V\ I \end{cases}$$

The third stage, establishment of the new key, is accomplished by means of the cadence which ends the phrase, although there

may occur strong progressions in the key before the cadence. The
cadence may be any one of the types studied in Chapter 12.

EXAMPLES OF MODULATING PHRASES

EXAMPLE 14–3: Mozart, *Sonata,* K. 332, II

This is a modulation up a perfect fifth, or from a given key to the key of its dominant. The key of F is convincingly established by the progression V–VI–II⁶–I₄⁶–V–I, even though there are some mode changes along the way. I of B flat is identical with IV of F, so it is taken as the pivot chord, and it introduces the V of the new key, making a strong tonal progression IV–V in F. The phrase ends with the authentic cadence strengthened by the II–I₄⁶ preceding.

The example is taken from a passage used to prepare the second theme of an abbreviated sonata form. In most such second-theme situations, especially in sonata-form movements, the preparation of the new key would be a little more protracted, extending over several phrases, with the cadence repeated. The concise modulation here can be attributed to the very slow tempo.

215

EXAMPLE 14–4: Bach, Chorale No. 320, *Gott sei uns gnädig*

This phrase modulates down a minor third (or up a major sixth), a change from a major key to its relative minor. After the strong tonic and dominant chords of A major, the key previously established, the supertonic triad is used as a pivot chord and looked upon as the subdominant of F-sharp minor. As such it introduces the cadential six-four chord in the fourth measure. The authentic cadence in F sharp is made more conclusive by the plagal cadence acting as an extension of the final tonic. The major third in the tonic chord is a Picardy third (see Example 5–32).

EXAMPLE 14–5: Bach, *French Suite No. 3*, Menuet

Here the modulation is up a minor third, from a minor key to its relative major. The I–V progression in itself would not be sufficient to establish B as the tonic, if it were not for the numerous repetitions and the fact that B was the tonic of the preceding phrase. The pivot chord here is IV, which is translated into II of D, and proceeds to V.

EXAMPLE 14–6: Beethoven, *String Quartet*, Op. 18, No. 3, III   MODULATION

A modulation up a major third. The progression II–V–I confirms the key of D. The pivot chord is VI of the major mode and is taken to be the equivalent of IV in F sharp, minor mode. Then follows the strong progression IV–V–I in the new key.

EXAMPLE 14–7: Bach, Chorale No. 200, *Christus ist erstanden*

In this excerpt modulating up a major second, the first phrase is shown with its strong cadence in F major. Therefore the first chord of measure three may be taken as V, and at the same time as subdominant of G minor, with a major third, sixth degree of the ascending minor scale. The new key is here affirmed by a deceptive cadence.

LEVELS OF TONALITY:
TONICIZATION AND INTERMEDIATE MODULATION

The examples of modulations shown in the previous section are taken out of context, the unspoken assumption being that the sec-   217 ond key is well-established as a new key. Presumably the new key would be established as firmly as was the old key, and in the same way—by the appearance and reappearance of tonic harmony and its reinforcement by the dominant. Observation of numerous modulations shows, however, that the establishment of the new key is not necessarily that simple. In most music, the factor of musical time is an essential consideration in modulation. The first key has a special tonal advantage for its having been first. The new key must compensate for this; if it does not project the new tonic sufficiently strongly, over a long enough time, the ear will retain the memory of the first key, and a return to the first key by reverse modulation will make it appear that no real modulation has taken place.

EXAMPLE 14–8: Mozart, *Fantasy*, K. 397

The above example contains all the necessary ingredients for a modulation, and is analyzed as modulating from D major to A major. On the other hand, the authentic cadence on A is followed immediately by a return to D major, both before and after the repeat. The A major tonic cadence is certainly strong, and is heralded in the phrase by more than just its dominant; nevertheless, its appearance is only momentary relative to the surrounding D major. Rather than a real modulation, the A major here is a tonicization which has been extended. It has more tonal weight than the tonicization of III in Example 5–33, in the chapter where we first encountered the concept of tonicization by means of a secondary dominant; in that example, the III was tonicized only by V of III, whereas in the Mozart example above, the A major tonic is strengthened by an entire consequent semiphrase interpretable in A major.

A comparable illustration is given below. No more definite immediate appearance of D major could be imagined; yet the composer shows at once that it is not meant to last.

EXAMPLE 14–9: Schubert, *Sonata in C minor*, Op. posth., II   MODULATION

The tonal strength of a tonicization is in direct proportion to the musical time in which it extends. In the Mozart example the tonicization of A first appeared in the sixth measure, the remaining measures serving as a prolongation. The continuation of A major throughout the length of the next phrase ought to be sufficient to confirm the new key, and to establish that a modulation has indeed occurred; but in this case, with D major returning immediately in the next phrase, it would be more accurate to say that the A major is only an intermediate modulation, or "false modulation," as the phenomenon has also been called. Similarly, in the Schubert example, the departure from A major begins in the second half of the phrase with a secondary dominant tonicizing F-sharp minor, and the appearance of D major is strengthened by a prolongation of the tonic by reference to the minor subdominant, as a plagal cadence.

In this way we may define tonicization of a secondary tonic as something that occurs within a short length of musical time, the reappearance of the original tonic occurring within the same phrase; intermediate modulation extends for a long enough time that the return to the tonic is delayed until the next phrase. The distinction is arbitrary, but it will nevertheless be found to be useful in most cases where a distinction is to be made.

What these examples show is that the ear is capable of comprehending different tonalities at different structural levels, levels that are measured by different scales of musical time. On a chord-to-chord basis the ear can perceive these progressions as modulating, without knowing for certain that the original key will reappear until it actually does so. On a phrase-to-phrase basis, with a longer time scale, the overall tonal scheme is that of a single key, with the apparent modulations actually existing as temporary tonal emphases on nontonic harmonies, assisted momentarily by harmonies drawn from outside the key.   219

At a more remote level we could employ a still longer time scale, for instance extending on a section-to-section basis throughout the length of a sonata-form movement. At this level, modulations occur between subsections of considerable length, as for instance between the tonic first theme and the dominant second theme in a major-mode exposition. The ear would be satisfied to relinquish the first key in favor of the second, simply on the basis of the durations involved, without having the feeling of certainty as to when the original key would return. Nevertheless, the eventual return of the first key, even after several different modulations, is a vindication of the principle of tonal unity of form in common-practice harmony. In this most fundamental sense, modulations can only be secondary tonal events in a piece beginning and ending in the same key. Certainly this is plain enough in shorter pieces employing only one or two keys different from the main key; it is revealed by analysis in larger works as well, even when there are many modulations.

THE MODULATION CHAIN

When the modulation from the main key is not followed by a return but by another modulation to a third key we have a different situation, a succession called a *modulation chain*. The ear's memory of the original key is progressively weakened by continued modulations to other keys, only to be reaffirmed when the original key finally reappears. Modulation chains are a resource of musical development, and are most dependably found in the development sections of sonata-form movements, where they may traverse six or seven different keys or even more before returning to the original tonic. Sequential modulations are very common in such passages; these will be discussed more fully in Chapter 19, although one example is seen later in this chapter (Example 14–12). Abrupt modulations may also be found in modulation chains; these also will be illustrated shortly. The extreme tendencies of modulatory practice are represented by continuous chromatic modulation, which came to be favored by composers in the latter part of the nineteenth century.

The separate time elements in the modulation chain may be quite long, in which case the appearance of new keys may be relatively stable, or they may be short, with only fleeting assertions of new tonics until the end of the chain. Some modulating sequences, as will be seen in later chapters, proceed by dominants alone, allowing for no stable tonics, even temporarily, until the sequence ends.

An example of systematic continuous modulation is afforded by a curious early work of Beethoven, the two *Preludes,* Op. 39, for piano or organ. Each of these pieces modulates through all twelve major keys via the circle of fifths, from C to C, with some digressions. The student is urged to analyze these preludes as examples of modulation over the most uncomplicated route, albeit not necessarily the shortest, between any two major keys. The designation for piano "or organ" suggests the practical use of these pieces as a substitute for improvisational skill in church services, where the organist might wish to provide an orderly transition from the key of one piece to that of the next. Other composers and theorists have written modulation manuals for much the same purpose, the modulations making use of all types of progressions involving secondary dominants, modal mixtures, and chromatically altered chords as well as the simpler relationships which we have been studying.

As the student's vocabulary of chordal procedures and types increases, he should make an effort to incorporate them in modulatory schemes realized at the keyboard. At this point it will be a sufficiently challenging task to master the simpler pivot-chord relationships between closely related keys in all possible positions and transpositions. Later the student should have in mind the ultimate goal of being able to work out at the keyboard a modulation between any two keys, using any given chord as a pivot, with a maximum of harmonic efficiency and smoothness.

Related Keys

All keys are related. It is only a question of the degree of relationship. The common expression "related keys" means always those most closely related.

The relationship of keys has two aspects of definition. The first conception is based on the number of tones in common between two keys. Thus it is plain that the keys C major and G major are very closely related since they differ in scale only as to F and F sharp. By this definition the keys of nearest relationship to a given key are those having one sharp (or flat) more or less in the signature.

EXAMPLE 14–10: Major Mode

C maj.   A m' 1.   G maj.   E min.   F maj.   D min.

It will be noted that the key-notes in the above example comprise the steps of the scale of C major, with the exception of VII, and that the modes of the keys, as shown by their tonic chords, are in agreement with the triads on the scale degrees of C major. The family of keys in the above illustration can be described in this way: tonic (major); dominant; subdominant; and the relative minors of all three.

EXAMPLE 14–11: Minor Mode

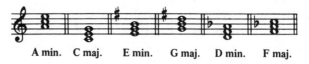

A min.   C maj.   E min.   G maj.   D min.   F maj.

The family of keys having one sharp (or flat) more or less than a given minor key shows two important differences from the scheme just described. The triad on the second degree does not appear. It will be remembered that II in the minor mode is a diminished triad and could not serve as a tonic chord. The seventh degree, however, is present, not in its form as leading-tone triad but as a major triad on the seventh degree found in the descending melodic scale. Its relationship is that of relative major of the dominant. This family of keys may be described thus: tonic (minor); dominant; subdominant; and the relative majors of all three.

INTERCHANGE OF MODES

During the nineteenth century, as more interest in harmonic color developed, the latent potentialities of another aspect of key relationship were exploited. This is the closeness of the major mode to the parallel minor mode, that is, the minor mode having the same tonic. Under the principles just outlined, the keys C major and C minor are rather distantly related since there is a difference of three flats in the signature. We have seen, however, that these two keys are practically identical, having as they do the same tonal degrees and really differing only in the third degree. Practice in the nineteenth century, and much individual practice in the eighteenth, tends to regard the two modes as simply two aspects of one tonality, so that the family of keys is greatly enlarged.

Rather than compile a list of related keys under this broader principle it is more practical to consider each pair of keys individually. The method of appraising the relationship of a second key to a main tonality is the same as that of relating a chord to a given tonality. The new tonic note is interpreted as in the fundamental key, together with its particular form as a chord.

These are a few examples:

D major is related to C minor as dominant of the dominant.

A-flat major is related to C major as the submediant of the parallel minor.

G minor is related to C major as dominant minor, or as subdominant of the second degree, or as supertonic of the subdominant, etc.

Cf. Ex. 12–20

The logic of modal interchange is governed in modulation by the same principles developed first in Chapter 5, wherein we saw that the change of mode is favored by some progressions but not by others. IV or VI in the minor can readily be followed by I in the major, for instance, but IV or VI in the major is seldom followed by I in the minor; major V proceeds to either a major or a minor tonic with equal ease regardless of the mode that has preceded it; and so forth. Modal interchange expands the scope of related tonalities available for modulation, and in a modulation chain can facilitate rapid modulation between otherwise distantly related keys.

In the following modulation sequence, the apparent remoteness of the keys involved is accounted for by the resolution of each successive dominant to the minor tonic, which serves as the mediant in the major mode of the key to follow; in other words, each modulation also occasions a change of mode. The pattern of keys travels all the way around the circle of fifths, and thus an enharmonic change (see below) occurs as well.

EXAMPLE 14–12: Schubert, *Symphony No. 9*, I

The steps given earlier show how the composer modulates by adopting a new tonal center for a given chord. The problem is slightly different when two tonalities are given and the pivot chord is to be found. Here, as in all branches of theoretical study, it is urged that no steps be omitted. They should rather be dwelt upon for what can be learned from them. It is natural to take advantage of the first good pivot chord that comes to mind, and it may happen that none better could be found. But the student should be advised and even required at least a few times to find all the possible pivot chords between two given keys, and then to select the one he considers the most effective to use.

Since we are still limiting ourselves to triads, while establishing fundamental principles, the exhaustive list of pivot chords between two keys will not be very large. The process of discovering these involves the attempted interpretation of all the chords of the first key in terms of the second key.

Assuming the two keys to be C and B flat, we first write all the forms of the triads we know in C and note those for which we find an explanation in the key of B flat.

EXAMPLE 14–13

C: I——— II——— III——— IV——— V VI——— VII———
B♭: II III IV V I

Looking at these possibilities, we can say at once that the B-flat V is not very good, since it is preferable to locate the pivot chord in advance of the dominant of the new key. The B-flat II would be excellent for the second key, but, as it is the minor of I in C, it would be convenient only if we wished to leave the impression of the minor mode in the first key. The B-flat I is not without objection—the note B flat would have to appear in C as part of the descending melodic minor scale, and to make that clear it would have to proceed next to A flat, a note we do not particularly welcome in B-flat. These considerations leave the two remaining possibilities B-flat III and IV. Since IV contains the troublesome note B flat, that leaves B-flat III, or in other words II of C, as best choice for the pivot chord.

ENHARMONIC CHANGES

In modulations between flat keys and sharp keys it will be necessary to invoke an enharmonic reading in one of the keys at some point. In Example 14–12 above, the pivot chord, I in A-flat minor (seven flats) is also III in F-flat major (eight flats), whose dominant is given as V_5^6 in E major (four sharps). If the dominant were to be notationally consistent with the old key it would have to be notated C flat, E flat, G flat, B double-flat. The practice of composers shows no great consistency in the employment of enharmonic notation for the sake of ease of reading, double sharps and double flats being freely used except where their density becomes clearly impractical.

ABRUPT MODULATIONS

Modulation means change of key. Hence there cannot be a "change of key without modulation." Some modulations sound sudden and unexpected, and sometimes one feels that the composer did not intend an overlapping transition between the two keys. But there can be no modulation in which the last chord of the first key cannot be analyzed in terms of the second key, at least theoretically. By this process the harmonic progression at the point of modulation is accurately described, and the degree of suddenness brought to light. Suddenness is a matter of rhythm when the modulation appears at some unexpected point in the phrase, as by deceptive cadence, but it is also a matter of remoteness of the tonal relationship. If the pivot chord has a close relationship to both keys and there is no modal change, the modulation should sound smooth and straightforward. The more distant the relationship to either key, the more abrupt will be the modulation.

EXAMPLE 14–14: Schubert, *Sonata in B flat,* Op. posth., I

The above example shows a modulation from F major to D-flat minor (enharmonic). This very unusual relationship involves two modal interchanges, first from F major to F minor to obtain the flat submediant triad, which is then itself changed to minor. The contiguous relationships of C and D flat (C sharp) and of A and A flat (G sharp) are strong enough to associate the chord as a submediant despite the anomalous association of F and F flat (E).

In the following example a pivot-chord relationship may be defined, but one could hardly say that it is easily heard if it is even heard at all, despite the common tone B.

EXAMPLE 14–15: Haydn, *Sonata No. 1*, I

The long-held cadential chord, the abrupt change of register, and the different textures all help to obliterate the sense of transition between the two keys. There is no modulating process; there is only a modulated state. Instances such as the above, where no real pivot chord can be heard, are best described by the term *shift* rather than *modulation*.

A fairly common type of shift in the nineteenth century is the chromatic shift to a key a semitone higher. In many cases the actual shift will take place in a single voice, to avoid the appearance of parallels.

EXAMPLE 14–16: Beethoven, *Andante in F*
("Andante favori"), WoO 57

Andante grazioso con moto

226

The analysis of the passage above is written as a direct shift between the two keys, without a pivot chord.

The following example of chromatic shift, not avoiding the parallel feeling, is a well-considered joke.

EXAMPLE 14–17: Schumann, *Faschingsschwank aus Wien,*
Op. 26: III, Scherzino

Semitonal modulations using pivot chords are more common; generally these employ chromatically altered chords and thus are the subject of later chapters of this book. Some semitonal modulations make use of simpler relationships. In the following example, the modulation to the key a semitone lower uses a pivot chord which is the dominant of the first key and the submediant of the second.

E.g., Ex. 27–29

EXAMPLE 14–18: Schubert, *Winterreise:* No. 7, *Auf dem Flusse*

The reverse of the above relationship is seen in the following example.

227

EXAMPLE 14–19: Beethoven, *Symphony No. 3* ("Eroica"), I

EXERCISES

1. Interpret the triad below in as many keys as possible, using roman numerals.

2. Label the triad below as a pivot chord in as many modulations as possible.

3. Work out the following figured basses:

4. Using only triads, construct phrases according to each of the following specifications:

   a. The pivot chord is II of the second key.
   b. The pivot chord is V of the first key.
   c. The pivot chord is III of the first key and II of the second key.
   d. The pivot chord is VI of the first key and IV of the second key.

5. Using as models the phrases by Schumann and Schubert given below, carry out the following steps:

   a. Analyze the phrase and write out the pattern of harmonic rhythm.
   b. Construct the four-part harmonic scheme.
   c. Using this harmonic pattern, construct a new phrase different from the original.

Schumann, *Album for the Young,* Op. 68: No. 17, *The Little Morning Wanderer*

Schubert, *Last Waltzes,* Op. 127, No. 15

6. Show by roman numerals the relationship of all the chords in A major to the tonality of C-sharp minor.

7. Write in four parts the following phrases:

   a. C min. $\frac{2}{2}$ VI | IV II | V | { I
   III | IV II | V | I ||

   b. E maj. $\frac{3}{4}$ I V I | IV II | { V
   IV I IV | V | I ||

   c. B♭ maj. $\frac{4}{4}$ V VI II | V I | { VI
   II VI IV | V |·I || 229

8. Construct musical sentences in two phrases, each beginning with the progression VI–II–V–I in the key of C major, modulating, and concluding with:

    a. II–I$_4^6$–V–I in D-flat major
    b. IV–V–VI–V–I in A major
    c. IV–I^6–II^6–V–I in G-sharp minor
    d. V–VI–II–V–I in E-flat minor

9. Harmonize the two chorale phrases given below, modulating from B minor to D major:

Herzliebster Jesu

10. Project: Examine twenty sonata-form movements in the major mode by Haydn and Mozart, for instance from the piano sonatas and string quartets, and determine in each where the second theme appears, the type of cadence that prepares it, and the type and extent of the modulation preceding.

CHAPTER 15

The Dominant
Seventh Chord

ORIGIN OF THE HARMONIC DISSONANCE

Although seventh chords may be built by superposing an interval of a third upon a triad, it must not be concluded that
these chords originated by that process. It should be repeated
that chords are made by moving voices. The seventh, the factor
which gives its name to the seventh chord, first appeared as a
melodic, nonharmonic tone. In the case of the seventh chord on
the dominant, the seventh is often seen in this purely melodic
capacity.

EXAMPLE 15–1

EXAMPLE 15–2: Handel, *Suite No. 8:* IV, Courante

The next evolutionary step was naturally the inclusion into the harmonic vocabulary of the vertical cross-section G–B–D–F as a chord, which we call V⁷. Its complete figuring is $V_{5\atop3}^{7}$ if we wish to show all the factors by numerals. We call the dominant seventh a chord in its own right because it possesses a certain independence from preparation. Common practice continued to use the seventh above the dominant root as a nonharmonic tone as just shown, but it also permitted the seventh to appear without preparation, that is, by skip from above or below.

EXAMPLE 15–3

IV V⁷ I   II V⁷ I   II V⁶₅ I   I⁶ V⁴₃ I

The adoption of V⁷ as an independent chord brings to the vocabulary the first unequivocal harmonic dissonance. With three exceptions all dissonances we have been using are nonharmonic, contrapuntal dissonances, tones foreign to the chords with which they are sounded. The seventh of V⁷ adds a dissonant element to the chord itself, so it is a harmonic dissonance. Historically this must be regarded as a novel concept, since the rules of sixteenth-century counterpoint prescribed proper preparation and resolution for all dissonances. (The period after common practice witnessed a comparable historical novelty, the emergence of the fully independent vertical sonority, that is, the dissonant chord which is both unprepared and unresolved.)

The three exceptions are the dissonant diminished triads VII and II (in minor) and the rarely used augmented triad III (in minor). The leading-tone triad may be disposed of at once by declaring it to be an incomplete dominant seventh. Certainly it sounds and acts as a dominant; the resolutions and voice-leading characteristic of V⁷ in general apply equally to VII.

E.g., Ex. 11–6

It has been argued that II of the minor mode is used chiefly in first inversion, with the second degree standing as a nonharmonic tone for the tonic note in a chord of the subdominant. Likewise, though it is much less often seen, the third degree in III of the minor mode, also in first inversion, is described as an appoggiatura in a dominant chord.

232

EXAMPLE 15–4

DOMINANT
SEVENTH

$$\text{II}^6\ (\text{IV}) \qquad \text{V} \qquad \text{III}^6\ (\text{V}) \qquad \text{VI}$$

Whatever the theoretical explanation, we are bound to report the occasional use of these dissonant triads by composers, even in root position, where the above reasoning is more difficult of application.

There are present in the dominant seventh chord two dissonant intervals: the diminished fifth between third and seventh, and the minor seventh between root and seventh. It has been common practice to resolve these dissonances. The principle of resolution has two aspects, harmonic and melodic. Harmonically, the dissonant intervals are followed in resolution by consonant intervals. Melodically, that is to say contrapuntally, the tendency tones set up by the dissonant intervals move in the direction of their tendencies to a point where they are no longer dissonant and no longer have the tendency to move.

The tendency of the diminished fifth is to contract to a third, major or minor, both voices moving inward by step. If the leading-tone, the lower of the two voices, alone moved, the following interval would still be dissonant, the perfect fourth.

In the case of the seventh, it would be possible for the upper voice alone to move, downward by step according to its tendency. This would leave an imperfect consonance, the major or minor sixth. When the lower note, the dominant, moves up to the tonic a more satisfactory interval is reached, the third.

EXAMPLE 15–5

$$5 \quad 4 \quad 5 \quad 3 \quad 7 \quad 6 \quad 7 \quad 3$$

Inversion of these two dissonant intervals gives an augmented fourth and a major second, or ninth if the voices are further apart. The tendencies of the tones remain the same, so that the augmented fourth will expand to a sixth and the major second will become a third.

EXAMPLE 15-6

Let us consider the contrapuntal consequences of disregarding the tendency of the seventh to descend. The following relative melodic movements would result:

EXAMPLE 15-7

The two fifths (*a*) should not be referred to as parallel fifths. Strictly speaking, the voices are not parallel, one fifth being smaller than the other. The characteristics to be noted in this progression are, first, the improper resolution of the tendency of the two voices in the dissonant interval, and, second, the prominence of the perfect fifth approached by similar motion. The same comment applies to the resolution of the seventh by similar motion to the fifth (*b*). These melodic progressions are generally avoided, though a common exception permitting *a* is shown below (Example 15-22); they are always avoided, however, between the outer voices, soprano and bass.

The resolution of the second into the unison (*c*) is used only when it is a minor second, and the upper voice is a nonharmonic anticipation.

EXAMPLE 15-8

*"Corelli clash,"
see Ex. 8-22*

G: V   I

EXAMPLE 15-9: Bach, Chorale No. 153, *Alle Menschen
müssen sterben*

An interval of a ninth is followed by an octave (*d*) only when
it is the upper voice that moves.

EXAMPLE 15–10

The motion shown in *e* above is found only when the dominant seventh chord changes position or spacing, as in *a* in the
example below, where the seventh reappears in some other voice.
The seventh is not used as a neighbor note (*b* below), harmonic
or nonharmonic, unless an ornamental resolution is to follow
it (*c*).

EXAMPLE 15–11

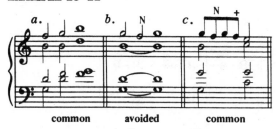

It is a generally valid principle that the seventh of V[7], once introduced, must have a resolution outside the chord. Examples like
a below are rarely found in common practice; typical resolutions
of the seventh by arpeggiation are shown in *b* and *c*.

EXAMPLE 15–12

See Exx. 6–13,
7–18

REGULAR RESOLUTION

All dissonant chords in common practice have what is called a
regular resolution. Harmonically, the term means the chord to
which the dissonant chord usually progresses. It is best expressed
in terms of root progression.

235

The regular resolution of V⁷ to I is probably the most fundamental harmonic progression in music. It is without doubt the
commonest, and it seems to be felt instinctively as a natural musical word even by an unmusical person.

The presence of the fourth degree, subdominant, supplies the
only important tonal factor that was missing in V–I; hence this is
the perfect progression for the definition of tonality.

In the resolution, the seventh descends one degree. The third
ascends to the tonic, and the fifth of the chord, having no tendency, descends to the tonic rather than double the modal third
degree. This results in an incomplete chord of resolution. It is to
be remarked, however, that the tonal balance of three roots and
one third is always preferred to that of two roots and two thirds,
quite apart from the precedence of contrapuntal movement that
caused the doubling. The principle of doubling tonal degrees in
preference to modal degrees is thus corroborated.

EXAMPLE 15–13

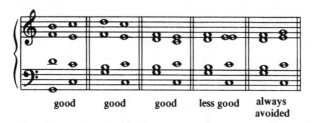

good   good   good   less good   always
                                                  avoided

EXAMPLE 15–14: Mozart, *Symphony No. 41*, K. 551
("Jupiter"), III

The second degree, fifth of the chord, is not essential to the
satisfactory sonority of the dominant seventh chord, and is frequently omitted. The consequent doubling of the root gives a
convenient common tone between the two chords, and the repetition of this common tone supplies the missing fifth to the tonic
236 chord.

EXAMPLE 15–15

DOMINANT
SEVENTH

Omission of the third is less often practiced, but there are occasions when the melodic outline of the voices brings about such a disposition. The chord is clearly recognizable as a dominant seventh and is a little less thick in sonority.

EXAMPLE 15–16: Chopin, *Prelude*, Op. 28, No. 21

If it is particularly desired that the tonic chord contain the fifth, as for instance in the final chord of a movement, the leading-tone is made to descend to the dominant—only, however, when it is in the alto or the tenor voice. Here the harmonic aspect assumes more importance to the composer than the melodic aspect (see Example 15–2).

EXAMPLE 15–17

G: V⁷   I   E♭:   V⁷   I

When the dominant seventh chord resolves to a tonic chord in first inversion, the bass may be said to have taken over the resolution of the seventh. The seventh may not resolve as usual because of the resultant direct octave on the third degree. It therefore moves upward, making the direct fifth and also the incorrect resolution of the diminished fifth, unless this interval happens to be in its inversion as an augmented fourth.

EXAMPLE 15–18

F : V⁷   I⁶   V⁷   I⁶

This resolution, which is not at all uncommon, is classified as a variant of the regular resolution, but it contains the irregularities of contrapuntal movement described above.

The following example shows the dominant seventh in a very unusual form, with the third omitted and the seventh doubled. The peculiar spacing, the syncopation, the lack of leading-tone, the irregular upward resolution of the seventh in the soprano, and the sustaining of the bass into a tonic six-four all combine to create a feeling of tonal mystery.

EXAMPLE 15–19: Beethoven, *String Quartet*, Op. 127, II

Adagio, ma non troppo e molto cantabile

pp sempre

cresc.

A♭ : V⁷   I⁶₄ I

THE FIRST INVERSION

The first inversion of the dominant seventh chord is commonly called the *dominant six-five*, its complete figuring being V⁶₅. The
3 is often omitted as understood.

Factors are rarely omitted from inversions of seventh chords. The root, since it is in an inside voice, will be repeated in the next chord so that the tonic chord of resolution will be complete. All other circumstances aside, the dominant six-five-three is most effective when the original seventh of the chord is in the soprano
voice.

EXAMPLE 15–20

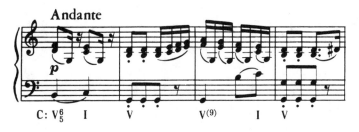

V^6_5 I V^6_5 I V^6_5 I

*See also Exx.
4–8, 5–34, 12–5,
12–9, 12–12,
13–9, 14–8,
17–3, 26–7*

EXAMPLE 15–21: Haydn, *Symphony No. 94* ("Surprise"), II

Andante

C: V^6_5 I V V(9) I V

It will be noticed that the tendency tones move just as they did in the root-position resolution.

This inversion is useful in constructing a melodic bass and also as a relief from the weight of the root-position progression.

THE SECOND INVERSION

The inversion with the fifth in the bass is called the *four-three* chord. The complete figuring shows the intervals six, four, and three: V^6_4 (with subscript 3). The four-three inversion is thus equivalent to the dominant six-four with the seventh present, and like its parent sonority has a somewhat restricted usage. It is generally considered weaker rhythmically than the other inversions, and it is very often used as a passing chord between I and I⁶. In this case, the bass is normally treated as a passing tone between the tonic and the third degree, moving either up or down. The other voices follow their tendencies as before, the exception being that when the bass moves up to I⁶ the seventh resolves upward in the same way and with the same contrapuntal results as in the progression V⁷–I⁶.

239

DOMINANT
SEVENTH

See also Exx.
6–14, 6–27, 9–6,
11–8, 13–7, 13–8,
13–15, 18–26,
19–3, 22–22,
26–11, 27–32

EXAMPLE 15–22

I^6 V^4_3 I I V^4_3 I^6

EXAMPLE 15–23: Beethoven, *String Quartet*, Op. 130, V

E^b: I V^6 of II V^4_3 I V^4_3 I^6 II^6 V^o_9 of V V   I V^4_3 I^6 V^4_3 I

EXAMPLE 15–24: Bach, *St. Matthew Passion*, Part I, No. 27

so schla - fen un - sre Sün - den ein,

F: V I^6_4 V I^6_4 V^7 I^6_4 V I^6 V^4_3 I V I^6_4 V^7 I^6_4 V

The following example shows the V^4_3 chord as a neighbor chord, the bass being melodically a neighbor note.

EXAMPLE 15–25: Haydn, *String Quartet*, Op. 76, No. 4, II

Adagio

240   E^b: I V^4_3 I V $\frac{6}{I}$ II V^4_3 of II II V of II $\frac{6}{II}$

In the example below, by Schubert, this inversion of the dominant seventh is used for its characteristic sound, as an important chord in the phrase.

EXAMPLE 15–26: Schubert, *String Quartet*, Op. 29, II

C: I   I⁶   V⁴₃   V⁶₅   I   V⁴₃   I⁶   V⁶₄ V⁷ of V V

THE THIRD INVERSION

The third inversion, with the seventh in the bass, is a strong chord. The bass is here dissonant with two of the upper voices and is thereby given a strong tendency to move. A significant comparison can be drawn between the dissonant quality of this bass with that of the bass of the second inversion. In the second inversion the bass is the lower note of the dissonant perfect fourth, in which the top note possesses the tendency to descend. The bass is therefore free to move up or down. In the third inversion the bass is the lower note of two dissonant intervals, the augmented fourth and the major second, and in each case has the obligation to move downward one degree. Hence this is a strong chord with an unusually strong tendency in a certain direction.

The other voices move as before, except that a favorite soprano part for this progression is one that moves from supertonic up a fourth to dominant, doubling the fifth in I⁶.

The full figuring of the chord is V⁶₄₂, usually abbreviated to V², or V⁴₂.

EXAMPLE 15–27

V⁴₂   I⁶   V⁴₂   I⁶

*See also Exx.
6–14, 6–29, 14–6,
17–18, 17–24,
17–26, 19–3,
19–5, 23–15,
24–25, 25–5,
25–23, 26–20*

EXAMPLE 15–28: Beethoven, *Sonata*, Op. 13, II

A♭ :   I   V²   I⁶   V⁶₅   I   V⁶   VI   V⁴₃ of V   V

The following apparent resolutions are but the effect of auxiliary chords over a static harmony.

EXAMPLE 15–29: Mendelssohn, *Symphony No. 4* ("Italian"), III

E: V²   (I⁶)   V²   (I⁶)   V²

THE MELODIC TRITONE

A melodic fragment that is included in the limits of an augmented fourth, from subdominant to seventh degree, is almost invariably resolved in the melodic line, either by the leading-tone continuing to the tonic, or, in descending, by the fourth degree continuing to the third. The direct skip downward from the leading-tone to the fourth degree is generally avoided in any case.

EXAMPLE 15–30

See Ex. 16–16   The following unresolved melodic tritones are avoided:

EXAMPLE 15–31

In accordance with the general rule for all wide skips, the skip of a diminished fifth, if it is not to continue in arpeggiation, is best followed by stepwise motion in the opposite direction. The following example shows the melodic resolution of the tritone to be in accordance with the ordinary resolution of the dominant seventh: the seventh descends, the leading-tone ascends.

EXAMPLE 15–32: Schubert, *Moments musicaux*, Op. 94, No. 1

C: V of III III   V of V   V(min.)   V(maj.)

Formulae, to be played in all keys:

EXAMPLE 15–33

V^7 I V^6_5 I V^4_3 I^6 V^2 I^6 I V^6_5 I V^2 I^6 V^4_3 I

EXERCISES

1. Work out in four parts the following figured basses:

2. Construct a musical sentence of two phrases according to the following specifications:

    a. The first phrase begins in G major and ends with an authentic cadence in E minor.

    b. The second phrase returns to G major by means of a pivot chord which is the supertonic triad in G.

    c. One example of each of the three inversions of the dominant seventh chord is introduced appropriately.

3. Construct a musical sentence of two phrases according to the following specifications:

    a. The first phrase ends with a deceptive cadence, without modulation.

    b. The first phrase shows the resolution of V^7 to I^6.

    c. The second phrase shows two uses of the V^2 chord—with the seventh prepared and with the seventh unprepared.

4. Harmonize the following basses, introducing dominant seventh chords and inversions:

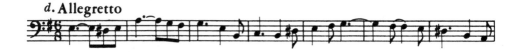

d. Allegretto

5. Harmonize the following soprano parts:

a.

b.

c. Allegro

d. Andantino

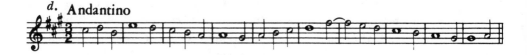

CHAPTER 16

Secondary Dominants

IMPORTANCE AND DEFINITION OF
THE SECONDARY DOMINANT FUNCTION

Almost any page of music chosen at random will show the presence of numerous accidentals, sharps, flats, and natural signs, which indicate alterations of the tones other than the qualifications announced by the key signature. We know that these chromatic signs do not necessarily signify that a modulation has taken place. Some of them are accounted for as the required notation of the major sixth and seventh degrees in the minor mode. Others are seen to be chromatic nonharmonic tones, like the neighbor note acting as a temporary leading-tone beneath the principal note.

Perhaps the largest source of these accidental signs lies in the tendency of composers to prefer the sound of dominant harmony to that of nondominant function, a tendency which prevailed until the end of the nineteenth century. Next to the dominant function in the main key itself, the secondary dominant principle, which we first encountered in Chapter 5, is the most important generator of dominant harmony. The principle expanded the range of harmonic color by the addition of new notes and thereby new chords; moreover it increased the sense of direction and movement in harmonic progression. In its most extended form the principle produced a sequential harmonic scheme in which each chord became the dominant of the next.

EXAMPLE 16–1: Mozart, *Sonata*, K. 283, III

Cf. Ex. 19–12

From observation of this practice of composers the following rule may be stated: any degree of the scale may be preceded by its own dominant harmony without weakening the fundamental tonality.

These temporary dominant chords have been referred to by theorists as *attendant chords, parenthesis chords, borrowed chords,* etc. The designation *secondary dominants* in this book reflects the belief that the term is fully descriptive of their function. The chords for which they serve as secondary dominants may be called *secondary tonics;* the function itself is thus one of *tonicization.*

Far from weakening the tonality, the secondary dominants can be a distinct aid in strengthening it. If we imagine a tonal center, supported on either hand by subdominant and dominant, it is easy to see that if these two important tonal degrees are in turn supported by their respective dominants the whole tonal edifice is made stronger thereby. This is essentially the scheme used by Beethoven in the opening measures of his first symphony. The actual tonic chord is delayed in its arrival, but it is made the more inevitable by the strong secondary tonics established beforehand. (It is only fair to add that this beginning was criticized in Beethoven's time for being tonally vague—a verdict which we could hardly justify today, after more than a century of evolution of complex tonality.)

EXAMPLE 16–2: Beethoven, *Symphony No. 1*, I

I^6

The secondary dominants have not only a functional value but are an important source of harmonic color as well. Composers of the eighteenth and nineteenth centuries were interested in the expressive advantages of new notes which could logically be included in the tonality. The harmonic vocabulary was greatly enriched through the introduction of these chords.

All the forms in which the regular dominant of the key may appear are also employed as secondary dominants. That means, at the present stage, major triads, dominant seventh chords, and the dominant seventh without root (leading-tone triad), with all inversions. For example, the chord V of V in the key of C may have these forms:

EXAMPLE 16–3

C: V of V   (VII of V)

Triads having a secondary dominant function in the key of C are shown below, compared with the normal triads of the major and minor modes. Four dominant sevenths, derived from major triads, are included in parentheses because their parent triads cannot readily be understood as having a secondary dominant function unless the seventh is present. It will be noted that the diminished-triad forms of II and VI in the minor mode can be interpreted as incomplete secondary dominants, just as VII in its diminished form is interpreted as an incomplete V^7. None of these incomplete sevenths, however, can serve as secondary tonics, and their dominants are not found. The major triad on VI in the minor mode is sometimes used, as well as its seventh chord, as the dominant of the chromatically lowered supertonic, known as the *Neapolitan sixth* (Chapter 26).

EXAMPLE 16–4

I V^7 of IV   II(VII of III)   II   V of V   III(V of VI) V^7 of VI   III   V of VI   IV(V of VII)

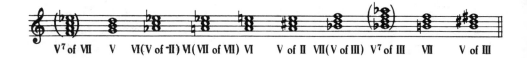

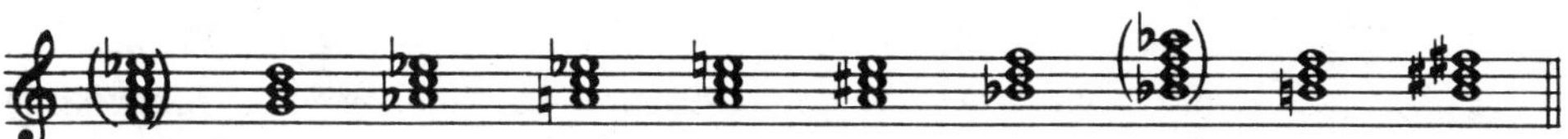
V7 of VII
V
VI(V of -II)
VI(VII of VII)
VI
V of II
VII(V of III)
V7 of III
VII
V of III

RESOLUTION

The principles of resolution in the dominant-to-tonic progression are equally valid in the treatment of secondary dominants. The secondary dominant and its tonic are considered a tonal unit of two chords for all purposes of voice leading. Thus, in Example 16–3, the F sharp is for the moment not the subdominant of C but the leading-tone of G, and so it is not doubled. The D is temporarily the tonal degree in the chord.

An important principle of chromatic alteration will be seen active in the treatment of secondary dominants. That is, a note chromatically raised is given thereby a tendency to proceed upward, and, conversely, a note chromatically lowered is given a tendency to proceed downward.

EXAMPLE 16–5

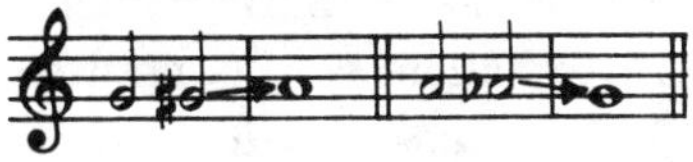

METHOD OF INTRODUCTION

The smoothest and most natural way that a secondary dominant may be introduced is when it follows a chord that itself could be interpreted in the key of which the secondary dominant is the actual dominant. In this case the group of three chords (the secondary dominant as the second chord of the group) could be regarded as in the temporary tonality, but the first and third chords would still be equally strong members of the true tonality.

EXAMPLE 16–6

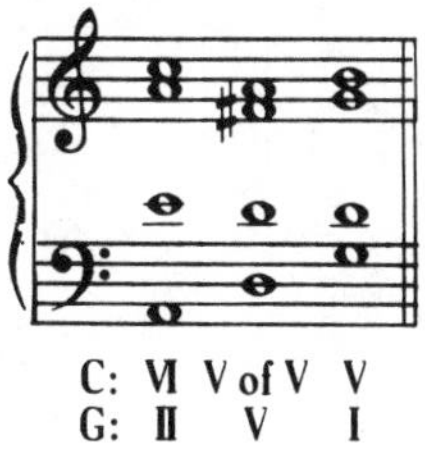
C: VI V of V V
G: II V I

Such a duality of tonal meaning facilitates the chord connection and guarantees the logical sound of the harmonic progression. (More will be said about dual-function chords in Chapter 18.)

Often, however, the preceding chord is incapable of natural analysis in the temporary key. This will ordinarily mean that a chromatic relationship exists between the two chords. A tone of one will appear in chromatically altered form in the other.

CROSS-RELATION

When this chromatic relationship is found between two different voices the effect is called *cross-relation*, indicating that the relationship exists across the voices.

EXAMPLE 16–7

cross-relation

Cross-relation, both simultaneous and not, is found in the works of all composers of the harmonic period, but never indiscriminately used. The various accepted uses of cross-relation will be discussed in connection with the relevant material. Here it will suffice to mention the most common. That is when the two tones involved are treated as scale degrees of the melodic and harmonic minor. In *E.g., Ex. 8–32* the example above, the cross-relation would be acceptable if the key were G minor, with F natural as descending seventh degree. A passing tone E flat would be either written or understood between F and D. The F sharp is, of course, the ascending leading-tone.

In C major, however, no such logic exists and this cross-relation is generally avoided. The chords would be arranged in a manner to allow the chromatic progression to take place in a single voice.

EXAMPLE 16–8

C: IV V of V V

A succession of V⁷ of V to V⁷ would generally be arranged in like manner, even though keeping the chromatic succession in the same voice means that the leading-tone of the secondary dominant, and sometimes the seventh as well, resolve contrary to their normal tendencies. Accordingly this is an irregular resolution, a subject to be covered in detail in the next chapter. The formulae given below are different forms of the "barber-shop" progression.

EXAMPLE 16–9

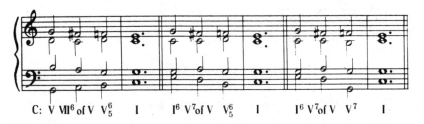

The student is advised to connect such chords at first without cross-relation, but to experiment with the sound of other arrangements and to observe instances of cross-relation encountered in the works of composers.

EXAMPLE 16–10: Bach, *Well-Tempered Clavier, II,*
Prelude No. 12

EXAMPLE 16–11: Bach, *St. Matthew Passion,* No. 1

EXAMPLE 16–12: Schumann, *Liederkreis,* Op. 39: No. 5,
Mondnacht

See also Exx.
22–23, 31–60

V OF II

See also Exx.
9–8, 15–25,
16–12, 17–16,
17–26, 18–8,
20–21, 24–11,
24–28

The dominant of the second degree has for its root the sixth
degree of the major scale. It is not used if the minor mode is
prevalent, since in that mode the supertonic is a diminished
triad and hence does not act as a tonic, even temporarily. The
tonic note of the key is chromatically raised to make it the
leading-tone of II.

The following example shows V of II as a triad both in root
position and as a passing six-four chord.

EXAMPLE 16–13: Schumann, *Novelette,* Op. 21, No. 1

As a dominant six-five-three chord:

EXAMPLE 16–14: Liszt, *A Faust Symphony,* II

V OF III

As there are two third degrees, major and minor, so there will be
two dominants available, a semitone apart in pitch. Needless to
say, the dominant of the third degree of the minor mode does not
progress to the third degree of the major mode, and vice versa.

*See also Exx.
18–9, 18–10*

In the major mode two alterations are necessary. The second
degree is raised to become leading-tone of the third, and the
fourth degree is raised to form a perfect fifth with the seventh
degree root.

EXAMPLE 16–15: Schubert, *Symphony No. 8*, II

In the following instance, the chord V of III is given the
rhythmic prominence of the final chord in a cadence, as though
there were a half cadence in C sharp. The entire chorale is,
however, clearly in A, so that a change of key so soon seems
hardly logical.

EXAMPLE 16–16: Bach, Chorale No. 216, *Es ist genug*

If the minor third degree is employed, its dominant will be
found on the lowered seventh degree, and the two chords will
sound like a V–I progression in the relative major key. This extremely common relationship was also discussed at length in
Chapter 5.

*Exx. 5–33, 5–34,
20–17*

253

EXAMPLE 16–17: Beethoven, *Sonata,* Op. 2, No. 1, IV

F: I   V⁶₅ of III   III   V⁶₅ of III   III   V⁶₅ of III VII⁶   I⁶   V   I   It.   V

See also Exx.
4–8, 7–7, 8–49,
8–55, 12–15,
12–24, 12–26,
13–19, 14–4,
17–27, 18–3,
18–11, 18–13,
20–18, 20–19,
20–20, 24–14,
25–23, 28–5

V OF IV

The major tonic triad actually stands in relation of dominant to the subdominant, although it needs the addition of a minor seventh to clarify this relationship to the hearer. This is one of the commonest of the secondary dominants and is very often used toward the end of a piece, where emphasis on the subdominant is desired to balance previous dominant modulations.

EXAMPLE 16–18: Mendelssohn, *String Quartet,* Op. 12, III

B♭: I   V⁷ of IV   (IV⁶₄)   IV   I

The subdominant is likewise frequently emphasized at the beginning of the movement by the use of V of IV, as in the example above from Beethoven's *First Symphony* and in the following:

EXAMPLE 16–19: Beethoven, Overture to *Prometheus*

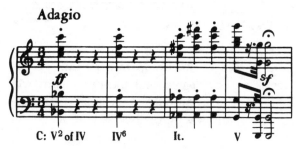

C: V² of IV   IV⁶   It.   V

254

F: I　　　　V⁷ of IV　　IV⁶₄　　　　　　　　V/I　　　　　　I

In an established minor mode it is, of course, necessary to raise
the third degree chromatically to create the leading-tone of the
subdominant.

EXAMPLE 16–21: Mozart, *Piano Concerto,* K. 466, III

Allegro assai

d: I⁶₄　　V⁷　　　VI　　V⁴₃ of IV　IV　IV(II)⁶₅　I⁶₄　V⁷

V OF V

The dominant of the dominant has already been mentioned in
connection with its use in half cadences (see Example 12–12).
The following is a typical case in which a modulation to the dominant key would not be called for in the analysis. The seventh
in the final chord of the half cadence provides an element of
continuity, implying the resolution to the tonic at the beginning
of the next phrase.

*See also Exx.
15–28, 6–14,
6–36, 8–11, 9–1,
9–12, 11–24,
12–2, 12–22,
17–11, 17–25,
18–10*

EXAMPLE 16–22: Schumann, *Album Leaves,* Op. 124:
　　　　　　　No. 16, *Slumber Song*

Allegretto

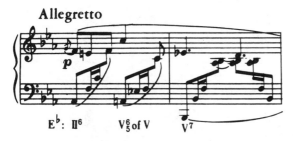

E♭: II⁶　　　V⁶₅ of V　　V⁷

In the following example the cross-relation is to be remarked between the A sharp, leading-tone of V, and the A natural in the bass of the chord of resolution. This type of cross-relation is characterized by the fact that the first of the two notes is a leading-tone, which follows its tendency upward, while the lowered tone enters as a strong appoggiatura-like dissonance, with downward tendency, in the bass of a seventh chord in its third inversion.

EXAMPLE 16–23: Wagner, Overture to *Tannhäuser*

$$E: \quad I^6 \ IV \ I^6 \ II \quad V \text{ of } V \quad V^2$$

V OF VI

*See also Exx.
8–21, 8–31, 9–2,
11–11, 13–7,
14–9, 17–9,
19–4, 25–21*

Like the mediant, the submediant exists in two forms, minor in the major mode and major in the minor mode, and thus there are different forms of dominant for these. In the major mode, the dominant note is chromatically raised to form the leading-tone in V of VI.

EXAMPLE 16–24: Wagner, *Siegfried Idyll*

$$E: \quad I \quad IV^6 \ I^6_4 \ II^6 \quad I^6 \ VI^6 \ V^6 \ VI \quad V \text{ of } VI \ VI \quad V \text{ of } VI \ VI \quad V$$

EXAMPLE 16–25: Schubert, *Piano Quintet*, Op. 114
("Trout"), III

256

$$D: \quad I \qquad V^7 \text{ of } VI \quad VI \qquad IV \qquad I^6_4$$

In the minor mode, the dominant note is not altered in V of VI, but its function changes from that of tonal degree to leading-tone. If the chord contains a seventh, a new tone—the chromatically lowered second degree—is introduced into the key.

EXAMPLE 16–26: Bruckner, *Symphony No. 7*, II

Unlike the mediant, the submediant of the minor mode is fairly common amid major harmonic surroundings. Its dominant seems rather remote from the major scale, as shown in Example 16–27.

V OF VII

The leading-tone is not considered a possible temporary tonic, so that its dominant is not employed. The lowered melodic seventh degree of the minor scale can, however, be found attended by a dominant harmony. Used in connection with an established major mode, as in the following example, it demonstrates the coloristic possibilities of this interchangeability of the modes.

Cf. Exx. 19–12, 19–15, 27–28

EXAMPLE 16–27: Bizet, *L'Arlésienne*, Suite No. 2: I, Pastorale

The sequential pattern of this example should be noted; the modulating sequence of an ascending cycle of fourths is a common device in the eighteenth and nineteenth centuries. (See the last of the following formulae.)

Formulae, to be played in all keys:

EXAMPLE 16–28

VI V⁶₅ of V V   I⁶   V(⁶₅)of IV IV V⁷   I   V⁶₅ of VI VI II⁶   V   V⁴₃ of II II V   I

V of IV IV⁶ V   I⁶   V of III III V⁴₃   I   V of III V of VI V of II V of V   V   I

EXERCISES

1. Work out the following figured basses:

a.

6#   6   6   5 6   6 7
         5   4 #

b.

6   6   6
5   5   7

c.

4   6   2 6 6   6
2   5   5
              3♮

d.

6   4   6 6♭   3 7
     5   2

e.

6   7 5 6#   # 6   6 #
5   4   4
            3

f.

6#   4#   6 7
     4   2
     3

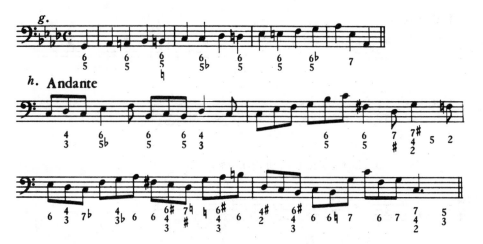

g.

h. Andante

2. Realize the following figured bass in four parts, with continuous eighth notes in the soprano except at the half cadence and the final cadence. Some nonharmonic tones are indicated by figures; others may be included in the added parts.

Allegretto grazioso

3. Construct a musical sentence of two phrases according to the following specifications:

    a. The prevailing mode is minor; the meter is three-four; the rhythmic texture contains eighth notes.

    b. The first phrase modulates to the subdominant of the relative major.

    c. The second phrase starts in that key and modulates to the original tonality.

    d. The sentence ends with a plagal cadence introduced by V of IV and finishing with a *tierce de Picardie.*

4. Harmonize the following unfigured basses:

a.

b.

c.

259

d. **Moderato**

5. Harmonize the following soprano parts:

a.

b.

c.

d. **Allegretto**

e. **Tempo giusto**

CHAPTER 17

Irregular Resolutions

DEFINITIONS OF IRREGULARITIES

The regular resolution of the dominant seventh chord is to the tonic triad. Consequently all other resolutions are irregular. It is essential that the two aspects of irregular resolution be clearly appreciated before generalizations regarding the practice of composers can be made. The irregularity may consist in a departure from the customary practice in voice leading, or it may be a purely harmonic matter of root progression.

In the example below, the harmonic progression is typical of the regular resolution of a dominant seventh chord. V^7 of V proceeds to its tonic, V. On the other hand, the voice leading is as irregular as could be.

EXAMPLE 17–1: Schubert, *String Quartet*, Op. 29, II

C: I^6 V^6_5 of V V^7

The progression V⁷–VI is properly regarded as an irregular resolution, but the voice leading characteristically exemplifies the rules for this progression, differing from V⁷–I only in the motion of the root.

EXAMPLE 17–2: Mendelssohn, *Andante con variazioni*, Op. 82

*See also Exx.
7–24, 8–33,
12–20, 12–23,
16–2*

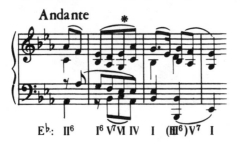

E♭: II⁶   I⁶ V⁷VI IV   I (III⁶)V⁷ I

The leading-tone moves to the tonic to emphasize the key. The second degree also moves to the tonic, as to ascend would form parallel fifths with the bass. The seventh of the chord resolves down, according to its tendency, but could not move up to the sixth degree, as that would make a poor direct octave on the resolution of a dissonance. One concludes that this progression, with the voice leading as shown, is essentially no different in its effect from the V–VI progression without the seventh.

It is customary to include the fifth in the V⁷ chord in this progression. The V⁷ in its incomplete form does not conveniently connect with VI, as the student may see by experiment.

EXAMPLE 17–3

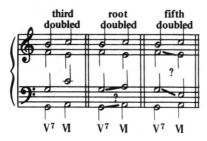

V⁷ VI   V⁷ VI   V⁷ VI

The extra root can only move by the skip up to the tonic. Otherwise it would move either in parallel octaves with the bass, or to the direct octave with the resolution of the seventh.

The examples given show that a regular resolution may be made with extreme irregularity of melodic movement, whereas an irregular resolution may show strict regularity of voice leading. In most irregular resolutions it will be found that the chord of resolution has at least two notes in common with the regular resolution;

or, to put it another way, under ordinary conditions the departure from regularity will be made in such a way as to conserve most of the expected chord.

All chord progressions are undoubtedly the product of melodic movement, as has been often stated; but since we are examining the practice of a particular period, in which it may be said that a vocabulary of chords exists, it seems reasonable to describe harmonic progressions in terms of root succession, considering as details the variants in form of the chords and the contrapuntal divergences.

Such a detail would be represented by the resolution of V^7 to V^7 of IV. The minor seventh above the tonic is in chromatic relationship with the leading-tone, so that usually the latter descends (*a* in the example below), although the cross-relation is sometimes used when the lowered tone is in the bass (*b*).

EXAMPLE 17–4

Cf. Exx. 12–24,
16–23

V^7 V^7 of IV V^7 V^2 of IV

The "barber-shop" progression, already noted in the previous chapter (Example 16–9), is an example of type *a* above.

It is to be noted that when two seventh chords occur in succession in root position, one of them is usually incomplete, with doubled root. The melodic progression of the voices to the nearest position brings this about. Inversions of seventh chords, however, are almost always in complete form with all factors present. The above example (*b*) shows a progression from a V^7 in root position to an inverted seventh chord. Hence the V^7 is constructed with doubled root so that the second chord will be completed naturally by the voice leading.

These two examples also show a dissonant chord resolving to another dissonant chord, an effect of frequent occurrence. One of the dissonant intervals, the minor seventh, resolves normally, while the other, the augmented fourth, moves in parallel motion to an equivalent dissonant interval, the diminished fifth. In all successions of dissonant chords it is important to notice the progression of the dissonant intervals.

In the following arrangement the chromatic bass is especially   263 effective, and the minor third degree as passing tone gives the color of cross-relation with the leading-tone of the subdominant.

EXAMPLE 17–5: Bach, *Magnificat:* No. 5, *Et misericordia*

$$e: \text{I} \quad (\text{IV}_4^6) \quad \text{II(IV)}_2^4 \quad \text{IV}_4^6 \quad \text{V}_5^6 \quad \text{V}_2^4 \text{ of IV}$$

VARIETY OF CHORDS OF RESOLUTION

The supertonic triad makes a weak resolution for the dominant seventh, since it is in effect similar to a dominant ninth minus root and third. The seventh of V^7 is common to the two chords so it does not resolve. In the following example, the presence of the seventh of II supplies a note of resolution for the leading-tone and thus strengthens the progression.

EXAMPLE 17–6: Brahms, *Intermezzo*, Op. 76, No. 3

$$\text{A}^\flat : \text{V}^2 \qquad \text{II}^7 \qquad \text{II(IV)}_5^6$$

The alteration of II to V of V gives a more satisfactory chord of resolution, since the seventh may then proceed chromatically upward. In the following example, showing a junction of phrases, the omission of the root in V of V eliminates another common tone.

EXAMPLE 17–7: Mozart, *Sonata*, K. 533, I

$$\text{C: } \text{I}_4^6 \qquad \text{V}^7 \qquad \text{V}_6^8 \text{ of V (: VII}^6 \text{ of V)}$$

Chords on the third degree tend to become less independent when associated with dominant harmony. The major third degree sounds more like a nonharmonic melodic tone than like a real resolution of the seventh. The resolution to the major triad on the minor third degree is not often found.

EXAMPLE 17–8

V⁷ III⁶   V² III   V⁷ III

Comparatively common as a chord of resolution, however, is the form of III which is dominant of the sixth degree. Here again there is a chromatic relationship involved.

EXAMPLE 17–9: Beethoven, *String Quartet*, Op. 18, No. 1, I

Allegro con brio

F: V⁷   V⁷ of VI   VI

In the resolution to IV the seventh may be prolonged into the second chord (or repeated). When both chords are in root position, the leading-tone is placed in an inside voice, to avoid prominence of the false relation of the tritone.

EXAMPLE 17–10: Chopin, *Prelude*, Op. 28, No. 17

Allegretto

Aᵇ : IV   V⁷   IV

The following example shows V⁷ of V resolving irregularly to I, followed by V⁷ to IV, in both cases with the leading-tone uncustomarily in the soprano, so that the false relation is not avoided; rather it is deliberately stressed for dramatic effect.

EXAMPLE 17–11: Schubert, *Symphony No. 9*, II

Andante con moto

a: III of III, V of V of III, V of V of III, V of V, V⁷ of V   I   V⁷   IV   I⁶₄   V

More often the subdominant is found in first inversion, allowing a choice of doubling either tonic or fourth degree.

EXAMPLE 17–12

See also Exx. 12–22, 25–8

V⁷   IV⁶   V⁷   IV⁶

In the Mozart example below, the dynamic change and the sudden leap in the upper melody add to the surprise of the irregular resolution.

EXAMPLE 17–13: Mozart, *Sonata*, K. 279, II

Andante

F: II⁶   I⁶₄   V⁷   IV⁶   V⁶₅   I

EXAMPLE 17–14: Chopin, *Ballade*, Op. 47

Allegretto

266   Aᵇ: IV⁶   V⁶₅   IV⁶   V⁶₅ (⁷₅)   V⁶₅ of II

The voice leading in the V⁷–VI progression, described in connection with Example 17–2, will of course be the same for the minor mode. In the following example the broken chords in the left-hand part stand for three sustained melodic parts. Hence in the V–VI progression A moves to G, D sharp to E, and B to C. The eighth note E in the right hand is an anticipation.

EXAMPLE 17–15: Rameau, *Harpsichord Pieces, Book II*, Suite No. 1: No. 5, *Gigue en Rondeau*

e: I   V⁷   VI   I⁶

The example below, of V⁷ resolving to V⁷ of II, is unusual for its parallel motion. Also to be noticed is that the melody notes in the second and third measures outline the scale of G minor, the temporary tonality of the second degree of F major.

EXAMPLE 17–16: Mozart, *Sonata*, K. 533, II

F: V⁴₃   V⁴₃ of II   II⁶   I⁶₄   V

The examples given are by no means an exhaustive accounting of the irregular resolutions of V⁷, even to the chords already studied. New chords will offer new resources in irregular resolutions, especially the diminished seventh chord.

The student is urged to experiment with resolutions of V⁷, in root position and in inversion, to all chords in his vocabulary in a single tonality. Some resolutions will prove to be unsatisfactory, but the experience will show the degree of practicability of the various chords as possible resolutions.

E.g., Ex. 25–5

267

IRREGULAR RESOLUTIONS OF
THE SECONDARY DOMINANTS

The practice of irregular resolution is applicable to the secondary dominants, in a somewhat lesser scope. These chords are generally identified by their resolution to their temporary tonic. When such resolution is lacking it may be that a modulation has taken place, or that the chord appears as enharmonic notation of a chord of quite different harmonic significance, as for instance an augmented sixth chord. If, however, the resolution is to a chord unquestionably of the initial key, the secondary dominant is plainly understood as such, without weakening the tonality. The best example of this principle is the progression V⁷ of VI to IV, which supports the original tonic better than the regular resolution by virtue of the tonal importance of the second chord.

EXAMPLE 17–17

*Cf. Exx. 11–5,
13–7, 22–22*

V⁷of VI   IV   II   V   I
(VI of VI)

As in the regular resolution, the secondary dominant and its chord of resolution are considered temporarily in the key of the secondary dominant for purposes of voice leading and doubling. Thus, in the example above, V⁷ of VI to IV is identical with V⁷ to VI in the key of VI, here A minor, so the voice leading is carried out as in V⁷–VI, resulting in the doubling of A, a tonal degree in the key of VI, but a modal degree in the main key of C. The same voice leading is seen in the example below, with the two chords in first inversion.

EXAMPLE 17–18: Bach, Chorale No. 268 *Nun lob',
mein' Seel', den Herren*

268   C: V⁶₅ of VI   IV⁶   I   V⁷   VI   I⁶₄   V⁷   I

Hardly less common is the progression V⁷ of V to I, particularly when I is in the six-four position in a cadence. The principle of the tonic six-four substituting for a dominant is confirmed by this strong progression.

IRREGULAR
RESOLUTIONS

See also Exx.
6–29, 6–38,
11–25, 18–13,
25–10, 30–17

Cf. Ex. 17–11

EXAMPLE 17–19: Saint-Saëns, *Piano Concerto No. 2, I*

In the following example, V⁷ of VI is approached from V, with tenor and bass moving in parallel fifths and the voices overlapping. The subsequent resolution is perfectly orthodox.

EXAMPLE 17–20: Cherubini, Overture to *Anacréon*

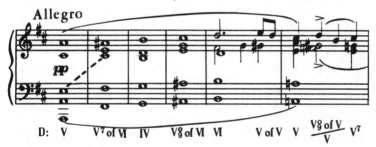

The same relationship is found between V⁷ of III and its irregular resolution to I. Analysis as an appoggiatura chord is ordinarily possible, or the chord may result from other melodic tones, such as the neighbor note used in several voices. In the following example, tenor and bass, here viola and cello, move in parallel octaves to effect the resolution, with a momentary change to three-part texture.

EXAMPLE 17–21: Beethoven, *String Quartet*, Op. 18, No. 5, III

269

The dominant of the supertonic progresses quite naturally to V⁷, the altered tonic following its tendency as leading-tone of the second degree.

EXAMPLE 17–22: Franck, *Symphony*, III

Such is not the case with the fairly common resolution of V⁷ of VI to I. In this progression the raised dominant turns back to its original form, not a usual procedure with chromatic alteration. It is as though it were really a lowered sixth degree in a kind of dominant effect.

EXAMPLE 17–23

EXAMPLE 17–24: Schubert, *Sonata*, Op. 53, III

Among the irregular resolutions of V⁷ of V, that to the triad on the third degree is a progression similar to V⁷ of VI going to IV, and V⁷ of III going to I. The voice leading produces a doubled third in the chord of resolution.

EXAMPLE 17–25: Chopin, *Mazurka*, Op. 7, No. 4

F: V   I   V⁷ of V   III   V   I

With the resolution of a secondary dominant to another secondary dominant, the validity of the harmonic functions in tonality is
demonstrated. The chords as dominants represent degrees of the
key, but each contains at least one note foreign to the scale. It
will be readily appreciated that the secondary dominants are a
source of much harmonic enrichment and a remarkable extension
of the unity of a single tonal center. The following are two examples out of numerous possibilities.

EXAMPLE 17–26: Schubert, *String Quintet*, Op. 163, III

C: I   V² of IV V of II   II⁶₄   V of II   II   I⁶   V

EXAMPLE 17–27: Franck, *Prelude, Aria, and Finale*

A♭ : V   I   V⁶₅ of V   V⁴₃ of IV   IV   I

In these examples the tonal unity of the phrase is assured by
the reappearance of the tonic. Consecutive secondary dominants,
as in Example 17–4, may, however, be used sequentially in modulation, each chord appearing as the dominant of the next, with
tonal stability not being reached until the sequence is broken off.
(See Chapter 19 for examples and amplified discussion.)

The student should try resolutions of each of the secondary   271 dominants to the various chords in a key, translating the progressions into terms of the tonality of the secondary dominant to clarify the voice leading.

The irregular resolutions vary widely in the frequency of their use. Only by the continued experience of observation of the circumstances affecting their employment by composers can knowledge of the practice be acquired. It is suggested that examples of the resolutions be collected gradually as they are seen in actual music, and that the student play them in all keys until their individual characteristics are assimilated, at the same time attempting to classify each as to its commonness or rarity.

Formulae, to be played in all keys:

EXAMPLE 17–28

V⁷ VI   V⁷ IV   V⁷ IV⁶   V⁷ IV⁶   V² III   VI   V⁷ V⁷ of II   II⁶   V⁷ V⁷ of V   V

V² V⁷ of VI   IV   I   V⁷   V⁶₅ of IV

Formulae of resolutions of secondary dominants are not given, as they would differ from the above only in the analysis. For example, V⁷–VI in C would be exactly like V⁷ of III–I in A flat, V⁷ of VI–IV in E flat, etc.

EXERCISES

1. Write four irregular resolutions of each of the following chords: E-flat V⁷; E-flat minor V⁷ of IV; F major V⁷ of VI; C minor V⁷ of V.

2. Write single phrases according to the following harmonic schemes, employing chords in root position and inversions.

a. D major, I–V⁷ of IV–IV–I–V⁷ of II–II–V⁷–I.
b. E minor, V⁷–V⁷ of IV–IV–I–V⁷ of V–V⁷–I.
c. A-flat major, I–V⁷–IV–V⁷ of VI–VI–V⁷ of V–I–V⁷–I.
d. G major, I–V⁷ of III–V⁷ of VI–V⁷ of II–V⁷ of V–V⁷–I.

3. Work out the following figured basses:

a.

b.

c.

d.

e. Andante cantabile

4. Harmonize the following soprano parts:

a.

b.

c.

273

d. **Andante**

5. Harmonize the following basses:

a.

b.

Molto moderato

c.

CHAPTER 18

Problems in
Harmonic Analysis

PURPOSE OF ANALYSIS

Musical composition is a process of synthesis of different elements into a whole. Analysis is also a process, but it begins with the finished piece, and the analyst is someone other than the composer.

One asks inevitably what the purpose of musical analysis is. Any answer that is framed for this question must be both specific and general. The specific answer addresses the specific composition. One applies one's skills to the analysis of a particular piece in order to understand it better. "Understanding" in this sense means revelation of details of structure both large and small, and this kind of understanding necessarily means more coherent and meaningful hearing. The general answer addresses more than the composition itself; analysis leads to an appreciation of aspects of the composer's style, and even to a comparative stylistic appraisal of works by different composers.

In the compositional process, the composer considers melody, rhythm, harmony, counterpoint, and form, all more or less simultaneously. His technique and imagination enable him to hold all of these at once in his mind, even though he may not be able to realize them all at once on paper without a laborious sketching process. The finished product displays these elements as a unified whole; it does not appear as though, for example, the succession of tones in the melody was conceived first, then a rhythmic element applied to it, and after that a harmonization fitted to the line. The 275 analyst knows that any separation of the whole into its elements is bound to be a somewhat artificial act, one that does not retrace the composer's steps in reverse.

Though this book is about harmony, the reader is already aware that it does not treat the subject of harmony as a fully detached component of musical thought. Considerations of melody, rhythm, and counterpoint will always have to be weighed against the harmonic element. "Pure" harmony is a creature of theory, and it has value for demonstrating relationships; but when we analyze the harmonic relationships of a particular piece of music, that is no longer theory but practice, application of theory, and must be considered in relation to other musical elements.

In his practical analysis of compositions so far, the student will have concentrated on the identification of particular chords and chord successions (musical words), their relationship to each other and within the larger structure of the phrase, the extent to which chords reinforce or weaken the prevailing tonality, and the musical meaning of various applications of nonharmonic tones. This chapter will attempt to give these aspects a somewhat broader view.

MELODIC ANALYSIS OF HARMONY

It often happens that what appears as a nonharmonic tone may also be interpreted as a factor in a different chord. The question then arises as to which chord is the true harmony. In a case like the following there is no problem in hearing that the second half of the third beat of the first measure is a true passing tone, not a VI⁶. VI⁶ is a harmonically weak chord, and if it were the principal harmony, with the G on the strong part of the beat, the upper voices would form parallel perfect fifths. But the harmonic answer to the question is simply that I is much stronger than VI⁶ as a follower to V⁶.

EXAMPLE 18–1: Bach, Chorale No. 104, *Wer nur den lieben Gott lässt walten*

b: I   V⁶ I(VI⁶?) V(min.)IV⁶ II⁶ V

The problem posed by the next example is only slightly more complex.

EXAMPLE 18–2: Bach, Chorale No. 6, *Christus,
der ist mein Leben*

Cf. Exx. 5–14,
15–9

In the above example, the chord on the second beat, coming between I^6 and I in root position, is either a II^7 with suspended seventh or a VII^6 with fifth doubled (the seventh above the missing dominant root). We know from experience that II in root position does not often progress to I, whereas VII^6 is a customary passing chord between I^6 and I or vice versa. On the other hand, the VII^6 is on the weak part of the beat, whereas the II is not only rhythmically stronger but is in root position, the harmonically strongest position. It is difficult to hear in this passage an actual II–VII succession, since the surrounding harmonic rhythm is in quarter notes and the bass does not change. (The harmonic question would indeed be different if the bass moved from G up to C for the second eighth note.) Ultimately, one probably comes to feel that in this case the harmonic ambiguity cannot be resolved in favor of either II or VII; but also it does not seem as important as the contrapuntal structure of the succession. It is not that the harmony between I^6 and I does not exist as a harmony, but rather that it is only an incidental sonority in the change of position between I^6 and I. In the reduction, the principal tones of the reduction are given in white notes, subsidiary tones in stemless black notes. Solid beams indicate connected motions between different tones, with slurs to indicate that the transit proceeds stepwise. Broken beams indicate that pitches thus connected are the same.

In the following example one might ask why the VI^6_4, a weak chord in any case, appears as a passing six-four on the third beat of the measure, rhythmically stronger than either the preceding or the following dominant.

277

EXAMPLE 18–3: Bach, Chorale No. 21, *Herzlich
tut mich verlangen*

The answer is to be found by an appreciation of the relative
levels of harmonic rhythm. At the foreground level of chord to
chord, the phrase contains three dominant chords within one
measure, but when these are reduced (*b*) to the level of a single
dominant sonority, represented by the dominant on the downbeat,
the other two dominants and the intervening VI$_4^6$ appear as mere
ornamentations, leading melodically to the I^6 on the next downbeat. To project this middleground model back onto the foreground requires that we hear a slowing of the harmonic rhythm in
this single measure from the quarter-note pace of most of the rest
of the chorale to a full-measure pace, but this slowing is easy to accept because V–I is a strong progression. If there is any drawback
to hearing the measure in this way, it is that the whole measure
now sounds like an extended perfect cadence, occupying too
much of the phrase; that feeling, however, is offset by the tonic
chord's first inversion, and its prolongation by a plagal cadence.

EXTENSION OF THE SECONDARY DOMINANT
PRINCIPLE: DUAL-FUNCTION CHORDS

The secondary dominant principle, as we have seen, presents what
appears to be a paradox: the secondary dominant supports a secondary tonic, not the actual tonic of the key, and thus would seem
in some way to actually change the key momentarily. Nevertheless,
the returning tonic is actually strengthened even more by virtue
of its associated harmonies having been tonicized. It would seem
that the stronger the emphasis on the secondary tonic, and the
greater its degree of remoteness from the main key, the greater
is the satisfaction of the return of the main tonic—though it is
plain that this idea can be carried too far, dislocating the sense of
the main tonic altogether.

The idea of a secondary dominant applied to a secondary tonic, creating as it were a miniature tonal region of its own within the larger context of a surrounding tonality, is analogous on a smaller scale to a modulation in a modulating piece. It should be conceptually possible, then, to extend the secondary dominant principle to other degrees of the scale; if, for instance, there can be V of V proceeding to V, then there should be the possibility of II of V proceeding to V of V and thence to V, exactly like the musical word II–V–I, but applied to V as a secondary progression. This is exactly like what happens in an ordinary modulation to the dominant key where the pivot chord is VI in the first key; the difference is that a modulation is not deemed to have taken place. The following examples show how the principle operates.

EXAMPLE 18–4

C: IV I   VI V of V V (7)   I   C: IV   I   VI
                                    G: II   V   I   V⁷ I

C: IV I   VI V of V   V V⁷of V V (7)

In *a* and *b* the phrases are identical except for their endings, in *a* an authentic cadence in C major and in *b* an authentic cadence in G major. We already know from experience that our perception of modulation depends on more than the immediate successions of chords. On the time scale of only two measures, only a brushstroke must be added to *b* to mark the whole phrase definitely in C major (*c*); whether a modulation to G has taken place in *b* has to be determined by what happens afterward.

In *a* above, the third chord is seen by the analysis to be a *chord of dual function* (compare Chapter 16, Example 16–6); with respect to I it is VI, but with respect to V it is II. We define a chord of dual function as having the function of a pivot chord without an actual modulation. In *b*, the third chord is the actual pivot chord. In neither case does the meaning of the chord become clear until the remainder of the phrase has either confirmed the initial key or established a new key. Both the dual-function chord and the pivot chord serve to relate the before-stage and the after-stage of an apparent tonal departure. The extension of the secondary dominant principle permits the theoretical existence of these dual-function chords, allowing the hearer to perceive within 279 the key a wide variety of tonal relationships from outside it, borrowed as it were for the duration, without upsetting the main perception of tonality.

EXAMPLE 18–5: Beethoven, *Violin Sonata*, Op. 47
("Kreutzer"), I

In the above example, the function IV of VI shows the relationship of the chord to what has already been heard, whereas the function VI of IV shows the relationship to what is about to be heard. The relationship of the B-flat triad to F major and to D minor is closer in both cases than the relationship to A minor, in which the B-flat triad would be the chromatically lowered supertonic, the Neapolitan sixth (Chapter 26).

It is not necessary that the borrowed chord have a clear function in both keys, but the relationship to either the preceding or the succeeding harmony must be clear, and it is likely to be perceived with less abruptness if it is to the latter. In the following example the direct relationship of the G minor triad to A (as minor VII) or to III of A (as minor V) is in neither case very satisfactory, but is entirely satisfactory to D minor, relating secondarily to A minor as IV of IV.

EXAMPLE 18–6: Brahms, *String Quartet*, Op. 51, No. 2, I

The minor triad on the fifth degree is quite lacking in dominant feeling. When it stands in subdominant relationship to the supertonic it may be called IV of II, as below.

EXAMPLE 18–7: Beethoven, *Symphony No. 9*, III

Adagio

B♭: V   IV of II   II   IV   I⁶₄

The diminished triad on D exists in B flat as V of IV, but as used in the example below the expression II of II better describes its function in the sequential harmony. To invoke a modulation to C minor on account of this one triad would be to exaggerate its importance.

EXAMPLE 18–8: Krebs, *Minuet*

B♭: II of II   V of II   II   V⁷   I   V I   I⁶₄ V

Mendelssohn's Wedding March begins with the formula IV–V–I as of E minor, but, as everyone knows, the piece is in C major. The first chord is, then, properly designated as IV of III rather than V₆⁰/₅ of V in C.

EXAMPLE 18–9: Mendelssohn, *A Midsummer Night's Dream*, Wedding March

Allegro vivace

C: IV(II)₅⁶   V of III   III   II⁶   I⁶₄   V⁷   I
of III

The analysis of the next example goes a step further, in suggesting that VI of E, the second chord, take part in a grouping of four chords as of G-sharp minor, actually III of E.

281

EXAMPLE 18–10: Bach, Chorale No. 278, *Wie schön
leuchtet der Morgenstern*

E: I   IV of III V of III IV of III III   IV⁶   I   V⁶₅ of V V⁷   I

*See also Exx.
9–5, 17–11*

In another Bach chorale three such groupings are shown, center-ing about III, VI, and IV of the fundamental key B-flat. The last chord in the second measure from the end, F minor, is obviously here II of IV rather than V of B flat, so that its dominant before it has been given the somewhat awkward but nonetheless accurate designation as V of II of IV.

EXAMPLE 18–11: Bach, Chorale No. 279, *Ach Gott und Herr*

B♭ : V⁶₅ IV⁶₅ of III V⁶₅ of III(V⁶ of IV)III VI of VI V⁰₉ of VI VI V of II II of IV V of IV IV
of IV   I

Four alternative analyses of the next example are presented for consideration of their relative merits.

EXAMPLE 18–12: Bach, *Well-Tempered Clavier, I*, Fugue No. 4

a. as modulating:

c♯: I { c♯: VI | { e: I | { b: I | { f♯: I |
       { e: IV V { b: IV V { f♯: IV V { c♯: IV V I |

b. literal roots in C♯:

c♯: I   VI | VII   III | IV   VII | I   IV | V I |

282

c. with secondary dominants:

   c♯: I   VI | VofIII   III | VofVII   VII | VofIV IV | V I |

d. unitonal functions by extension of secondary dominant principle:

```
        ─────────→    ─────────→    ─────────→   ──→
   ⎛  I    IVof    |    IVof     |    IVof     |  IV(of) |   I
   ⎪
   ⎪
c♯:⎨  I  IVofIVofIV  VofIVofIV      VofIV        VofIV  IV  V I
   ⎪        ofIV       ofIV          ofIV
   ⎪                           IVofIV         IVofIV
   ⎝                            ofIV
```

Each analysis is correct from its own point of view, and it should be said that a preference for one should not mean a rejection of what the others may offer. The modulating sequence in *a* is clear at a glance, although one feels that the changes of tonal center happen too quickly, and that each key noted does not remain long enough to justify the analysis as a modulation. The pattern is not readily discernible in *b,* whereas *c* tells more about the grouping of the harmonies in the sequence. In *d* the organization of the passage is exactly set forth as in effect a step back from the tonic to a thrice removed subdominant, in order to return symmetrically by means of four IV–I progressions, with intervening dominants.

The extension of the secondary dominant principle to include other secondary tonal functions is of course an analytical construction, but it reflects an important observation: that the feeling of modulation is received by the experienced ear with a certain inertia, together with a tendency to interpret the foreign harmony in terms of the key already established. Modulation, then, is something that happens on a relatively broad level of musical perception, whereas the incorporation of harmonies from outside the key belongs to a relatively immediate level, even when analysis shows the broad and the immediate to coincide at a particular point. As so often in musical analysis, the term *relatively* here is very wide in its scope. There are countless instances when the hearer is uncertain whether what he is hearing is an actual modulation or a temporary tonicization, and this uncertainty may not disappear on repeated hearings or detailed study, even when these tend to support intuition.

The following example shows a modulating passage from a subsidiary section, beginning in F major, of a movement whose main tonality is A minor. The passage is analyzed with two changes 283 of key, subsidiary analyses being given in parentheses for dual-function progressions. Some listeners might hear more changes of tonal center than the given analysis indicates; others might hear fewer. What is brought out by the alternate analyses is the large amount of plagal motion, IV–I being equivalent intervallically to I–V.

EXAMPLE 18–13: Schubert, *Symphony No. 9*, II

VIOLATIONS OF RULES OF VOICE LEADING

The student will sometimes encounter in his analyses what appear to be violations of the rules of voice leading. There is often a simple explanation to be had for these. One of the commonest is doubling, and the ubiquitous practice of melodic doubling in octaves needs no comment. Some types of doubling are, to be sure, more common than others, but all types and dispositions may be seen in orchestral music, even a melodic line doubled in three or four octaves with only a relatively narrow-spaced harmonic layer in between. Such doublings are a matter of instrumentation, and do not waken the ear to violations unless the part writing is unclear.

E.g., Exx. 17–21, 21–8

The following example of irregular doubling is apt to be puzzling. The texture seems to shift back and forth between melodic doubling (in the "tenor") and an independent four-voice texture with occasional extra chordal voices.

EXAMPLE 18–14: Schubert, *Sonata*, Op. 53, II

There is no doubt that an ambiguity of texture can be perceived here, but nevertheless such seemingly casual textural changes, with one voice or another appearing to drop out or to shift from independent line to doubling, are found everywhere in instrumental music.

Another common source of apparent violations, particularly of the parallel-fifth prohibition, is contrapuntal writing. Even in such a simple progression as the following, the combination of passing tone and anticipation gives rise to this parallel motion.

EXAMPLE 18–15: Bach, Chorale No. 121, *Werde munter,*
mein Gemüte

See also Exx.
15–2, 15–9,
16–26, 6–23

This type of motion was prohibited in the strict counterpoint of the sixteenth century, but is of frequent occurrence in the works of Bach and his contemporaries. The anticipation and the passing tone are both rhythmically weak with respect to the harmonic rhythm, and would be avoided on the strong part of the beat.

The appoggiatura in the following example forms parallel fifths with the bass on the strong part of the beat, but is of short duration and is hardly noticed.

EXAMPLE 18–16: Mozart, Overture to *The Magic Flute*, K. 620

285

Parallel perfect fifths between successive offbeats are freely permitted over short distances, and octaves likewise. Between successive strong beats, with melodic motion intervening, they are best treated cautiously in contrapuntal writing. In the following sequence, the suspensions effectively offset the parallel fifths.

EXAMPLE 18–17: Bach, *Prelude and Fugue in A minor for Organ*

See also Ex. 8–7

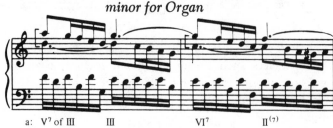

a: V⁷ of III III VI⁷ II⁽⁷⁾

Parallel fifths, but not octaves, may sometimes occur as a result of ornamental resolution, or in the combination of melodic tones with accompanimental patterns.

EXAMPLE 18–18: Chopin, *Etude*, Op. 10, No. 3

Lento ma non troppo

See also Ex. 15–26

E: V⁷ of IV IV II⁶

A fairly common type of consecutive octave between the outer voices is that found in V–I cadential patterns, particularly final cadences where the cadential harmonies are repeated several times, or where otherwise detached from the phrase. In such cases the octaves will generally be in contrary motion. Examples such as the following can be justified as instances of a cadential mannerism, where the dominant note followed by the tonic note is wanted in the soprano for the appearance of greater finality. The octaves are thus in a sense doubling octaves, and by usage are not really considered as independent voices.

EXAMPLE 18–19: Mozart, *Sonata*, K. 332, I

Allegro

See also Exs. 5–34, 25–14

F: I⁶ V⁷ I V⁷ I V⁷ I

EXAMPLE 18–20: Beethoven, *Symphony No. 4*, IV

Allegro ma non troppo

Bb: V   I   V   I   V   I

The following instance of parallel fifths is the result of miscalculation in orchestration. The apparent voice leading would surely not be heard in an orchestral *tutti* with many doublings, were it not that these fifths occur between the highest and lowest parts of the strings. The uppermost voices are given to two flutes and two harps, which are completely overbalanced by the first violins in fortissimo and are scarcely heard at all.

EXAMPLE 18–21: Berlioz, *Symphonie fantastique*, II: *A Ball*

Allegro ma non troppo (con fuoco)

A: III   VI   V   I   V   I

One may surmise a literalistic purpose—not without a touch of arcane wit—in these fifths in Verdi's Requiem Mass, to the text of "I pray in supplication on my knees."

EXAMPLE 18–22: Verdi, *Messa da Requiem, Dies irae*

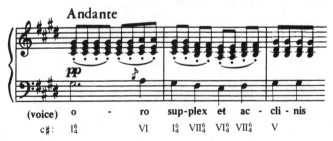

Andante

(voice)   o   -   ro   sup-plex   et   ac   -   cli   -   nis
c#:   I⁶₄   VI   I⁶₄   VII⁶₄   VI⁶₄   VII⁶₄   V

Parallel fifths achieve a greater degree of freedom in Chopin's works than anywhere else until the late nineteenth century, actually becoming a minor aspect of his style. Sometimes he seems to have chosen them for their open-string–like bass sound, such as in the mazurkas and other pieces suggesting the style of folk   287 music. The following remarkable passage is unique for its time in its systematic chromatic succession with fifths in the outer voices.

EXAMPLE 18–23: Chopin, *Mazurka*, Op. 30, No. 4

Cf. Ex. 30–20

Elsewhere one can find fifths in the outer parts occurring seemingly as intrusions in an otherwise independent texture, not to be readily accounted for other than as part of the melodic continuity.

EXAMPLE 18–24: Chopin, *Scherzo*, Op. 39

By the end of the nineteenth century parallel fifths became integrated into several post–common-practice styles, which will be studied in detail in Part Two of this book. At the same time, even composers whose techniques were essentially rooted in common practice began to accept parallel fifths as an occasional normal component of tonal part writing. The subtle use of fifths in the following cadence makes a fine effect.

EXAMPLE 18–25: Mahler, *Ich atmet' einen linden Duft*

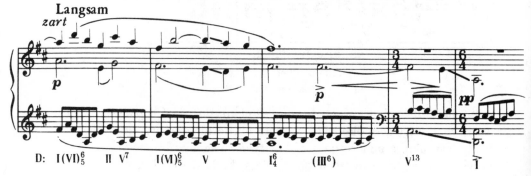

Finally there are examples of parallel fifths that can probably be attributed to inadvertence, even on the part of the masters. One such instance may be seen in Example 14–4, a four-part chorale by Bach; another is this often-cited passage by Beethoven.

EXAMPLE 18–26: Beethoven, *Symphony No. 6* ("Pastorale"), I

Allegro ma non troppo

F: I   V⁴₃   I   IV   I   V

Below are two examples of V–I progressions in which the leading-tone in the upper voice resolves downward by skip to the fifth degree instead of upward to the tonic.

EXAMPLE 18–27: Bizet, *L'Arlésienne*, Suite No. 1: No. 2, Minuet

Allegro giocoso

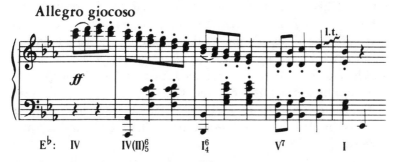

E♭:   IV   IV(II)⁶₅   I⁶₄   V⁷   I

EXAMPLE 18–28: Brahms, *A German Requiem*, II

Etwas bewegter (Langsam)

So seid nun ge - dul - dig, lie - ben Brü - der, bis auf die Zu - (kunft)

G♭:   I   V   I   V   I   V   IV   VII⁶   I

In the long run it is hard to say that any of these examples, though they may be technical violations of contrapuntal rules, represents a defect in the music. Certainly in every case these violations represented sounds that were satisfactory to the composer; 289

had they not been, the composer would have changed them. The music itself is always more important than rules, and it is only in the work of lesser composers that violations appear as defects, when they will actually seem to be inhomogeneities of style or lapses in technique.

HARMONIC ANALYSIS AND MUSICAL FORM

Analysis in depth of compositions in large forms, such as the sonata-form movement of a symphony, will not normally be a topic encountered in the first year of harmonic study; the student's analytical efforts will principally be involved with short forms such as songs, dances, and compositions in aria da capo form, and occasionally excerpts from the longer movements of sonatas and symphonies or from contrapuntal forms. In all his analyses, the student should make an effort to relate the individual harmonic progressions to the larger tonal context. This will mean the necessity of determining, perhaps with the aid of a chart or sketch, the principal tonalities of the piece and all subsidiary tonalities together with modulatory schemes. In pieces of any substantial length, the tonal scheme thus outlined will have to be considered on an equal basis with the thematic layout and phrase structure, which should indeed be examined first. Where time allows, much can be learned from differential comparison of several works of the same formal type, even by different composers, such as minuets by Haydn and Mozart, or waltzes by Schubert and Brahms.

In all types of analysis the conscientious student will sooner or later come to experience the sometimes bewildering and sometimes exciting feeling of discovery, when as many questions are newly raised as are answered by dint of thorough work. It is the authors' conviction that this sense of discovery, though not to be fully satisfied in a lifetime of effort, is one of the chief pleasures of musical study.

SCORE READING

The student should make an effort to acquire as early as possible a familiarity with orchestral scores. In a course in orchestration he will naturally do this to gain knowledge of instrumental techniques and orchestral styles, but he should already know the value of orchestral-score study as an aid in the study of harmony as well. The principles of harmony become visible in the most realistic way possible when they are seen at work in orchestral music, where their action is distributed between a variety of instrumental types and textures and over long stretches of musical time.

Orchestral works of the period of Haydn, Mozart, and Beethoven, including opera full scores, should be studied first, beginning with pieces in which the complement of woodwind and brass instruments is relatively small. In this way the student will learn to become automatically familiar with the layout of instruments in the score, even in editions where the instruments are not always labeled on every page. The most difficult problem at first in reading scores will be the transposing instruments. Various ways of deciphering these have been devised, such as clef equivalents, but all require constant practice. One infallible rule of transposing instruments may be stated here: for any instrument "in X," the note C appearing in the part sounds X. The note D will sound a major second above X, E will sound a major third above X, and so forth, allowing for octave differences.

Another essential part of fluent score reading is a working knowledge of the alto clef, the regular clef used by the viola. The tenor clef· is nearly as often met with, in upper-register writing for instruments normally using the bass clef (cello, double bass, bassoon, etc.). Fluency in the use of these clefs is best acquired through sight singing and sight reading, but listening to orchestral music while following the score is also valuable here, as it is generally.

It will be noticed that in most orchestral music up until Beethoven's time the main harmonic and melodic elements will most often be entrusted to the strings. In part this is because the strings provide a remarkable homogeneity of sound quality and strength over virtually the entire orchestral range; another reason is that the woodwind and brass instruments, particularly the horns and trumpets, had not been perfected in their design and playing technique, and consequently could not be used as freely or over as wide a range as later became possible. Recognition of this reality becomes of practical value in reading orchestral scores at the piano.

PROJECTS IN ANALYSIS

1. Examine the passage in the first movement of Schubert's *String Quintet in C major*, Op. 163, where the second theme is stated   291

(measures 60–99). As a rule in sonata form of this period, the second theme is in the dominant key, and in fact this theme is preceded by a full cadence in G major. How does one account for this theme's beginning in E-flat major? In what ways can you analyze the tonal stresses of the melody itself?

2. Analyze the tonal scheme of the exposition of the first movement of Mozart's *Symphony No. 40, K. 550.* Then analyze that of the recapitulation, and compare the two.

3. Explain why the first movement of Schubert's *Symphony No. 5* and the first movement of his *"Trout" Quintet,* Op. 114, are said to have subdominant recapitulations, and why these are unconventional. What advantage is there to such a tonal plan?

4. It was stated in Chapter 5 that relative minor and major are an association of special importance in a tonal composition in the minor mode. One work that shows this association with particular intensity is Chopin's *Scherzo,* Op. 31, usually referred to as the *Scherzo in B-flat minor* although it ends in D-flat major. Trace the course of these two keys, and compare their relative emphases, throughout the work.

5. Compare and contrast the tonal organization, sectional structure, cadential types, and modulatory schemes if any, of twenty different minuet movements chosen from the symphonies, piano sonatas, and string quartets of Haydn and Mozart. Show the results of this investigation in tabular form.

6. Analyze the minuet (really a scherzo) movement of Beethoven's *Symphony No. 1* and make a chart showing the modulatory scheme.

7. Chabrier's *España* for orchestra has a simple overall tonal plan, involving only a single modulation and return. Determine the larger tonal outlines of the piece, and the proportion of tonic–dominant harmony relative to other types. (The more complex harmonic types may be ignored.)

8. The second movement, *Andante poco moto,* of Schubert's *Piano Sonata in A minor,* Op. 42, is a theme with variations, the theme being in two sections of 8 and 16 measures, each repeated. A comparison of the theme with the first variation shows that the second half of this variation, with twelve measures, is apparently four measures too short; the second variation, with sixteen measures in the second half, confirms this deduction. Determine by analysis where the measures are missing, and what sort of harmonic structure they might be expected to have. As a special additional exercise, compose four measures to fill the gap, making them as close as possible stylistically to the context. (The manu-

script of this sonata has not been found. All published editions follow the first edition, which was printed in 1825 or 1826, during Schubert's lifetime; but it is not known whether he corrected the mistake or even noticed it. Of course, it is also not unthinkable that Schubert, who habitually composed with incredible speed, may simply have forgotten to compose them; but it is very unlikely that he deliberately left them out.)

CHAPTER 19

The Sequence

The harmonic sequence, the systematic transposition of a melodic, rhythmic, and harmonic pattern, is a resource of development in music. The change of pitch adds the element of variety to the unity of repetition. While the sequence may readily become a refuge for the composer of lesser talent, it has been used with great effectiveness by the best composers. On close analysis it is often discovered to be the basis for many passages which do not at first seem sequential, notably in the fugue and in symphonic developments and transitional sections.

We are here concerned primarily with the harmonic background of the various kinds of sequence and will give our attention to those sequences which do not attempt to conceal their fundamental structure. By way of introduction to this chapter, the student will find it helpful first to review the material on sequences given in Chapters 9 and 14.

THE INITIAL PATTERN

The pattern chosen for systematic transposition in the sequence may be of a variety of forms. Its length may vary from a single short motive on a single chord to a whole phrase. Although it is possible to construct a pattern of musical significance with but one chord as background, this kind of pattern is less interesting harmonically and the sequence is mainly dependent for its effect on the contrapuntal arrangement.

EXAMPLE 19–1: Beethoven, *Trio*, Op. 1, No. 3, IV

c: I   VI   IV   II

Most often the pattern contains two chords. In the following example they are simple triads with roots a fourth apart, the commonest strong progression.

EXAMPLE 19–2: Mozart, *Sonata for Two Pianos*, K. 448, II

A: I   IV   II   V   III   VI IV   I

If the pattern is of much length it is not so readily recognized as sequential as the shorter group, which can be heard as a unit. A short phrase may be successfully used as pattern in a sequence.

EXAMPLE 19–3: Beethoven, *Sonata*, Op. 10, No. 1, I

A♭: V²   I⁶   V⁴₃   I
     F: III   V²   I⁶   V⁴₃   I
     D♭: III

(D♭): V²   I⁶   V⁴₃   I

295

Example 25–25 shows a pattern twenty measures long, with five chord changes, and much longer patterns have been used successfully.

HARMONIC RHYTHM

The harmonic formula upon which the pattern is based has its rhythmic form, arising from the choice of root progressions, time values, and other contributing elements. Example 19–2 shows a simple rhythm of strong-to-weak in the pattern. In Example 19–3 the rhythm is strong-weak-weak-strong. If the rhythmic pattern begins with an anacrusis a more fluent sequence will result.

EXAMPLE 19–4: Beethoven, *Sonata*, Op. 106
                ("Hammerklavier"), II

The anacrusis may be strong enough to give the effect of syncopation in the melodic rhythms. It should be noted in the following example that the harmonic rhythm is in agreement with the meter, whereas the preponderance of melodic rhythmic stress is on the third beat of the measure.

EXAMPLE 19–5: Mozart, *Quintet*, K. 593, III

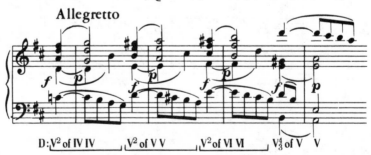

The rhythmic impression of pressing forward is heightened if the anacrusis is long, followed by a short downbeat.

EXAMPLE 19–6: Brahms, *Intermezzo*, Op. 10, No. 3

THE
SEQUENCE

LENGTH OF THE SEQUENCE

It is generally agreed that a single transposition of the pattern does not constitute a full sequence, the systematic transposition not being established until the third appearance of the initial group; in other words, three separate appearances, involving two transpositions, are necessary to show that the interval of sequentiation is consistent. Certainly there are many examples of what might be called half sequences, with only a single transposition, the two patterns being antecedent and consequent in a phrase and not continuing sequentially (Examples 9–8 and 9–13). On the other hand, it is remarkable that composers seldom allow the symmetry to extend beyond the third appearance of the pattern without breaking it up by variation or abandoning it altogether. This rule may be stated as an observation without presuming to deduce a principle of aesthetics therefrom.

Exceptions to the above rule may of course be found, and in certain types of musical expression, such as virtuoso cadenzas and compositions intended for technical study or display, sequences are sometimes written to extend by numerous repetitions throughout the entire range of the instrument.

DEGREE OF TRANSPOSITION

The pattern may be transposed by any interval, up or down. The interval of sequentiation chosen depends upon two factors, the desired harmonic destination of the sequential passage, and the feasibility of connecting the pattern to itself when transposed. Construction of a sequence necessitates consideration of both of these problems.

Most sequences will use the same interval of sequentiation throughout. Stepwise transposition in nonmodulating sequences, where the step may be a major or minor second, is not held to be a violation of this property. Sometimes, however, the transpositional interval changes markedly in midcourse (Examples 19–6 and 19–14).

THE NONMODULATING SEQUENCE

The sequence is either a *modulating sequence*, changing the tonal center with each transposition of the pattern, or a *nonmodulating sequence*, sometimes called a *tonal sequence*, with one tonal center throughout.

In the nonmodulating sequence the transpositions are made to degrees of the scale of the key. This causes some variation in the pattern since the intervals between the degrees of the scale are not always the same. For instance, in Example 19–2 the harmonic background is as follows: I–IV, II–V, III–VI. The initial pattern consists of two major triads, the second of a minor and a major triad, and the third of two minor triads. Note that the transposition is upward the interval of a step, while the root progression at the joint between the patterns is down a minor third.

The nonmodulating sequence is likely to contain variation, too, in the interval of transposition of the pattern. In Example 19–4 the first transposition is down a minor third, while the second is down a major third, resulting from the intervals between I, VI, and IV in the major scale.

Both of these variations are present in the sequence shown below, descending by seconds. The root progressions are by fourths throughout the entire passage, all perfect fourths except from VI to II.

EXAMPLE 19–7: Paradisi, *Sonata in A major*, II

The employment of secondary dominants in the nonmodulating sequence adds the harmonic color of tones foreign to the scale of the main tonality, contributes the rhythmic element of dissonance, and emphasizes the unity of the group of chords comprising the pattern.

*See also Exx.
8–38, 16–10*

EXAMPLE 19–8: Beethoven, *Sonata,* Op. 7, I

Bb: V of VI   VI ⌐ V of IV   IV ⌐ V of II   II ⌐ I6/4   V   I

EXAMPLE 19–9: Schubert, *Symphony No. 5,* III

g: I6 V of V V7 I ⌐ V of V V7of VI VI ⌐ V V7of IV IV I ⌐ Ger. I6/1   V7   I
           of VI   (V of V
                           of IV)

The following short sequence shows roots in progression by perfect fourths throughout, at one-beat time intervals. The secondary dominants with their resolutions divide the harmonic rhythm into a meter of two-four against the prevailing three-four meter.

EXAMPLE 19–10: Chopin, *Mazurka,* Op. 24, No. 3

Ab: V0/9 of III III ⌐ V0/9 of II II ⌐ V0/9 I

299

EXAMPLE 19–11: Beethoven, *Symphony No. 3* ("Eroica"), I

Allegro con brio

Eb: I⁶   V⁴₃   I⁶   V⁶₅ of IV   IV   V⁴₃ of II   II   V⁴₃ of V   V   It. of VI

V of VI   VI   V⁴₃ of IV   IV   VII   VII⁶ of V   V   I   V⁴₃ of VI   VI   V⁶₅ of VI   VI   V²of IV   IV of   V of VI
                                                      of VI   VI   of VI

Sequences in which each harmony is a dominant of the next are of uncertain tonality and may or may not be felt as being in a single key. The commonest sequence of this type is the cycle-of-fourths sequence, moving by successive subdominants, with alternating rising fourths and falling fifths in the bass.

*Cf. Exx. 8–8,
16–1, 16–27*

EXAMPLE 19–12: A. Scarlatti, *Fugue in F minor*

Andantino

Bb : V of II   V of V   V (of I)   V of IV   V of VII   V of III   V of VI   VI   II
or F :   V of V   V   Eb:V of V   V   Db: V of V   V

In the following sequence the secondary dominant is not used on the third appearance of the pattern because the supertonic triad in minor, being a diminished triad, does not act as a temporary tonic.

EXAMPLE 19–13: Haydn, *String Quartet*, Op. 76, No. 4, III

Allegro

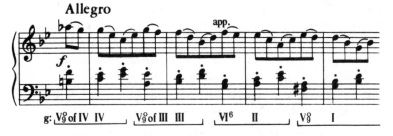

Cf. Ex. 21–17

g: V$^{\circ}_9$ of IV IV | V$^{\circ}_9$ of III III | VI^6 II | V$^{\circ}_8$ I

The sense of intermediate modulation is common in sequences, even when successive secondary dominants are present that themselves have the same roots as temporary tonics in the phrase. The prominent harmonic feature in the example below is undoubtedly the sense of a strong half cadence in the keys of B, A, and D. The subdominant character of the first chord in each group is not taken into account by its analysis as a plain triad in the fundamental key. This suggests the possibility of extension of the secondary dominant principle to other secondary tonal functions. II of D is used here as IV of VI, and I as IV of V.

EXAMPLE 19–14: Mozart, *Menuet*, K. 355

D: II(IV of VI)   V of VI V of II   V of V   I(IV of V)   V of V   V   V of IV   IV

V   V of IV   IV   VII$^6_4$ I^6 (IV) I$^6_4$ V   I

When the temporary tonics are themselves unsatisfactory chords of the main tonality, the impression of modulation is given, although in many cases these modulations are so fleeting that even a far-fetched explanation of the relationship of the chord to the main key is preferable. In the following example two anal- 301 yses are offered. The first is nonmodulating, but necessitates reference to the minor triad on the dominant and the triad on the lowered seventh degree as temporary tonics. The second, on the other hand, shows four changes of tonal center in as many measures of rapid tempo, only to return to the original key of C. The student is advised to make similar alternative analyses in similar cases, weighing for himself their advantages and disadvantages as descriptions of the harmonic effect.

EXAMPLE 19–15: Weber, Overture to *Der Freischütz*

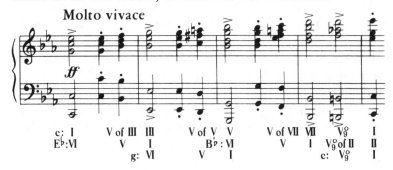

THE MODULATING SEQUENCE

The commonest form of modulating sequence embraces three keys. There is no return to the tonality of the initial pattern. The modulation does not take place within the pattern, but the final chord of the pattern is the pivot chord. The modulation to the second key is called a *passing modulation* since there is no permanence to the key. It represents a stage in the modulation to the third, or ultimate, key. Passing modulations are not necessarily sequential, but the modulating sequence does contain a passing modulation in its most common form.

Cf. Ex. 18–12

EXAMPLE 19–16: Bach, *Well-Tempered Clavier, I*, Fugue No. 18

In this example the modulation to E is a passing modulation. The suspension in the inside voice is helpful in avoiding the cadential effect at each final chord of the pattern. The first transposition moves down a major third and the second down a minor third, it being impossible to divide the interval of a perfect fifth (from the initial key, G sharp, to the desired destination, C sharp) into two equal parts. Moreover, there is a change of mode in the second key. The E minor triad is a poor chord in both the other keys, so E major is chosen.

The pattern used in a modulating sequence is usually constructed on a clearly tonal harmonic basis. This does not mean of necessity the inclusion of the tonic chord. In the example below the progression II–V serves very well to establish the tonal centers of three keys not closely related.

EXAMPLE 19–17: Brahms, *Symphony No. 2*, I

The modulating sequence has more possibilities as to the degree of transposition than the sequence with one tonal center. The following example shows a chromatic relationship between the keys.

EXAMPLE 19–18: Wagner, *Die Walküre*, Act I, Scene 1

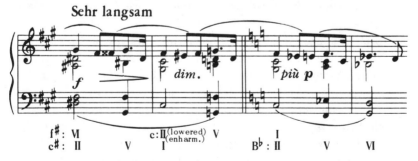

The chromatic modulation may involve difficulties of analysis, as the following example shows.

303

EXAMPLE 19–19: Berwald, *Symphony No. 5*
("Sinfonie Singulière"), III

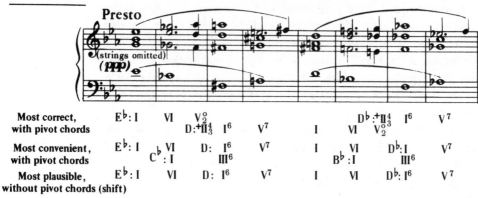

Most correct, with pivot chords	E♭: I	VI	V$_2^o$					D♭:+II$_3^4$	I^6	V^7	
			D:+II$_3^4$	I^6	V^7	I	VI	V$_2^{o3}$	I^6	V^7	
Most convenient, with pivot chords	E♭: I	VI	D: I^6	V^7		I	VI	D♭:I	V^7		
		C♭:I	III^6				B♭:I	III^6			
Most plausible, without pivot chords (shift)	E♭: I	VI	D: I^6	V^7		I	VI	D♭:I^6	V^7		

THE SEQUENCE IN HARMONIZATION

A sequence in a melodic voice is not always accompanied by sequence in the other voices or in the harmony. It is nevertheless
advisable in the study of harmony to treat sequences in given parts
as harmonic sequences, until the facility is acquired of arranging
these sequences whenever desired. Above all, the avoidance of
sequential treatment should not be due to failure to notice the
suggestion in the given part. Let it be understood as a convention
that melodic sequences in the exercises of this book are to be
treated as harmonic sequences.

KEYBOARD PRACTICE

The sequence is an extremely useful device for the practice of
harmonic progressions at the keyboard. The student should try to
form sequences of all the harmonic formulae at his disposal, playing them throughout the length of the keyboard. His first problem
will be to make a smooth connection between the pattern and its
transposition. While there are some cases in which no really satisfactory connection can be made, it may be accepted as a principle that a solution always exists and is to be found by searching.
Weak progressions can be used if they are properly placed in the
rhythmic scheme. Lengthening of the time values facilitates
change of position of the voices. In the modulating sequence the
last chord of the pattern is taken as pivot chord for the modulation.

It is strongly urged that the entire sequence not be written out. Two appearances of the pattern are enough to show the plan. The continuance of the sequence will then be a mental exercise rather than a mechanical reading or memorizing. As in all keyboard exercises, rhythmic playing (meaning rhythmic thinking) is essential, and a steady beat should be adhered to at all times, even though it must be very slow at first.

The literal extension of a nonmodulating sequential pattern throughout all its possible transpositions will often bring about one or two progressions which would not otherwise be employed, as for instance IV–VII, with its diminished-fifth relationship and use of root-position VII with doubled leading-tone. Such progressions are considered justified by the logic of the symmetrical melodic movement of the voices and need not be avoided in exercises.

EXAMPLE 19–20

II V I IV VII III

The following are a few examples of beginnings of sequences, to be played the length of the keyboard, and in all keys.

EXAMPLE 19–21

a. I V VI III etc.

b. I V⁶ I II⁶ V IV⁶ VII I⁶ IV etc.

c. I V⁶ I IV⁶ VII etc.

d. C: I V I E♭:V⁶ of V V
B♭:V of V V I etc.

305

F: V of V   V⁶   I   *etc.*

B♭ : V⁶ of V   V

E♭ : V of V   V⁶   I⁶

C: V VII⁶ of V V⁶₅ I   B♭ : V   VII⁶ of V V⁶₅ I   *etc.*

F : V   VII⁶ of V V⁶₅ I

EXERCISES

1. Work out the following figured basses:

2. Construct different sequences on the same harmonic back-
grounds as those in Examples 19–2, 19–3, 19–12, and 19–16. Vary
the tempo and the general melodic texture.

3. Construct phrases containing sequences fulfilling the following requirements:

    a. A nonmodulating sequence in which the pattern contains three different chords and the transposition is upward by intervals of a third.

    b. A modulating sequence in which the final chord of the pattern is V of V in the second key.

    c. A modulating sequence which starts in the key of D and ends in the key of A flat.

    d. A nonmodulating sequence which employs secondary dominant seventh chords.

4. Harmonize the following unfigured basses:

a.

b.

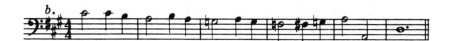

c.

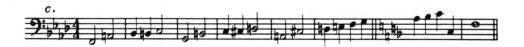

d.

5. Harmonize the following melodies:

a.

b.

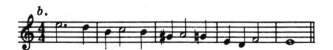

c.

CHAPTER 20

The Diminished
Seventh Chord

DEFINITIONS

With the superposition of another third upon the dominant seventh chord, the group of chords known as dominant harmony is extended to include two dominant ninth chords, major and minor.

EXAMPLE 20–1

The dominant ninth chords are most often found with root omitted, their dominant implication being sufficiently strong whether or not the actual fifth degree is present. Composers have shown a distinct preference for the incomplete forms of these chords over the comparatively thick and heavy effect of the ninth chord with root.

Dominant harmony consists, then, of the following group of chords:

EXAMPLE 20–2

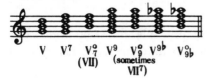

By far the commonest of the dominant ninths is the last of the group shown in the example, the *incomplete dominant minor ninth,* known as the *diminished seventh chord.* The intervals making up this chord are minor third, diminished fifth, and diminished seventh. Examination of these intervals will show the dissonant characteristics of the chord.

When it is arranged as a series of thirds, its lowest tone is the leading-tone, which, in addition to its inherent tendency, is found to be in dissonant interval relationship to the fifth and seventh. (Note that the terms *fifth* and *seventh* are here applied to the chord as a seventh chord on the leading-tone. Those factors would be the seventh and ninth of the original ninth chord. It would, however, be illogical to refer to the leading-tone as root of the chord.)

The third, the second degree, forms with the sixth degree a diminished fifth, so that all the factors of this chord are involved in dissonant relationships.

EXAMPLE 20–3

A chord made up entirely of tendency tones would seem to be a chord of very definite tonal significance, but, paradoxically, the diminished seventh chord is the most ambiguous of chords. The thirds are all minor thirds, and the inversion of the diminished seventh, the augmented second, is the equivalent of the minor third in our tempered scale system. The diminished fifth interval has likewise an equivalent sound in its inversion, the augmented fourth. In consequence the ear cannot distinguish the factors of a diminished seventh chord until its resolution shows which is the leading-tone. The chord and its inversions have the same sound harmonically.

EXAMPLE 20–4

ENHARMONIC EQUIVALENTS

By application of the enharmonic principle, the same diminished seventh chord can be written in four different ways, taking each note in turn as leading-tone.

EXAMPLE 20–5

DIMINISHED
SEVENTH

The leading-tone is readily found in each case by arranging the chord in a series of thirds, when it will appear as the lowest tone.

Such changes in notation, by designation of the leading-tone, mean change of tonality and also change of root of the chord. The root is found a major third below the leading-tone. It is interesting to observe that the four roots of one diminished seventh chord in its enharmonic changes form in themselves the notes of another diminished seventh chord.

EXAMPLE 20–6

C: V   E♭: V   F♯: V   A: V

Players of string instruments know that these different interpretations of one chord involve an actual change of pitch. The note A flat with destination G is perceptibly lower than the leading-tone G sharp with destination A. It is likewise the experience of many musical persons that the pitch of the notes seems actually to change when the different roots are struck in the bass against a diminished seventh chord sustained on the piano.

EXAMPLE 20–7

RESOLUTION

The regular resolution of the diminished seventh chord, as an incomplete dominant ninth, is to the tonic triad. It is customary to resolve the two intervals of the diminished fifth, contracting each to a third, without regard for the doubling that results. If the diminished fifth is inverted, the augmented fourth will, of course, 311 expand to a sixth. The diminished seventh chord resolves with equal frequency to either a major or a minor tonic.

EXAMPLE 20–8

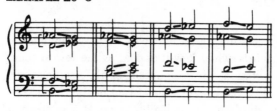

The augmented fourth may, however, abandon its natural resolution so that the three upper voices will descend in parallel motion. Such procedure is less often followed if the interval is a diminished fifth, which would then approach the perfect fifth by similar motion.

EXAMPLE 20–9

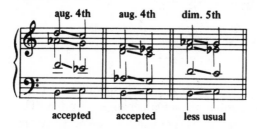

aug. 4th   aug. 4th   dim. 5th

accepted   accepted   less usual

EXAMPLE 20–10: Bach, Chorale No. 4, *Es ist das Heil uns kommen her*

E: I   I⁶   IV
    f♯: III   V   V°₉ I   V

Nonharmonic resolution often occurs with the diminished seventh. The ninth resolves internally as a melodic tone without change of root. (See also Example 20–19.)

*See also Exx.
26–11, 26–26*

EXAMPLE 20–11

V°₉ (⁶₅)

As shown above, in Example 20–4, the inversions of the diminished seventh chord and the position with the leading tone in the bass all sound alike harmonically. They vary contrapuntally in the orientation of the factors, the bass being especially important; but this is realized by the hearer only through the manner of resolution.

Since the root of the chord is not present, there can be no root position, strictly speaking, although the grouping in which the leading-tone is the lowest tone is often called root position. In this book the symbol V^o_9 will be used for this position. For the inversions the V will be used to indicate a dominant root which is not present in the chord, and the arabic numerals will show the intervals formed between the bass and the upper voices.

EXAMPLE 20–12

By strict figuring, the ninth of these chords, wherever situated, should be indicated by a flat sign or other appropriate accidental next to the arabic numeral, as in Example 20–2. Other than in that example, however, we will not use this indication, since the differentiation between major and minor ninth is easy enough to make by referring to the score itself, and omission of the accidental makes for less fussiness in the analysis.

The inversions resolve in the same way as the root position. When the second degree is in the bass it usually resolves to the third degree to avoid a direct fifth on the resolution of the diminished fifth.

EXAMPLE 20–13

See Ex. 6–15

The six-four-three inversion, with the subdominant in the bass, ordinarily resolves to the first inversion of the tonic triad, but it may also resolve to the root position.

313

EXAMPLE 20–14

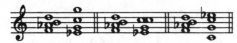

When the second inversion resolves to the root position, the fourth degree and minor sixth degree, by their resolution, have a strongly subdominant feeling. The leading-tone and second degree, on the other hand, still have their characteristic dominant values. The diminished seventh chord in this position, therefore, seems to combine dominant and subdominant functions into a single sonority. The following example shows a perfectly prepared cadence of this type.

EXAMPLE 20–15: Schumann, *Toccata*, Op. 7

See also Ex. 30–1

Più mosso (Allegro)

(V/IV)

C: IV   IV(II)$^6_5$ V$^o_{\substack{4\\3}}$ I

When the lower tone is the ninth, or submediant, the natural resolution is to the tonic six-four, which means dominant followed by a dominant substitute, a rhythmically weak progression. Furthermore, the disposition of the voices will be likely to produce a doubling of the sixth or the fourth in the chord of resolution, rather than the customary bass. This grouping is, therefore, less useful than the others.

EXAMPLE 20–16

6
4

As a rule, in four-part writing no factor of a diminished seventh chord is omitted in any position. Occasionally the third or fifth may be omitted in contrapuntal passages, though in such cases the omitted factor will usually appear later, in melodic succession.

THE SECONDARY DOMINANTS

The diminished seventh chord is employed as a secondary dominant wherever such chords are used, whether the secondary tonic is major or minor. The following examples show some of the secondary dominants in the form of diminished sevenths.

DIMINISHED
SEVENTH

*See also Exx.
4–8, 6–26, 8–36,
11–30, 11–32,
12–19, 13–11,
17–19, 17–20,
19–10*

EXAMPLE 20–17: Brahms, *Waltz,* Op. 39, No. 3

e: V°₉ of III III   V°₉   I   II⁶   V⁷   I

EXAMPLE 20–18: Bach, *Well-Tempered Clavier, II,*
Prelude No. 12

f: II²   V°₄₃ of IV   IV⁶   I⁶₄   V°₉ of V   V⁷   I

EXAMPLE 20–19: Bach, *Mass in B minor,* Kyrie

Adagio   app.

b: I   V°₆₅   V°₉ of IV   IV   V⁶₅   I   V⁶   IV⁶   II₄₃   V

EXAMPLE 20–20: Schumann, *Piano Concerto,* Op. 54, I

Allegro affettuoso

G: I   V°₉ of V V   V°₉ of IV IV   V°₉   I

315

EXAMPLE 20–21: Haydn, *String Quartet*, Op. 76, No. 1, II

C: I V♭⁰₉ of VI VI V♭⁰₄ of II II⁶ VII⁶ of II II VI⁶ V⁶ V⁶₅ I V

IRREGULAR RESOLUTION

Since it is the resolution that establishes the tonal identity of the diminished seventh chord, most apparently irregular resolutions will be discovered to be regular when the notation of the diminished seventh chord is revised. Composers have never been over-scrupulous as to the grammatical notation of this chord, especially in writing for keyboard instruments, so that the student must be prepared to judge the chord by what it does rather than by its appearance on paper.

The following is cited in a harmonic treatise as an instance of irregular resolution of a diminished seventh chord:

EXAMPLE 20–22

In this case the B natural has no leading-tone function relative to the second chord. If it were written C flat the true nature of the two chords would be clear. They are both derived from the same root, B flat, the ninth C flat resolving into the B flat, so there is no harmonic resolution.

EXAMPLE 20–23

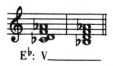

E♭: V_____

Although detailed study will have to await a later chapter, it is necessary to call attention to two diminished seventh chords which do not fall in the category of dominants. They are II⁷ and VI⁷ with root and third chromatically raised, acting as appoggiatura chords to I and V⁷ respectively.

316

EXAMPLE 20–24

$+\text{II}^7$ I^6 $+\text{VI}^{o7}$ V^6_5
(not V^o_9 of III) (not V^o_9 of V of III)

Like other diminished sevenths these two chords are identified by their resolutions. They are mentioned here to avoid confusion with irregular resolutions and incorrect notations of other chords.

The diminished seventh chord will seldom be found without either the dominant relationship to its chord of resolution, or a relationship such as the two shown above. Only if these are lacking can the resolution be called irregular harmonically, in terms of root progression. The II chord in the example below is a substitute for a V^o_9, differing from it only by the substitution of E for D sharp.

EXAMPLE 20–25: Mendelssohn, *A Midsummer Night's Dream,* "Notturno"

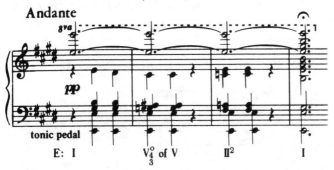

Often the chord preceding the diminished seventh, or the general sense of the tonality, will give it a meaning other than that defined by the resolution, that is, the diminished seventh will be a chord of dual function. The effect may be explained as irregular resolution, or by enharmonic change in the chord.

Cf. Exx. 22–25, 23–24

EXAMPLE 20–26: Rameau, *Nouvelle Suite No. 2:* No. 5, *The Hen*

Irregularity of voice leading is common in the treatment of the diminished seventh chord. Voices are allowed to move freely by arpeggiation among the chord tones, over such "unmelodic" intervals as the augmented second and fourth, and diminished fifth and seventh. It should be remembered, however, that in examples like the following these are really instrumental voices.

EXAMPLE 20–27: Schubert, *Symphony No. 5*, III

CONSECUTIVE DIMINISHED SEVENTHS

Sequences of more than two diminished sevenths are often employed, the vagueness of the chord causing a momentary uncertainty of tonality.

EXAMPLE 20–28: Beethoven, *Sonata*, Op. 10, No. 3, II

EXAMPLE 20–29: Beethoven, *Piano Concerto No. 4*, II

In rapid harmonic movement, successive diminished sevenths progressing by half step in similar motion give the effect of chromatic passing tones, although the chords are related harmonically. In the following example the parallel movement is disguised by the changes of position in the right-hand part. Each chord may be considered a dominant of the next, with some enharmonic revision. In actual performance the ear grasps as harmony only the first and last chords of the group.

EXAMPLE 20–30: Chopin, *Etude,* Op. 10, No. 3

MODULATION USING THE DIMINISHED
SEVENTH CHORD

The tonal ambiguity of the diminished seventh chord is turned to versatility when it is a question of modulation. This versatility is unmatched by any other chord. A single diminished seventh chord, without enharmonic change, is capable, like any dominant chord, of the following analyses: V, V of II, V of III (in minor), V of III (in major), V of IV, V of V, V of VI (in minor), V of VI (in major), V of VII (in minor). Add to these the nondominant forms II⁷ and VI⁷, and the dominant of the lowered second degree (V_9^0 of N^6), and we have twelve interpretations for the one chord. Moreover, since the chord may be enharmonically written in four different ways without changing the sound, we may multiply the above by four, making a total of forty-eight possible interpretations.

There are, however, certain limitations upon the usefulness of the diminished seventh as an effective pivot chord in modulation. To begin with, it is not advisable to employ the dominant of the new key as a pivot chord, the chord before it being a better common ground between the two keys. Further, if a secondary dominant is selected, it may happen that its chord of resolution is still a good chord in the first key and would be a more logical pivot chord than the diminished seventh.

EXAMPLE 20–31

In the above example, the modulation may be effected in theory by the diminished seventh chord; but actually its chord of resolution is the real pivot chord, as it is both I in A and II in G, and it introduces the dominant of the new key. If we wish to use V_9^o of A as pivot chord in a modulation to G it is better to assume an enharmonic change (G sharp = A flat), making the dominant of IV in G. By resolving to the minor form of IV the key of A is excluded from the harmony following the diminished seventh chord.

EXAMPLE 20–32

A modulation employing the diminished seventh chord as a pivot chord through enharmonic reinterpretation, as in the example above, but by means of remote relationships, is shown below.

EXAMPLE 20–33: Bach, *Mass in B minor,* Credo: *Confiteor*

Such uses of the diminished seventh are uncommon before the nineteenth century. Bach's use of it here is particularly striking in its unusual tonal direction, wherein the pivot chord is a secondary dominant in both keys, V_9^o of IV in D and V_9^o of V in F-sharp.

The following example from late in the period is similar, except that the dominant ninth of the first key is in the complete form with root F sharp, and the resolution is to the dominant seventh of the second key. This is an example of modulation by pivot tones, without an actual pivot chord.

EXAMPLE 20–34: Grieg, *Piano Concerto*, I

Formulae, to be played in all keys:

EXAMPLE 20–35

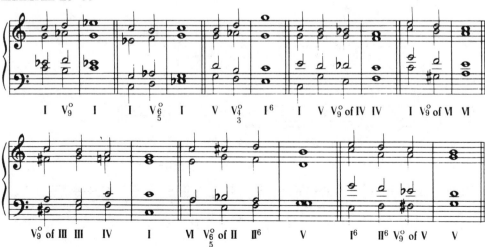

C: II⁶   I₄⁶   V₉° of VI   VI   D : II

G: II   II⁶   I₄⁶   V₉° of VI   VI

etc.

EXERCISES

1. Correct the notation of the following diminished seventh chords, to agree with the resolutions given.

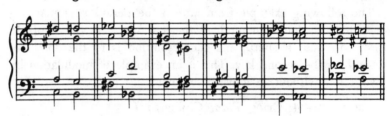

2. Work out in four parts the following figured basses:

a.

   ⁶₅   7   6   7♮   7   #‾7
                  #

b.

  6   7   7   ⁶₅   6   7♭   2   6
      #

c.

  7♭   7♮   5♮   ⁴₃♭   6   7   7   7♮   7

d.

  ⁶₅   6   ⁴₃   6   7♭₅♮   7   #   6   ⁴₃   6   ⁶₅
                   ♮

e.

  7♭   7   ⁶₅   7   ‡₇   7♭   7♭₅♭   7♭‾   7   7
                                  #   #

3. Interpret the following chord as a dominant or secondary dominant in the keys named, using enharmonic change when necessary, and showing the resolution of the chord in each key.

Keys: G, A flat, B flat, C, E.

4. Construct a phrase using four diminished seventh chords in succession.

5. Harmonize the following melodies, introducing diminished seventh chords:

6. Harmonize the following unfigured basses, introducing diminished seventh chords:

a.

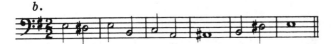

b.

c.

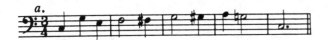

d.

CHAPTER 21

The Incomplete
Major Ninth

The Half-Diminished
Seventh Chord

The seventh chord constructed on the leading-tone and using the major mode bears a striking contrast to that from the minor mode, the diminished seventh. These chords are both dominant ninths without root, and they both resolve regularly to the tonic triad, but they are different in several respects.

Whereas in the diminished seventh chord the intervals between the factors were the same, and enharmonically equivalent in the inversions, the use of the major sixth degree gives a major third between the two upper factors. The resulting seventh chord has been called the *half-diminished seventh chord*, a term now widely accepted. Because of the nonequiintervallic structure there is a marked difference in the character of the inversions.

EXAMPLE 21–1

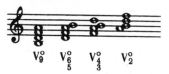

$$V^{\circ}_{9} \quad V^{\circ}_{6 \atop 5} \quad V^{\circ}_{4 \atop 3} \quad V^{\circ}_{2}$$

E.g., Ex. 23–25

The designation VII⁷ has been used by some writers to distinguish the major V°_{9} from the diminished seventh chord. We will use VII⁷ only to indicate such chords where the dominant feeling has been weakened, as before III.

The last inversion (ninth in the bass) is rarely found except as a dominant seventh chord in which the sixth degree appears as a suspension in the bass, resolving to the root. Indeed, a tendency is noticeable throughout the period of harmonic common practice to treat the upper tone of the major ninth interval, with or without root, as a melodic tone, resolving it to the tone below before the resolution of the chord takes place (nonharmonic resolution). The very characteristic sonority of the major ninth, however, makes a harmonic effect, especially when the leading-tone is present and the chord is in root position.

E.g., Exx. 8–53, 19–13

EXAMPLE 21–2: Schubert: *Sonata,* Op. 120, II

In the resolution, the presence of the perfect fifth between second and sixth degrees may lead to parallel fifths in the voice leading. This is usually avoided by moving the second degree up to the third or by skip of a fifth down to the dominant. In neither case will the root be doubled in the tonic triad.

EXAMPLE 21–3

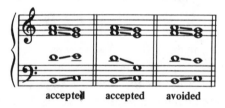

EXAMPLE 21–4: Bach, Chorale No. 11, *Jesu, nun sei gepreiset*

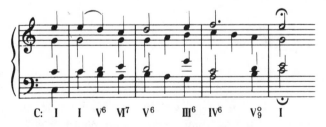

If the upper voices are so arranged that the interval of a fifth is inverted to a fourth, all three may descend in parallel motion.

326

However, this contrapuntal advantage has not been valued above the typical sound of the major ninth when heard in the top voice. Compare the sonority of the following with the disposition shown above.

EXAMPLE 21–5

In the example below, the instrumental writing actually creates seven melodic parts, hence the direct fifth in the resolution, between the two lower voices.

EXAMPLE 21–6: Dvořák, *String Quartet*, Op. 96, I

Allegro ma non troppo

A: IV(II)$^6_5$ I^6 V$^{o}_9$ I

INVERSIONS

The six-five-three inversion must resolve to the first inversion of the tonic chord to avoid parallel fifths between the bass and the resolution of the ninth.

EXAMPLE 21–7

But see Exx.
8–42, 11–5

The following resolution is like the above. The apparent multiplicity of parts is due mainly to instrumental octave doublings. Parallel octaves are the result of this duplication and are not defects of voice leading.

EXAMPLE 21–8: Mendelssohn, Overture to *A Midsummer Night's Dream*

The six-four-three inversion is more useful as there are more alternative possibilities of its arrangement. It may resolve to either root position or first inversion. The arrangement in *d* below, with the ninth below the leading-tone, is somewhat less often found.

EXAMPLE 21–9

EXAMPLE 21–10: Haydn, *Sonata No. 24*, I

EXAMPLE 21–11: Grieg, *Lyric Piece*, Op. 43: No. 1, *Butterfly*

Allegro grazioso

Unlike the diminished seventh chord, the incomplete major ninth is not equally appropriate to both modes. The major sixth degree as a dissonance tends to descend, which it could not normally do in the minor scale without undue prominence of the false relation of the tritone between sixth and third degrees. If the sixth degree were purely melodic, it could ascend as a step of the melodic minor scale but would lose its harmonic significance as a ninth.

EXAMPLE 21–12

avoided   uncommon

IRREGULAR RESOLUTION

The incomplete major ninth is not capable of greatly varied resolution. The progression to supertonic harmony is weak because all the tones of II are common to both chords.

In the resolution to III the chord loses its identity as a dominant ninth without root and becomes a seventh chord on the leading-tone (VII⁷). This progression is most often seen in harmonic sequences.

EXAMPLE 21–13: Brahms, *Ballade,* Op. 118, No. 3

Resolutions to IV may be made, but if the subdominant chord has the tonic in the bass there is really a regular resolution in disguise.

329

EXAMPLE 21–14

The submediant is not more satisfactory as a chord of resolution. If the tonic is in the bass the VI chord is really I (regular resolution). If the VI chord is in second inversion it represents III, and the V_9^0 is really a VII^7. The latter nondominant quality is likewise strongly felt in the progression to VI in root position, the two chords sounding like II–I in the relative minor.

EXAMPLE 21–15

See Ex. 24–12

SECONDARY DOMINANTS

The incomplete dominant major ninth is far less useful as a secondary dominant than the diminished seventh chord. This is due to its inability to act as dominant of a minor tonic. The degrees which may be preceded by a major ninth are I, IV, V, in the major mode, and III, V, VI, in the minor mode. In the case of III, its dominant in this form would be identical with the seventh chord on the second degree.

EXAMPLE 21–16

*See also Exx.
15–23, 17–27*

C: II^7 III

The dominant of the subdominant with major ninth resolves to the major form of IV.

From the foregoing it will be evident that the incomplete dominant major ninth offers somewhat limited opportunities as a pivot chord in modulation. There are no possibilities of enharmonic change as with the diminished seventh chord. The interpretations of the V_9^0 chord of the key of C are these: V of IV in G major; V of V in F; V of VI in E; II^7 in A.

Formulae, to be played in all keys:

EXAMPLE 21–21

$$V_{6\ 5}^{0} \quad I^6 \quad V_{4\ 3}^{0} \quad I^6 \quad V_{4\ 3}^{0} \quad I \quad V_9^0 \text{ of IV} \quad IV \qquad I \qquad V_9^0 \text{ of V} \quad I_4^6 \quad V^7 \quad I$$

EXERCISES

1. Construct three separate original phrases, illustrating three different modulations in which the pivot chord is the incomplete dominant major ninth of the first key.

2. Work out the following figured basses:

$a.$

$$7 \qquad {6 \atop 5} \quad 6 \quad {4 \atop 3} \quad 6 \qquad 6 \quad {6 \atop 4} \quad 7$$

$b.$

$${4 \atop 3} \quad 6 \qquad {6 \atop 5} \quad 6 \ 7 \qquad {6 \atop 5}\flat$$

$c.$

$${4 \atop 3} \quad 6 \qquad 7 \qquad {6 \atop 5} \quad 6 \ 7 \qquad 7\natural$$

$d.$

$${7 \atop 5\natural \atop 3} \qquad 7 \qquad 7 \qquad {6 \atop 4} \ 7 \quad 5$$

EXAMPLE 21–17: Mozart, *String Q*...

Moderato

B♭: V♮₉   I   V♮₉ of VI VI   V♮₉ of IV I

Most common of the secondary do...
V♮₉ of V.

INCOMPLETE
MAJOR NINTH

EXAMPLE 21–18: Franck, *Symphony*, I

Allegro

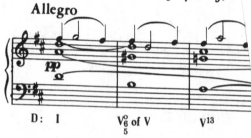

D: I   V♮₆₅ of V   V¹³

V♮₉   I   V♮₉ I

V♮₉ of V may be found in irregular resolutio...
lowing are two examples.

EXAMPLE 21–19: Brahms, *Capriccio*, Op. 116

Allegro

E♭: I   V♮₆₅ of V   I   V♮₉ of V

EXAMPLE 21–20: Schubert, *Sonata*, Op. 164, II

Allegretto quasi andantino

E: I⁶   V♮₉ of V   II₅⁶   V⁷   I

3

3. Harmonize the following melodies, using the chord V_9^o and its inversions where appropriate:

4. Harmonize the following basses:

333

CHAPTER 22

The Complete
Dominant Ninth

DIFFERENT FUNCTIONS OF THE NINTH

Far less frequently employed than the incomplete forms is the complete dominant ninth chord in its two forms, major and minor.

EXAMPLE 22–1

Reduction of this chord of five factors to four-part writing necessitates omission of one factor, which is usually the fifth. The fifth is unimportant contrapuntally compared to the other chord members, as it has no strong tendency, and the characteristic sound of the dominant ninth seems unaffected by its omission.

The regular resolution of the chord takes place as follows:

EXAMPLE 22–2

In practice, however, it is rare that the voices do not contain some melodic movement in the course of which all the factors of the chord may be touched upon.

Treatment of the complete dominant ninth chord by composers of the eighteenth and nineteenth centuries has three important aspects:

1. The ninth may appear as any of the types of nonharmonic melodic tones, resolving into the fifth degree before the chord itself resolves. It is often an appoggiatura, in which case the harmonic color is very pronounced, but even when it is rhythmically weak its harmonic significance is recognized by the ear.

EXAMPLE 22–3: Brahms, *Intermezzo*, Op. 76, No. 3

See also Exx.
5–12, 5–16, 8–27,
8–30, 8–57,
14–3, 15–21,
16–27, 18–17,
18–27, 26–25,
26–27

EXAMPLE 22–4: Bach, *Well-Tempered Clavier, II*, Fugue No. 5

2. The ninth may be used in a true harmonic sense as a chord tone but it may be absent from the chord at the moment of change of harmony. This is an important aspect of harmonic treatment of the ninth fairly common in the classics. It actually consists of the resolution through arpeggiation of a dissonant factor, a principle applied in common practice to no other dissonant chord (it is also called *dissolution* by some theorists). It is as though the ninth were regarded as an overtone in the dominant sonority, too high in the series to need to take part in the resolution effected by the seventh of the chord. Such treatment of the ninth implies a slowly moving root progression in comparison with the melodic activity.

See also Exx.
8–55, 17–14

335

EXAMPLE 22–5: Mozart, *Symphony No. 40*, K. 550, II

$E\flat$: I I^6_4 V

EXAMPLE 22–6: Beethoven, *Piano Concerto No. 3*, III

c: V^9 I

EXAMPLE 22–7: Beethoven, *String Quartet*, Op. 18, No. 1, II

d: V^9 I

EXAMPLE 22–8: Schubert, *Mass No. 6 in E flat*, Kyrie

$E\flat$: I I^6 II V^9 I

Cf. Ex. 23–41

3. Finally, the ninth may act as a normal dissonant chord tone
336   resolving to a tone of the following chord.

EXAMPLE 22–9: Franck, *Violin Sonata*, I

Allegretto ben moderato

A: V⁹   I

EXAMPLE 22–10: Beethoven, *Symphony No. 3* ("Eroica"), II

Adagio

c: I   V⁹   I

In the example below the voice leading is more or less lost in the piano pedal effect. The resolution of the ninth chord is accompanied by a dynamic change from loud to *dolcissimo,* as well as a change of register and of movement.

EXAMPLE 22–11: Liszt, *Années de Pèlerinage,* II, No. 4,
        Sonetto 47 del Petrarca

Sempre mosso

G: V⁹♭   I

The excerpts above show the minor ninth resolving to either a major or a minor tonic. The major ninth, complete or incomplete, is used only before the major tonic.

The major dominant ninth has further limitations with respect to the common practice of composers. It represents a harmonic 337 color and style of the end of the common-practice period rather than of the eighteenth century. Employed as in the third of the three aspects described above it cannot be said to be of frequent use until the latter part of the nineteenth century. We will meet the dominant major ninth again in Part Two of this book in connection with impressionistic harmony, in which it is of great importance both as an independent quasi-consonant sonority and as an adjunct to the triad in modal harmony. In the latter case the dominant major ninth owes the flexibility of its use to the dual dominant-nondominant nature of its structure, wherein its lower three factors support a dominant feeling but its upper three coincide with the supertonic triad.

PREPARATION

Dominant ninth chords, like all chords of dominant harmony, are introduced with or without preparation.

SPACING

When the root of the ninth chord is present, and the chord is used in the usual harmonic sense (aspect no. 3, above), care is taken to place the ninth at least a ninth above the root. It is practically never found below the root and preference is shown for the arrangement of the chord in which the leading-tone is below the ninth rather than above it.

It is, of course, possible to place the factors close together, all within the range of an octave (a below). In a chord which contains all but two of the seven tones of the scale the effect of this is not of a ninth chord, but more that of a chord built with intervals of a second, or what is known in the twentieth century as a tone-cluster.

EXAMPLE 22–12

Considering the above dispositions: *a* is not heard as a ninth
chord; *b* is usually avoided since the root is higher than the ninth;
c has more of the characteristic sound of the dominant ninth chord
although not ideal, as the ninth is below the leading-tone; *d* shows
the importance of the leading-tone, by its omission, in the typical
ninth chord sound; *e* is the most usual arrangement. It will prove
instructive to the student to play these chords and note carefully
their comparative harmonic effect.

The peculiarly strident sound of the following minor ninth chord
is largely due to the spacing, as well as to the placing of the root
D close to the ninth E flat.

EXAMPLE 22–13: Beethoven, *Symphony No. 9*, IV

The root may appear above the minor ninth in a nonharmonic
function as appoggiatura to the seventh. This effect is not uncommon and should be regarded as a diminished seventh chord, the
root nonharmonic.

EXAMPLE 22–14: Chopin, *Mazurka*, Op. 56, No. 3

INVERSIONS

The complete dominant ninth chord in inversion is not often found
in the common-practice period, but there are occasional examples. It is important that the spacing in the inversions follow the
restrictions regarding the relative positions of ninth, root, and
leading-tone, if the characteristic sonority of the chord is desired. 339

In figuring basses for the inversions the spacing is not taken into account, the arabic numerals simply identifying the notes to be used in arranging the chord.

EXAMPLE 22–15

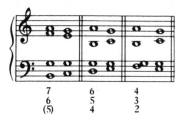

7
6
(5)

6
5
4

4
3
2

The fourth inversion is not used as that would place the ninth below the root. The second inversion, with the fifth in the bass, is less used than the other two.

EXAMPLE 22–16: Lalo, *Symphonie espagnole*, Op. 21, IV.

d: I   3   V⁷₆   i   3   V⁷₆   i   3

EXAMPLE 22–17: Haydn, *Sonata No. 7*, II

F: IV(II)⁶₅   V⁴₃₂   I⁶   II⁶   I⁶₄   V⁷   I

IRREGULAR RESOLUTION

The student should experiment with the connection of V⁹ to other chords in the key, judging the result both contrapuntally and for its harmonic effect. Irregular resolutions found in the works of composers should likewise be noted. These successions cannot always be called resolutions because the ninth may be unresolved or treated nonharmonically. A few examples are given below.

EXAMPLE 22–18: Haydn, *String Quartet*, Op. 64, No. 2, II

B: V   I$^6_4$ V^9 VI

EXAMPLE 22–19: Schubert, *Sonata*, Op. 122, III

E$\flat$: V^7 I$^6_4$ V   I^6 V^9 VI

EXAMPLE 22–20: Franck, *Symphonic Variations*

f$^\sharp$:   V^9 IV^6 V$^{\circ 6}_{5}$ of V   VI^6 V   I

EXAMPLE 22–21: Liszt, *Sonata*

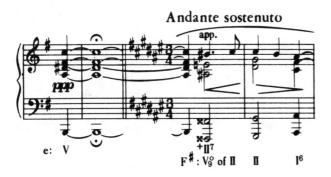

e: V

F$^\sharp$: V$^{\circ}_9$ of II   II   I^6

+II^7

SECONDARY DOMINANTS

The complete ninth chord is used as a secondary dominant, the limitation being that the major ninth is not used to introduce a minor tonic. Irregular resolutions of secondary dominant ninths are occasionally employed, as shown in the first of the following examples.

EXAMPLE 22–22: Wagner, *Die Meistersinger*, Act III, Finale

C: V^7 I^6 V^4_3 V^9 of VI IV V^o_9 of V
(VI of VI)

EXAMPLE 22–23: Chopin, *Nocturne*, Op. 72, No. 1

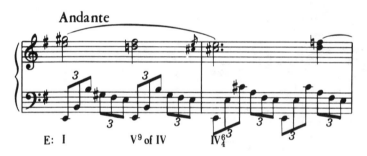

E: I V^9 of IV $IV^{6\,3}_4$

EXAMPLE 22–24: Bach, *Well-Tempered Clavier, I,*
Prelude No. 12

342 f: V^9 of IV   IV   V IV^6 V   I   V

EXAMPLE 22–25: Franck, *Symphony*, II

EXAMPLE 22–26: Mussorgsky, *Songs and Dances of Death:*
No. 3, *Death's Serenade*

MODULATION

The ninth chord has the disadvantage of all dominant chords in
modulation in that the pivot chord is preferably not the dominant
of the new key. It is, therefore, more effectively used as a secondary
dominant in the second key, or even in both. Irregular resolution
of the pivot chord is an added resource. The presence of the root
takes away the possibilities of enharmonic change which were so
numerous in the incomplete minor ninth chord.

In the following example, the ninth chord appears as the chord
of resolution in the deceptive cadence in D. Hence it is taken as
the pivot chord in the sudden modulation to B-flat, in order that the
formula of the deceptive cadence may be preserved in the analysis.

EXAMPLE 22–27: Franck, *Symphony*, I

Formulae, to be played in all keys:

EXAMPLE 22–28

V⁹ I   V⁹ I   V⁹ I   V⁷₆ I   V⁶₅₄ I⁶   V⁹   V°₉ of VI VI

V⁹ of V V⁷ V⁹ of IV   V⁹   V°₉ of II   V°₉   I

EXERCISES

1. Work out the following figured basses:

344

2. Construct original phrases showing the treatment of the dominant ninth chord in the following three ways:

    a. With the ninth as a melodic nonharmonic tone;

    b. With the ninth as a harmonic factor resolved through arpeggiation;

    c. With the ninth as a normal harmonic dissonance.

3. Write in four parts the following irregular resolutions:

    a. E flat: V^9–V^9 of II

    b. G: V^9 of II–V^9 of V

    c. A: V^{9b}–V^{9b} of V

    d. F: V^9 of VI–IV

    e. B flat: V^9–VI

4. Construct a phrase modulating from G major to F major, in which the pivot chord is a major ninth chord, secondary dominant in both keys.

5. Harmonize the following unfigured basses, introducing complete dominant ninth chords:

a.

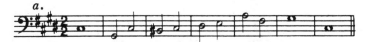

b.

c.

d. Andante

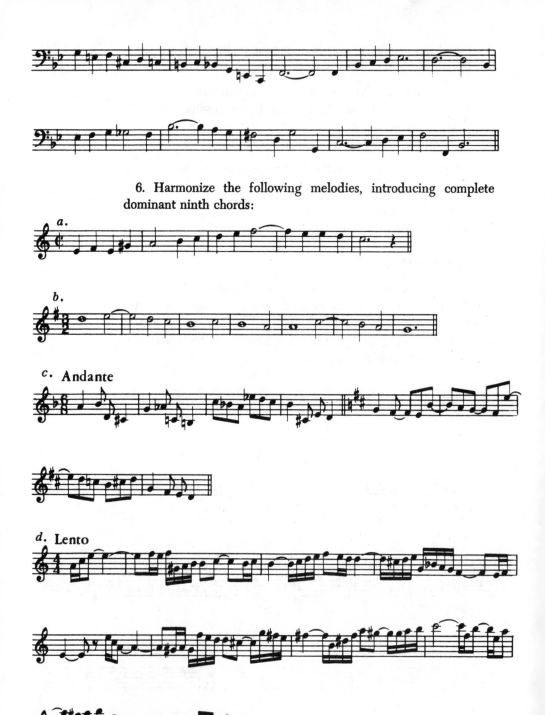

6. Harmonize the following melodies, introducing complete dominant ninth chords:

a.

b.

c. Andante

d. Lento

CHAPTER 23

Nondominant Harmony—
Seventh Chords

FUNCTION OF DISSONANT
NONDOMINANT CHORDS

It was stated earlier that most of the chordal types in the common-practice period are either triads or various kinds of dissonant chords of dominant effect. Chromatically altered chords, to be discussed in later chapters, account for some of the remaining types. In this chapter we will begin to examine the various kinds of nondominant harmony.

Dissonant chords of nondominant character are found to be comparatively unusual, when the whole period is considered. Throughout the period they appear fairly often as the result of contrapuntal writing, especially as suspensions or appoggiature and in sequences. Not until the nineteenth century do they begin to appear independently, that is, with their dissonant factors introduced without preparation. That kind of independence is nevertheless a harbinger of the much more central role achieved by nondominant harmony in the period after common practice; in the works of the impressionist composers, nondominant seventh chords, as well as more complex nondominant types, become fully independent sonorities, their dissonant factors being neither prepared nor resolved.

Dominant harmony occupied such an important place in common practice that its characteristics became sharply defined 347 through over two centuries of usage and convention. The presence of the leading-tone a major third above the root, with its strong tendency toward the tonic, is no doubt the strongest characteristic of the dominant effect, and the root succession of V to I, whether up a fourth or down a fifth, is hardly less strong. A further reinforcement of the dominant effect is provided by the addition of a seventh to the chord, a diminished fifth above the leading-tone, and the combination of the leading-tone and the seventh often suffice to sustain the dominant effect even when the dominant root is absent, as in the two types of V_9^0.

It follows that harmonic formations that do not show these characteristics are by definition nondominant, although observation shows that the distinction can sometimes be a subtle one. The family of nondominant seventh chords, which will concern us first, is large and various, and in some ways their structure and function may be compared with dominant harmony. The nondominant seventh chords, whatever their type, are distinguished from the dominant seventh above all by sound. Beyond that they are distinguished from each other by structural type.

COMPARATIVE TABLE OF SEVENTH CHORDS

The dominant seventh chord is the only seventh chord that can be constructed from the degrees of the major scale that has the structure of major third, perfect fifth, and minor seventh above the root, as the following table shows.

EXAMPLE 23–1

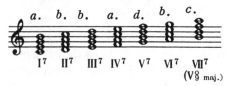

The nondominant seventh chords that can be formed from the minor scales, including the mixed-mode types, are much more numerous. All the possibilities are shown here.

EXAMPLE 23–2

The chords in the two tables can be categorized in seven structural types, indicated by the letters.

  a. Major third, perfect fifth, major seventh: these are called *major seventh chords.*
  b. Minor third, perfect fifth, minor seventh: these are called *minor seventh chords.*
  c. Minor third, diminished fifth, minor seventh: these are called *half-diminished seventh chords.*
  d. Major third, perfect fifth, minor seventh: these are the familiar dominant seventh chords.
  e. Minor third, perfect fifth, major seventh: some writers call this form the *major-minor seventh chord.*
  f. Major third, augmented fifth, major seventh: this form has no specific name in common use.
  g. Minor third, diminished fifth, diminished seventh: this is the familiar diminished seventh chord.

Forms shown in square brackets are already familiar and will not be discussed further. They include the various dominant sevenths (d) and the two forms of V_9^0 (c, g). Very infrequently, some of these may be found as nondominants (e.g. Example 5–33, third measure).

The other c forms in the table are equivalent to the incomplete major ninth used as a secondary dominant, but because this type of dominant has less dominant strength than the dominant seventh or the complete dominant minor ninth, these forms have an important value as nondominant sevenths as well. Their true identity becomes clear only on resolution.

The chords grouped under a have the major seventh, a sharper interval than the minor seventh, and these chords thus have a certain pungency. The mixed-mode e chords have the added dissonance of the augmented fifth interval between their fifth and seventh, and a correspondingly greater pungency. By contrast, the minor seventh chords, b, are of generally softer effect, because the only dissonant interval between any of the factors is the minor seventh.

The chords with the augmented fifth, f, have a dissonance value comparable to the e chords. All seventh chords with strongly dissonant intervals have both typical and atypical resolutions, depending on the extent to which the dissonant factors are considered as harmonic or nonharmonic tones.

349

The question of deciding whether a tone is a chord factor or a nonharmonic tone often comes to the fore in the study of harmony. More important than the decision of this question is the appreciation of both sides of the issue. As we have often said before, harmony results from the coincidence of melodic parts, but certain coincidental forms become established through usage and recur constantly under different melodic conditions, whereas others seem to depend on the assumption of a simpler harmonic form as a basis.

The extremes of theoretical explanation of chords might be illustrated as follows:

EXAMPLE 23-3

C : I^{13} I   I____

In the first case the A has been taken to be the top factor in a thirteenth chord of which the seventh, ninth, and eleventh are missing! In the second case the D, B, and F have been diagnosed as appoggiature on the tonic triad. Without denying the theoretical validity of these analyses, one must concede their practical absurdity. In most music the differentiation between harmonic and nonharmonic factors will be relatively unambiguous; sometimes the differentiation will be subtle, but it should never require one to stretch the analysis to the point of the above examples.

Some of the nondominant seventh chords appear ordinarily in a form which does not necessitate analysis as a seventh chord, but their relative importance as harmonic effects should be taken into account.

RESOLUTION

The seventh of a nondominant seventh chord resolves customarily by moving down one degree, just as in the case of the dominant seventh. This rule applies to the major seventh as well as the minor, with the qualification that the major seventh also occurs fairly often as an upward-resolving appoggiatura, to the octave of the root. Harmonically, the regular resolution is to the chord whose root is a perfect fourth higher, except in the case of IV⁷ and the minor VI⁷, where the perfect fourth above would lie outside the scale. The resolutions are shown below.

Irregular resolutions are also employed, although not as often in practice as the possibilities would lead one to expect.

The fifth, or the third, is sometimes omitted when the chord is in root position, especially when the resolution is made to another seventh chord. In such a case the root is doubled.

The inversions resolve contrapuntally in much the same way as the root position, except that the root will usually remain stationary rather than move up a fourth.

THE TONIC SEVENTH

EXAMPLE 23–4

The regular resolution of the tonic seventh is to IV. In the minor mode the lowered seventh degree is used in order to descend melodically to the minor sixth degree.

EXAMPLE 23–5: Brahms, *Intermezzo*, Op. 117, No. 2

The commonest irregular resolution is to II⁷, the root remaining in position to become the seventh of the second chord.

In the following example, too, the root remains static, making a six-four chord of the subdominant triad. Note the apparent descending scale motion across the voices, from C down to G.   351

EXAMPLE 23–6: Grieg, *Sonata*, Op. 7, II

Andante molto

C: IV$^6_4$ I^7 IV$^6_4$ I

THE SUPERTONIC SEVENTH

See also Ex. 7–19   The supertonic seventh regularly resolves to V. This chord is common in cadences, before the dominant or the tonic six-four chord. The minor form of II^7, obtained by adding A flat to the following illustrations, is employed in both major and minor modes, but the major form is used only in major surroundings. Irregular resolutions are to I, III, VI, and the secondary dominants.

EXAMPLE 23–7

II^7 V   II^7 V^7 II$^6_5$ V   II$^4_3$ V   II^2 V$^6_5$ II^7 I^6 II$^6_5$ I$^6_4$ II^7 III   II^7 VI

More will be said about the minor form in the remarks on the half-diminished seventh chord later in this chapter.

EXAMPLE 23–8: Bach, *Three-Part Invention No. 11*

susp.

B♭: VI   II$^6_5$ V^7

EXAMPLE 23–9: Schumann, *Symphony No. 1*, II

Larghetto

p

c: VI^6 II^7 V   I

352

EXAMPLE 23–10: Berlioz, *Symphonie fantastique*, I:
Reveries, Passions

Allegro agitato e appassionato assai

C: IV⁶   V⁶₅ of V   IV(II)⁶₅   I

THE MEDIANT SEVENTH

The regular resolution of the mediant seventh is to VI. The two
minor forms differ in the action of the fifth, which ascends when it
is the leading-tone and descends when it is the lowered seventh
degree. Irregular resolutions of III⁷ are to IV, II, and the secondary dominants.

EXAMPLE 23–11

III⁷ VI   III⁶₅ VI   III⁴₃ VI   III⁷ VI   III⁷ VI

EXAMPLE 23–12: Chopin, *Etude*, Op. 10, No. 1

Allegro

cresc.

C: III⁷   VI⁷   II⁷   V⁷

EXAMPLE 23–13: Mattheson, *Gigue*

Allegro

d: III⁷   VI⁷   II⁷   V⁷ of V   V   I

353

EXAMPLE 23–14

| IV⁷ | II⁶₅(IV) | V | IV⁷ | II⁶ | V | IV⁷ | II⁶₅(IV) | V | IV⁷ | II⁶₅(IV) | V | IV⁷ | V | IV⁷ | V |

(rare: V⁷ of VII)

See also Exx.
8–52, 20–34
The regular resolution of IV⁷ is not to the root a fourth above, which would be VII. In the majority of cases the seventh moves down before the progression of the other tones of the chord, making a form of II⁷, which then proceeds to V. The seventh is therefore usually considered an appoggiatura.

EXAMPLE 23–15: Bach, Chorale No. 59, *Herzliebster Jesu*

g: I IV⁷ II⁴₃ V V² I⁶ VII⁶ I   V°₉ I V
        (IV⁶)

EXAMPLE 23–16: Schubert, *Moments Musicaux*, Op. 94, No. 6

Allegretto

A♭: V⁷of V/V   I   IV⁷   IV(II)⁶₅   I   IV⁷   IV(II)⁶₅

EXAMPLE 23–17: Bach, *Well-Tempered Clavier*, I,
Prelude No. 1

354

G: I⁶   IV²   II⁷

The alternative analyses in these examples, where II is given parenthetically with IV, will be explained in the section on neighbor-note harmony later in this chapter.

When the fifth is omitted the root is doubled and the supertonic chord which usually follows is a triad in first inversion.

EXAMPLE 23–18: Haydn, *String Quartet*, Op. 20, No. 4, I

The direct resolution of IV⁷ to V is less common and calls for care in the arrangement of the voices to avoid parallel fifths. Two such arrangements are shown in Example 23–14. In the following example the progression is made smoother by the use of a tonic six-four chord.

EXAMPLE 23–19: Brahms, *Violin Sonata,*
            Op. 108, III

Irregular resolutions are practicable to I and to several of the secondary dominants. The example below shows an unusual progression by parallel motion to III⁷.

EXAMPLE 23–20: Bach, *Sonata No. 1 for*
             Unaccompanied Violin, IV

EXAMPLE 23–21

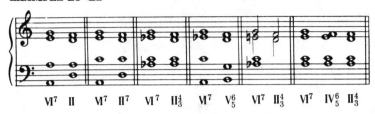

$$\text{VI}^7 \quad \text{II} \quad \text{VI}^7 \quad \text{II}^7 \quad \text{VI}^7 \quad \text{II}_3^4 \quad \text{VI}^7 \quad \text{V}_5^6 \quad \text{VI}^7 \quad \text{II}_3^4 \quad \text{VI}^7 \quad \text{IV}_5^6 \quad \text{II}_3^4$$

The regular resolution of VI⁷ is to II. When the third is present it is extended or repeated, becoming the seventh of II.

EXAMPLE 23–22: Handel, *Suite No. 8:* III, Allemande

f: VI⁷   II   V   I

As in the last of the progressions shown in Example 23–21, the voices may pass over a form of IV⁷ before reaching the II chord, or the resolution may sound like both IV and II. The harmonic rhythm may be either weak-to-strong or strong-to-weak. In the latter case the seventh will sound as appoggiatura to its note of resolution.

EXAMPLE 23–23: Mendelssohn, *Symphony No. 3* ("Scottish"), I

Cf. Ex. 13–1

Andante con moto

a: III   VI⁷   II₅⁶ (IV⁹)   I₄⁶   V⁷   I

Although the form of VI⁷ which combines the major sixth degree with the minor third degree ordinarily occurs when the sixth degree is part of an ascending melodic minor scale, it may also be found resulting from a descending chromatic movement.

Gracieux

g: V⁰₉ (V⁰₉ of III) III⁴₃   VI⁷   II⁴₃   V

THE LEADING-TONE SEVENTH

This chord, usually an incomplete dominant ninth, partakes of
nondominant characteristics when it proceeds to III.

EXAMPLE 23–25: Bach, *French Suite No. 5:* VII, Gigue

G : VII⁷   III   VI⁷   II

NONDOMINANT SEVENTHS IN SEQUENCE

The continuous series of seventh chords is a favorite device in
nonmodulating sequences. The sevenths usually enter as suspensions, and when the chords are in root position every other chord
will be incomplete, with its root doubled.

*See also Exx.
8–37, 21–13,
23–12, 24–8*

EXAMPLE 23–26

All inversions may be employed in these sequences, as well as
ornamental resolutions of the suspensions and other melodic devices.

357

EXAMPLE 23–27: Krebs, *Partita No. 6*, Allemande

B♭: VI⁷   II⁷   V⁷   I⁷   IV⁷   VII⁷   III⁷   V of V   V

MODULATION

The nondominant seventh chords are useful as pivot chords in modulation. Since they are not of dominant effect they do not strongly suggest the key, and for each of these chords there is at least one other of identical sound. For instance, the II⁷ of C major may be interpreted also as I⁷ of D minor, III⁷ of B-flat major, IV⁷ of A minor, or VI⁷ of F major.

Irregular resolutions are sometimes useful in confirming the interpretation of the second key. For example, in a modulation from F to B flat, if the pivot chord is VI⁷ in F becoming III⁷ in B flat, the regular resolution will be heard as a chord still in F.

EXAMPLE 23–28

F : VI⁷   II
B♭: III⁷   VI

If, on the other hand, the irregular resolution III⁷ to IV is employed in B flat, it will be evident to the ear that a modulation has taken place, since the chord of resolution is not a usual chord in the key of F.

EXAMPLE 23–29

358   B♭: III⁷   IV
       F : VI⁷

NEIGHBOR-NOTE HARMONY:
THE TRIAD WITH ADDED SIXTH

An important category of nondominant chords originates in the harmonic relationship of the consonant neighbor note. Mention has already been made (Chapters 5, Example 5–8, and 12, Examples 12–17 and 12–18) of the use of the first inversion of the supertonic triad, especially with the seventh present, as a substitute for the subdominant triad. In such uses, one tends to hear the root-position triadic component of the chord as the most stable part of it, and the fourth degree, not the second degree, as the actual root.

EXAMPLE 23–30

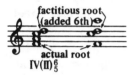

This chord is an excellent example of the imbalance between composers' practice and established theory. According to theory, the root of this sonority should be D, the tones being rearranged in the archetypal chord to form a stack of thirds with D at the bottom. But usage of this chord ever since the eighteenth century, especially in certain spacings, consistently has shown that composers have in the main thought of it as a subdominant chord with root F, the D originating as a neighbor note or passing tone, or even as a purely harmonic dissonance analogous to the seventh in the dominant seventh chord. (It will be observed that in the major mode, the only dissonance in this triad with added sixth is a major second, the harmonic inversion of the minor seventh, which in turn is the only dissonant interval in the dominant seventh structure; the dissonance values of the two chords are therefore comparable.)

EXAMPLE 23–31: Schumann, *Phantasiestücke,*
Op. 12: No. 6, *Fabel*

See also Exx.
5–33, 5–34,
8–31, 11–5, 15–2,
18–27, 26–11

EXAMPLE 23–32: Brahms, *In stiller Nacht*

The chord regularly proceeds to the dominant, as in the Schumann example above, or to the tonic, as in the Brahms example.
These are normal root progressions for II when in the first inversion, or for IV in any position.

Whether one hears the chord as II or IV will ordinarily depend
on which tone is stressed as a root. IV has the advantage as a root
because it is in the bass, but this may be offset by other conditions.
One might compare two examples from earlier in the chapter for
their relative harmonic effect. In Example 23–8, the root C of the
II_5^6, the sixth above the bass, is repeated three times in the measure, while the fifth (B flat) above the bass is suspended at the
beginning; moreover the sequential pattern tends to reinforce C as
the true root. On the other hand, in Example 23–10, the root D of
the II_5^6 is suspended while the F is sounded much more prominently, and one would more likely hear the harmony as a subdominant with added sixth.

If the triad with added sixth thus represents a chord with two
roots, one real in the sense of actually perceived, and the other
factitious, there remains a problem of what to call the chord. In
this book we will use the designation $IV(II)_5^6$, whenever it seems
that the chord actually appears to have a function that is more
strongly subdominant than supertonic.

The subdominant feeling of this chord is rather stronger when
the minor form is used. This is because the supertonic component in the minor mode is a diminished triad, which being
dissonant is relatively less stable than the minor triad.

A complete series of triads with added sixth can be constructed
upon the notes of the major scale, thus:

EXAMPLE 23–33

Added-sixth chords constructed on the second and seventh degrees are seen to be identical with VII$^6_5$ and V$^6_5$ respectively, the
well-known dominant forms. As for the others, the chords constructed on the third, fifth, and sixth degrees are not perceived
with a dual root, and are employed only as first-inversion seventh chords of I, III, and IV respectively. That leaves the added-
sixth chord constructed on the tonic, equivalent to the first inversion of VI^7. This chord is employed as a tonic chord with some
frequency in the common-practice period.

*See also Ex.
18–25*

EXAMPLE 23–34: Chopin, *Sonata,* Op. 35, II

EXAMPLE 23–35: Chopin, *Prelude,* Op. 28, No. 23

EXAMPLE 23–36: Wagner, *Five Poems of Mathilde
Wesendonk:* No. 5, *Träume*

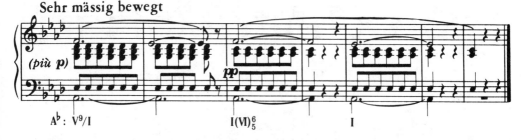

The two Chopin examples show the sixth degree on the one
hand as a neighbor note and on the other as a harmonic factor
freely touched upon by arpeggiation. The Wagner example seems
to show both aspects, the appoggiatura effect lasting for a long 361

time and interrupted by a rest before finally resolving. The final stage of evolution of this sonority can be seen in the last measures of Mahler's *Das Lied von der Erde*, where it is left unresolved (Example 30–30).

The minor form of this chord, employing the major sixth degree, is less frequent in common practice, because it is a mixed-mode chord whose major-scale component is of less harmonic strength than the minor. One is most likely to encounter this chord as a triad with nonharmonic sixth degree, from the ascending melodic minor scale.

EXAMPLE 23–37: Beethoven, *Symphony No. 7*, II

In the works of several Russian composers in the latter half of the nineteenth century, the tonic sonority with added sixth became virtually a nationalist mannerism, even to the point of omission of the fifth, with VI⁶ substituting for the tonic triad.

EXAMPLE 23–38: Borodin, *Polovetsian Dances*
from *Prince Igor*, I

EXAMPLE 23–39: Rimsky-Korsakov, *Scheherazade*, III

Such usages reflect the interest of the Russian nationalists in harmony involving the natural minor scale, which appears more strongly in their works than it does in the western European music of the time. We noted in Chapter 5 that common practice recognized a strong association of relative-major harmony in a surrounding minor-mode context; the Russian nationalists were the first to explore the reverse association to any great extent, as they explored a wide variety of modal harmony.

The major tonic with added sixth also shares a kinship with the pentatonic scale; it forms a basic sonority in pentatonic writing of the period following common practice.

THE HALF-DIMINISHED SEVENTH CHORD

EXAMPLE 23–40

Of the four half-diminished seventh chords that can be formed out of notes of the major or minor scales, VII⁷ is already familiar, and the second chord in the example above is given the somewhat clumsy designation of VII⁷ of IV because it has no other ready interpretation within a single mode. This leaves II⁷ and VI⁷, of which only the former is of common occurrence. As we have just seen, VI⁷ in the first inversion is relatively uncommon, while II⁷ in the first inversion, as IV(II)$^6_5$, is very common. In root position, II⁷ with diminished fifth is freely used in strongly tonal contexts like any other seventh chord, especially in the early part of the period.

In the nineteenth century, however, composers began to exploit the half-diminished II⁷ for its apparent tonal ambiguity. The principle suggested earlier, that in the first inversion this chord may appear to have two different roots in different contexts, seems to apply even when the chord is in root position; the diminished-triad component is harmonically less strong than the minor-triad component. This ambiguity makes the half-diminished seventh chord a useful nondominant adjunct in passages that modulate rapidly and repeatedly, where the composer wishes to avoid temporarily a stabilization of the tonality.

A characteristic use of the half-diminished II⁷ occurs in the following example, showing the famous "Tristan chord." At first the

II⁷ resolves to a dominant with major ninth, the modal mixture adding a chromatic relationship to the progression; at the climax, the II⁷ is reinterpreted enharmonically as an augmented sixth chord with appoggiatura, the pivot chord in a modulation to a remote key. (Compare Example 27–19.)

EXAMPLE 23–41: Wagner, Prelude to *Tristan und Isolde*

In the following example the half-diminished seventh moves upward by parallel chromatic motion, much as the diminished seventh might do, with a comparable temporary suspension of the tonality. At the cadence, the stable harmony seems to be the F-sharp minor triadic component of the chord, even though the D sharp is firmly established in the bass.

Cf. Ex. 30–25

EXAMPLE 23–42: Dvořák: *Symphony No. 9*, I

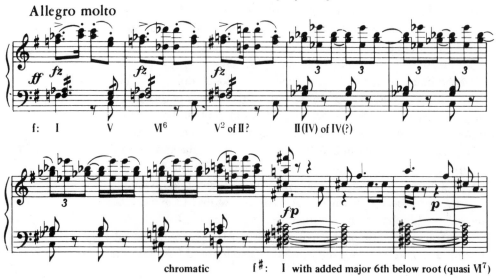

The two examples following may be compared for their relative atmospheric quality in their use of the half-diminished seventh chord. In one example, the chord is in the $\frac{6}{5}$ position; in the other, in root position.

EXAMPLE 23–43: Wagner, *Das Rheingold*, Interlude
before Scene 2

Etwas langsamer (Ruhig)

EXAMPLE 23–44: Schoenberg, Prelude to *Gurrelieder*

Mässig bewegt

FORMULAE

The numerous formulae for keyboard practice afforded by the nondominant seventh chords are by no means exhausted by those given in Examples 23–4, 23–7, 23–11, 23–14, 23–21, and 23–26. The student is expected to add others to his repertory, especially formulae using inversions and irregular resolutions, either originally constructed or gathered from musical literature.

EXERCISES

1. Work out the following figured basses:

a.

365

2. Construct a phrase containing a sequence, the pattern of which has for its harmonic background the progression II²–III⁴₃.

3. Construct a musical sentence of three phrases, fulfilling the following specifications:

a. The first phrase modulates from D major to F-sharp minor by means of a nondominant seventh chord as pivot chord.

b. The second phrase contains a modulating sequence ending in some key other than D.

c. The third phrase returns to D major by a modulation using a nondominant seventh as pivot chord.

4. Harmonize the following unfigured basses, introducing nondominant seventh chords:

f. Moderato

5. Harmonize the following melodies, introducing nondominant seventh chords:

CHAPTER 24

Ninth, Eleventh,
and Thirteenth Chords

It would seem a natural process in the evolution of harmonic usage to continue superposing intervals of a third in order to
increase the vocabulary of chords. However, conscious efforts to
accomplish this are not observed in the works of composers of the
common-practice period in harmony. One important influential
factor in this result is the firm establishment of the principle of
three- and four-part writing as the norm of melodic texture. Despite the apparent complexity of much instrumental music it will
usually lend itself to a reduction to not more than four real parts.
Writing in less than three parts is not at all uncommon, but it is
rare that a composer employs more than four parts, or five at the
most. This fact is consistently borne out in harmonic analysis, the
continued practice of which on the part of the student is here taken
for granted.

When a chord of five factors, like the ninth chord, is rendered
by four parts, one factor must be omitted unless one of the parts
sounds two factors successively. It has been seen that in the dominant ninth the ninth is often either a melodic or a harmonic tone,
depending upon its prominence as a harmonic ingredient. Similar
attributes have been noted in the nondominant seventh chords,
especially IV. This ambiguity of function becomes even more 369

marked in the nondominant ninth chords, and the so-called chords of the eleventh and thirteenth. The omission of factors weakens the sense of structure in thirds and allows the ear to accept the higher factors as melodic tones dependent on a simple harmonic background, usually a triad, or dominant seventh chord.

In the following example, a thirteenth chord is shown (*a*) with all its factors, a sonority quite foreign to the period of harmonic common practice. It is also shown (*b*) as it usually occurs. Playing of this second arrangement will demonstrate the high improbability of the missing thirds, especially A and C, and will also show the strong implication in the note E that it represents D, whether or not it actually resolves to it.

EXAMPLE 24–1

The nondominant ninth chord effects used by composers are generally found on the roots I, II, and IV, less often on III or VI. They are brought about in nearly all cases by the presence of one or more appoggiature or suspensions.

THE APPOGGIATURA

The appoggiatura to the octave above the bass, if sufficiently prominent harmonically, will create the effect of a ninth chord. If the seventh is not present the true chord is a triad in root position.

EXAMPLE 24–2

(I⁹) I   (II⁹) II   (IV⁹) IV

When the seventh is included and both seventh and ninth resolve, as a double appoggiatura, the fundamental harmony is a triad in first inversion.

EXAMPLE 24–3

(I⁹) VI⁶ (II⁹) VII⁶ (IV⁹) II⁶

Cf. Ex. 23–23

Both fifth and seventh may be included with the ninth, representing a seventh chord in first inversion.

EXAMPLE 24–4

(I⁹) VI$_5^6$ (II⁹) VII$_5^6$ (IV⁹) II$_5^6$

All of the appoggiature shown may occur in the form of suspensions, in which case they would enter as tied-over notes from the preceding chord and would, of course, be weak instead of strong rhythmically.

These effects are also used in the minor mode, the lowered seventh degree being employed when it descends to the sixth.

III⁹ and VI⁹ have been omitted from the above examples as they are little used, but these effects may be seen in the following examples.

EXAMPLE 24–5: Brahms, *Ballade*, Op. 10, No. 4

Andante con moto

B: VI(I)$_5^6$ (VI⁹)   V⁷of V   V

In the example above, the ninth of the VI⁹ chord is a passing tone, rather than an appoggiatura. The following excerpt shows what might be called a III⁹ chord, created contrapuntally by two suspensions. It is difficult, however, to hear this as a true mediant ninth, because the dominant-to-tonic resolution of the double suspension is so strong.

371

EXAMPLE 24–6: Bach, *Well-Tempered Clavier, I,*
Prelude No. 7

$E\flat$: VII^2 III^6 IV$^6_5$ VII (III^9) I^6 V   I^7 (VI^6) V^2 of V V^6

The ninths representing harmony of II or IV are the commonest of the nondominant ninths.

EXAMPLE 24–7: Beethoven, *Violin Sonata,*
Op. 30, No. 2, II

Adagio cantabile

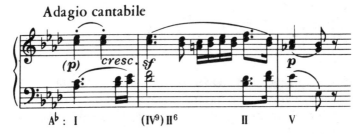

$A\flat$: I   (IV^9) II^6 II   V

In the following sequence, the ninths arise by suspension from
the fifth of the preceding chord, the sevenths from the preceding
third.

EXAMPLE 24–8: Verdi, *Messa da Requiem, Requiem aeternam*

a: II^{7}of III V^9 of III (V^7 of III)III^7 VI^9(IV^9 of III)(VI^7) II^7 V^9 (V^7) I II^7 of V V of V V V

APPOGGIATURE WITH DELAYED RESOLUTION

Sometimes the appoggiatura, or suspension, is delayed in its resolution so that a change of harmony takes place before the melodic
tone is resolved. The nondominant ninth seems under these cir-

cumstances to possess more independence as a chord, although its contrapuntal origin is still apparent.

EXAMPLE 24–9: Beethoven, *Symphony No. 2*, I

Allegro con brio

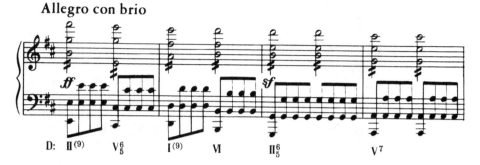

D: $II^{(9)}$ $\qquad$ V^6_5 $\qquad$ $I^{(9)}$ $\qquad$ VI $\qquad$ II^6_5 $\qquad$ V^7

EXAMPLE 24–10: Schumann, *Symphony No. 3* ("Rhenish"), IV

Feierlich

$E\flat$: III   V of IV IV^9 II V^6_5 V of IV   IV $I^6 V^7$ of V IV^6

The following is an unusual example in that all factors of the ninth chord are sounded, so that the effect is that of a true supertonic ninth.

EXAMPLE 24–11: Grieg, *Sonata*, Op. 7, II

Andante molto

C: V of II   II II^9 V^7

THE UNRESOLVED APPOGGIATURA

As a final stage in the evolution of a chord the contrapuntal tone is left unresolved. It is nevertheless essential in the nondominant ninth chord, as well as in the chords of the eleventh and thirteenth,   373 that the character of these higher factors, as contrapuntal tones whose resolution is not sounded but implied, be recognized. The effect is somewhat different from that of the dominant ninth similarly treated, in which case the sense of the harmonic structure in thirds is strongly felt.

In the following example, the ninth is resolved in the accompaniment but this resolution is barely audible by comparison with the melody as orchestrated by the composer. The syncopated chords are given to divided violas while all the violins, both first and second, play the melody.

EXAMPLE 24–12: Schumann, *Symphony No. 2*, III

The ninth in the example below cannot in any sense be said to resolve. Note also that the chord is in the first inversion. Inversions of these chords are not common, the interval of a ninth being ordinarily formed with the bass.

EXAMPLE 24–13: Franck, *Quintet*, I

Part of the charm of the cadence in the following example derives from the uncertainty as to the contrapuntal significance of the double appoggiatura, E and C sharp. It is as though the seventh and ninth of the subdominant were held over from the tonic chord and the group of sixteenth notes were decorated auxiliaries.

374

EXAMPLE 24–14: Mozart, *Piano Concerto*, K. 488, I

The same combination is very frequently arranged rhythmically so that the dominant chord is heard as an appoggiatura chord to the tonic, an effect conveniently described as "five over one."

ELEVENTH AND THIRTEENTH

The effects generally referred to as eleventh and thirteenth chords are brought about by the melodic means of the appoggiatura and the suspension, and also by the use of the pedal. The pedals usually employed are tonic and dominant.

The tonic eleventh effect may be created by a dominant seventh chord superimposed upon a tonic pedal.

EXAMPLE 24–15: Brahms, *Variations*, Op. 21, No. 1, Variation 3

The same combination is very frequently arranged rhythmically so that the dominant chord is heard as an appoggiatura chord to the tonic, an effect conveniently described as "five over one."

See also Exx. 5–27, 8–12, 12–12

EXAMPLE 24–16: Bach, *Partita No. 5:* I, *Preambulum*

EXAMPLE 24–17: Beethoven, *Violin Sonata,*
Op. 30, No. 1, I

It may happen that the tonic part of the above sonority is represented by an actual chord or arpeggio while the dominant chord
is still sounding. We then have all the factors of a tonic eleventh
chord, but there can be no doubt that the upper factors are heard
as contrapuntal tones over a simple triad, rather than as chord
members.

EXAMPLE 24–18: Beethoven, *Sonata,* Op. 2, No. 2, IV

What is commonly referred to as the dominant eleventh is ordinarily the subdominant triad sounding over a dominant pedal.

EXAMPLE 24–19: Brahms, *Sonata,* Op. 5, II

*See also Ex.
25–16*

Or the dominant eleventh may include the fifth, in which case the chord may be considered to include a supertonic-seventh element.

EXAMPLE 24–20: Grieg, *Piano Concerto,* I

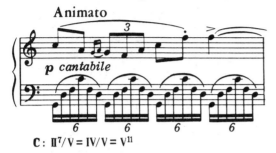

C: II⁷/V = IV/V = V¹¹

In the following example the dominant pedal lies both above and below the subdominant triad.

EXAMPLE 24–21: Brahms, *Intermezzo,* Op. 118, No. 2

A: V   IV/V(V¹¹)   V⁷   I

The eleventh may appear as a nonharmonic tone over the dominant ninth.

EXAMPLE 24–22: Beethoven, *Symphony No. 9,* I

*See also Exx.
8–54, 13–3*

d: V   V of V   II⁴₃   V¹¹   V⁹

Eleventh-chord effects may be found on II, and IV, resulting from appoggiature.

377

EXAMPLE 24–23: Mascagni, *Cavalleria rusticana, Regina coeli*

EXAMPLE 24–24: Liszt, *Sonata*

Ninth and eleventh may both be present in the form of a double appoggiatura.

EXAMPLE 24–25: Beethoven, *Symphony No. 2*, II

EXAMPLE 24–26: Brahms, *Symphony No. 3*, III

Andante espressivo

The thirteenth is as high as it is possible to go in the series of thirds, since the fifteenth would coincide with the double octave. The dominant thirteenth of contrapuntal origin is a fairly common chord effect. It has been pointed out that the third degree, that degree being the thirteenth above the dominant, tends to be absorbed into the dominant harmony when it stands above a dominant bass, as in III^6 and I$^6_4$. It is this third degree which gives rise to the expression "dominant thirteenth," especially when it occurs in combination with a dominant seventh chord (see Example 24–1).

See Ex. 23–31

In the following example the thirteenth appears as an appoggiatura, really a sixth, to the fifth of the chord. (At a slightly more remote level, the thirteenth here is a neighbor note to the C sharp.) A measure and a half later, the minor thirteenth appears and is not resolved, but is unobtrusively incorporated into the secondary tonic which follows.

Cf. Ex. 18–25

EXAMPLE 24–28: Chopin, *Prelude*, Op. 28, No. 13

Lento

The same type of appoggiatura is shown below in its minor form, and over the dominant minor ninth. It is to be noted that in both of these chords the fifth is omitted until supplied by the resolution of the third degree.

EXAMPLE 24–29: Wagner, *Parsifal*, Act I, Scene 1

Schneller (mässig bewegt)

The third degree may enter as escape tone interpolated between the second degree and its destination, the tonic.

EXAMPLE 24–30

Although not strictly speaking an escape tone, the third degree in the example below is of similar effect. The D may also be explained as an anticipation.

EXAMPLE 24–31: Schumann, *Carnaval*, Op. 9, No. 4,
Valse noble

Un poco maestoso

Cf. Ex. 27–15

The unresolved appoggiatura, often the means of suggesting the dominant thirteenth chord, is also clearly understood as a contrapuntal rather than a harmonic factor.

EXAMPLE 24–32: Brahms, *Intermezzo*, Op. 76, No. 4

g: V of V/V   V⁷⁽¹³⁾   I   IV

EXAMPLE 24–33: Chopin, *Polonaise-fantaisie*, Op. 61

B: I V of V/V V⁷⁽¹³⁾   I

If the following example contained a leading-tone in the first three measures the chord would sound as a real thirteenth. Without that factor the separation of subdominant harmony from the dominant bass is quite marked, so that a pedal effect is clearly present, continued from the preceding measures.

EXAMPLE 24–34: Dvořák, *Symphony No. 9*, I

Cf. Ex. 21–18

dom. ped.
G : IV⁷   II⁷   IV⁷   II⁷   IV⁷   II⁷   V⁷   I

The following example is a clearer instance of a true dominant thirteenth, with only the eleventh missing. The thirteenth resolves, somewhat deviously, by downward arpeggiation to the major ninth, which in turn resolves upward. The spacing of the 381 chord is warm and sonorous, comparable to the distribution of natural overtones.

EXAMPLE 24–35: Wagner, *Die Meistersinger*, Act III, Finale

So-called thirteenth chords may be found resulting from the placing of the dominant ninth over the tonic bass as a pedal.

EXAMPLE 24–36: Chopin, *Mazurka*, Op. 24, No. 1

The dominant ninth used thus may be either major or minor and may occur without root.

EXAMPLE 24–37: Bach, *Well-Tempered Clavier*, II, Prelude No. 9

Cf. Ex. 20–15

The dominant ninth may appear as an appoggiatura chord over the tonic root, making a tonic-thirteenth effect.

EXAMPLE 24–38: Mendelssohn, *Song without Words,* Op. 85: No. 5, *The Return*

In the following example the complete tonic thirteenth is formed by a combination of the dominant ninth and the tonic triad. The dominant is represented by four suspensions which subsequently resolve into the tonic harmony.

EXAMPLE 24–39: Brahms, *Intermezzo,* Op. 119, No. 1

Formulae, to be played in all keys:

EXAMPLE 24–40

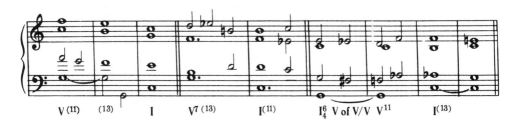

1. Work out the following figured basses:

2. Construct original examples of the following harmonic effects, showing their introduction and resolution:

    a. II⁹ in G major, without seventh;

    b. IV⁹ in E-flat minor, with fifth and seventh;

    c. I⁹ in A major, resulting from an appoggiatura with delayed resolution;

d. IV⁹ in F minor, the ninth an unresolved appoggiatura;

e. An inner dominant pedal;

f. A tonic eleventh chord;

g. A subdominant eleventh chord made by a double appoggiatura;

h. A dominant thirteenth chord in which the thirteenth is an unresolved appoggiatura.

3. Harmonize the following unfigured basses, using some chords of the ninth, eleventh, and thirteenth:

a.

b.

c.

d. Largo

4. Harmonize the following melodies, introducing effects of chords of the ninth, eleventh, and thirteenth:

a.

CHAPTER 25

Chromatically Altered Chords:
The Raised Supertonic
and Submediant

In a literal sense an altered chord is any chord affected by an accidental, signifying that one of its tones is changed from its original form as established by the key signature. There are three sources of these accidentals or chromatic alterations.

The first reason for the use of an accidental may be said to arise from the deficiency of our system of key signatures, inasmuch as the signatures do not permit the interchangeability of the modes as practiced by composers. Hence it is hardly necessary to speak of a chromatic alteration when a sharp, flat, or natural is used to indicate a normal scale degree. For example, we shall not apply the term *altered chords* to the following:

EXAMPLE 25–1

c: III VI⁷ VI⁷ V₉°

In the second category of chords affected by accidental signs are all the secondary dominants. These chords are not really altered chords. The process of deriving a secondary dominant chord is not that of altering a chord in the scale of the main key, but rather of adopting a temporary tonality in which the second-   387 ary dominant exists as a normal, unaltered chord. Some theorists use the expression *borrowed chords* for the secondary dominants. This category accounts for the greater part of the accidentals seen in music, except perhaps for actual modulations when the key signature has not been changed.

Keeping to the vocabulary of chords in the common practice of composers, there remains the group of chords which have chromatic signs not derived from the above sources. The important members of this group are the raised supertonic and the raised submediant, the Neapolitan sixth, the chords of the augmented sixth, and the chords with altered fifth.

II⁷ AND VI⁷ WITH RAISED ROOT AND THIRD

The seventh chords on supertonic and submediant, derived from the major mode, and having root and third chromatically raised, are nondominant diminished seventh chords. It was pointed out in Chapter 20 that the identity of a diminished seventh chord is determined by its resolution. These two chords resolve to I and V⁷ respectively. It will be noted that ⁺VI⁷ has the same

EXAMPLE 25–2

$$^+\text{II}^7 \quad \text{I}^6 \quad ^+\text{II}^6_5 \quad \text{I}^6_4 \quad ^+\text{II}^4_3 \quad \text{I}^6_4 \quad ^+\text{II}^2 \quad \text{I} \qquad ^+\text{VI}^7 \quad \text{V}^6_5 \quad ^+\text{VI}^6_5 \quad \text{V}^4_3 \quad ^+\text{VI}^4_3 \quad \text{V}^2 \quad ^+\text{VI}^2 \quad \text{V}^7$$

relationship to V as ⁺II⁷ does to I, the voice leading being different in only one factor. If the fifth of the ⁺VI⁷ were to resolve downward, doubling the fifth of V and omitting the seventh, it would be more accurate to describe the progression as ⁺II⁷ of V going to V. In resolving to V⁷ the raised submediant strengthens the tonality by making the dominant harmony more certain.

The resolutions illustrate the principle that a chromatically altered tone receives a tendency to continue movement in the direction of its alteration. Both chords contain raised tones whose tendency is upward. They are like leading-tones or appoggiature. (Sometimes these chords are called appoggiatura chords, but this name is inaccurate since the harmonic rhythm of the resolution is often weak-to-strong.) The root being thus altered does not seem like a harmonic root, but more like a melodic tendency tone. Thus the names ⁺II and ⁺VI are really more a matter of convenience than an accurate designation for independent super-

388

tonic and submediant harmony. These chords are like V_9^0, or II^7 and VI^7 (ascending) in the minor mode, in that the lowest factor of a diminished-triad component is not heard as a true root.

For use in root analysis, we shall here adopt plus and minus signs to indicate chord factors which have been chromatically raised or lowered. A plus sign placed at the upper left of the Roman numeral indicates that the root is raised. Thus $^+II^7$ and $^+VI^7$ will be sufficient to designate the chords discussed in this chapter, the third being understood as also raised.

NOTATION

Composers have shown indifference to the grammatical notation of these diminished seventh chords, not only in writing for keyboard instruments but also in music for strings or wind instruments. The raised second degree is often written as minor third degree and the raised sixth as lowered seventh degree.

EXAMPLE 25–3

$^+II_5^6 (E^\flat = D^\sharp) \quad I_4^6 \qquad ^+VI^7 (B^\flat = A^\sharp) \quad V_5^6$

As written, V of V appears in place of $^+II^7$ and V of II for $^+VI^7$. The resolutions show both to be incorrect.

EXAMPLE 25–4: Bach, *Well-Tempered Clavier, I*, Prelude No. 3

$C^\sharp:\quad I_4^6 \qquad\qquad ^+II^2 (E^\natural = D^\times) \quad I_4^6 \quad V^7 \quad I$

EXAMPLE 25–5: Beethoven, *Symphony No. 2*, II

Larghetto

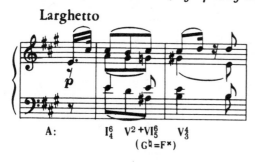

$A:\qquad I_4^6 \quad V^2 + VI_5^6 \qquad V_3^4$
$\qquad\qquad\qquad (G^\natural = F^\times)$

Music is fortunately a matter of sound rather than symbols, and there is no doubt that the second violins in the Beethoven example instinctively give the G natural its proper meaning, that of an F double-sharp.

The problem is more difficult in the example below.

EXAMPLE 25–6: Schubert, *String Quintet,* Op. 163, I

A comparable problem in Ex. 12–4

Here the viola part is obviously incorrectly written E flat, for D sharp. But the melodic outline of the first violin part would be strange, indeed, if D sharp were substituted for E flat. A compromise must be effected in performance between the harmonic and the contrapuntal, a compromise that is continually necessary in music of chromatic style and especially where enharmonic changes operate.

RHYTHM

When the chord and its resolution are in the rhythmic relation of strong-to-weak, the chord has the character of an appoggiatura chord, or three appoggiature over a single harmonic root.

EXAMPLE 25–7: Tchaikovsky, *The Nutcracker:*
Waltz of the Flowers

EXAMPLE 25–8: Chopin, *Impromptu*, Op. 36

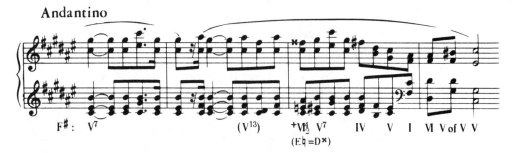

Andantino

F♯: V⁷   (V¹³)   ⁺VI⁴₃ V⁷   IV   V   I   VI V of V   V
(E♮=D×)

The voices may move as auxiliary tones, making an auxiliary chord of weak rhythmic value.

EXAMPLE 25–9: Rossini, Overture to *William Tell*

Andante

See also Ex. 8–17

G: I   ⁺II²   I

When the altered tones enter as chromatic passing tones the chord is a passing chord.

See also Ex. 24–23

EXAMPLE 25–10: Weber, Overture to *Oberon*

Adagio sostenuto

D: II⁶₅ ⁺II⁶₅   I⁶₄ IV⁶   V of V   I⁶₄   V

EXAMPLE 25–11: Chopin, *Valse brillante,* Op. 34, No. 1

Vivace

A : V⁹   ⁺VI⁶₅ V⁴₃

These chords may also serve as independent chords of equal rhythmic value with the surrounding harmony. $^{+}$VI^{7} is a useful chord for introducing the dominant half cadence to emphasize the key, and $^{+}$II^{7} often appears prominently before the cadential six-four chord.

EXAMPLE 25–12: Brahms, *Intermezzo,* Op. 119, No. 3

C: V_9° of VI   IV$_5^6$ $^+$VI^7 V$_5^6$ (II^6)   V^7 I

EXAMPLE 25–13: Mozart, *Concerto for Two Pianos,* K. 365, III

E$^\flat$: IV $^+$II$_5^6$ (G$^\flat$ = F$^\sharp$)   I$_4^6$

EXAMPLE 25–14: Beethoven, *Sonata,* Op. 10, No. 2, II

D$^\flat$: $^+$II$_5^6$ I$_4^6$ V^7 I

CROSS-RELATION

The two altered tones of either chord are sometimes found in a melodic group of double thirds or sixths forming a double reaching tone. In this case the resulting cross-relations are not avoided. The altered tones may be first or second in the group.

392

EXAMPLE 25–15

RAISED II
AND VI

The above progressions contain not only the cross-relation, but also the unusual melodic interval of the diminished third, F to D sharp and C to A sharp. In the example below there are two cross-relations, A flat to A natural and F natural to F sharp. The melodic diminished third, A flat to F sharp, is accompanied in the top voice by the interval of a diminished fourth, D flat to A natural. It is the reaching-tone quality of the altered tones that makes this acceptable.

EXAMPLE 25–16: Wagner, *Die Meistersinger*, Act II, Scene 4

Sehr mässig

MODE

The raised supertonic and submediant chords are more suggestive of the major mode than of the minor. $^+$VI^7 contains the major third degree and $^+$II^7 implies it by the raised second degree. Both chords may, however, be employed in the minor mode. If the resolution of $^+$II^7 is treated not as tonic, but as V of IV, there is no difficulty in continuing in minor. The following example shows $^+$VI^7 used in surroundings predominantly minor.

EXAMPLE 25–17: Haydn, *String Quartet*, Op. 76, No. 4, I

Allegro con spirito

393

Irregular resolution of diminished seventh chords in the harmonic sense of progression to an irregular root is rare. Variations in the form of the chord of resolution can be employed, however, without destroying the identity of the diminished seventh.

In the resolution of II⁷ raised, V of IV may be used, either as a dominant seventh chord or as an incomplete ninth, usually minor. The second case results in diminished seventh chords moving parallel.

EXAMPLE 25–18

EXAMPLE 25–19: Beethoven, *Symphony No. 3* ("Eroica"), III

Allegro vivace

The submediant chord may also resolve to an incomplete ninth.

EXAMPLE 25–20: Bach, *Well-Tempered Clavier, I,*
                Prelude No. 8

The following example of apparent irregular resolution is comparable, in its enharmonic notation of the doubled root, to the Schubert example above (Example 25–6). Note the effect of color produced by the combination of raised II⁷ with an appoggiatura.

394

EXAMPLE 25–21: Schumann, *Symphony No. 2*, III

MODULATION

The use of the diminished seventh chord in a nondominant function adds greatly to the already numerous resources of that chord as a pivot chord in modulation. The modulation in which a dominant becomes a nondominant is especially effective and somewhat unexpected. For instance, if the incomplete dominant minor ninth of C is left as II⁷ raised, the new key will be A-flat major. If it is left as ⁺VI⁷ the distant key of D flat will be introduced.

See also Ex. 19–19

EXAMPLE 25–22

If it is desired that the pivot chord be ⁺VI⁷ or ⁺II⁷ in the first key, there are two problems. Since the identity of these chords depends upon their resolution, it is necessary that their function in the first key be made clear before the point of modulation. The best method of securing this clarity is to present the chord with its resolution in the first key, using it as a pivot chord only after its identity has been thus established to the hearer. The second problem is to avoid weakening the modulation by allowing the pivot chord to be the dominant of the second key. This can be arranged by using a secondary dominant.

395

Both of these procedures are seen in the following example:

EXAMPLE 25–23: Beethoven, *Symphony No. 7*, II

The pivot may be a nondominant diminished seventh chord in both keys. In the following example analysis reveals it to be based on the same degree in both tonalities, but with enharmonic change.

EXAMPLE 25–24: Franck, *String Quartet*, I

The following example, from the coda of the finale of Schubert's *Ninth Symphony*, shows both the raised II⁷ and VI⁷ used in a modulating sequence. It is given here in reduced form because the tempo is very fast and each harmony stretches over four measures; the entire sequence, with some deviations from the pattern, lasts for eighty measures, or twenty measures per unit, modulating from D minor to C major.

EXAMPLE 25–25: Schubert, *Symphony No. 9*, IV (reduction)

Formulae, to be played in all keys:

EXAMPLE 25-26

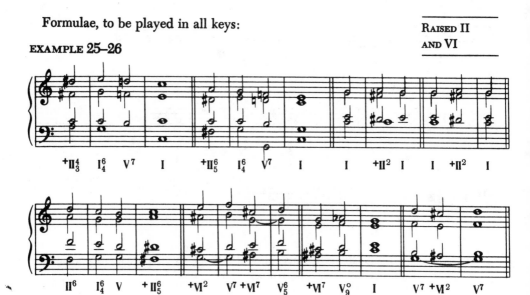

+II$_3^4$ I$_4^6$ V^7 I   +II$_5^6$ I$_4^6$ V^7 I   I +II^2 I   I +II^2 I

II^6 I$_4^6$ V +II$_5^6$ +VI^2 V^7 +VI^7 V$_5^6$ +VI^7 V$_9^o$ I   V^7 +VI^2 V^7

EXERCISES

1. Work out the following figured basses:

a.

6 7 6 6̷ 6 6 7
   #   5 4 4̸

b.

6# 6 6× 6 2 6 6 7
4× 4 5 4   #
3   3

c.

6 7 7 7 7♭ 6 6 6♮ 6 7♭
4̷   ♮   5 4 5♭

d.

6 3 6 7 6 7♮ 4̷ 6 7♮
4̸   #   2

397

2. Construct a musical sentence of three phrases according to the following specifications:

    a. The first phrase shows a diminished seventh chord used first as V of V, then as +II⁷ (with enharmonic change).

    b. The second phrase modulates by means of a pivot chord which becomes +VI⁷ in the second key.

    c. The third phrase returns to the original key by a pivot chord which is +II⁷ in the final key.

3. Construct a modulating sequence, the pattern of which contains the chord +VI⁷.

4. Harmonize the following unfigured basses, introducing chords of the raised supertonic and submediant:

e. **Andante**

5. Harmonize the following melodies, introducing chords of the raised supertonic and submediant:

CHAPTER 26

The Neapolitan Sixth

DEFINITION, RESOLUTION, PREPARATION, AND DOUBLING

The major triad having for its root the chromatically lowered second degree of the scale is known everywhere as the *Neapolitan sixth*. It is difficult to say wherein this chord is "Neapolitan," but the fact is that the name is of universal acceptance. In the earlier part of the period it was usually found in first inversion, hence the term *sixth*. Later, however, the term *Neapolitan sixth* was applied to any arrangement of the triad, even root position.

Far from wishing to discard a definition so securely established by usage, we shall welcome the convenience of the identifying label attached to this chord. In this way we may be permitted the unscientific but quite understandable expression, "the Neapolitan sixth in root position," and the occasional use of the commonly accepted symbol N. If the Roman numeral II is used instead of N for the Neapolitan, it should be preceded by a small minus sign at the upper left, indicating chromatic lowering of the root.

The Neapolitan sixth is a major triad and is, therefore, not a dissonant chord. However, the chromatic alteration of the second degree gives that tone a downward tendency so that when it proceeds upward there is a feeling of irregularity of movement, if not of irregular resolution.

Although derived from the minor scale, the Neapolitan sixth is freely used in either major or minor mode. It is a chord of strongly subdominant character, progressing most frequently to some form of the dominant chord.

EXAMPLE 26–1

Note that the bass is the best tone to double, as it is a tonal degree. The altered second degree is normally not doubled in the first inversion, but this is a rule less strictly followed in the case of the Neapolitan sixth than with any other chromatically altered chord.

The progressions shown in the example contain the cross-relation between D flat and D natural. It cannot be said that this cross-relation is avoided by composers, although there are many arrangements of the progression to V without it, as will be shown. The cross-relation may be seen in Examples 26–3, 26–5, 26–7, and others.

In any resolution to V, the preferred voice leading of the altered second degree is downward by a skip of a diminished third. Examples such as *d* and *e* above, where the altered tone moves contrary to the direction of alteration, are less often found (Example 26–4).

When the dominant chord contains a seventh, its fifth will very likely be omitted so that no cross-relation will occur.

EXAMPLE 26–2: Beethoven, *Sonata quasi una fantasia,*
　　　　　　　Op. 27, No. 2, I

Adagio sostenuto

401

The bass may remain in place as the harmony changes, making the third inversion of V⁷.

EXAMPLE 26–3: Bach, *Orchestral Suite No. 2:* VII, *Badinerie*

Allegro

*See also Ex.
26–21*

b: ⁻II⁶   V²

If the sixth degree, fifth of the chord, is continued into the next harmony, a ninth chord will result.

EXAMPLE 26–4: Beethoven, *Sonata,* Op. 90, I

Mit Lebhaftigkeit

e: I   IV   ⁻II⁶   V⁹

The dominant ninth chord may be in its incomplete form, without root, most often as a diminished seventh chord. Unless the lowered second degree progresses upward, contrary to its tendency, the cross-relation will occur in this case.

EXAMPLE 26–5: Mozart, *String Quartet,* K. 421, IV

Allegro ma non troppo

d: ⁻II⁶   V⁰₉   I   II⁶   I⁶₄   V⁷

Very often the dominant chord will first be represented by the cadential tonic six-four chord, the sixth and fourth as double appoggiatura. This allows a smooth stepwise progression in all voices, the three upper parts moving in contrary motion to the bass. The root succession is, of course, still II to V. The cross-relation is not noticeable because of the intervening harmonic effect of I.

EXAMPLE 26–6: Mozart, *Piano Concerto*, K. 488, II

Adagio

f♯: I   VI   ⁻II⁶⁴   I⁶₄   V⁷   I

Other chords are sometimes interpolated between the Neapolitan sixth and the dominant. These are for the most part different forms of supertonic harmony. The problems of voice leading vary with the form chosen. If the chord is dominant of the
dominant, there will be several chromatic progressions in the
voices. Note, in the example below, that the cross-relation between
the two forms of the second degree is permitted so that the lowered tone G natural may descend according to its tendency. The
other two chromatic progressions are effected each in a single
voice.

See also Ex. 28–30

EXAMPLE 26–7: Schumann, *String Quartet*, Op. 41, No. 3, II

Un poco adagio

p

f♯: ⁻II⁶   V⁶₅ of V   V⁷   I

These problems of voice leading are sometimes obscured by the
texture of instrumental writing, especially in music for keyboard
instruments. In the following the altered second degree appears to
be doubled and it is questionable whether the ear will follow
the upward or the downward progression of that tone.

EXAMPLE 26–8: Mozart, *Fantasy*, K. 397

Andante

3   3   3   3

3   3   3   3

d: ⁻II⁶   V of V   V

403

The following excerpt is clearer as to the melodic progression of the parts, and it is evident that the lowered second degree moves upward. Doubling of the tone A, the sixth degree, avoids the cross-relation by allowing the progression A to A sharp to be made in one voice. In the first measure it is to be remarked that the melodic figuration over the Neapolitan sixth harmony takes the form of the scale of the temporary tonality of the lowered degree, here D major.

EXAMPLE 26–9: Beethoven, *Sonata quasi una fantasia,* Op. 27, No. 2, III

The altered tone may appear as appoggiatura to the tone below. The fundamental harmony will then be subdominant, although the peculiar color of the Neapolitan sixth should be recognized harmonically. It is also reasonable to consider the tonic as a passing tone, as in the following example:

EXAMPLE 26–10: Mozart, *String Quintet,* K. 515, I

The above example shows the adaptability and coloristic effect of this chord employed in a passage which is prevailing in the major mode.

The harmonic rhythm of the following cadential passage gives unusual prominence to the Neapolitan six-four.

EXAMPLE 26–11: Weber, Overture to *Der Freischütz*

The use of the Neapolitan sixth is not limited to cadential formulae. It may be found in any part of the phrase, and may even begin the piece.

EXAMPLE 26–12: Chopin, *Ballade*, Op. 23

In its subdominant capacity it progresses occasionally to I or V of IV.

EXAMPLE 26–13: Handel, *Concerto Grosso*, Op. 6, No. 5, IV

See also Ex. 12–28

EXAMPLE 26–14: Beethoven, *Trio*, Op. 1, No. 3, I

The Neapolitan sixth may be used as subdominant harmony in a plagal cadence, followed by either major or minor tonic harmony.

EXAMPLE 26–15: Brahms, *String Quartet*, Op. 51, No. 1, I

405

Another example by Brahms shows the chord in combination with the tonic note, making a seventh chord.

EXAMPLE 26–16: Brahms, *Symphony No. 4*, II

Andante moderato

E: VI   I   ˉII²   I

*Note Phrygian
relationship
(cf. Ex. 5–3)*

In the nineteenth century the Neapolitan sixth chord was employed with increasing frequency as a triad in root position. This gave the chord much more independence and stability, the lowered second degree being treated in this case not as a melodic tendency tone, but as a true harmonic root and so doubled. The doubled root and the augmented fourth relationship to the dominant help to emphasize the remoteness of this harmony from the main tonal center.

EXAMPLE 26–17: Brahms, *Violin Sonata,*
Op. 108, IV

Presto agitato

(piano
only) *f*

d: V of IV   IV   ˉII   I$^6_4$ V

SECONDARY RELATIONSHIPS

Cf. Ex. 20–34

In the example below by Chopin, the root-position D-flat major triad in the second measure is clearly IV of VI, the two measures being sequentially related. At the end of the piece, however, the identical triad is in Neapolitan relationship to C minor.

406

EXAMPLE 26–18: Chopin, *Prelude,* Op. 28, No. 20

c: I   IV⁷ V⁷ I   VI IV of VI V⁷of VI VI   VI ⁻II V⁷ I

The above secondary-subdominant relationship accounts for the occasional appearance of what could also be interpreted as the minor Neapolitan.

EXAMPLE 26–19: Schubert, Overture to *Fierrabras*

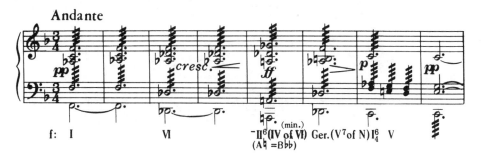

f: I   VI   ⁻II⁶(IV of VI) Ger.(V⁷of N)I⁶₄ V
                               (A♮ =B♭♭)

V OF N⁶

The Neapolitan sixth may be preceded by its dominant, thus adding another to the list of secondary dominants available in one tonality.

EXAMPLE 26–20: Mozart, *Clarinet Quintet,* K. 581, III

a:⁻II⁶ V²of N ⁻II⁶   I⁶₄   V⁷   I   407

EXAMPLE 26–21: Schubert, *Symphony No. 9*, II

Andante con moto

pp

a: V² of N   ⁻II⁶   V²   i⁶   ⁻II⁶   I⁶₄   V

See also Exx.
11–33, 30–17

The independence of the root position chord is greatly strengthened by the presence of the secondary dominant, V of N⁶. It is plain, however, that the two chords constitute an extension of the bounds of the main tonality rather than a weakening of it.

EXAMPLE 26–22: Chopin, *Mazurka*, Op. 7, No. 2

Vivo

p

a: V⁷ of N   ⁻II   V   I

INTERMEDIATE MODULATION

The Neapolitan sixth chord is often felt to be of sufficient tonal strength to cause a momentary shift to its root as a tonal center. This may be due simply to the length of time it occupies.

EXAMPLE 26–23: Chopin, *Prelude*, Op. 28, No. 6

Lento assai

p

b: I   VI (V of N)   ⁻II (or I in C)

V   I

Or it may be because of the attendant harmonies. In the following example the last chord in the first measure is the raised
supertonic in the key of G, followed by the tonic six-four. The
use of the subdominant of G confirms this impression, but we know
that the G-natural triad is but the Neapolitan sixth chord of the key
of F sharp.

EXAMPLE 26–24: Beethoven, *Sonata*, Op. 106
              ("Hammerklavier"), III

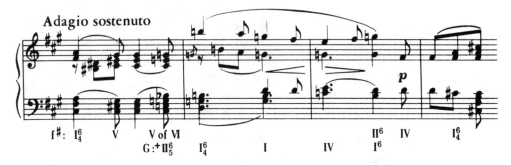

The intermediate modulation may be analyzed without invok-
ing the symbols of an actual modulation; the chords foreign to
the tonality may be referred to a secondary tonic, such as the
Neapolitan in the following example. Enharmonic equivalents are
frequently employed, as here, so as to avoid notating such triads as
B-double-flat major.

EXAMPLE 26–25: Chopin, *Etude*, Op. 10, No. 6

MODULATION WITH THE NEAPOLITAN

Cf. Ex. 5–26

The Neapolitan sixth is a useful pivot chord in modulation. As a
simple major triad it is capable of many interpretations. It is common ground between distantly related keys, as in the following
modulation from F to E.

EXAMPLE 26–26: Beethoven, *Sonata*, Op.14, No. 1, III

See also Ex.
19–18

Such modulations as the above, to keys a semitone distant, are often accomplished with the aid of the augmented sixth chord, the enharmonic equivalent of the dominant of the Neapolitan; augmented sixth chords are discussed in the next chapter.

The Neapolitan six-five appears as a pivot chord in the dramatic and dissonant climax of the following well-known passage:

EXAMPLE 26–27: Beethoven, *Symphony No. 3* ("Eroica"), I

Formulae, to be played in all keys:

EXAMPLE 26–28

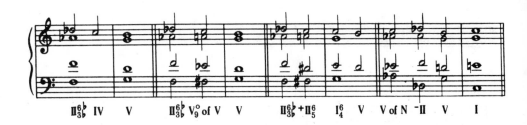

$$\text{II}_3^6\flat \quad \text{IV} \quad \text{V} \qquad \text{II}_3^6\flat \quad \text{V}_9^\circ \text{ of V} \quad \text{V} \qquad \text{II}_3^6\flat + \text{II}_5^6 \quad \text{I}_4^6 \quad \text{V} \quad \text{V of N} \quad {}^-\text{II} \quad \text{V} \quad \text{I}$$

EXERCISES

1. Work out the following figured basses:

a.

2. Construct a modulating sequence in which the pivot chord is the Neapolitan sixth in the second key.

3. Explain the relationship of the Neapolitan sixth chord of the key of G to the tonalities A, F, E, F sharp, and B flat.

4. Show the progression of the Neapolitan sixth to five different chords in the key of D flat.

5. Harmonize the following unfigured basses, introducing Neapolitan sixth chords:

a.

b.

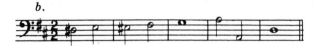

c.

d.

e. **Andantino**

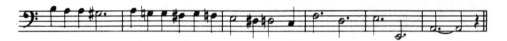

6. Harmonize the following melodies, introducing Neapolitan sixth chords:

a.

b.

c.

CHAPTER 27

Augmented Sixth Chords

The four chords comprising the group known as *augmented sixth chords* have in common the interval of the augmented sixth created by the minor sixth degree and the chromatically raised fourth degree. The name *augmented sixth chord* derives from the commonest arrangement of the chords, in which this characteristic interval is found between the bass and an upper voice; but, as in the case of the Neapolitan sixth, it is often applied to other positions.

ORIGIN AS SECONDARY DOMINANTS

The raised fourth degree, as leading-tone to the dominant, is the clue to the secondary-dominant function of three of the four augmented sixth chords. The interval of the augmented sixth expands in its normal resolution to an octave which is the octave on the dominant. This principle of tonality inherent in the aug-

EXAMPLE 27–1

V

414

mented sixth chords is important to an understanding of their use by composers of the common-practice period. Only exceptionally is the octave of resolution anything other than the dominant. The augmented sixth interval does not come from a subdominant with raised root, but from a dominant with lowered fifth. The following example shows its contrapuntal origin.

EXAMPLE 27–2

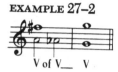

V of V__ V

DEFINITIONS

The normal position of all four augmented sixth chords is that with the minor sixth degree in the bass and the raised fourth degree in any upper voice. Another voice is always the tonic, making three voices common to all four chords. Each member of the group will then be distinguished by the fourth voice. The four augmented sixth chords are shown below with their regular resolutions.

EXAMPLE 27–3

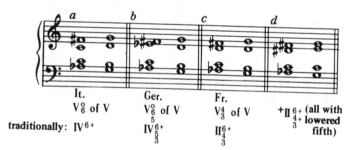

a is called the *augmented sixth;*
b is called the *augmented six-five-three;*
c is called the *augmented six-four-three;*
d is called the *doubly augmented fourth.*

The names *Italian sixth* (*a*), *German sixth* (*b*), and *French sixth* (*c*) have won wide, if not universal, acceptance over the years. As in the case of the Neapolitan sixth, there seems to be no good explanation for the origin of these names.

Many harmony texts, including earlier editions of this book, have customarily described *a* and *b* above as chords having the raised fourth degree as root, and *c* as an altered supertonic seventh. The difficulty with the traditional labeling of *a* and *b* as 415

IV is that the presumptive underlying triad is diminished and therefore not easily heard as a true subdominant. It is probably more accurate, then, to think of a above as a type of VII^6 (V_6^0) of V, that is, an incomplete V^7 of V with lowered fifth. The actual root of the chord would then be D, as in the complete form, c in the example above. As for b, it may be considered an altered diminished seventh chord, V_9^0 of V with lowered fifth. If c, traditionally called II_4^6, is interpreted in a similar manner it is seen to be V^7 of V with lowered fifth. Thus all three chords a, b, and c have a family resemblance as various types of V of V, as their usual resolutions imply.

Because the exact labelings "V_6^0 of V with lowered fifth," "$V_5^{0\,6}$ of V with lowered fifth," and "V_3^4 of V with lowered fifth" are somewhat cumbersome, it is more practical to use "It.," "Ger.," and "Fr." respectively, regardless of inversion; the national abbreviations are readily understood as indicating augmented sixth chords, and there is no danger of confusing the roman-numeral labels with those of unaltered forms of V of V.

The doubly augmented fourth (d above) has no special national name, but is readily seen to be the result of chromatically lowering the fifth of the raised supertonic seventh.

Note that b is like a with minor seventh added; d sounds like b, but the difference between E flat and D sharp becomes clear on the resolution of the chord; c is distinguished from b by the presence of the second degree in place of the minor third degree; a, b, and d sound like dominant sevenths of the Neapolitan, which property makes them useful as pivot chords in modulation.

RESOLUTION

The regular resolution of the augmented sixth chords is to V or, in the case of the doubly augmented fourth, to major I_4^6. The raised fourth degree moves up a half step, the minor sixth degree moves down a half step, and the tonic either moves down directly to the leading-tone or remains in place as a suspension or appoggiatura before descending.

The fourth voice will, of course, vary in movement according to its identity. In a, the plain augmented sixth chord, since there are but three factors the tonic will be doubled. It is not customary to double either of the tones making the interval of the augmented sixth. The fourth voice usually moves up by step.

EXAMPLE 27–4

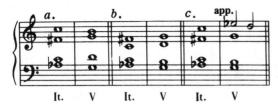

AUGMENTED
SIXTHS

*See also Exx.
16–17, 16–19,
19–11*

The fourth voice is free to move up by the interval of a fifth to the dominant, often a desirable melodic skip when in the upper voice.

EXAMPLE 27–5: Beethoven, *Symphony No. 5*, I

In the augmented six-five-three (*b*) the fourth voice forms with the bass an interval of a perfect fifth. The parallel fifths arising from the natural progression to the dominant are practiced except when occurring between soprano and bass. They are most often seen between tenor and bass. The third degree is, however, more frequently tied over as a suspension, or repeated as an appoggiatura, before continuing down to the second degree.

The augmented six-five-three is strongly indicative of the minor mode, since it contains both minor third and minor sixth degrees.

EXAMPLE 27–6

Cf. Ex. 11–27

EXAMPLE 27–7: Mozart, *Sonata*, K. 332, I

The parallel fifths are more noticeable in the following example:

EXAMPLE 27–8: Franck, *Symphony*, I

d: V⁷ of V   Ger.   V⁷

*See also commen-
tary to Ex. 17–19*
This form of secondary-dominant harmony is very common preceding the cadential six-four chord. Its tonal clarity is especially useful after a modulation.

EXAMPLE 27–9: Mozart, Overture to *Don Giovanni*, K. 527

d: IV⁶   Ger.   I⁶₄   V

EXAMPLE 27–10: Brahms, *Intermezzo*, Op. 117, No. 2

f: Ger.   I⁶₄   V⁹

The augmented six-four-three is the most obviously secondarily dominant in function of the augmented sixth chords. The presence of the actual root, the second degree, affords a common tone between this chord and the dominant chord, so that factor will usually be repeated or tied over in the chord of resolution, although it may progress to an appoggiatura of the second degree, as in a cadential six-four chord.

418

EXAMPLE 27–11

See also Exx.
6–31, 12–10

EXAMPLE 27–12: Schubert, *String Quartet*, Op.125, No. 1, IV

The augmented six-four-three is employed in connection with chords characteristic of the major mode as well as those of the minor, contributing to the impression of interchangeability of the two modes.

EXAMPLE 27–13: Chopin, *Nocturne*, Op. 48, No. 2

In the chord of the doubly augmented fourth (*d*) the distinguishing factor is the raised second degree, implying a resolution to the major third degree. This interval of the doubly augmented fourth, formed between the minor sixth degree bass and the raised second degree, is enharmonically identical with the perfect fifth. The chord can be told from the augmented six-five-three only upon its resolution.

See also Ex.
13–11

EXAMPLE 27–14

419

EXAMPLE 27–15: Chopin, *Ballade*, Op. 47

Allegretto

A♭: VI   +II⁶⁵₄₃ I⁶₄ V⁷

Composers frequently write the doubly augmented fourth incorrectly as an augmented six-five-three. It will be recalled that the same indifference as to the notation of the raised second degree was observed in the supertonic seventh chord with raised root and third. The two chords are closely related, differing only in the form of the sixth degree.

EXAMPLE 27–16: Haydn, *String Quartet*, Op. 64, No. 5, II

Adagio, cantabile

A: IV   I⁶₄   +II⁶₄₃   I⁶₄   V⁷   I

When the augmented sixth is followed by a dominant seventh chord, the raised fourth degree descends chromatically, somewhat in the manner of the irregular resolution of a leading-tone. If the augmented six-five-three is used, the progression sounds like a succession of dominant seventh chords and is often so written, though incorrectly. The steps in the evolution of this progression might be outlined as follows:

EXAMPLE 27–17

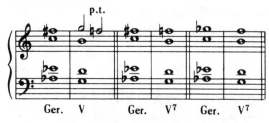

Ger.   V   Ger.   V⁷   Ger.   V⁷

In the following example, the parallel motion is interrupted by the appoggiatura in the upper voice.

EXAMPLE 27–18: Beethoven, *Sonata,* Op. 57
("Appassionata"), II

Andante con moto

D♭: I   IV   I   Ger.   V⁷⁽¹¹⁾   I

Coloristic possibilities of the augmented sixth combined with chromatic nonharmonic tones are suggested in the following well-known quotation.

EXAMPLE 27–19: Wagner, Prelude to *Tristan und Isolde*

Langsam und schmachtend

a: I   (VI)   Fr.   V

Cf. Ex. 23–41

The appoggiatura forming the interval of a diminished octave with the raised fourth degree is of fairly frequent occurrence.

EXAMPLE 27–20: Mozart, *Sonata,* K. 576, II

Adagio

f♯: I   VI⁷   Ger.   V

INVERSIONS

Dispositions of the factors of these chords with other than the sixth degree in the bass does not seem to destroy their identity as chords of the augmented sixth, even though the characteristic interval is found between less prominent voices, or inverted to   421 become a diminished third. This accounts for such expressions as "the augmented six-five-three in the six-four-three position," meaning that the chord normally found making the intervals six, five, and three has been rearranged so that it makes the intervals six, four, and three.

When the raised fourth degree is in the bass the resultant interval of a diminished third resolves with no less emphasis to the octave of the dominant. The diminished third is usually found as its compound interval, the diminished tenth; it less often appears as a simple diminished third in contiguous voices, with resolution to a unison.

EXAMPLE 27–21: Brahms, *Waltz*, Op. 39, No. 7

EXAMPLE 27–22: Bach, *Mass in B minor*, Credo: *Crucifixus*

In the above examples, the position of the chord is a natural consequence of the melodic progression of the two outside voices in contrary motion chromatically. The melodic movement of the bass is usually the reason for a choice of some factor other than the sixth degree as a bass note.

A static bass on the tonic or third degree may hold through an augmented sixth appearing above as double neighbor or double

appoggiatura.

EXAMPLE 27–23: Brahms, *Violin Concerto*, Op. 77, I

Allegro non troppo

a: I   Ger. I⁶ I   Ger.   I⁶

As a dissonant chord over a dominant pedal the augmented sixth
is strikingly effective.

EXAMPLE 27–24: Chopin, *Scherzo*, Op. 20

Presto con fuoco

b: Ger./V

Like the Neapolitan sixth, the augmented sixths may be found.
anywhere in the phrase, even at the beginning of the piece.

EXAMPLE 27–25: Schumann, *Dichterliebe*, Op. 48: No. 12,
Am leuchtenden Sommermorgen

Ziemlich langsam

B♭:   II⁶⁺₄₊₃   I⁶₄   V⁷

IRREGULAR RESOLUTION

Harmonically, the augmented sixth chords have few irregular resolutions. Smooth progressions to tonic harmony, as in Examples 27–
6b, 27–9, 27–10, and 27–11c, are strong and easily understood,   423

and cannot really be called irregular. Most of the irregularities encountered with resolutions of these chords will be those of voice leading. With the sixth degree in the bass, the progression to I in root position, the augmented sixth interval resolving in a direct fifth, was rarely used until late in the period, when it is recognized as a characteristic feature of the harmonic style of César Franck.

EXAMPLE 27–26: Franck, *Violin Sonata*, I

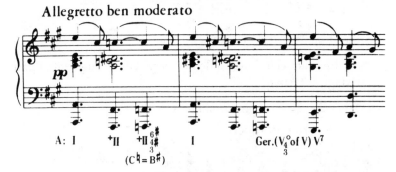

Many irregularities in voice leading are possible in the regular root progression to V, because of the variety of forms of dominant harmony and the added resources of nonharmonic tones (see Example 27–19). In the following example the doubly augmented fourth leads to an effect of dominant thirteenth.

EXAMPLE 27–27: Schumann, *Symphonic Etudes*, Op. 13

The irregular resolution in the fourth measure of the following example is merely a change of harmonic color, from the augmented six-five-three (which, let us remember, is a $V_{6\atop5}^{0}$ of V with lowered fifth) to the unaltered V^7 of V. The appoggiatura ninth, G flat, resolves downward to the root; the lowered fifth, B (enharmonically C flat), rises to the unaltered fifth; the tonic note and raised fourth degree remain where they are, as seventh and third respectively of V of V.

EXAMPLE 27–28: Brahms, *Schicksalslied*, Op. 54

E^b: V^2 of IV IV^6 V^7 of VII VII$^6_4$ V^7 of VII V^6 of V $+$II$^6_5$ I$^6_4$ Ger. V^7 of V V   I

MODULATION

As a pivot chord in modulation the augmented sixth is most often employed for the advantage of its enharmonic similarity to a dominant seventh chord. The raised fourth degree then becomes the seventh of the chord, a tone of downward tendency. Since the minor sixth degree is interpreted as a dominant the two tonalities involved will be a half tone apart.

EXAMPLE 27–29: Chopin, *Polonaise*, Op. 40, No. 2

A^b: I   V   (+II^7)   I$^6_4$ +II$^{6+}_{4+}$$_3$ I$^6_4$ +II$^{6+}_{4+}$$_3$

A: V^7 I

In the above example the modulation as well as the pivot chord is enharmonically notated. Modulations to semitonally higher keys using the augmented sixth are very common in the nineteenth century. Because the pivot chord is the dominant of the new key, the modulation is felt as abrupt, like an actual shift between the keys, with the feeling of a pivot chord being somewhat lost in the process. This is especially true when the modulation occurs sequentially, since the dominant relationship to the tonic is more strongly perceived than the augmented sixth.

Example 27–30: Schubert, *Symphony No. 9*, III

Of somewhat different effect is the reverse arrangement, that is, in modulation to the key a semitone lower, where the pivot chord is the augmented sixth chord in the second key. Both modulations may be described as unusual, however, in that the changes are to distantly related tonalities.

Example 27–31: Schubert, *Symphony No. 8*, II

Exceptional Forms

A few cases may be found of chords having the same interval structure as chords of the augmented sixth group but derived from other degrees of the scale. One of these has been mentioned —that formed by the lowered second degree in a dominant seventh chord. Although properly considered a chord with altered *See Ex. 28–15ff* fifth, it may be cited here as an instance of the comparatively rare treatment of the augmented sixth as a dominant.

Example 27–32: Schubert, *String Quintet*, Op. 163, IV

e seventh chord with major sixth degree and
metimes used in progression to I. It is equivalent
ated six-five-three in the relative minor, but with
lution.

.7–33: Schubert, Symphony No. 9, IV

gro vivace

cresc.

I^6 (I^6_4)

C: $II^{6+}_{5\ 3}$ (E♭ = D♯)

In addition to the four-part formulae given in Examples 27–4,
27–6, 27–11, and 27–14, the following sequences are recommended for keyboard practice. They should not be written out,
but played from the patterns given.

EXAMPLE 27–34

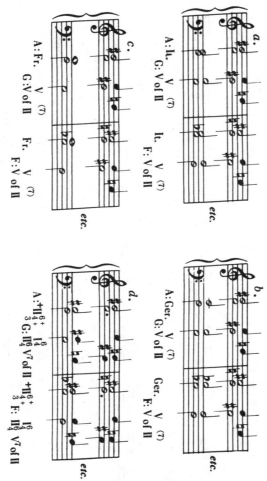

a.
A:II.   V (7)
G:V of II   It.
F:V of II
etc.

b.
A:Ger.   V (7)
G:V of II   Ger.
F:V of II
etc.

c.
A:Fr.   V (7)
G:V of II   Fr.
F:V of II
etc.

d.
A: $^+II^{6+}_4$ I^6_4
G: II^6_4 V^7 of II $^+II^{6+}_4$
F: II^6_4 V^7 of II I^6_4
etc.

EXERCISES

1. Work out the following figured basses:

a.

6   6   6   #   7♮   7♮   #
5   6×   4♯
2

2. Write a modulating sequence in which the pivot chord is V⁷ of IV becoming the chord of the doubly augmented fourth in the second key.

3. Construct a musical sentence of two phrases according to the following specifications:

    a. The first phrase modulates from B to B-flat by means of a pivot chord which is an augmented sixth in the second key.

    b. The second phrase returns to B by means of a passing modulation through a third key.

4. Harmonize the following unfigured basses, introducing augmented sixth chords:

a.

b.

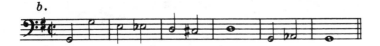

c.

d.

e. Marcia funebre

5. Harmonize the following melodies, introducing augmented sixth chords:

a.

b.

429

CHAPTER 28

Other Chromatic Chords

ENHARMONIC RESTRICTIONS OF
ALTERED SCALE DEGREES

The appearance of chromatic tones has been studied thus far in these harmonic groups: the secondary dominants; the altered chords II⁷ and VI⁷, the Neapolitan sixth, and the augmented sixth group. There remain but few altered chords that we can include in the vocabulary of harmonic material in the common practice of composers. It is physically possible through the process of chromatic alteration to create a large number of new forms, just as one can spell new words with the letters of a language; but our purpose in this study is to define the harmonic vocabulary as composers have used it.

Much can be learned about this common practice by experimenting with the possible alterations of existing chords with a view to discovering reasons why some forms were used in preference to others. The student should go about this systematically, taking each chord in turn and applying to it various chromatic alterations of the factors, appraising the results for the combination of intervals obtained and the relation of the chord to the tonality.

It will be observed immediately that a large proportion of the chords made by this method are really heard enharmonically as other more familiar chords, so that the apparent new form exists only on paper. A few such results are given here:

EXAMPLE 28–1

The harmonic interpretation of these forms depends upon the acceptance by the ear of the tones as particular scale degrees of a particular key and mode. In the above example the key of C is arbitrarily chosen but, as we know, it can be established aurally only through association with other harmonic elements. So the context will influence strongly the interpretation of chromatic tones. The following example contains a chromatic passing tone creating the augmented triad on C. If, however, the third of the chord is minor, the passing tone will be heard as the minor sixth degree instead of the raised fifth, and the progression is diatonic rather than chromatic.

EXAMPLE 28–2

The following observations are made as to chromatic alteration of the scale degrees:

The tonic may be raised, but if lowered it is heard as seventh degree.

The supertonic may be either raised or lowered. When raised it is sometimes heard as minor third degree.

The minor mediant if raised becomes the major mediant; if lowered it is heard as supertonic.

The major mediant if raised is heard as subdominant; if lowered it becomes minor third degree.

The subdominant may be raised, but if lowered it is heard as third degree.

The dominant may be raised, sometimes being heard thus as minor sixth degree. When lowered it will usually be heard as leading-tone of the dominant.

The minor submediant when raised becomes the major submediant; if lowered it is heard as dominant.

The major submediant may be raised, sometimes being heard thus as lowered seventh degree. When lowered it becomes minor sixth degree.

The leading-tone if raised is heard as tonic. It may be lowered.

THE AUGMENTED FIFTH

Chords with fifth raised to make the interval of the augmented fifth above the root are found on I, IV, and V.

The tonic chord so altered is practically always the major form. The altered tone is of course not doubled and the chord resolves regularly to the subdominant.

EXAMPLE 28–3

$\text{I}^{5\sharp} \quad \text{IV} \qquad \text{I}^{6}_{3\sharp} \quad \text{IV}$

It also leads smoothly into the supertonic seventh chord, especially when the third degree is doubled.

EXAMPLE 28–4: Bizet, *L'Arlésienne Suite No. 1:* No. 3,
Adagietto

$\text{F: V}^{7} \qquad \text{I}^{6}_{3\sharp} \quad \text{II}^{6}_{5} \quad \text{I}^{6}_{3\sharp} \quad \text{II}^{7} \quad \text{II}^{2}$

The presence of the tendency tone brings out the inherent quality of the major tonic as dominant of the subdominant. Many examples are found of V⁷ of IV with augmented fifth. Note the interval of the augmented sixth between the two upper voices as they are arranged in the following example.

EXAMPLE 28–5: Beethoven, *String Quartet*, Op. 18, No. 4, II

Andante scherzoso quasi allegretto

$\text{C: V}^{6}_{5} \quad \text{V}^{2}\text{ of IV} \quad \text{IV}^{6} \quad \text{V}^{6}_{5}\text{ of IV} \quad \text{IV} \quad \text{II} \quad \text{I}^{6}_{4} \quad \text{V}^{7} \qquad \text{I}$
$\qquad\qquad\qquad\qquad\qquad\quad 3\sharp$

433

In the following example of this chord, the upper voice, here first and second violins, divides into two parts, one of which proceeds upward by a diminished fourth to the tonic. The expansion of the number of voices to six adds to the expressive and colorful effect.

EXAMPLE 28–6: Strauss, *Till Eulenspiegel*

Gemächlich

F: I   V$_5^7$# of IV IV   I$_4^6$ V^7 I

In dominant harmony the raised degree is the supertonic, suggesting the major mode by its implied resolution to the major third degree.

EXAMPLE 28–7

*Note enharmony
with III (aug.) in
minor mode
(Chapter 4)*

V$^{5\sharp}$ I   V$_7^{5\sharp}$ I

EXAMPLE 28–8: Brahms, *Piano Concerto No. 2*, IV

Allegretto grazioso

B♭: I   V$^{6\sharp}$ I   V$^{6\sharp}$ I

The raised supertonic is a tendency tone added to those already present in the dominant seventh chord. Resolution of these tendency tones results in doubling the third of the tonic triad. The augmented sixth interval between two of the factors, as noted also in V^7 of IV, does not mean that these chords should be regarded

434

as augmented sixth chords. The characteristic interval here is the augmented fifth, not the sixth.

EXAMPLE 28–9: Beethoven, *Symphony No. 9*, III

Adagio molto e cantabile

Bb: II$^6_5$ I$^6_4$ V   V$^5_7$$\sharp$ I

Added tendency reduces the number of practicable irregular resolutions. The student should try resolving this chord to all others and note examples of irregular resolution encountered in music. The following shows an effective resolution of the augmented triad V to the incomplete major ninth V of V.

EXAMPLE 28–10: Wagner, *Siegfried*, Act III, Scene 3

Sehr ruhig und mässig bewegt

Ab: V^5$\natural$ V$^o_9$ of V V^2 I^6 VII^6 I   IV^6

The subdominant chord with raised fifth differs rhythmically from the two chords described above in that it is nearly always an appoggiatura chord. The raised tonic is an appoggiatura to the second degree, and if seventh and ninth are present they act as appoggiature to the third and octave of a II chord in first inversion.

EXAMPLE 28–11

IV^5$\sharp$ II^6 IV$^7_5$$\sharp$ II^6 IV$^9_7$$_{5\sharp}$ II^6

(II^6____)   (II^6____)   (II^6____)

435

EXAMPLE 28–12: Liszt, *Sonata*

The augmented triad has a certain vagueness due to the fact that the inversions sound like the root position. It is composed of two major thirds which divide the octave into three equal parts, the upper interval—the diminished fourth—being the enharmonic equivalent of the major third. This symmetry suggests the origin of the whole-tone scale.

EXAMPLE 28–13

A chromatic succession of augmented triads loses the sense of definite tonality. The following passage continues for twenty-two measures before augmented-triad harmony yields to a minor triad; this justly famous beginning sets the tone for the entire work.

EXAMPLE 28–14: Liszt, *A Faust Symphony*, I

THE DIMINISHED FIFTH

See also Ex. 27–32 Chromatic lowering of the fifth is found in dominant harmony. In the second inversion of the dominant seventh this produces a chord similar to the augmented six-four-three, but of dominant function.

EXAMPLE 28–15

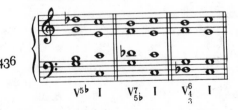

436

EXAMPLE 28–16: Brahms, *Symphony No. 4*, IV

Allegro energico e passionato

e: V⁷of V   I⁶   V⁴₃   I

This chord may resolve to a minor tonic as well.

EXAMPLE 28–17: Chopin, *Nocturne*, Op. 27, No. 1

Larghetto

c♯: I   ⁻II⁶   V⁷₅♮   I

If this alteration (lowered second degree) is applied to the dominant minor ninth without root, the chord sounds like the augmented six-five-three but with dominant function.

EXAMPLE 28–18: Schubert, *Schwanengesang*: No. 13,
Der Doppelgänger

Sehr langsam

Der Mond zeigt mir mei-ne ei - g'ne Ge - stalt._____   Du Dop-pel-

b: I   V   III   V⁰₉   I
(lowered 5th)

The following example shows the same kind of chord, but in the four-three position, which, like the ordinary diminished seventh in this position, has a subdominant effect when it resolves to root-position I (compare Example 20–15). Here the chord sounds rather like a Neapolitan. In combination with the tonic pedal it gives the unusual result of A, B flat, and C flat, all sounding simultaneously.   437

EXAMPLE 28–19: Beethoven, *Fidelio*, Act I, Finale
(Prisoners' Chorus)

THE RAISED AND LOWERED FIFTH

It may so happen that the altered chord contains a factor which has been both raised and lowered. Usually this will be the fifth of a dominant triad or dominant substitute, combining the effects of V with lowered fifth and V with raised fifth.

EXAMPLE 28–20

In the example below, the altered chord is the pivot chord in an unexpected modulation to G major, showing that the B flat must be reinterpreted as A sharp. The expected resolution would be to IV⁶ in B-flat major.

EXAMPLE 28–21: Schumann, *Dichterliebe*, Op. 48: No. 12,
Am leuchtenden Sommermorgen

438

The minor triad with raised and lowered fifth is enharmonically equivalent to a dominant seventh chord or to an augmented sixth chord, either of which would resolve irregularly. Its commonest use is as an altered tonic in a progression to II⁷ or to V · of V, a harmonic gesture which became popular in the nineteenth century.

EXAMPLE 28–22: Liszt, *Piano Concerto No. 2*

EXAMPLE 28–23: Duparc: *Lénore*

EXAMPLE 28–24: Chabrier, *Souvenirs de Munich: II, Été*

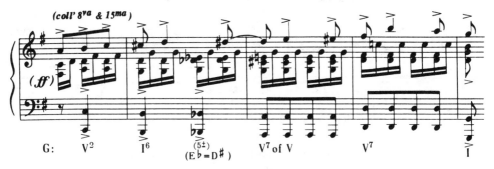

The raised and lowered fifth may also occur in other functions, such as the supertonic. The notation in the following example indicates that the altered II might also be thought of as V⁷ of III in minor, with irregular resolution.

439

EXAMPLE 28–25: Schubert, *Rosamunde, Entr'acte No. 1*

The above description of altered II offers a possible harmonic explanation for a favorite chromatic progression of the common-practice period which has been called the *omnibus*.* The succession *a* below is the commonest form of the omnibus.

EXAMPLE 28–26

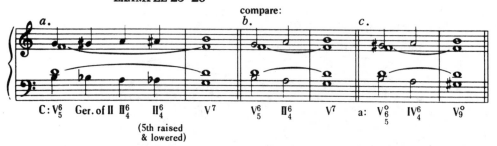

It is easy to see how the addition of chromatic passing tones to the contrary-motion voice exchange in progression *b* brings about the omnibus. Composers have traditionally avoided the doubly augmented octave in their notation of the omnibus.

EXAMPLE 28–27: Schubert, *Sonata*, Op. 42, I

The simplicity of the voice leading of the omnibus is in starkest possible contrast to the cumbersomeness of the purely harmonic analysis of it. One can easily enough understand the second step of the progression as an augmented six-five-three of II, but the fourth step is more problematic. With the voice leading given, it

---

440   * This designation is due to Victor Fell Yellin.

is a supertonic six-four chord with raised and lowered fifth; considered enharmonically, with B flat in the soprano and G sharp in the bass, it is an inversion of the second-step chord, but resolving irregularly, the diminished tenth expanding to a major tenth. However it is notated, the progression is very unorthodox, perhaps not even comprehensible, when considered merely as a succession of roots and altered factors. But as the product of linear chromatic motion over sustained tones it is entirely transparent to the ear. The omnibus serves as an excellent illustration of the power of clear and simple chromatic motion to generate harmonic relationships that are only tenuously related diatonically, a phenomenon that is increasingly characteristic of the chromatic harmony of the later nineteenth century.

The five-step omnibus begins and ends with the same dominant seventh chord but in different positions, and can thus be called a prolongation of dominant harmony. The three-step sequential omnibus, on the other hand, is used as a modulating device. In this sequence, the successive dominant sevenths are enharmonically reinterpreted as the augmented sixth chords of the next key. The model below is given in strict (that is, not enharmonic) notation, a process which cannot be carried very far without encountering triple sharps.

EXAMPLE 28–28

The following example from a work on the borderline of common practice carries the three-step omnibus through two cycles and the beginning of a third before breaking off; as reference to the model above will show, this is the farthest that a pedal can be sustained in the progression.

EXAMPLE 28–29: Mussorgsky, *Boris Godunov*, Act III, Scene 1

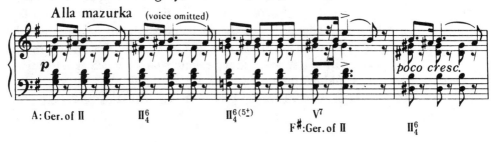

Many variants of the omnibus preserving the general pattern can be found. Usually these are seen to be departures from the strict chromatic motion made for one reason or another.

EXAMPLE 28–30: Schubert, *Winterreise:* No. 20, *Der Wegweiser*

APPOGGIATURA CHORDS

It is customary to speak of a combination of appoggiature as an *appoggiatura chord*. The name is retained here for want of a better general term, but it should be strongly emphasized that the chords commonly called appoggiatura chords most often form the weak part of a weak-to-strong progression, in which case the members could hardly be called appoggiature.

442   The method of forming these chords is that of preceding some

The following chord is like VI⁷ except for the presence of the subdominant E.

EXAMPLE 28–33: Franck, *Prelude, Chorale, and Fugue*

In the following closely related example, the G flat is incorrectly written for F sharp, the raised submediant, while the F flat is an appoggiatura to the seventh, not a lowered root.

EXAMPLE 28–34: Wagner, *Die Götterdämmerung*, Act I, Scene 2

The following example shows a chord which might properly be called an appoggiatura chord because of the rhythm. It is questionable whether a weak-to-strong progression can be heard here, as the placing of the barline tends to suggest. The leading-tone in both chords creates a dominant feeling throughout.

EXAMPLE 28–35: Brahms, *Capriccio*, Op. 76, No. 8

Grazioso ed un poco vivace

444   C: V

or all of the factors of a given chord by tones a half step ab
below, so that they resolve into the chord factors somewl
leading-tones. The possibilities of forming new chords by thi
lodic process are very numerous and the individual combina
do not appear often enough to become part of the harm
vocabulary, but a few characteristic examples can be given.

In the following example the first chord is an unusual form
IV⁷, but its function is readily understood. Compare its effect w.
that of the raised submediant seventh as an introductory chord
the dominant.

EXAMPLE 28–31: Brahms, *Intermezzo*, Op.116, No. 6

Andantino

B♭:   IV⁷   V⁷

When the subdominant triad appears with all its factors raised,
to lead into the dominant, it becomes a chord whose root is distant from the tonic by an augmented fourth, the farthest possible.

EXAMPLE 28–32: Liszt, *Sonata*

Quasi adagio

dimin.   *pp*

F♯:   V⁹   IV⁶(raised; enharm.) V⁹
                                        or perhaps   V⁶ (lowered)?

One might well ask why the altered chord above might not,
with equal validity, be considered to be a V with all its factors
lowered, as Liszt's notation implies. Our argument here is based
on the assumption that an appoggiatura relationship, even of one
entire triad to another (raised IV resolving in the direction of its
alteration), is more plausible to the ear than a false dominant
(resolving contrary to the direction of its alteration). But it must
be conceded that here, in an extreme instance of tonal chromaticism, a good case for the alternate interpretation can certainly be made. Ultimately, only careful and repeated listening
will enable the analyst to decide the question.

True appoggiatura chords are found in this example from Mozart, shown by asterisks. They are unquestionably harmonic in effect, but a root analysis seems less appropriate than a melodic description. Literally, both are augmented triads on the minor sixth degree, the third of the triad appearing simultaneously in both raised and unaltered form.

EXAMPLE 28–36: Mozart, *Symphony No. 40*, K. 550, I

The lowered tonic in the submediant triad, used by Franck as in the example below, imparts a dominant quality to the chord since it sounds like a leading-tone.

EXAMPLE 28–37: Franck, *Piano Quintet*, I

The examples given above by no means represent an exhaustive list of these altered chords, but they will serve to indicate the circumstances in which such chords appear. It is suggested that the student should note down examples of similar chords discovered in music of the eighteenth and nineteenth centuries, taking special notice of those combinations found used several times.

LIMITATIONS

New chords are the result of harmonic and melodic, vertical and horizontal, influences. Harmonically, they arise from a desire to add to the harmonic interest and variety by the creation of a 445 sonority hitherto unheard, or by the use of an established form in an unaccustomed position in the tonality. Melodically, the altered tones forming the new chord are introduced for their value as tendency tones imparting melodic direction and continuity.

These two aspects are not entirely separate. Some of the altered chords appear most often as the effect of chromatic passing tones or other melodic tones. Some, like the raised supertonic, are almost entirely made up of tones capable of analysis as nonharmonic factors. Those vertical combinations which by their recurrence in music seem to have been brought about deliberately should be recognized as chords, albeit with certain qualifications.

All the same, one becomes aware that, in the expanded chromatic harmony of the late nineteenth century, particularly in the music of the Austro-German composers after Wagner, the formation of such chords becomes increasingly a matter not of common practice but of the individual composer's practice, or even of the idiosyncrasies of an individual work. The student should try to single out such individualities and relate them to common practice, insofar as this is possible; but it will nevertheless be apparent that harmonic analysis of such music becomes inseparable from questions of contrapuntal relationships, and indeed becomes involved in the relationships of tonality and form in different ways in different works. Much of that analysis is beyond the scope of this book; some of it will be discussed later, in Part Two.

EXERCISES

1. Work out the following figured basses:

2. Construct a musical sentence of three phrases according to the following specifications:

  a. The first phrase modulates by means of a pivot chord which is a chromatically altered chord in both keys.
  b. The second phrase contains a modulating sequence whose pattern includes a dominant chord with lowered fifth. The phrase ends in a key not found in the first phrase.
  c. The third phrase returns to the initial key by a pivot chord which is an augmented triad.

3. Harmonize the following unfigured basses, introducing chromatically altered chords:

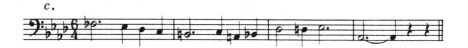

4. Harmonize the following melodies, introducing chromatically altered chords:

448

After Common
Practice

CHAPTER 29

Harmonic Practice
Historically Considered

In the first part of this book we sought to define the common
practice of composers over a period of about one and a half
centuries, assuming arbitrarily that time stood still for composers,
that Bach, Mozart, Chopin, and Dvořák were contemporaries and that harmonic practice did not even change, let alone
evolve. While conceding these assumptions for their value in the
study of harmonic practice, let us also concede that this book is not
the place for a thorough historical consideration of harmony. A
few general observations, nevertheless, will be useful before we
take up the extremely varied developments of the last century.

At the time of J. S. Bach's first compositions (about 1703),
twelve-tone equal temperament (see Appendix I) had not yet
achieved wide acceptance. In the tuning systems then popular,
music was ordinarily restricted to the simpler keys, that is, those
having at most two or three flats or sharps in the key signature.
Keys and chromatic tones further around the circle of fifths were
too out of tune to be used effectively. Equal temperament did
away with these limitations. By distributing the collective intonational defects of the circle of fifths equally over the chromatic
scale, equal temperament made every interval (except the octave) out of tune by an equal but tolerable proportion. This   451

meant that, for instance, the C-sharp major triad or the C-flat major triad sounded no more out of tune than the C major triad, and that therefore composers were free to write in any key they wished. Bach himself did much to popularize equal temperament and demonstrated his belief in it by composing the two books of the *Well-Tempered Clavier* (1722, 1744), each book containing a prelude and a fugue in each of the twelve major and twelve minor keys.

Most of the music of Bach's time and for some years thereafter nevertheless kept not only to the simpler keys but also to the simpler relationships among the keys. Composers apparently felt that the tonal unity of their individual works would be best ensured by not modulating very far from the main tonality, with the nearest keys being particularly favored—dominant, subdominant, and relative major or minor. Part of this can be attributed to the relative brevity of individual pieces and movements, and to the preference of late Baroque composers for musical forms whose basis was melodic rather than motivic (such as the concerto forms and dance forms) and contrapuntal rather than harmonic (such as the fugue). With the subsequent emergence in the Classical period of the more homophonic forms, the close association of tonic–dominant and relative-minor–relative-major key relationships became part of the very basis of the sonata allegro form, thus confirming the long-established preference for closely related keys.

Throughout this time there existed some notable exceptions to one or the other of these tendencies. For example, the episodic form of the keyboard fantasia, where continuity of themes was not a concern, permitted a freer succession of keys. Thus Bach's *Fantasia in G minor for Organ* modulates as far afield as D-flat minor (which must have had a frightening sound on the nontempered organs of the time). This work, as well as the opening section of Mozart's *Fantasia for Piano in C minor*, K. 475, which has a similarly wandering quality of tonality, is comparable to the operatic recitative in not being formally tied to a closed phrase structure, and in its essential freedom to move from chord to chord. Mozart's *G minor Symphony*, K. 550, composed in 1788, is a good example of the extent to which one of the most innovative composers of the time was willing to explore the resources of chromatic modulation. The key relationships between the first and second themes of the sonata-form movements are according to the usual patterns, but the development sections show a tendency toward rapid and far-reaching modulation.

We have already seen how the era of tonal counterpoint was

Review Chapter 5 (last sections) and Chapter 14 (first section)

Cf. Ex. 20–33

452

able to justify on contrapuntal grounds the momentary vertical concurrence of practically any diatonic combination of four or five tones. The same could be said for a large number of possible chromatic combinations of tones that would hardly be conceivable as self-standing harmonies. The vocabulary of independent harmonies that we have studied was basically complete even in Bach's time, even though, for instance, complete dominant ninths and augmented sixth chords are quite rare. The incidence of such usages at different times in the period of common practice is just one of the complex questions that must be considered in a historical study of harmony.

*See also Ex.
31–61*

See Ex. 27–22

Another such question would be the differences between common practice and individual practice. This question, let us repeat, is never fully answered by the attempt to define common practice. Some generalizations are easy enough to make intuitively, but would require a good deal of effort to test analytically. For instance, one tends to think of Beethoven as somewhat less interested in the possibilities of chromatic harmony even than his predecessors, if only because one finds a number of examples in Bach and Mozart that seldom have a counterpart in Beethoven. At the same time it is demonstrable that Beethoven habitually used a wider range of keys in his developmental structures than any composer before him; this is less a question of harmony than of tonality. Similarly, Schubert, who achieved few innovations in musical form comparable to Beethoven's, nevertheless shows a remarkable degree of harmonic originality, including a personal chromaticism that often goes beyond Beethoven's. Some of Schubert's harmonic practices are, for their time, so individualized that they are a distinguishing characteristic of his music; not until Chopin does history again reveal a composer so trademarked by his harmony.

E.g., Ex. 14–19

E.g., Ex. 26–19

Like Beethoven before him, but on a much larger scale, Wagner achieved a revolution in musical form, and part of this revolution included an extension of the very comprehensiveness of tonality as a structural principle. Before Wagner, the tonal unity of even a multiple-movement composition could be sensed as a background for the entire work, such as C minor—C major in Beethoven's *Fifth Symphony*. Even in an opera like Mozart's *Magic Flute*, which begins and ends in E-flat major, the individual numbers in a variety of keys represent stable tonal units, perceivable as related, to one extent or another, to each other and to the "main" tonality. But in Wagner's music-dramas the dimensions are so large and the changes of key so numerous that the idea of a "main tonality" becomes virtually meaningless. While it may be possible to speak of *Die Meistersinger* as being "in C major" just because that is the key in which the opera begins and ends and has some important episodes, the C major tonality is more symbolic than actual. In the same way D-flat major comes to symbolize Valhalla in Wagner's *Ring*, if only because of the association of the key with certain leitmotives and scenes and, at the end of *Die Götterdämmerung*, with the destruction of Valhalla.

See Exx. 5–31,
23–41, 27–19,
30–17

From the harmonic standpoint Wagner's *Tristan und Isolde* is in every way the most remarkably innovative achievement of the last part of the common-practice period. Though when considered on a chord-to-chord basis the harmony of *Tristan* is no more radical than the chromatic explorations of Chopin, the dimensions and continuity of the work carry the conceptions of tonality far beyond anything that had been realized before in closed, tonally self-limited symphonic forms. What was pointed to in *Tristan* at the time as "unending melody" might better be called "unending progression," in which the listener is led on a journey from one key to another for over four hours. Some points of tonal stability or referability exist, but always only relatively; deceptive cadences, abrupt modulations, motivic chord progressions, and chromatic alterations are so ubiquitous that the listener is forced to accept them as the harmonic norm, abandoning any expectation that a particular key, defined by simple root progressions, will be established for more than a relatively short time. All of this radical approach to tonality, which in its day was considered destructive of the very idea of tonality, was at the heart of the psychological necessities of the drama, exactly as Wagner intended. What was not immediately understood was that Wagner accomplished it entirely within the resources of classical voice leading; other than the chromatic context, there is no essential difference between the counterpoint of *Tristan* and that of the C-major Prelude of Book I of Bach's *Well-Tempered Clavier*. The essentials of this counterpoint are contiguity, controlled motion, and restricted harmonic relationships.

The mature music of Debussy offers the severest contrast to Wagner's chromaticism, although that was one of its aesthetic influences. While it was influenced to some extent also by his somewhat older countrymen, such as Franck, Lalo, Fauré, and Chabrier, Debussy's style is essentially original, the originality residing above all else in its anticlassical approach to harmony, counterpoint, and form. Parallel motion of perfect fifths, triads, seventh chords, and ninth chords, in any succession, in any position, and to any degree of the chromatic scale, is a fundamental characteristic. So is the use of all manner of scales, including major, minor, chromatic, modal, pentatonic, and artificial scales, as well as the whole-tone scale (whose use in Debussy's music, though abundant, has been overemphasized by many writers). In his later works Debussy added quartal, quintal, and polychordal sonorities to his vocabulary. Debussy's distinctive harmonic language was a conscious attempt to do away with what he perceived as the restrictively systematic relationships of classical tonality, and as such was as genuinely revolutionary as anything in the history of music. At the same time it succeeded, in ways that are difficult to define, in creating a tonal logic of its own, which depends not on counterpoint or ordinary root relationships (the V–I relationship, for instance, rarely appears) but on the maintenance of tone-centers, nonclassical "tonics," and an essentially diatonic, triadic background.

At about the same time that Debussy was using his carefully controlled nonsystematic tonal language to create a new and essentially French musical aesthetic, Wagner's successors in Austria and Germany were continuing to explore the world that *Tristan und Isolde* had opened up for them. The more adventurous of these probed into chromatic counterpoint of ever-increasing complexity, in which the harmonic element, at least in the classical sense, was progressively attenuated until, in the works of Schoenberg, Berg, and Webern, beginning about 1907–08, tonality disappeared altogether. Remaining in its place was a dense nontriadic chromaticism regulated by various abstract means which were usually intrinsically bound up with the autonomous structures of the individual works. Eventually a principle called serialism emerged, which was based on the composer's precompositional definition of certain different pitches to be projected in a stated intervallic succession. Schoenberg's invention, in the early 1920s, of what came to be called the twelve-tone system, was an application of the serial principle to the twelve different pitch-classes of the chromatic scale, which would be ordered by the composer in a certain way, the entire composition then being referable to the initial ordering, subject to certain conditions and defined states. The twelve-tone system, as its best practitioners demonstrated, allowed for a remarkable degree of compositional freedom, and clearly was a convincing way of regulating atonality; it has been enormously influential in the music of the last half-century.

While the revolution in chromatic harmony initiated by *Tristan*   455 *und Isolde* represented one pole of the development of Austro-German music after Wagner, another pole was destined to serve as an international restorative force in twentieth-century tonality. This was the aesthetic movement that came to be called neo-classicism, which drew its inspiration from the masters of the eighteenth century. As early as the middle of the nineteenth century we find composers like Brahms, and a short time later several French and Russian composers, reacting against what they regarded as the excessive tendencies of Wagner in general and the Wagnerian music-drama in particular, in favor of "absolute" music, classical forms and contrapuntal devices, and restrained chromaticism. Wagner himself contributed to the movement with *Die Meistersinger,* which in keeping with its historical subject is much more diatonic than his other mature operas. Nevertheless, as a genuinely forceful trend in music, neoclassicism did not begin to flourish until the third decade of the twentieth century, when an entire generation of composers, led by Ravel, Stravinsky, Hindemith, and Prokofiev, wrote an impressive body of works that projected a new kind of diatonic tonality. (Oddly enough there was also at the same time a chromatic neoclassicism, led by Schoenberg, but it was not tonal; this is just one aspect that makes neoclassicism a complex historical phenomenon.)

Even if it is roughly true, it is an oversimplification to say that diatonicism and chromaticism, or tonality and atonality for that matter, represent the broad categories of twentieth-century harmony. Neither in theory nor in practice does such a division account for the abundance of harmony wherein the two domains merge, and we have already seen numerous instances in eighteenth- and nineteenth-century music where diatonic harmony is colored or elaborated by chromaticism. Nor does the categorization give much idea of the tremendous variety, both possible and actual, of diatonic and chromatic harmony.

For it becomes obvious at once that the evolution of harmony after Wagner is unparalleled in its richness, in its wealth of new discoveries, and in the variety of individual practices. The period ending about 1914 was particularly fruitful in these respects. At the same time, it must be admitted that all this harvest of originality has posed a problem for theorists and historians of music because of the increased complexity of tonality and formal structure that it embodies. The decline of nineteenth-century common practice was not followed by a twentieth-century one, nor even by several, but more like dozens of practices which could be said to have some kind of acceptance at one time or another, and which in many cases overlapped.

In the remainder of this book we shall concern ourselves with aspects of post–common-practice harmony that can in some ways be accounted for, analyzed, or described. What is given in the following chapters should not be thought of as forming more than a relatively small part of the harmonic cosmos after common practice. Rather, it should be thought of as an introduction to just a few of the many ways by which the student may begin to be familiar with the equally many modes of compositional thought that have marked the past century. As has been noted before, theory does not precede practice but follows it, and is never complete; if it were, presumably we would have a consistent theory of twentieth-century music as well as of earlier music. The student will find ample opportunity, in examining the examples that follow, to find alternative explanations and interpretations; he may be reassured that, on many of the questions posed here, no substantial agreement has been achieved today even by the most accomplished analysts.

Exercises are not given for these chapters. The standard exercises in harmonization and figured bass, of use in common-practice training, do not as a rule lend themselves well to complex diatonic or chromatic harmony. It is assumed that most of the student's work on these chapters will consist of analysis of the examples and comparison with examples drawn from other works. Nevertheless, the student will find it instructive to compose phrases or short pieces incorporating some of the harmonic types described, and testing the range of possibilities inherent in some of the generative procedures shown. Analysis in the classroom should include study of complete works as a supplement to the examples given in the text.

CHAPTER 30

Extensions of
Common Practice

No simple dividing line separates common-practice harmony from what came after it. The individualities of the common-practice composers reveal numerous instances of uncommon practice, in some cases forerunners of much later kinds of harmony; these exceptions, seen in increasing numbers in the later part of the period, are found to be extensions or extremes of established procedures more often than direct violations. Some composers, like Mussorgsky, Fauré, and Mahler, can be said to have begun in common practice and gradually developed away from it; others, like Debussy and Schoenberg, gained this liberation more quickly and completely, in both cases achieving a new kind of harmonic language whose ties to the past are nevertheless apparent. And indeed, many features of common practice persist in some way even in much music of the present day.

One of the striking features of the period extending approximately from 1880 to 1920 is the way common practice gave way to individual practice, at first gradually and later more rapidly. Even composers who were close contemporaries came increasingly to develop styles that were characterized in large part by individualities of harmony. Fauré's harmony, for example, often

458   does not resemble Chabrier's; Mahler's harmony is significantly dif-

ferent from Richard Strauss's. On examination, the works of even two such popularly associated composers as Debussy and Ravel are seen to be clearly distinct in their harmonic languages, despite many aspects common to both.

In some ways it is possible to argue convincingly that the forty-year period which supplies most of the examples in this and the following chapters represents the climax of the "harmonic period," for it certainly includes the most music wherein composers seem to have been interested in the independent expressive qualities of harmony in its own right, that is, kept relatively free from contrapuntal considerations. With the revitalization of counterpoint in neoclassical tonality after the First World War, that tendency markedly declined. This does not mean that the new counterpoint was in itself any less harmonic, but it does mean that the era of new discoveries in harmony had by then essentially passed. This fact of history will necessitate one more limitation on our study. Much of the music of this century—as indeed of previous centuries—is less meaningfully analyzed as harmony than as counterpoint, and in laying a groundwork for twentieth-century harmonic analysis we do not wish to go beyond the announced scope of this book.

The purpose of this chapter will be to describe the early manifestations of the new tendencies and to relate them in various ways to each other and to the common background from which they arose. For when all is said and done, even the most radical of the harmonic discoveries after common practice to appear to be an evolutionary result of the past.

Modal Scales and Modal Harmony

The use of modal scales is a convenient subject with which to begin our departure, because it represents a tendency, even though only an occasional one, that persisted through the common-practice period. The church modes, a legacy from pretonal music, can be viewed in common practice as variants of the major-minor system, having different harmonic effects in their application. Thus the Dorian and Phrygian modes, with minor third degree, yield a minor tonic triad, and thus should be regarded as essentially minor in sound, whereas the Lydian and Mixolydian, with major third degree, are essentially major for the same reason. The Dorian and Mixolydian modes form a minor dominant triad,

Review Chapter 5, beginning

459

whereas the Phrygian mode, with lowered second degree, produces a diminished triad on the dominant. From the standpoint of the major-minor system the effect of all these modal scales is to weaken the perception of the classical tonic.

The deliberate use in the common-practice period of modal scales, or at least of some of their distinguishing characteristics, seems to have reflected composers' desires to increase harmonic possibilities on the one hand, and, on the other, to provide a certain feeling of archaic style, especially in religious music. The Bach fughetta furnishing the example below, based on a sixteenth-century Mixolydian chorale melody, could be said to be in G major with a Mixolydian flavor. The F-sharp leading-tone, absent from the key signature, is worked into the harmony at some points and replaced by F natural at others. The final measures emphasize G by repetition of the tonic note; at the same time, subdominant harmony is stressed by the presence of F natural as the *Cf. Ex. 20–15* seventh of V^7 of IV. The final cadence ingeniously partakes of both tonal regions: the leading-tone rises to G as in V–I, while the C bass and E flat proceed as in IV–I.

EXAMPLE 30–1: Bach, Fughetta on *Dies sind die heil'gen zehn Gebot'*

G: I   IV V^7 I   V^7 I (V of IV)   IV   II   I (V of IV)   IV   V$^4_3$ I
tonic pedal   (V/IV)

The "Dankgesang" movement of Beethoven's *String Quartet,* Op. 132, pointedly labeled "in the Lydian mode," is perhaps the most famous example in the common-practice period of a systematic attempt to employ a modal scale. In that piece, as well as in the example below by Chopin, tonal functions are often obscure; it is hard to say where the tonic is. Strong dominant-to-tonic relationships occur seldom, and when present are interfered with by the increased emphasis on root-position modal-degree triads, the latter occurring without preceding secondary dominants. The modal feeling is increased by the avoidance of the leading-tone relationship in the dominant of the relative minor, which would introduce an accidental. The Chopin example is drawn from the beginning of the work, where fifty-six measures appear consecutively without a single accidental.

EXAMPLE 30–2: Chopin, *Mazurka*, Op. 24, No. 2

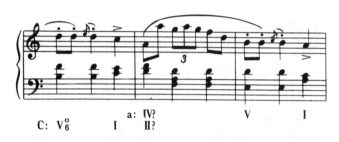

The increasing prevalence of such "modal harmony" in the later nineteenth century can be traced to the use of modal scales in folk music, which had a wide influence on the so-called nationalist composers. The tendency was perhaps greatest in eastern Europe, most notably among the Russian composers, whose homophonic styles reflect the influence of the a cappella choirs of the Orthodox Church. In the example below, a pentatonic melody is accompanied by chords that first stress VI, V, and III, and only then turn toward the tonic; the V of V abruptly following suggests a touch of Lydian mode.

Review Chapter 23: Neighbor-Note Harmony

EXAMPLE 30–3: Mussorgsky, *Pictures at an Exhibition,* Promenade

The familiar March from Tchaikovsky's *Nutcracker* begins and ends on the G major triad, but contains numerous references to E minor throughout. Several phrases end on either the E minor triad or the E minor half cadence; the entire middle section is based on an E pedal. Like Chopin's B flat minor *Scherzo* and a number of other works of the nineteenth century, this March seems to merge relative major and minor into a tonality that is simultaneously single and dual.

EXAMPLE 30–4: Tchaikovsky, *The Nutcracker*, March

The following example illustrates a typical use of the Aeolian mode, that is, the natural minor, without the leading-tone.

EXAMPLE 30–5: Borodin, *Symphony No. 3*, I

In the example below, the use of differently inflected modal degrees is entirely harmonic and coloristic; because of the inflected third degree, the passage projects an alternating quasiminor and quasi-major, with no single modality prevailing.

EXAMPLE 30–6: Balakirev, *Symphony No. 1*, II

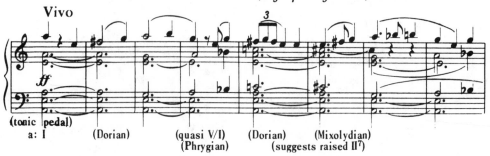

The following example of Lydian mode sounds like an alternation between I and V of V, irregularly resolving.

EXAMPLE 30–7: Mussorgsky, *Boris Godunov*, Act III, Polonaise (Rimsky-Korsakov version)

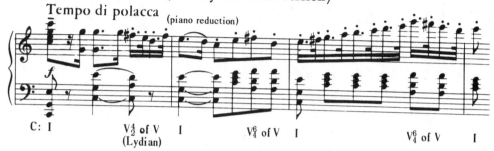

The following examples incorporating the minor seventh degree show different ways of circumventing dominant harmony.

EXAMPLE 30–8: Berlioz, *Requiem, Dies irae*

EXAMPLE 30–9: Dvořák, *Symphony No. 9*, IV

Cf. Ex. 30–4

The Phrygian mode, as used in the opening measures of Debussy's *String Quartet*, projects a feeling of E-flat major that is only offset by the repetition of the G-minor triad and by the use of the leading-tone at the end of the second measure. Later in the movement Debussy changes the harmonization of the melody so as to emphasize an actual E-flat major.

463

EXAMPLE 30–10: Debussy, *String Quartet*, I

Animé et très décidé

As the examples given here demonstrate in various ways, the most important determinant of modal perception is the extent to which a strong tonic is felt, for if the tonic is made clear by reiteration, all the modal functions will relate to it even if they weaken it in the classical sense. More comprehensive examples can be found, of course, particularly in twentieth-century popular music, where systematic use of a single mode within a simple repetitive harmonic scheme is a common procedure.

THE DECLINE OF DOMINANT HARMONY

Review also
Chapter 23

It was stated earlier (Chapter 16) that the common-practice era was marked by a definite preference for dominant harmony over nondominant harmony, and we have already seen many examples of how this preference was projected. Tonicizing chords, such as secondary dominants progressing to their respective tonics, and including diminished seventh chords and the various chromatically altered chords which are either secondary dominants themselves or intensifiers of dominants, form the most significant general category of chord functions in common practice.

Though the period after common practice did not dispense with dominant harmony, even introducing more complex forms not previously employed, it must be acknowledged that a number of composers sought and achieved ways of weakening the dominant effect, even to the point of extinction. In part this can be accounted for by the resurgence of interest in modal harmony, in which triads on modal degrees were used more frequently and prominently. A natural concomitant of this was the appearance of the cadential minor dominant resolving to either a major or a minor tonic.

EXAMPLE 30–11: Grieg, *Piano Concerto*, III

Poco più tranquillo (Allegro marcato)

F: I   V⁷(min.)   (V⁹)   I

EXAMPLE 30–12: Chabrier, Overture to *Gwendoline*

Allegro con fuoco

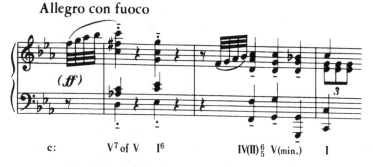

c: V⁷of V   I⁶   IV(II)⁶₅ V(min.)   I

EXAMPLE 30–13: Ravel, *Menuet antique*

Majestueusement

en élargissant

f#:   IV(II)⁶₅ V   (min.)   I

The above examples differ from common practice only by their substitution of the minor seventh degree for the leading-tone.

The anticlassicism of Debussy included, as forcefully as anything else, an attack on dominant-to-tonic progressions everywhere in the phrase. His works furnish the most consistent and abundant examples of avoidance of the dominant in its most traditionally dependable usage, the final cadence.

465

EXAMPLE 30-14: Debussy, *Suite bergamasque, Clair de lune*

Andante

pp morendo

D♭: III (I)$^6_4$^{3} I

Debussy's final cadences range over a variety of types during the course of his development. In the early works dominant chords in other than root position or with nonharmonic tones may precede the final tonic; in the later works even the final tonic may be an independent, unresolved dissonant chord. All of this is not to say that V–I relationships cannot be found in Debussy, but they are rarely found unmixed with extra factors, and in any event they are infrequent.

The following example, from the final measures of the movement, shows a dominant seventh with unresolved chromatic appoggiatura (the C in the third measure) reinterpreted enharmonically as the dominant seventh of a tritone-related key. The root of V⁷ in C-flat major is the lowered fifth of V⁷ in F major, and the raised fourth above the root of the V⁷ in C flat is the root of the V⁷ in F. This progression illustrates a harmonic substitution often used in jazz.

Cf. Ex. 31–68

EXAMPLE 30-15: Debussy, *Sonata for Flute, Viola, and Harp*, II

Tempo di menuetto

(app.)

dolce e tristamente

p

C♭: V⁷

F: V$^4_3$(5-)

REMOTE TONAL RELATIONSHIPS

Music of the eighteenth and early nineteenth centuries is rich in examples of harmonic successions between distantly related triads and modulations between distantly related keys. These are accomplished by a variety of well-established and coherent means, such as pivot tones, enharmonic relationships, chromatically altered chords, and mode change, as well as by unorthodox types of dissonance preparation and resolution. The use of such means does not ordinarily result in more than a momentary weakening of tonality—which may indeed be the effect desired by the composer—because the context of the remote tonal relationship is ordinarily a well-established key both before and after. It was only when these means were applied continuously, frequently, and in combination, with the result of straining the sense of tonal predictability, that common practice was exceeded.

EXAMPLE 30–16: Fauré, *Nocturne No. 6*, Op. 63

A: I   IV⁷   IV/V (V¹¹) I (V⁷ of IV) V⁷ of IV
                                    D♭: Ger.   V⁴₃ of V   V⁷ ⁽¹³⁾   V⁷/I   I
                                    (V of V)

The example above contains few, if any, instances of harmonic progression or dissonance treatment that considered separately could not be found widely in common practice, but the phrase when considered as a whole constitutes a chain of events that would hardly be likely to occur before Fauré. The irregular voice leading in the resolution of the dominant eleventh, the ambiguity of I and V⁷ of IV, the enharmonic reinterpretation of the V⁷ of IV as an augmented sixth chord, the interpolation of an unaltered V of V between the augmented sixth and its resolution, and the presence of an unresolved thirteenth in the resolution itself—these are all a distinctive succession, an example of the individuality of Fauré's style. It is worth noting that the passage contains only a single chromatic alteration (the augmented sixth chord) and a single chromatic motion (the resolution of V of V to V).

The following excerpt from Wagner's *Tristan und Isolde* illustrates the continuous chromatic modulation for which the opera is famous. It shows how the principle of contiguity operates to bring about the association of remote keys by contrapuntal means. Nearly every harmony in the passage has at least one tone in common with the preceding or following harmony; most of the tones 467 that move in succession move stepwise. The reduction shows this more clearly than does the example itself. S-shaped curves shows the connections where an octave change is involved. The harmonically stronger triadic formations are indicated by white notes; except for the G major triad, the only triad in the excerpt that is preceded by a strong dominant, they are related by the interval of a minor third (triads beamed together). The motivic sequential progression, I–V–III, involves a mode change between V and III.

EXAMPLE 30–17: Wagner, *Tristan und Isolde*, Act II, Scene 2

REDUCTION, omitting doublings and some nonharmonic tones

The example shows that even the most remote harmonic relationships, in an advanced chromatic idiom, can result from the smooth connection of melodic lines, even under the elementary contrapuntal restrictions of suspension and stepwise motion, and can be fully comprehended as harmonic progressions. The chromaticism of the post-Wagnerian composers is often seen to pro-

ceed just as smoothly, though the root motions may be only tenuously related from chord to chord or from cadence to cadence.

EXTENSIONS

The passage by Berlioz given below, composed in 1830, may be
cited as an example of freakishly uncommon practice, deliberately
written for its grotesque effect. From the standpoint of common
practice, the root relationships are so remote as to have no apparent connection. The noncontiguous harmony may indeed be
unique for its time, but before the end of the nineteenth century
such progressions came to be heard frequently, and within a few
years (see the Satie example following) were commonplace.

*Examine the
complete score
and find the
D-flat major
passage earlier
in the movement*

EXAMPLE 30–18: Berlioz, *Symphonie fantastique*, IV:
March to the Scaffold

EXAMPLE 30–19: Satie, *Three Pieces in the Shape of a Pear*, No. 7

Contrapuntal technique in the nineteenth century can be described as embodying the following general principles:

a. Smooth connection of harmonies;
b. Regulation of parts, even in the most complex figurations and textures, by elementary voice leading, and by the characteristics of nonharmonic tones;
c. Avoidance of prohibited motions.

The explanation and elaboration of these principles have already been a major concern of this book. We will now examine the ways in which music after common practice set new values on these principles and departed from them.

Review Chapter 18

The traditionally prohibited parallel motions were the first to be set free, to be employed as a resource in new kinds of harmony. We have already seen some examples of parallel perfect fifths in common practice that can be explained in various ways, such as those resulting from the combination of nonharmonic tones, from the resolution of the German sixth chord, or even sometimes from inadvertence or extramusical reasons.

Cf. Ex. 18–25

An example like the following probably cannot be attributed to any such causes. The fifths in the first measure are part of a smooth motion from a tonic triad with doubled third. Certainly the fifths are not overlooked as fifths by the discerning ear, but the listener should think of them as a manifestation of a self-consistent style, not as a flaw in common-practice harmony.

EXAMPLE 30–20: Fauré, *Pelléas et Mélisande*, Prelude

The doubling of a melody in fifths is a coloristic device of impressionist harmony. Instances like the following abound in the works of Debussy, Ravel, and later composers.

The systematic application of parallel fifths will also be considered shortly in the discussions of independent sonorities, block-chord harmony, and quintal harmony.

EXAMPLE 30–21: Debussy, *La Mer*, I

Modéré sans lenteur

The following is an extreme instance of parallel dissonant intervals, resulting from the addition of a countermelody to a minor-mode version of the well-known round *Frère Jacques*. The passage occurs in a funeral march which contains a number of such deliberately grotesque gestures.

EXAMPLE 30–22: Mahler, *Symphony No. 1*, III

Feierlich und gemessen

The counterpoint of the following example is anything but smoothly connected.

EXAMPLE 30–23: Mahler, *Symphony No. 4*, I

Gemächlich

The two upper melodies and the bass line are all variants of themes that have already been extensively developed earlier in the movement in many versions; thus in part it is the hearer's recognition of the themes that supports the counterpoint. Nevertheless, the note-to-note connections in the melodic lines, with so many wide leaps, multiple appoggiature and reaching tones, and irregular resolutions, make it difficult for the ear to form a harmonic connection between them. Only on repeated hearing does it become clear that the passage is a complex elaboration of the following melodic progression, in which all the chromatic tones are passing tones. The harmony, and the underlying melodic motion, are characteristic of common practice; the actual contrapuntal realization, however, is not.

EXAMPLE 30–24

THE INDEPENDENT VERTICAL SONORITY

A piece of tonal music presupposes a context of selected keys, and a beginning and ending with continuity in between. Thus in one sense there could be no vertical arrangement of tones completely independent of a context, except perhaps in the case of a work that consisted of a single chord. We will use the term *independent sonority* to indicate a harmony whose origin and resolution are for the most part independent of voice-leading considerations.

We have already seen a hierarchy of chordal types, beginning with the dominant seventh, whose dissonant factors may arise without preparation. Some of these chords, such as ninth chords, may have their dissonant factors resolved internally by arpeggiation, and a few examples may be found in common practice in which such dissonances have no apparent resolution. There are *E.g., Ex. 20–30* also many instances of chords "resolving" by parallel chromatic motion over a distance, as in the case of the sequential diminished seventh chord, where in most cases it is the final chord of the series that carries the resolutionary weight. More complex sonorities have been treated similarly:

EXAMPLE 30–25: Wagner, *Die Götterdämmerung,*
Act III, Scene 2

EXTENSIONS

The above passage, occurring after an uncomplicated authentic
cadence in C major, initiates a complex series of chromatic mod- *Cf. Ex. 23–42*
ulations that eventually returns to C. The pedal point provides
a tonal anchor without which the tonality would be momentarily
suspended.

Chromatic succession of root-position chords in parallel mo-
tion is a characteristic invention of the end of the common-prac- *Cf. Ex. 27–17*
tice period.

EXAMPLE 30–26: Fauré, *Impromptu No. 2,* Op. 31

This example could be explained as a modulating sequence of
augmented sixth chords, but it is not really heard that way. It is
rather a dominant seventh moving as one line up the chromatic
scale, not only against the tendency of the natural resolution of
the seventh but with parallel motion of root and fifth; the figuration helps to conceal the parallel motion. The chromatic scale *For a "horrible*
serves as a regulating influence on parallel motion of this sort, *example," see Ex.*
even permitting, as we saw in Chapter 27, the chromatic resolu- *18–23*
tion of parallel fifths in the augmented sixth chord.

The next departure was to allow dissonant chords to move
diatonically in parallel motion. 473

EXAMPLE 30–27: Debussy, *Nocturnes*: I, *Nuages*

This is a typical example of block-chord writing, a type which will be discussed more thoroughly in the next chapter. What is notable about it in the context of the present discussion is that all the chords are independent dominant major ninths. The sevenths and ninths move along with their supporting triads, but do not resolve. The chords have the dominant-ninth structure, but they are not dominants that refer to actual tonics. They are purely chordal, their dissonant factors being treated as though they were consonant.

Debussy's use of the dominant major ninth as an independent sonority is one of the distinguishing characteristics of his style; later composers also used it, though rather less abundantly. The Ravel example below shows the chord in its commonest spacing.

EXAMPLE 30–28: Ravel, *Pavane pour une Infante défunte*

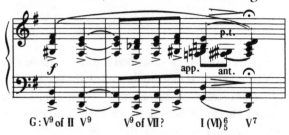

Another quasi-consonant sonority is the triad with added sixth, which had already achieved some degree of independence in common practice but was later much more widely and freely used. The following examples show the tonic triad with added sixth used at the beginning of one work and at the end of another.

474

EXAMPLE 30–29: Debussy, *Fantasy for Piano and Orchestra*, I

EXAMPLE 30–30: Mahler, *Das Lied von der Erde*, VI

Students of jazz techniques will recognize that an entire harmonic vocabulary based on the complete set of added-sixth chords and nondominant sevenths and ninths exists in that art, indeed defining the normative chordal states in a harmony where pure triads are rare. Examples such as those shown here illustrate the ancestry of such harmony.

The chordal types shown thus far have been cited as harmonies established in common practice which came to have an independent existence. More complex independent sonorities include chords with various kinds of unresolved nonharmonic tones, to be discussed later.

NEW DEFINITIONS OF TONALITY

Tonality without effective dominant relationships is difficult to envision in common-practice terms. Strongly modal harmonic relationships, in contexts that avoid the V–I relationship, tend to weaken the tonic and to bring about a fluctuating sense of relative-major–relative-minor mixture, as we have seen even in common-practice instances. Whatever confusion this may cause for the harmonic analyst, it is clear that the unsettled tonality of such   475 music was not looked on as a drawback by its practitioners. But even in the period after common practice, the evidence indicates that in many cases composers were intent on preserving the feeling of some kind of tonal center, a point of harmonic gravitation fully comparable to the classical tonic but defined by a nonclassical array of harmonic conditions.

The most important means of defining a tonal center, in the absence of a preceding dominant, became and remained the tonic itself, either as a triad or as a single pitch used somewhat like a pedal point, asserted vigorously or subtly but always definitely.

EXAMPLE 30–31: Mussorgsky, *Boris Godunov*, Prologue, Scene 2 (Rimsky-Korsakov version)

The above well-known example illustrates the establishment of the tonic C through nondominant means. The two harmonies are related enharmonically as V⁷ of D flat and V⁷ of G, with C and F sharp (G flat) as common tones, but the tonic triads of D flat major and G major do not appear anywhere in the constant oscillation of the two dominants, which continues beyond the above quotation for thirty-four measures more without harmonic change. In the classical sense the two dominants are independent sonorities, but they nevertheless reinforce the common tone C as a nonclassical tonic. (F sharp–G flat is also a common tone but C is stressed as a pedal much more strongly.)

Cf. Ex. 28–32

The following example shows the first sixteen measures of a remarkable pedal-point passage.

EXAMPLE 30–32: Debussy, *Nocturnes: II, Fêtes*

Modéré mais toujours très rhythmé

quasi A: VII⁷   V⁶₅

VII⁷   V⁶₅   VII⁷   V°₉

⌐repeated⌐   ⌐repeated⌐

first sixteen measures   **next sixteen measures**

The A-flat–G-sharp pedal remains in the bass throughout. In the initial harmony it is the root of a triad with added major sixth; the avoidance of the leading-tone in the first four measures gives the melodic parts a touch of Dorian harmony. The next four measures have the A-flat pedal as the seventh of an independent secondary dominant sonority. Then comes an alternation of what could be called a VII⁷–V relation in A major, or a II–V, over the G-sharp pedal which is the quasi-root of a half-diminished seventh chord; this yields at the end of the phrase to a diminished seventh chord on G sharp. The reduction of the entire thirty-two-measure succession, given below the example, shows clearly the considerable amount of common-tone association and contiguity between the successive chords; next to the A-flat–G-sharp pedal itself, the strongest contributor to the tonal centricity of the A-flat-minor triad is the C flat–B. Not a single functional dominant is present. The entire passage is characteristic of Debussy's quite original approach to tonal organization of larger contexts.

The first of Debussy's *Nocturnes, Nuages,* shows if anything a more radical tonal outlook, and the student would find it a profitable exercise to analyze the entire piece. Part of the tonal organization depends on Debussy's use of a special scale, discussed in the next chapter, which has a diminished tonic triad on B and   477 no functional dominant. Through subtle reiteration of the B and its companion F natural, Debussy defines and accumulates special harmonic regions related through one or the other of these tones, ultimately leaving only the single note B to define a tone center at the end (see Example 31–12.) The following example shows the beginning of the piece.

EXAMPLE 30–33: Debussy, *Nocturnes:* I, *Nuages*

Another means of defining the tone center is illustrated by the following example, which seems to project G (Mixolydian) major and A (natural) minor simultaneously, or at least interchangeably. The ostinato bass is more oriented towards G than A, the A seeming like a neighbor note to the G. On the other hand, the upper parts gravitate toward the pedal A, which is also the goal note of the first melodic phrase. The situation shown here may be compared with the uncertain tonal center of the Chopin example shown earlier (Example 30–2); on the other hand it is also comparable to bitonality, which will be discussed in the next chapter.

EXAMPLE 30–34: Stravinsky, *L'Histoire du soldat,* Music to Scene 1

More complicated questions of tonality in the twentieth century will be discussed in Chapter 32.

CHAPTER 31

Scalar and Chordal Types

THE PENTATONIC SCALE

The pentatonic scale, whose intervallic pattern corresponds to that of the black keys on the piano, is very ancient, having been used in the music of Eastern cultures perhaps longer even than the diatonic scale in the West.

EXAMPLE 31–1

It is also the scale used in many European folk songs, particularly those of the British Isles.

Cf. the major tonic triad with added sixth (Chapter 23)

Because the pentatonic scale corresponds to only five of the seven major-scale degrees, it is sometimes called a *gapped scale*. Only two triads are possible, corresponding to relative major and minor. Many pentatonic folk melodies, heard without accompaniment, seem to suggest a constant oscillation between relative major and minor modes.

See Ex. 11–21

Chopin's *Etude* for piano in G-flat major, Op. 10, No. 5, called the "Black Key" Etude, uses only the black keys in the right hand. The left hand, however, uses a number of white keys to complete the diatonic harmony. Thus although the piece at times suggests harmony made up entirely of pentatonic degrees. fundamentally it is diatonic. Debussy's *Pagodes* is a good deal closer to an example of "pure" pentatonic writing, even though parts of the piece often depart from the scale.

EXAMPLE 31–2: Debussy, *Estampes*: I, *Pagodes*

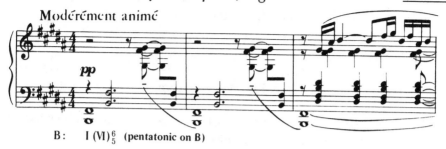

B: I (VI)$^6_5$ (pentatonic on B)

The absence of the leading-tone in the pentatonic scale is in keeping with Debussy's habitual aversion to dominant–tonic relationships.

In the following example a pentatonic melody is harmonized with only slight deviations from the scale, which nevertheless add suggestions of modal harmony to the passage.

EXAMPLE 31–3: Debussy, *Nocturnes*: I, *Nuages*

d♯:   I   (pentatonic melody)

(natural minor)   (Dorian)

The following example is based exclusively on the pentatonic scale. The second degree, F sharp, appears as a passing tone between E and G sharp; only the sixth degree dangles slightly, though it seems to be associated with the tonic triad like an added sixth. The passage, from one of Debussy's early works, is a good illustration of a subtle, rather than a radical, departure from common practice.

EXAMPLE 31–4: Debussy, *Arabesque No. 1*

Melodies using the pentatonic scale are found in many twentieth-century works in all types of harmonic contexts. Often the use has a programmatic significance, such as a connection with Oriental subjects (Ravel, *Mother Goose Suite*, No. 3; Stravinsky, *The Nightingale*; Bartók, *The Miraculous Mandarin*; Mahler, *Das Lied von der Erde*, No. 3).

THE WHOLE-TONE SCALE

As was mentioned before (Chapter 28), the six-note whole-tone scale is a symmetrical partitioning of the chromatic scale.

EXAMPLE 31–5

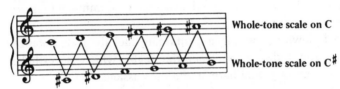

Whole-tone scale on C

Whole-tone scale on C♯

In this scale all triads are augmented, and no intervals except the octave are perfect. It is in fact pointless to speak of "major" and "minor" intervals, since these change depending on enharmonic notation. Reference to the semitonal-interval table in Chapter 1 establishes that the intervals of the whole-tone scale are only even-numbered.

The whole-tone scale is occasionally seen in the common-practice period, though never as an independent generator of harmony. Mozart used it for deliberately disruptive purposes in his *Musical Joke*, K. 522. At other times it appears as a companion to the chromatic scale, as in the bass line of the following example:

Cf. Exx. 20–29 and 20–30: similar motion

EXAMPLE 31–6: Chopin, *Prelude*, Op. 28, No. 19

The above passage, like most instances of consecutive diminished sevenths, suspends the tonality between the triads surrounding it, and can be regarded as a harmonic, though not triadic, thickening of the chromatic scale. A similar situation is found in the example below. All four parts move chromatically in two opposing layers, each vertical relationship coinciding with the whole-tone scale.

EXAMPLE 31–7: Schoenberg, *String Quartet*, Op. 7

The matching of chromatic and whole-tone scales here should be compared with the opening of Liszt's *Faust Symphony* (Example 28–14).

The use of the whole-tone scale by Debussy is just one of many distinctive characteristics of his style. In the earlier works it appears in augmented-triad harmony like that of the Schoenberg example above, or sometimes as an incidental detail in prevailing diatonic harmony, growing out of the dominant seventh with raised fifth, or the augmented six-four-three, as here:

EXAMPLE 31–8: Debussy, *Prélude à l'Après-midi d'un faune*

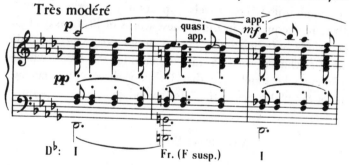

The use of the suspended third degree and the irregular resolution to the tonic would be unlikely to be found in common practice; the sonority contains five of the six possible whole-tone degrees.

In Debussy's more typical use of the whole-tone scale, tonality can hardly be defined in terms of classical triads and progressions. Only two triads are possible, both of them augmented, and, as has already been noted, all inversions sound alike. All "progressions" tend to have the same tonal character. What one hears are tone centers rather than tonics, and only when these are 483 stressed in some way, such as by repetition, like the low B flat in the following example:

EXAMPLE 31–9: Debussy, *Préludes*, Book I: No. 2, *Voiles*

Modéré

It cannot be denied that the small number of possible different intervals and nonequivalent chords available in the whole-tone scale results in a soft-edged, neutral kind of sound lacking in tonal contrast. For certain types of atmospheric effects, however, whole-tone harmony suited Debussy's purposes admirably. Though he used it often, he seldom used it for very long, for more than a few measures at a time, always contrasting it with more conventionally diatonic harmony. Example 31–9 above is drawn from Debussy's most thoroughgoing whole-tone work; with the exception of four chromatic passing tones and a short middle section using the pentatonic scale, the entire piece is constructed on the whole-tone scale.

Whole-tone harmony only rarely appears in the works of Ravel, and with some frequency in the earliest works of Stravinsky. It is found occasionally in Schoenberg's and Berg's early works, within a context of advanced tonal chromaticism. Since the 1930s, whole-tone harmony, like much else that Debussy discovered, has become one of the platitudes of the "Hollywood style."

ARTIFICIAL SCALES

It is apparent that the major and minor scales and the modal scales do not exhaust the possibilities of diatonic scales, that is, seven-note scales composed of successive half-steps and whole-steps in various distributions. An *artificial scale* is defined to be a scale that is neither major, minor, chromatic, nor one of the church modes. We will concern ourselves in this section with artificial scales that are subsets of the twelve-tone tempered scale, leaving aside the whole-tone and pentatonic scales just discussed, as well as nontempered scales, such as those found in Oriental music, and microtonal scales, such as the quarter-tone scale (24 tones to the octave) and others that even today are considered experimental.

Already in the common-practice period we have encountered the use of the harmonic minor scale, with one augmented second, as a basis of melody, even though in such cases it is usually possible to think of this as the result of alternating between the different melodic minor forms. The so-called Hungarian scale (Chapter 5, Example 5–1), with two augmented seconds, turns up occasionally in the melodic writing of the Hungarian nationalists, beginning with Liszt, but not as a basis for harmony. Other comparable patterns may be occasionally found in nineteenth-century melodic writing, in isolated instances where the appearance of one or more nonclassical interval successions is likely to be brought about by momentary chromatic alteration in the major or minor scale, and we have seen how the use of the chromatically lowered second degree in the Neapolitan sixth does not of itself proclaim the use of the Phrygian mode.

A more compelling instance of an artificial scale is afforded by Debussy's *Nuages*, the first of his three *Nocturnes* for orchestra, in which the following scale appears as the basis of both melody and harmony during a large part of the piece.

EXAMPLE 31–10

At a glance this is no more than the B natural-minor scale with lowered fifth degree, but that one difference has a considerable effect on the tonality. The tonic triad is diminished, being absorbed into the sound of the submediant seventh chord, which itself sounds like the dominant of C, a tone not present in the scale.

EXAMPLE 31–11: Debussy, *Nocturnes: I, Nuages*

Debussy never considered the exclusive use of a particular scale in a composition to be an imperative, and *Nuages* is no exception; the extensive passages in which the artificial scale appears are contrasted with projections of various kinds of ordinary B minor, with F sharp as the fifth degree. But it is precisely that condition that makes *Nuages* such an important departure from common practice. The distinction between B–D–F sharp as the tonality-organizing triad and G–B–D–F as the companion chord of the tone B becomes blurred, and eventually any classical association with B minor vanishes, leaving at the end only the single pitch B as a tone center.

EXAMPLE 31–12: Debussy, *Nocturnes:* I, *Nuages*
(final measures)

One of the "Six Inventions" that constitute the final act of Berg's opera *Wozzeck* is a scene designated by him "Invention on a six-note chord," that chord being the D-flat pentatonic scale with an additional note, the minor third degree:

EXAMPLE 31–13

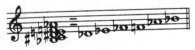

From this collection of pitch-classes (including their enharmonic and octave equivalents) most of the pitches of the scene are drawn. (Some parts of the scene use the transposed collection, others add chromatic passing tones; one climactic point uses the collections as one chordal layer, adding below it, in a cluster, the other six tones of the chromatic scale, forming a twelve-tone chord.) Thus the six-note "chord" is also to be considered a scale in the same sense that only its pitch-classes are used, in a variety of combinations with each other, triadic and otherwise, and in both scalar and nonscalar order. The convergence of this scale with the pentatonic scale lends a loose quasi-tonality to the scene, one of the relatively few places where such a thing occurs in this mostly atonal opera.

EXAMPLE 31–14: Berg, *Wozzeck*, Act III, Scene 4

Langsamer (piano reduction)

BLOCK CHORDS

Block-chord writing is a generalizing term that implies the parallel motion of chords without regard for common-practice considerations of voice leading, and with a constant homophony.

Block-chord motion may employ only triads in root position.

EXAMPLE 31–15: Bartók, *Bluebeard's Castle*

Larghissimo
coll'8va

The above passage, using all major triads, gives the impression of mixed modes on C.

The following example is not parallel in all parts, nor even between the outer voices, but would be called block-chord writing because all the triads are in root position.

EXAMPLE 31–16: Debussy, *String Quartet*, I

Block-chord motion of more complex sonorities will be found in many of the examples cited elsewhere in this and the previous chapter.

In cases where the parallel motion is continuous, it is possible to regard block chords as a harmonic expansion, or thickening, of a single line. An analogous procedure was widespread in common practice with parallel triads in the first inversion, as will be remembered from Example 6–11. The parallel chromatic motion of diminished sevenths in common practice is a somewhat different matter, because such motion is ordinarily connective rather than inherently melodic; it is somewhat as though the entire sequence were a prolonged passing chord from the initial harmony to the final. Only after common practice did block-chord motion come to include the intervals of perfect fifth or octave between the outer voices, with everything subordinate to the progress of the line itself. With these considerations in mind, it is not hard to imagine the possibility of lines in combination, each thickened by block chords.

EXAMPLE 31–17: Stravinsky, *Petrushka*, Tableau I

Such combined lines or layers naturally give rise to complex chords whose vertical relationship cannot be accounted for other than by such "contra-chordal" interpretations, just as certain complex sonorities in common practice result from the contrapuntal combination of nonharmonic tones.

The term *tertial harmony* means harmony based on chords constructed by superposing intervals of a third. In the larger sense this would include all of common-practice harmony, but we shall discuss here only harmony in which the superposition of thirds, and the treatment of the resulting chords, go beyond common practice.

Beginning with Debussy, composers came to realize the possibilities of nondominant seventh and ninth chords treated independently, without consideration of how these might be fitted into a context by classical voice leading. The following passage from Ravel's *Menuet antique,* for example, shows at least in part how Ravel imagined the voices to move, but this movement, though entirely smooth, is hardly what one would expect to find in common practice. It seems likely that Ravel was as fully interested in the sonorous peculiarities of the chord as in any contrapuntal considerations.

EXAMPLE 31–18: Ravel, *Menuet antique*

In the following example, the accumulation of thirds certainly does not arise from the counterpoint, but neither does it obscure the underlying classical root progression, probably because the passage is entirely diatonic in C major.

EXAMPLE 31–19: Ravel, *Le Tombeau de Couperin:*
No. 4, *Rigaudon*

Stacks of thirds can also result from the intersection of melodic layers.

EXAMPLE 31–20: Holst, *The Planets:* II, *Venus*

The example above can be analyzed strictly in the manner shown, but one does not really hear this as a succession of true roots any more than one hears a succession of parallel first-inversion triads as moving roots, independently of other features of the music. It is more realistic to think of it as the convergence of two lines thickened by layers of superposed thirds.

Nor would one be likely to perceive the following admittedly extreme example as an independent supertonic twenty-seventh chord, where the bass is just one more factor that happens to be the "root."

EXAMPLE 31–21: Stravinsky, *Petrushka*, Tableau II

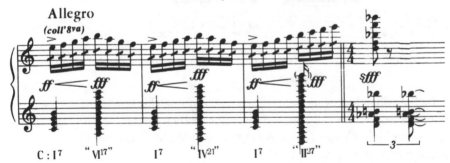

QUARTAL HARMONY

In triadic music the interval of the perfect fourth is a consonant component only of triads in the first inversion, or when the root is doubled in root position. As a dissonant interval it is marked by its tendency to shrink to a third. Perfect fourths heard in superposition seem to compound this tendency and thus are sel-

heard in common practice. In the absence of a triadic , the ear finds it difficult to determine a root unless other harmonic elements are involved.

The apparent structure of superposed fourths in the following example, ingeniously arranged to account for the open strings of Beckmesser's lute, is actually a II⁷ over a dominant pedal, as the resolution shows.

EXAMPLE 31–22: Wagner, *Die Meistersinger*, Act II, Scene 5

The regular use of chords built of superposed fourths does not appear until the early twentieth century, with works like Schoenberg's *Chamber Symphony,* Op. 9, which remains an isolated phenomenon in Schoenberg's output but had a considerable influence elsewhere. In the following example, a chromatically descending series of fourth chords settles on a five-tone quartal sonority (circled), whose factors then move variously into a whole-tone chord having the structure of a dominant seventh with raised fifth. (It was the practice of Schoenberg and his followers to provide accidental signs on nearly every note, even when a key signature was used.)

EXAMPLE 31–23: Berg, *Piano Sonata*, Op. 1

The following example shows separate lines doubled in fourths, becoming parallel, and finally moving as a single layer of fourths.

EXAMPLE 31–24: Bartók, *Sonata for Two Pianos and Percussion*, I

The harmonically neutral sound of superposed perfect fourths is not substantially affected by the addition or removal of factors in the chord. The alteration of one of the intervals within, however, revises the entire structure of the chord and introduces a definite coloristic change. The inclusion of an augmented fourth in the vertical structures of the following example gives the impression of a series of independent dominant thirteenths.

EXAMPLE 31–25: Satie, *Le Fils des étoiles*, Prelude

The limit of perfect-fourth superposition is reached in the following example.

EXAMPLE 31–26: Berg, *Three Pieces for Orchestra,*
Op. 6: No. 2, *Reigen*

Schwungvoll, fast roh

QUINTAL HARMONY

The sonority of superposed perfect fifths is similar to but different
from that of fourths. It seems to be qualitatively more stable, if
only because the ear can imagine a root in the bass, and sometimes a third in between the root and fifth. Beyond two superposed fifths, however, it is difficult to carry this process of mental
extrapolation; one does not hear three superposed fifths as a
thirteenth chord with third, seventh, and eleventh missing.

The beginning of Liszt's *Mephisto Waltz* is like the Wagner
example above in that it is a musical depiction of tuning up a
stringed instrument. Note how the tones in the stack of fifths
move so as to change the sonority to something more closely
related to triadic harmony.

EXAMPLE 31–27: Liszt, *Mephisto Waltz No. 1*

Allegro vivace (quasi presto)

In the example below, Debussy uses oscillating chords of two perfect fifths in the left hand, together with a melody doubled in perfect fifths and octaves, to give an archaic atmosphere to his impressionistic "sunken cathedral," in which he seems to be recalling parallel organum of the Middle Ages. A marking at the beginning of the piece says "in a gently sonorous fog."

EXAMPLE 31–28: Debussy, *Preludes*, Book I: No. 10,
La Cathédrale engloutie

The following comparable example combines fourth chords with a surrounding stack of six fifths.

EXAMPLE 31–29: Ravel, *Daphnis et Chloé* (beginning)

The following passage is firmly rooted on C, with an implication of alternating tonic and dominant.

EXAMPLE 31–30: Casella, *Sonata No. 2 in C major
for Piano and Cello*

Largo molto e sostenuto

The harmony of the following example is in two quintal layers in contrary motion. Sometimes these intersect to form octave doublings or an unbroken stack of fifths, while at other times the variable interval separating the two layers introduces a new color.

EXAMPLE 31–31: Bartók, *Piano Concerto No. 2*

SECUNDAL HARMONY

Chords built of seconds are of several types. When only major seconds are superposed, a whole-tone sonority results. Chords built of adjacent diatonic scale degrees will have major and minor seconds; these and chords built only of semitones are described as tone-clusters.

A melodic line in parallel major seconds was a device particularly favored by the impressionist composers.

EXAMPLE 31–32: Ravel, *Gaspard de la nuit*: III, *Scarbo*

The following example gives the impression of something between a C-major glissando and a C-major tone-cluster.

EXAMPLE 31–33: Prokofiev, *Piano Concerto No. 3*, III

The following pair of clusters for the piano, an important leitmotive in Berg's *Lulu,* uses all twelve pitch-classes of the chromatic scale. The example is given in Berg's notation.

EXAMPLE 31–34: Berg, *Lulu,* Prologue

A comparable passage is found in Ives's "Concord" Sonata, where the pianist uses a measured strip of wood to press the keys. Later in the same work the pianist is directed to play the following, using his fist "if he feels like it."

EXAMPLE 31–35: Ives, *Sonata No. 2,* "Concord, Mass., 1840–1860": II, *Hawthorne*

Tone-clusters containing many different chromatic pitches closely packed will ordinarily have no tonal basis. They are usually employed for rhythmic, percussive accents, only occasionally for soft, atmospheric color.

EXAMPLE 31–36: Bartók, *Piano Sonata,* III

PANDIATONICISM

In the previous section of this chapter we examined harmony in which the superposition of equal intervals is employed systematically to produce characteristic sonorities. These special harmonic types were thoroughly explored by composers beginning in the first decade of the twentieth century, and in varying ways became incorporated into the diatonic vocabulary. However, these sonorities account for only part of the nontriadic harmony of the twentieth century. Composers were equally cognizant of harmony based on the diatonic scale but not having any specifically intervallic organization. The terms *pandiatonicism* and *white-note harmony* have been coined in recognition of the entire spectrum of diatonic harmony that is not limited to chords originating from triads.

The opening measures of Stravinsky's *Octet* demonstrate E-flat major clearly enough at the very beginning by means of tonic triad and dominant seventh; the chords that follow combine elements of both, then proceed to a half cadence on V of VI.

EXAMPLE 31–37: Stravinsky, *Octet for Wind Instruments,* I

The dissonances in some of these chords are not to be explained by the conventional determinations of preparation and resolution, but by the composer's choice of individual harmonic and melodic relationships. Another passage from later in the piece shows a more contrapuntal genesis of the pandiatonic harmony; it has no chromatic tones at all.

Cf. Exx. 31–28, 31–30

497

EXAMPLE 31–38: Stravinsky, *Octet for Wind Instruments*, I

Copyright 1924 by Edition Russe de Musique. Renewed 1952. Copyright and renewal assigned to Boosey & Hawkes, Inc. Revised Version Copyright 1952 by Boosey & Hawkes, Inc. Reprinted by permission.

V, IV, I mixed   II, I/V I

The following example of melody and accompaniment can be said to be texturally pandiatonic. The overlapping layers of the three-note motive E–G–A and its transposition A–C–D are not heard canonically because there is no rhythmic differentiation; rather there is a blurring of all five different pitches into a single pentatonic harmony, which serves as a background to the A natural minor melody in the bass.

EXAMPLE 31–39: Holst, *The Planets: IV, Jupiter*

Copyright © 1921 Goodwin & Tabb Ltd. Copyright © renewed 1949 J. Curwen & Sons Ltd. Used by permission, G. Schirmer Inc.

POLYCHORDS AND POLYTONALITY

Review Chapter 8: The Pedal

Polychords result from the combination of two or more triads or other simple chords. Normally the term is used to designate only combinations of relatively remotely related triads. A chord resulting from superposition of a D-minor triad over a G-major triad, for instance, would normally be a V^9 of C major, and not a polychord. Nevertheless the differentiation is not always an easy one to make, because the effect of many polychords is to have one of the components harmonically predominating, and the other members heard to a greater or lesser degree as nonharmonic tones.

498

A wide variety of polychordal types can be found in the works of many composers, beginning in the first decade of the twentieth century. These types range from combinations of incomplete triads to combinations of seventh and ninth chords and altered chords. It is characteristic of the period that the polychords used by composers are chosen for their individuality of sound and not for their systematicity of structure. Thus it is not at all unusual to encounter harmonies in which a particular member of a polychord may be explainable as a factor of one particular triadic component, or as an altered factor of another, or as an unresolved appoggiatura, or a combination of these.

The extraordinary chord that appears seemingly out of nowhere in Mahler's *Tenth Symphony* is a good illustration of the insufficiency of our descriptive language in its present state.

EXAMPLE 31–40: Mahler, *Symphony No. 10,* I

It is possible to analyze this sonority as a combination of three groups, a diminished seventh (G sharp–B–D–F), a half-diminished seventh (B–D–F–A), and a minor triad (C–E flat–G), over a pedal C sharp. With equal validity it could be considered as a stack of thirds reaching as far as the nineteenth (though the omission of the third between the low C sharp and G sharp makes a big difference), but with several chromatic alterations; as a complex dominant over a C-sharp root the chord is directly related to the main tonality of the movement, F-sharp major. But neither of these analyses seems to go very far towards explaining why such a chord should be chosen at all; only a closer analysis of the context, perhaps including the entire movement, would be likely to illuminate that question.

The relationship of a tritone between two major-triadic components is the basis of Stravinsky's so-called Petrushka chord, although other composers, such as Ravel in his *Jeux d'eau,* used it at least ten years before *Petrushka.*

499

EXAMPLE 31–41: Stravinsky, *Petrushka*, Tableau II

From the standpoint of the circle of fifths, the tritone relationship is the remotest possible (cf. Example 28–32). One should compare the Petrushka sonority also with the "*Boris* chords" as shown in Example 30–31.

The following example is relatively simple to resolve into two layers, a sustained D-minor triad with most of its weight in the bass, and an oscillating pair of D-sharp and C-sharp-minor triads in the upper parts.

EXAMPLE 31–42: Stravinsky, *The Rite of Spring*,
Part II: Introduction

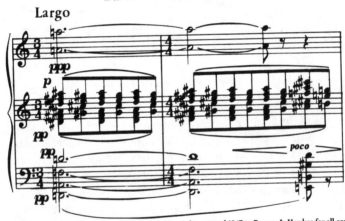

The melodic activity of the upper parts seems to define a Phrygian D-sharp minor tone center, strong enough to overbalance the D-minor bass, which acts as a sort of "false tonic," even the sustained upper-register A sounding like a leading-tone to A sharp. This interpretation is not the only possible one, however, nor even necessarily a preferred one. The outstanding characteristics of the harmony of this passage, as in so much music of the period, are its autonomous structure and individualized sound, and not the way in which it may or may not fit into some formal tonal scheme.

Polytonality is a somewhat different situation from the mere use of polychords. In polytonality, the intention is to create the impression of more than one key at the same time, a sort of counterpoint of keys.

EXAMPLE 31–43: Wagner, *Die Meistersinger*, End of Act I

In the above example, the listener has already heard the Apprentices' Song earlier, with the harmony shown. Here it is incorporated into a slower-moving passage over a dominant pedal in F major, a key that has been well-established for some time. The different meter and different texture make it possible to hear the song as a simultaneous different music, anchored by the C in the bass, and the impression of two keys, though delicate and fleeting, is not hard to hear.

In twentieth-century bitonality the key relationships are likely to be more remote and contrasting. It is easier to distinguish mentally the two keys if one of them is established first and then the other is added.

EXAMPLE 31–44: Poulenc, *Mouvements perpétuels*, I

By permission of J & W CHESTER/Edition Wilhelm Hansen London Limited.

In the example above, the G-flat-major scale shares most of its pitches with the B-flat-minor scale, so the difference between the 501 two keys (B flat and G flat) is not as great as the difference between the two modes (B-flat major and B-flat minor).

Another aid to aural separation of the two keys is to have one of them relatively inactive harmonically, like a pedal point.

EXAMPLE 31–45: Ravel, *L'Enfant et les sortilèges,*
Dance of the Shepherds

Sometimes one of the keys may be defined by as little as an ostinato bass of tonic and dominant. The following examples may be compared for their different effects.

EXAMPLE 31–46: Ravel, *Daphnis et Chloé*

EXAMPLE 31–47: Berg, *Wozzeck,* Act I, Scene 3

In another passage in *Daphnis et Chloé,* the upper layer of triads does not seem to define a single separate key because the triads are not all closely related to each other; rather there is the feeling of a series of polychords related by their melodic succession in the upper layer and by the sustained dominant seventh in the bass.

EXAMPLE 31–48: Ravel, *Daphnis et Chloé*

The sustained chord in the following passage is a polychord composed of a dominant seventh of A-flat and a C-major triad, though it could also be regarded as a single dominant ninth sonority (of F) with simultaneous major and minor third. The melody in the upper part suggests D major, implying three simultaneous keys, though one is hard put to account for the F-sharp drumbeat in the bass.

See below: The Inverted Ninth Chord

EXAMPLE 31–49: Stravinsky, *The Rite of Spring*, Part I:
Ritual of the Abduction   *ff marcatissimo*

When there is much harmonic activity in both bitonal layers the separate keys may be difficult to distinguish. One hears instead a synthesis of the two into a complex harmony that sounds more chromatic than diatonic.

EXAMPLE 31–50: Ravel, *L'Enfant et les sortilèges*, Final Scene

Examples like the foregoing make it apparent that the simultaneous perception of different keys is not necessarily easy, and that it depends on more than just the constitution of the chords involved. Rhythmic, melodic, and contrapuntal separation may have a good deal to do with how the different keys are heard, and spacing may be especially important.

MODAL MIXTURE

*Review Chapter
5: Mixed Modes*

The interchangeability of parallel major and minor modes, noted in Chapter 5 as a resource of common practice, continued into twentieth-century tonality. One perceives an actual change of mode when it is the tonic triad that changes, as in Example 5–28. Triads from the opposite mode, other than the tonic triad, do not usually create the impression of a shift in the main mode, but rather appear as chords lent temporarily from the other mode. IV from the minor followed by I in the major, for example, does not change the prevailing major mode; this progression is found everywhere in common practice. The prevalent use in the major mode of such chords as the various forms of dominant minor ninth, the Neapolitan sixth, and the augmented sixth chords, all of which contain the minor sixth degree, attests to the adaptability of the different modal degrees without disturbing the stability of the major mode. This property is comparable to the use of inflected triads with the ascending melodic minor scale, which do not in themselves alter the predominance of the surrounding minor mode. Hardly less frequent than these is the use of VI from the minor, progressing to I in the major, two major triads involving a change of the modal third degree. On the other hand, the reverse progression, VI from the major progressing to I in the minor (two minor triads) is definitely not common practice.

EXAMPLE 31–51: Mahler, *Symphony No. 3*, IV

Sehr langsam. Misterioso

a: VI   I   VI   I

Other such progressions entered the harmonic vocabulary at the end of the nineteeth century as the use of modal scales increased. As we have seen, the Lydian and Mixolydian scales are essentially "major" because the tonic triad is major; similarly the Dorian and Phrygian are essentially "minor."

Another aspect of modal mixture that has already been pointed out is the cross-relation of leading-tone with minor seventh degree in dominant harmony, the leading-tone ascending and the minor seventh descending as part of the melodic minor scale (Example 8–32). In common practice this is generally an appoggiatura relationship, but in the twentieth century it became an independent harmonic structure.

EXAMPLE 31–52: Bartók, *The Wooden Prince*

The addition of a minor third to dominant seventh and dominant ninth harmony is an example of what jazz musicians call a "blue note." The first composer to make systematic use of such harmony was Ravel, who made it a distinctive stylistic characteristic.

EXAMPLE 31–53: Ravel, *Miroirs:* No. 4, *Alborada del gracioso*

The following example shows a dominant with major and minor third, and another with major and minor seventh (the major seventh as chromatic neighbor-note).

505

EXAMPLE 31–54: Ravel, *Rapsodie espagnole:* I,
Prélude à la nuit

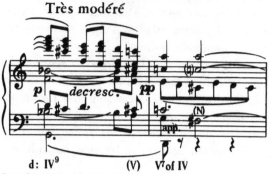

Très modéré

d: IV⁹   (V)   Vᵒof IV

The following example is more complicated. To the third, fifth, and seventh of each dominant is added an appoggiatura a major seventh (or diminished octave) above. This may be an extension of the principle of major-minor mixture, but the effect is of a polychordal sonority, rather like the *Daphnis et Chloé* example earlier (Example 31–48). Despite the complex dissonances in the upper register, the classical sequence of dominant basses is clear and effective.

EXAMPLE 31–55: Ravel, *Piano Trio:* II, *Pantoum*

Assez vif

g#: V

C#: I
V

f#: V
I

f#: I

b: V

THE INVERTED NINTH CHORD

Like its counterpart in common practice, the dominant minor ninth with major and minor third may appear as an incomplete chord without the root.

EXAMPLE 31–56

V^9 "V^o_9" V^7 "VII"   =   "V^7_4" (of III)

complete   (without   without   with neither   2

form   root)   ninth   root nor ninth   "inverted ninth"

In the spacing shown, the complete chord of six factors is not without some polychordal feeling, rather like V^7 in the lower four voices combined with V^7 of III in the upper four. When the root is left out, the chord no longer sounds like an incomplete dominant, but like a complete and different dominant, V^7_4 of III, with a different root (the upper voice, in the example). The chord called "VII" above, implying an incomplete V^7 with major and minor third, is often seen in the enharmonic notation shown. This enharmonic version is seen to have notationally the structure of a dominant minor ninth in the fourth inversion, with root but without seventh. In this inversion the ninth is below the root, a situation that does not occur in common practice (see Chapter 22), but that is characteristic for this sonority in the twentieth century.

*See also Ex.
31–49*

*See also Ex.
31–21*

*But see Ex.
22–14*

EXAMPLE 31–57: Ravel, *Gaspard de la nuit*: I, *Ondine*

Rapide et brillant

The following example contains three harmonic layers, the middle showing parallel inverted ninth chords. The upper layer (with a somewhat different chordal doubling) and the parallel-fifth ostinato bass have previously been heard together without a middle layer. The overall effect is generally one of dense major-minor polychords.

EXAMPLE 31–58: Stravinsky, *The Rite of Spring*,
Part I: *Round Dance*

Sostenuto e pesante

The following example is of somewhat similar effect, made particularly pungent by the B-natural–B-flat semitone in the middle of the cadencing sonority.

EXAMPLE 31–59: Berg, *Wozzeck*, End of Act I

Andante affetuoso

APPOGGIATURA CHORDS

Appoggiatura chords in common practice, defined in Chapter 28 as vertical combinations of appoggiature, are dependent for their meaning on expected resolution to consonant sonorities. By extension the term includes chords resulting from combinations of other types of nonharmonic tones. Many such chords are possible, and even the most mordantly dissonant combinations are well un-

508

derstood by the ear if the melodic motion and the surrounding harmonic context are clear.

EXAMPLE 31–60: Bach, *Brandenburg Concerto No. 1*, II

EXAMPLE 31–61: Mozart, *String Quintet*, K. 614, II

Common practice also included, as we have seen, a category of so-called harmonic dissonances—the seventh and ninth in dominant harmony, and the added sixth above a root position triad—which in some circumstances were appoggiature or suspensions, but in others were less restricted in their preparation and resolution, that is, closer to being autonomous chords. In our discussion of independent sonorities we saw that after common practice it was chords embodying these harmonic dissonances that were the first to achieve a freedom of motion and connection comparable to that enjoyed by pure triads.

Appoggiatura chords in the twentieth century are extensions of common-practice forms of chordal dissonance. They include several basic types. One type is represented by common-practice appoggiatura ninth, eleventh, and thirteenth chords and chords 509 over pedal points, the dissonant factors being left unresolved; some of these have already been discussed under the heading of tertial harmony. Another type includes chromatic appoggiature such as in altered chords, also unresolved. A third type includes appoggiature sounding simultaneously with their notes of resolution. These types also occur in various combinations, and certainly a number of the chordal phenomena we have already discussed earlier, such as major-minor chords and certain fourth chords, occur in contexts that permit them to be treated as appoggiatura chords.

EXAMPLE 31–62: Stravinsky, *The Firebird*, Finale

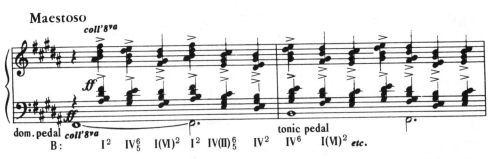

The vertical structure of the above example is no more complex than simple nondominant sevenths and added-sixth chords, framed by parallel sixths. It is their closely packed arrangement, in the form of triads with attached neighbor notes, and their nonsystematic resolution, that brands these as diatonic appoggiatura chords.

Short appoggiature in close texture with their notes of resolution appear as special ornaments called *acciaccature* (Italian, *acciaccare*, "to crush") in Baroque harpsichord music; Domenico Scarlatti's sonatas furnish some startling examples. Chopin's *Etude* in E minor, Op. 25, No. 5, is a later example of the acciaccatura style. In all these cases the appoggiatura, usually the semitone below, is sounded on the strong part of the beat like any other appoggiatura (in other words, it is not a true grace note), the note of resolution coming either simultaneously or immediately afterward. The developments after common practice extended this principle to allow appoggiature of equal duration with their simultaneous notes of resolution, a technique that seems to fore-

shadow tone-clustering.

EXAMPLE 31–63: Dvořák, *The Noon Witch*, Op. 108

Poco animato, non tanto

The following example suggests a roughly strummed guitar.

EXAMPLE 31–64: Albéniz, *Ibéria*, Book I: No. 3,
Fête-Dieu à Seville

Allegro gracioso

The augmented sixth chord over a dominant pedal, occasionally found in common practice, may be cited here as a type of appoggiatura chord, representing a secondary dominant sounding simultaneously with the root of its chord of resolution. As an unresolved appoggiatura chord, it may also be regarded enharmonically as a dominant seventh with pedal; as such it was a favorite chord of Ravel. The reader may compare the following example with Example 27–24.

EXAMPLE 31–65: Ravel, *Miroirs*: IV, *Alborada del gracioso*

Assez vif

In the example below, the sequence, which is not completely strict, gives the impression of a chromatically descending series of dominants, each an appoggiatura chord to the next. The starred chords are rhythmically stronger, however, and carry the harmonic weight as successive dominants with appoggiatura thirteenth (in the upper voice) and major and minor third.

EXAMPLE 31–66: Ravel, *Gaspard de la nuit*: III, *Scarbo*

The first harmony of the following example is a dominant seventh with appoggiatura thirteenth and appoggiatura leading-tone (E sharp) to the leading-tone; the second is a chromatic passing chord (D sharp from D to E; C sharp from C to D; A sharp from A to B); the third is a tonic triad with added sixth and appoggiatura ninth (A); the fourth is a superposition of raised supertonic (like the traditional raised supertonic seventh but without the seventh) over a dominant bass.

Cf. Ex. 30–28

EXAMPLE 31–67: Ravel, *Valses nobles et sentimentales*, I

A favorite resource of jazz harmony is the following sequence of appoggiatura dominants:

EXAMPLE 31–68

D: V¹³   V⁷ of IV⁽±3⁾   C: V¹³   V⁷ of IV⁽±3⁾
  G: V⁷⁽±8⁾   V¹³ of IV   F: V⁷⁽±3⁾

The upper voices move in parallel; the bass moves in downward fifths. An early use of the sequence is the following:

EXAMPLE 31–69: Ravel, *Gaspard de la nuit*: II, *Le Gibet*

The dominant seventh and dominant major ninth, both with raised fifth, were widely employed as independent sonorities in the atmospheric harmony of Scriabin, which in turn had an influence on the early chromatic harmony of Stravinsky. The examples below may be compared for their chromatic and whole-tone relationships.

EXAMPLE 31–70: Scriabin, *Poem of Ecstasy*, Op. 54

EXAMPLE 31–71: Stravinsky, *The Firebird*, Supplication Scene

The closely textured seconds, sevenths, and ninths of the following example partly result from appoggiatura-chord layers, partly
from pedal points, and partly from contrapuntal convergences.
It is instructive to compare the style of this example with that of
the preceding; the two are wholly different, although they were
composed only nine years apart.

EXAMPLE 31–72: Stravinsky, *Symphonies of Wind Instruments*

The following example could be cited as one paradigm of the
appoggiatura principle in the twentieth century. The first two
measures are an unadorned appoggiatura plagal cadence in E minor; the next two are an echo of it, beginning with a complex
tangle of notes which slowly slide their way (except for the bass)
to consonance.

514

EXAMPLE 31–73: Prokofiev, *Piano Concerto No. 3*, II

CHAPTER 32

Extended Chromaticism

The music of the twentieth century, considered as a whole, shows the widest possible range of different styles, techniques, and compositional philosophies, and we have shown in this book a large variety of examples of music that can in one way or another be called tonal. Tonality in music is in part a manifestation of form, and tonal harmony is one kind of intrinsic form, however it has been used by composers. By "form" we mean here a kind of organized relationship among tones, a system in all its variability and with all the exceptions that composers have been able to devise. That is what this book is about.

Nevertheless the most distinctive aspect, and the most interesting historical fact, of the music of our own century, is the appearance in music of atonality, or absence of key, the result of more than a century of harmonic evolution and ever-widening exploration of the expressive resources of chromaticism. Though atonal music has not been readily accepted by perhaps even the majority of listening audiences, at least so far, atonality and the compositional techniques which govern it have been the major interest of some composers for nearly seventy years, and of most composers for at least the past twenty years.

The disappearance of tonality was from the start attended, in the works of the first atonal composers, by a search for new formal relationships, for new modes of compositional thought that could support a new music without tonality, and this search was successful. The techniques of atonality are beyond the scope of this book, but it is worthwhile to follow some of the paths that eventually led to the emergence of atonality, if only because they form a logical conclusion to the present study.

We have seen that even in music of the common-practice era there are instances when the impression of tonality, at least on some level, can be temporarily suspended. This means that one or another element of the music causes the obliteration of tonality, or perhaps that the absence of some element results in a failure of the tonality to be sustained. Atonality would then be represented by the systematic application or suppression of these respective elements.

TONALITY-SUPPORTING AND TONALITY-WEAKENING ELEMENTS

The following elements tend to establish tonality, or to preserve it:

1. Tone centers, related intrinsically by scale, but established by the compositional process, and including the possibility of major and minor modes.
2. Harmonic progression of triads. In common practice, these are fundamentally the most important organizers of tonality. Dissonant harmonic factors reinforce progressions by their contrapuntal resolutions.
3. Clear cadences. A phrase need not immediately reveal its tonal center, and interest is to be gained by postponing the arrival.
4. Dominant and tonic pedal points and ostinati.
5. Avoidance of notes other than the major and minor scale degrees.
6. Reinforcement of a tone center by its restoration after a temporary departure.

The following elements tend to weaken or disguise tonality:

1. Complex chords, specifically: chords containing multiple nonharmonic tones; chords with obscured root functions (for instance, a ninth chord with the ninth below the root); chords of superposed fourths or fifths.
2. Multiple functions of chords from common practice having

517

neither a major nor a minor triad as the principal component, such as II in the minor mode, VII, V_9^0, etc.

3. Irregular resolutions.
4. Rapid harmonic rhythm.
5. Dense contrapuntal writing.
6. Remote tonal functions; dislocation of tonal center through extension of the secondary dominant principle.
7. Frequent and continual modulation.
8. Extensive use of modal mixture.
9. Fluctuation of tonal center about a single chord or pivot tone.
10. Use of scales other than major or minor: modal scales, whole-tone, pentatonic, chromatic, and artificial scales.
11. Polychords and polytonality.
12. Harmony chosen for other than grammatical or contextual significance; tone clusters.
13. Intentional avoidance of tonality-strengthening elements; atonality.

Most of these elements have already been dealt with at some length in this book; we know that not all of them are mutually exclusive categories. What is plain from the examples of the two preceding chapters is that the various new discoveries of the post–common-practice era were applied by different composers so as to alter, suspend, or even distort the classical perception of a tone center, but not to eliminate it entirely. Debussy's music, for instance, is full of examples of pieces beginning in one key and ending in another, or traversing many different keys within a short time without ever employing a V–I cadence, but we have seen that in all such pieces there is most of the time a clear sense of some kind of a tone center, even if that center is constantly shifting and even if there is no apparent single background tonality.

The idea of unified classical tonality replaced by nonclassical (in this case nondominant) centricity in a composition is perfectly demonstrated by Debussy's *Prélude à l'Après-midi d'un faune.*

EXAMPLE 32–1: Debussy, *Prélude à l'Après-midi d'un faune*

The opening melody begins unaccompanied on C sharp and returns to it, outlining the E major triad at the end. In several reappearances of this melody, the C sharp is differently harmonized, once as a major seventh above a D major triad (measure 11), once as an added sixth above an E major triad (measure 21), twice as a thirteenth above a V^9 of A major (measure 26, measure 94), and only near the end as the root of a chord, which, ambiguously enough, is equivalent to a V_3^4 of F-sharp major (measure 100). One reappearance of the melody does not even begin on C sharp but on E, whose presumptive tonality, the relative major of C-sharp minor, is like an "alter ego" in this work; the C sharp appears as the root of the accompanying VI^7 of E major (measure 81). This passage is followed a few measures later by a repeat in E-flat major, with no C sharp anywhere (measure 86). The only strong appearance of C sharp as a root-position sonority is in the middle section of the work (measure 55ff.), in connection with a new theme, with the main melody absent from the context; the only connection to the main theme suggested by this passage is the tritone span in the bass. Even the final measures of the piece treat the C sharp as a tone that dissolves rather than resolves. One concludes that the pitch-class C sharp is indeed central to the tonality of the work, but that its centricity is veiled by the varied harmonic functions which it is called upon to perform. The centricity derives from its being present so often and from its oblique but definite connection with every fiber of the harmony and the form, and not from any classical stature as the root of a systematically recurring triad.

A centricity of C sharp of an entirely different kind is illustrated by the following equally familiar example. The C sharp is maintained by constant recurrence in the outer voices, as a chordal component in a texture dominated by inverted ninth chords, polychords, and tone clusters. Were the C sharp not present, one would probably hear the passage as atonal, without any connection to a tone center. Whatever the chromatic density may suggest about the tonality, Stravinsky's own sketches refer to this

passage as "in C-sharp major."

EXAMPLE 32–2: Stravinsky, *The Rite of Spring,*
Part II: *Sacrificial Dance*

Rapid chromatic and augmented-triad relationships in the two-note figure repeated at various transpositions in the following example account for the mostly atonal impression.

EXAMPLE 32–3: Stravinsky, *The Firebird,* Supplication Scene

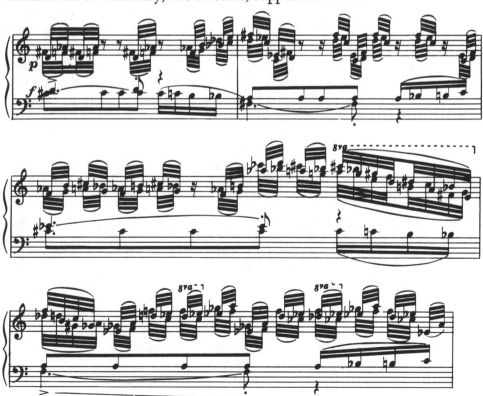

In the following example it is possible to discern a modulating pattern among the imitative entries of the main theme, indicated in the top and bottom voices by the wedge accents (compare Example 28–6). The harmony, however, only tenuously supports the tonalities suggested by the melodic entries, and soon any generalized appearance of tonality breaks down under the weight of the rapid harmonic rhythm and distantly related harmonic functions, not to be restored until the surprise appearance of D major. A partial analysis has been provided, but it is not meant to suggest anything definitive.

EXAMPLE 32–4: Strauss, *Till Eulenspiegel*

A comparable situation, but one in which the very slow tempo makes all the difference, is shown in the opening of the third

movement of Bruckner's *Ninth Symphony*.

EXAMPLE 32–5: Bruckner, *Symphony No. 9*, III

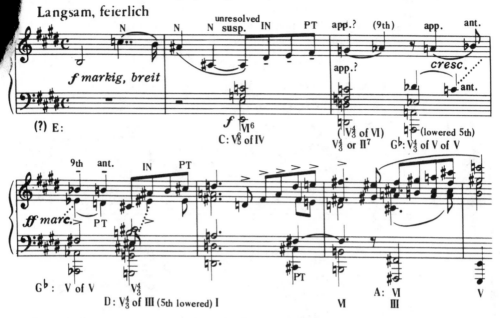

This is a characteristic example of late-nineteenth-century chromatic modulation, one that presents typical difficulties of hearing in terms of classical tonal progressions. Because of the slow tempo, the ear fixes on the individual chords; because of their apparent tonal remoteness from each other, the chord progressions sound like abrupt modulations, at least until the relatively more tonally stable climax on D major is reached. The distant harmonic relationships of the individual chords are further clouded by nonharmonic tones. The chord on the third beat of the third measure, for instance, is more likely to be thought of as an A-major triad (D flat = C sharp) with a D-sharp-(= E flat-) appoggiatura in the tenor voice, until its altered dominant relationship to A flat, the downbeat harmony of the next measure, is made clear. A reduced harmonic scheme makes it easier to follow the more distant progressions.

EXAMPLE 32–6

The problem of chromatic density in tonal harmony and counterpoint is most vividly illustrated in several transitional works of Schoenberg, who in his earliest works had already demonstrated consummate mastery of all aspects of tonal composition. The fol-

lowing is a typical passage from his *String Quartet,* Op. 7, a wor̶
in several continuous movements lasting nearly an hour. Th̶
tonality of the quartet as a whole is loosely organized about ̶
minor but is far-ranging, with relatively stable tonal areas con̶
trasting with chromatic harmony of the most extreme complexity.

EXAMPLE 32–7: Schoenberg, *String Quartet,* Op. 7

Etwas weniger bewegt (nicht zu rasch)

During the greater part of the last movement of Schoenberg's
Second Quartet, Op. 10, tonality is abandoned altogether, though
harmony unmistakably in F sharp, the nominal key of the work,
does reappear at the very end. Most of Schoenberg's music written
after this work can be classified as atonal simply on the basis of
its systematic elimination of triadic harmony and of relative consonance and dissonance. A characteristic example is given here.

EXAMPLE 32–8: Schoenberg, *Three Piano Pieces,* Op. 11, No. 3

In atonality as practiced by Schoenberg and his followers, it is irrelevant to speak of consonance and dissonance. By tonal standards nearly everything is dissonant, strongly tonal intervals such as the fifth generally being concealed within dense textures and intentionally avoided in thin ones. (Octaves occur in melodic doublings, as the above example shows.) There is no diatonic hierarchy; the pitch-classes of the chromatic scale are represented in the note-population on a generally equal basis, subject only to the structural postulates of the individual work.

EXAMPLE 32–9: Webern, *Five Pieces for String Quartet,* Op. 5, No. 4

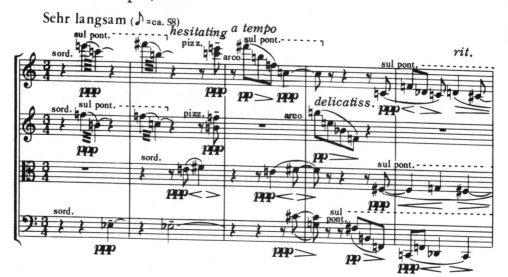

In atonality there can be no such thing as harmony in the traditional sense. It is obvious that even in atonality different tones sounding simultaneously create harmony, by definition, but a fundamental background for this harmony that is comparable to the assumption of a key, a scale, and roots in tonal music cannot be assumed in atonal music unless the composition in some way defines such a background. The attempt was made by Schoenberg, and to a greater extent by his pupil Berg, to provide comparable definitions by means of specific recurring vertical combinations of motives, or by the use of motivic chord progressions. In the following example, the initial motive group recurs at three later points in the piece, including the last measures, the open D–A fifth being a prominent underpinning, and the D alone appearing as a bass support at other points.

EXAMPLE 32–10: Schoenberg, *Five Pieces for Orchestra,*
Op. 16: No. 2, *Vergangenes*

It is possible, though not particularly important, to point to this motivic unit in its various transformations as constituting the basis of a vague D-major-minor background to the piece, with all the other pitch-classes hovering around a D-major-minor sonority even if not exactly gravitating towards it. It would be more accurate to say that the piece is "in D-*Vergangenes*," indicating that the occasional emphasis on D as a quasi tone-center is but one of the defining conditions of the piece.

The following example shows a progression of three chords (X, Y, Z) which, in a variety of compositional dispositions, underlie most of the musical substance of Act I, Scene 2 of Berg's *Wozzeck*, and reappear prominently at four later points in the opera.

EXAMPLE 32–11: Berg, *Wozzeck*, Act I, Scene 2

Berg's compositional practice differs from Schoenberg's most notably in that it regularly employs harmonies within an atonal context that derive in sound and structure from tonal harmony, even going so far as to include these on an important structural basis. 527

EXAMPLE 32–12: Berg, *Five Orchestral Songs on Picture-
Postcard Texts of Peter Altenberg*,
Op. 4, No. 2

In the above example, it is possible to relate much of the harmonic substance of the orchestral accompaniment to the successive and overlapping transpositions of a single intervallic cell, a major third plus a semitone in the opposite direction, or to the retrograde of the same cell. In the fifth measure the ascending overlapping statements outline two simultaneous diminished seventh chords, and this structuring seems to justify the appearance in measure 7 of a complete dominant ninth sonority, whose upper four factors are also a diminished seventh chord. This dominant ninth does not refer to any key, and it carries no express tonal implication other than its own isolated sound; nevertheless, it is the structural centerpiece of the song. The descending layer of thirds which follow it cleave to the pattern of the basic cell in reverse order, again outlining diminished seventh chords, and the final pitch of the accompaniment, like the initial, is identical with the "root" of the centerpiece chord. Thus within this atonal song one perceives a certain F-centricity, perhaps on an abstract, not easily heard basis. Certainly it is not a tonal centricity in any diatonic sense, but one could hardly deny that the F is structural, and that the diminished seventh structures are harmonic in the sense defined by the composition itself.

The influence on music of the twentieth century of the atonal works of Schoenberg and his followers has been enormous, not so much for the fact of atonality as for the comprehensive principles of form which evolved concomitantly with it in their music. The most potent of these has been the technique of the twelve-tone series, in which all the pitch relationships of a given composition are referable to a predetermined special ordering of the twelve pitch-classes of the chromatic scale. One of the first twelve-tone serial works by Schoenberg is shown in part in the following example. The series is used in all parts of the piece, most clearly in the upper melody of the first four measures. The order numbering beginning with zero is a convention of contemporary twelve-tone analysis.

EXAMPLE 32–13: Schoenberg, *Five Piano Pieces,*
Op. 23: No. 5: *Waltz*

Used by permission of EDITION WILHELM HANSEN, Copenhagen

Berg's last work, his *Violin Concerto*, provides a fitting close to this chapter on extended chromaticism and to this textbook on tonal harmony. The *Violin Concerto* is chiefly based on a twelve-tone series deliberately selected for its tonal implications. In this work tonality and atonality, as we have defined them, are merged in such a way that neither predominates; if the two domains are opposites by definition, Berg nonetheless has successfully combined them in a personal and compelling manner. The example below, from near the beginning of the work, displays the tonal harmony which the series implies. (Some expression marks have been omitted.)

EXAMPLE 32–14: Berg, *Violin Concerto*, I

By convention, the basic series of any twelve-tone work is the prime, abbreviated P_0, meaning prime without transposition.

The final movement of the *Violin Concerto* is a set of variations on the chorale *Es ist genug* (compare Example 16–16). Berg's twelve-tone harmonization makes use of the eleventh and third transpositions of the prime series and the ninth transposition of the inverted series, with a few slight modifications; the last four notes of the eleventh transposition give the first four notes of the chorale in B-flat major, the relative major of the basic "G minor" form of the series. Berg's phrase is answered by a repeat of the melody in Bach's own harmonization (Chorale No. 216, transposed to B flat).

530

EXAMPLE 32–15: Berg, *Violin Concerto*, II

Conclusion

This book has been conceived mainly as an introduction to the study of harmony, reflecting the authors' belief that what has been covered here will form the most important part of the college music student's general training in the theory of music; at the same time, the attempt has been made to give a broad application to the principles of harmony, with relation to counterpoint and to the formal structure of music both small and large. More advanced studies in music theory, such as tonal counterpoint, strict composition, orchestration, and analysis of musical forms, all depend on a thorough familiarity with the principles of tonal harmony; the understanding of the evolution of music in history is likewise greatly assisted by a knowledge of harmony. Regardless of specialty or generality in the student's undergraduate music study, what he learns from this book will have basic applicability in his later course-work.

College programs offering only two years of theory might cover Part I of this book in the first year, with the second year dedicated to counterpoint and to analysis of works from various periods, applying the principles developed here to the broader aspects of musical form. Part II would then be studied in connection with particular works from after the common-practice period, where time allows.

Where the program includes a third year of theory, one full year, either the second or the third, should be devoted to the study of counterpoint, preferably beginning with the strict counterpoint of the sixteenth century. When tonal counterpoint is studied, this book will be helpful for reviewing many necessary details.

It is recommended that the type of exercise drawn from actual compositions, described in Chapter 9, be extensively applied to all levels of theory study. The material should be judiciously selected, beginning with music that proceeds in normal fashion before introducing examples of unusual treatment. Exercises ought to be of considerable length, at least several phrases, so that experience may be acquired in problems of harmonic rhythm, modulation, phrase structure, melody writing, and the relation of the harmony to the form.

Some practice should be had in harmonic writing with three parts and with five parts. The student will use these in contrapuntal study, but there, the emphasis being on the lines, he will less often have the opportunity to use any but simple chords. No new principle is involved in arranging harmony for three or five voices. Comparison of such writing with the basic four-part background, supplemented by analysis of actual examples, will be helpful.

For exercises in harmonization, good material can be found in existing treatises, though by and large the given parts are too short to allow more than elementary invention. Better results are likely to be obtained with exercises designed by the teacher or by the student himself to fit a specific set of compositional conditions. Parts may be selected from standard works for harmonization and subsequent comparison with the composer's score. These parts may be soprano or bass, or sometimes both; for variety, even an inner voice may be chosen so that soprano and bass are to be constructed together.

When a fair degree of facility in manipulating the harmonic material is achieved, some writing may be done in instrumental styles, for the piano or for small instrumental combinations such as string quartet or wind quintet. Strict composition in small classical forms, such as the minuet with trio, is a very valuable exercise for this purpose.

Students gifted for original composition will naturally work on Part II of this book in more detail than will the noncomposers, as will those who have a particular historical interest in the late nineteenth and early twentieth centuries. It is self-evident, of

533

course, that the principles of common-practice harmony need to be mastered concomitantly with such study.

Many music students will make music their profession, and many others will make it their avocation. The serious musician, whether composer, performer, musicologist, teacher, or amateur, never loses sight of what is to be gained by constant study of the masterworks. A book like this one can be his valued and continuing guide, but only up to a point. Mere principles and pedagogy are only a beginning; they can never take the place of the technique, questioning judgement, and taste that can be acquired only through close study of the works themselves.

The writers are aware that what has been outlined briefly in a few sentences amounts to virtually an endless assignment. It is not denied that the acquisition of a consummate knowledge of the practice of composers is a lifetime's work. *Ars longa, vita brevis,* but consolation may be derived from the thought that intellectual and artistic rewards are to be had at all stages along the way.

Acoustical Basis of the Scale: The Harmonic Series and Equal Temperament

I t was known to the ancient Greek mathematicians that the simpler intervallic relationships between tones exactly correspond to simple ratios, in small whole numbers, of lengths of a vibrating string. If a plucked string sounding a certain tone is shortened, for instance, to exactly half its initial length, the resulting tone sounds an octave higher than originally, assuming that the tension on the string is kept constant. The same string shortened by only a third of its length (that is, so that two-thirds remain) sounds a perfect fifth higher; other simple proportions yield other intervals. The simple intervals and the ratios of their string-lengths can easily be correlated by using a monochord, which is essentially a string with one fixed bridge and one movable, mounted over a suitable ruler; many college physics departments possess one. If a monochord cannot be procured, intervals can be measured on a suitably long musical string, such as one of the strings of a double bass or cello, using a tape measure or yardstick (a tape measure graduated in centimeters is most convenient).

If we set up a string of arbitrary length (call it 1) between two fixed bridges and divide it by means of a third bridge placed between, we can obtain the tones represented by the lengths $\frac{1}{n}$ and 535

$1 - \frac{1}{n}$, that is, the lengths on either side of the movable bridge, n being an integer.

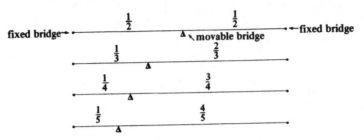

Let us say that the undivided string (length 1) sounds C two octaves below middle C, corresponding to the open string which is the lowest note of the cello. Then we will find that the lengths of the segments shown in the above diagram sound as follows:

The process of division cannot be carried much further without our running into impracticably short string-lengths. Assuming that we could accurately measure them, however, the increasingly smaller $\frac{1}{n}$ lengths would yield the following tones (sixteen of them are given here, but theoretically the number is infinite):

harmonic number: 1 2 3 4 5 6 7 8 9 10 11 12 13 14 15 16 *etc.*
sounding length: 1 $\frac{1}{2}$ $\frac{1}{3}$ $\frac{1}{4}$ $\frac{1}{5}$ *etc.*

These tones are called the *harmonic series* for low C; the numbers are the ordinals of the *harmonics* in the series. The number of each tone is also the denominator of the fraction representing the length of the string segment producing the tone. (The asterisks indicate tones that by musical standards are grossly out of tune, for reasons that will soon become clear.) An older terminology, still widely used, calls the series the *overtone series*, but numbers the notes differently: the second harmonic is the first overtone, the third harmonic is the second overtone, etc., while the first harmonic is called the *fundamental*.

Harmonics are generated by all natural vibrating systems. A vibrating string under normal conditions sounds not only the fundamental tone but simultaneously all the other harmonics together—at least theoretically. Harmonics above the fundamental are present in the tone, but only in much lesser strength than the fundamental, and their relative strength decreases with higher harmonic number, in most cases vanishing completely above the sixteenth harmonic. The strength of the harmonics above the fundamental, relative to each other, contributes to our perception of timbre and instrumental individuality; the distribution of these relative strengths results in a characteristic wave-shape that can be measured quite accurately in a modern acoustics laboratory. The shape of a sustained middle C on an oboe, for instance, is seen on an oscilloscope to be quite different from that of a middle C played on a piano. A "pure" tone, that is, a fundamental tone without any overtones, is represented by a sine wave (the graph of the expression $y = \sin x$), and can be generated electronically; it has a plain, undistinguished, humlike sound. (A tuning fork generates a nearly pure tone.)

HARMONICS, INTERVAL RATIOS, AND EQUAL TEMPERAMENT

The harmonic series as shown in the preceding example consists of tones related intervallically to a particular tone, the C two octaves below middle C. They are also related intervallically to each other, of course, but this intervallic relationship remains constant regardless of what the fundamental may be. For instance, the first six harmonics of F sharp below middle C would be:

1 2 3 4 5 6

It is easily verified by experimenting on differently tuned strings that the ratio of string-lengths for *any* particular interval must be constant, assuming that the tension and density of the string remain constant.

537

The Greek theorists beginning with Pythagoras (fl. c. 531 B.C.) were able to correlate intervals with numerical quantities only by measuring strings. In more modern times, when it was known that sound is propagated by waves in the air, it became possible to measure tones by their frequency of vibration; it was then ascertained that the ratios of the measured frequencies were identical with the Pythagorean ratios of string-lengths. For instance, two tones an octave apart differ in frequency by a factor of 2, as mentioned in Chapter 1.

On a somewhat more sophisticated level, we can determine that the frequencies of tones in the musical scale correspond logarithmically to the integers. This is easy enough to see with the octave relationships. If we start with a given tone of frequency f, the octave above it will have a frequency $2f$, the octave above that will have a frequency 2^2f or $4f$, the next octave 2^3f or $8f$, and so forth. These coefficients correspond to the numbers of the harmonic series, as the example on page 536 shows. To take another example, the interval of an octave plus a perfect fifth (that is, a perfect twelfth) is represented by the ratio of $\frac{3}{1}f$ or $3f$, that is, the upper tone has three times the frequency of the lower. The tone two octaves above that upper tone would then have 2^2 times that frequency, and thus $2^2 \cdot 3$ times the frequency of the original tone, or $12f$. (Refer again to the example on page 536.) The principle emerging from these empirical observations is that when intervals are added, their frequency ratios are multiplied. Likewise, when intervals are subtracted, their frequency ratios are divided. This is exactly comparable to a logarithmic procedure, using 2 as the logarithmic base.

The multiplication property suggests that it should be possible to obtain tones that are not found in the harmonic series on C, and thereby generate the entire chromatic scale over a given range. For instance, we might generate all twelve pitch-classes by starting with the lowest C of the piano, and tune upward with perfect Pythagorean fifths, thus:

$$1 \quad \frac{3}{2} \quad \left(\frac{3}{2}\right)^2 \quad \left(\frac{3}{2}\right)^3 \quad \left(\frac{3}{2}\right)^4 \quad \left(\frac{3}{2}\right)^5 \quad \left(\frac{3}{2}\right)^6 \quad \left(\frac{3}{2}\right)^7 \quad \left(\frac{3}{2}\right)^8 \quad \left(\frac{3}{2}\right)^9 \quad \left(\frac{3}{2}\right)^{10} \quad \left(\frac{3}{2}\right)^{11} \quad \left(\frac{3}{2}\right)^{12}$$

Since each of these fifths has the frequency ratio of $\frac{3}{2}$, by successively adding the fifths we multiply the lowest frequency by successive factors of $\frac{3}{2}$. The numbers in the preceding example are the multipliers, the lowest C being the unit frequency. (Its actual frequency according to international standard pitch is 32.70 cycles per second.) The series of eleven superposed fifths gives all twelve pitch-classes ending with the high E sharp, and if we tuned the corresponding notes of a piano to the indicated frequencies it would then be a simple matter to tune all the other notes from them by octaves up or down.

Unfortunately such a procedure yields very unsatisfactory results. To see why, let us compute the frequency of the next fifth up in the series, the high B sharp, whose frequency relative to the low C would be $(\frac{3}{2})^{12}$. Enharmonically this should be equivalent to the highest C on the piano, seven octaves above the lowest, corresponding to the C arrived at this way:

Working out the unwieldy fraction $(\frac{3}{2})^{12}$, or $\frac{531441}{4096}$, we obtain 129.746, which is significantly greater than 2^7, or 128. This means that the B sharp obtained by tuning upward from the low C by fifths will be audibly sharper than the C obtained by tuning upward by octaves. The difference between the two pitches obtained in this way, expressed as the intervallic ratio 1.014, is called the *comma of Pythagoras*. This is slightly less than $\frac{1}{4}$ of a semitone—an easily audible difference.

A comparable comma could not have been avoided by tuning instead by perfect fourths, as the following demonstration shows.

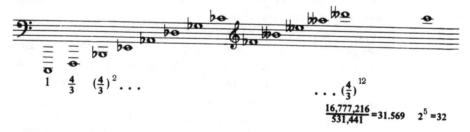

The ratio of the perfect fourth, $\frac{4}{3}$, multiplied twelve times, comes out to be less than five octaves by a factor of 1.014, just as in the previous instance, and the terminal D double-flat will be annoyingly lower than the corresponding C.

Only a little more exploration is necessary to ascertain that *none* of the ratios representing simple intervals will yield a division of the octave, or of a series of octaves, that is free from commas.

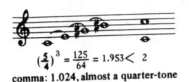

$$\left(\tfrac{5}{4}\right)^3 = \tfrac{125}{64} = 1.953 < 2$$

comma: 1.024, almost a quarter-tone

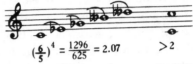

$$\left(\tfrac{6}{5}\right)^4 = \tfrac{1296}{625} = 2.07 \qquad > 2$$

comma: 1.037, more than a quarter-tone

The practical result of any of these tunings is that notes progressively higher in the stack of repeated intervals become progressively more out of tune. Even F sharp, the seventh tone of the perfect-fifth series, will be audibly sharp as the third of a D major triad, and D sharp, considered enharmonically, will be totally unacceptable as the third of a C minor triad.

The multiplicational inequities inherent in the intervallic ratios can be demonstrated within the harmonic series itself.

$$1 \quad 2 \quad 3 \quad 4 \quad 5 \quad 1 \quad \left(\tfrac{3}{2}\right) \quad \left(\tfrac{3}{2}\right)^2 \quad \left(\tfrac{3}{2}\right)^3 \quad \left(\tfrac{3}{2}\right)^4 = \tfrac{81}{16} > 5$$

The ratio of this difference, $\tfrac{81}{80}$, called the *syntonic comma*, reveals a startling fact. In the case of the other commas, it was plain that a notational difference existed between B sharp and C, and between D double-flat and C, and we might suppose that these notational differences resulted from the natural differences in the way the frequencies were generated. In the case of the two E's in the example above, no such notational difference exists; they are both the same, just as B sharp, D double-flat, and C all designate the same note-class on the piano. What, then, is wrong with the measurements? For plainly the ratios which we have computed represent different quantities.

Eventually we may come to reexamine the harmonic series as notated in the example on page 536. One property that may have escaped our attention is that the intervals between adjacent harmonics get progressively smaller, or seem to. Certainly this fact is plain enough from their frequency ratios; $\tfrac{10}{9}$ or 1.111 ..., for example, is obviously smaller than $\tfrac{9}{8}$ or 1.125. But this is not apparent notationally; in the example, the distance C to D is a major second as we know it, and D to E is also a major second. Thus there is an inequity between the harmonic series that we can generate and hear, and the musical notation we have chosen for it. To put it another way, our familiar notational system cannot accurately

540

represent the notes of the harmonic series, or at least not all of them. We know that the musical notation we use, though complicated and cumbersome to learn, is adequate to represent the music in our ordinary experience; it is perhaps not a little alarming to realize that it is intrinsically at variance with the acoustical realities of the physical world. It is disconcerting enough to know that we cannot tune a piano, or indeed any instrument with fixed pitches, by combining pure intervals; how can we rescue our notational system from the same kinds of defects?

The answer is found in the unique historical compromise known as *equal temperament,* invented in the early sixteenth century and perhaps earlier, but not put into wide use until Bach's time (Bach in fact did much to popularize it). In equal temperament, the octave is divided into twelve exactly equal semitonal intervals, meaning that every semitone in the octave, regardless of where it is situated, is represented by a constant ratio. This ratio is $\sqrt[12]{2}$ to 1, or 1.05946. . . . The tempered major second thus has the ratio $(\sqrt[12]{2})^2$ or $2^{\frac{2}{12}}$, the minor third $2^{\frac{3}{12}}$, and so on up the chromatic scale, so that the octave ratio becomes $2^{\frac{12}{12}}$, or 2. The multiplier $\sqrt[12]{2}$ is an irrational number and thus cannot be expressed as the ratio of two integers; therefore the tempered semitone cannot be the exact interval between *any* two tones in the harmonic series. (It can be pretty closely approximated, however, by $\frac{18}{17} = 1.0588$, as was suggested in 1581 by Vincenzo Galilei, a composer who was the father of the great astronomer.) What this means is that none of the intervals in the tempered chromatic scale will be precisely in tune with the intervals of the harmonic series, except the octaves. From the standpoint of "ideal" intonation, as measured by the harmonic series, this is a general disadvantage; from the standpoint of practical musical performance and notation, however, the advantage is immense. Commas vanish, the intonational differences between intervals being shared equally throughout the scales, and being too small to be readily noticed in performance. As for our system of musical notation, we realize that its diatonic basis permits a subsystem of chromatic notes with sharp signs and flat signs, and that equal temperament is perfectly accommodated by these notes when enharmonic equivalence is assumed. (Without the assumption of equal temperament and enharmonic equivalence there would, for one thing, be no circle of fifths, but rather a spiral of fifths, implying the theoretical possibility of key-signatures with infinitely many sharps or flats.)

A little calculation shows that the ratio of the tempered perfect fifth (7 semitones) is equal to $2^{\frac{7}{12}} = 1.498$ . . . , which is very 541 slightly flatter than 1.500, the Pythagorean fifth. The tempered major third is 1.2599 . . . , slightly sharper than the major third of the harmonic series, 1.25. The student will find it a profitable exercise, much facilitated by a pocket electronic calculator, to compute all the tempered multipliers and to compare them in various multiples with the interval ratios of the harmonic series as well as with those obtained by superposing different and like integral ratios. He may also find it interesting to study the obsolete tuning systems, such as mean-tone tuning and just intonation, comparing their intervallic ratios with the tempered ones, so as to see quantitatively how these systems were only partially satisfactory even in their own time; the relevant descriptions will be found in the various music dictionaries and in most treatises on musical acoustics.

DIFFICULTIES

Some considerable questions remain. The harmonic series, which is sometimes called the *chord of nature*, is more than just a physical fact; it also represents intervallic relationships that to a large extent agree with what we need for music. It is therefore natural to ask: how does the ear actually perceive "pure" intervals as opposed to tempered ones? How, for instance, does a singer, or a player of an instrument with adjustable pitches such as a violin or a trombone, actually manufacture the tuning of the notes he produces? Does he instinctively imagine and produce a tempered pitch, or a harmonic-series pitch, or something else? Is the hearing of the pianist, who most of the time will not have to worry about such matters, fundamentally different from that of a violinist? Why is it that in actual practice, pianos are not tuned to precise tempered pitches throughout their entire range? Most important of all, why do the scales and intervals of our music exist at all, or, to put it another way, why did Western music come to choose these particular relationships based on twelve pitch-classes per octave? (We must remember that throughout this book we have completely ignored, for no good reason other than Western practicality, the large repertory of non-tempered and unequal tunings in non-Western music.)

There are no simple answers to these questions. The results of many years of research in psychoacoustics have not yielded much that is not still subject to widespread debate. The subjective phenomena of hearing turn out to involve much more complex relationships than the relatively straightforward arithmetic we have dealt with here. Controlled acoustical measurements under actual conditions of performance have shown a great variability in the intonational preferences of highly skilled musicians, preferences that are influenced by a number of different factors but that are certainly not the product of chance. Furthermore, these preferences may be very different for even the same performers when measured in the laboratory with electronically synthesized tones. What is evident above all is that the musician attempts to solve his intonational problems by his musical sense. He is a practitioner, not a theorist; he does not measure and compute, but rather he compares and judges.

The complexities of acoustics and hearing are therefore inescapably different from the complexities of music itself. However systematic and simplifying the tempered system may be (or for that matter the Pythagorean or any other nontempered system), it is only a practical, and therefore partial, solution to the question of musical tuning. Thus equal temperament, like everything else in this book, is incomplete as a theoretical foundation on which the art of music is built. The inequities and incompletenesses we have been discussing indeed may have more to do with the philosophy of music than with anything else. The tempered system, so different from nature, is symbolic of the whole art of music: more than any other, music is the sublime artificial art, the creation of the mind of man.

543

Supplementary Exercises

CHAPTER 1: SCALES AND INTERVALS

1. Name the following intervals:

2. For each of the following intervals, determine at least two scales which contain both tones:

3. For each of the following four-note fragments, determine the scale which contains all four notes:

Keeping in each case the note G sharp as the soprano note,
write in four parts the following chord forms:

    a. a major triad in first inversion, with its fifth in the soprano
    b. a dissonant triad with its third in the soprano
    c. a triad in second inversion, in the key of E
    d. a triad whose root is the mediant of a major scale
    e. a triad in open position, with its root in the soprano
    f. a minor triad in close position
    g. an augmented triad with its third doubled
    h. a consonant triad in the key of B major
    i. a diminished triad in major mode
    j. a triad in first inversion, with subdominant in the bass

CHAPTER 3: HARMONIC PROGRESSION IN
THE MAJOR MODE:
RULES OF VOICE LEADING

Add soprano, alto, and tenor parts to the following basses, making four-part harmony. Use only triads in root position, and work
out two versions for each given bass.

Add three upper parts to the following basses, forming triads in root position. Work out two versions of each, using the ascending or descending melodic minor form of the scale where indicated.

CHAPTER 5: TONALITY AND MODALITY

1. In which tonalities is E flat a modal degree? a tonal degree? Answer the same questions for the notes F sharp, B, G sharp, and D flat.

2. Rewrite the following progressions, changing those that are major to minor, and those that are minor to major.

3. Work out the following basses according to the directions given in Chapter 5, Exercise 5.

c.

d.

Chapter 6: The First Inversion— The Figured Bass

1. Write out the four-part harmony indicated by the following figured basses.

a.

b.

2. Harmonize the following unfigured bass, introducing triads in first inversion where appropriate.

Chapter 7: Function and Structure of Melody

1. Construct two melodies in A major, each eight measures long, one in $\frac{3}{4}$ and the other in $\frac{4}{4}$, to the following specifications:

    a. each melody contains exactly twenty notes;
    b. the tonic note appears seven times;
    c. the dominant note appears six times;
    d. two notes are dotted;
    e. the overall range of the melody is not more than a twelfth.

2. Construct a melody in C major, $\frac{3}{8}$ time, eight measures long, in which the following fragments appear, not necessarily in the order given:

CHAPTER 8: NONHARMONIC TONES

1. Work out the following figured basses in four parts.

2. Harmonize the following basses. Note that the triads are not necessarily in root position.

Harmonize the following basses in four parts, using triads in root position. In these exercises pay particular attention to the differentiation of harmonic and melodic rhythms.

CHAPTER 10: HARMONIZATION OF A
GIVEN PART

1. Harmonize the following soprano melodies, using triads in root position and first inversion.

549

2. Add three upper voices to the following bass.

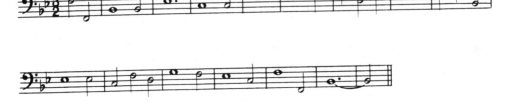

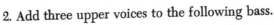

CHAPTER 11: THE SIX-FOUR CHORD

1. Work out the following figured basses in four parts.

2. Harmonize the following soprano and bass parts. At least five six-four chords are to be introduced into each exercise.

a. Siciliana

b. Moderato

c. Allegro

CHAPTER 12: CADENCES

1. Work out the following figured basses in four parts.

a. Moderato

b. Andante

2. Harmonize the following bass and soprano parts, after analyzing them to decide upon the types of cadences they contain.

a. Lento

b. Allegro

c.

d. Moderato

552

1. Harmonize the following basses in four parts.

2. Harmonize the following soprano melodies.

c. Andantino

CHAPTER 14: MODULATION

1. Work out the following figured basses in four parts. Determine by analysis in each case the location of the pivot chord or chords.

a. Andantino

b.

c. Allegro

2. Harmonize the following basses and soprano melodies. The location of the pivot chord for each modulation is shown by the asterisk.

a.

3. Harmonize the following bass and soprano melodies, determining appropriate pivot chords in each case.

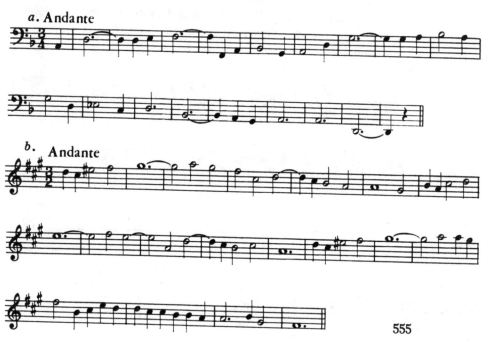

CHAPTER 15: THE DOMINANT SEVENTH
CHORD

1. Work out the following figured basses in four parts.

2. Harmonize the following bass and soprano parts, introducing dominant seventh chords where appropriate. Use at least eight dominant seventh chords in each exercise.

c. Allegro

d. Andante

Chapter 16: Secondary Dominants

1. Work out the following figured basses.

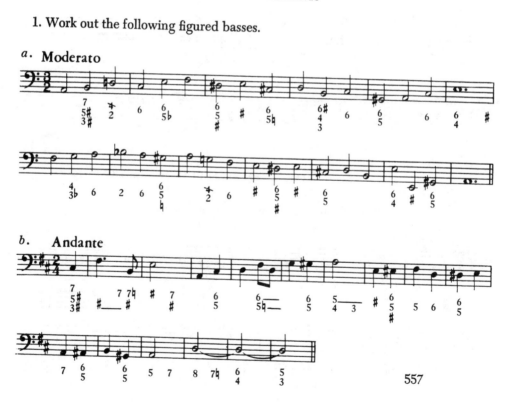

a. Moderato

b. Andante

2. Harmonize the following bass and soprano parts, employing secondary dominant chords where appropriate.

a. **Andantino**

b. **Allegro**

c. **Adagio**

CHAPTER 17: IRREGULAR RESOLUTIONS

1. Work out the following figured basses.

a. **Andante**

b. **Moderato**

2. Harmonize the following bass and soprano parts, introducing irregular resolutions of dominant seventh chords and of secondary dominants.

a. **Allegro**

b. **Lento**

c. **Andante**

559

1. Work out the following figured basses.

a. **Allegro**

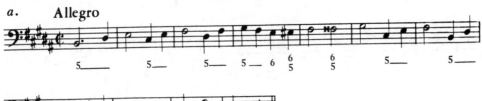

b. **Andante**

2. Harmonize the following basses, the first and third modulating, the second nonmodulating.

a. Adagio

b. Con moto

c. Lento

3. Harmonize the following soprano melodies.

a. Andantino

b. Moderato

c. Allegretto

CHAPTER 20: THE DIMINISHED
SEVENTH CHORD

1. Work out the following figured basses.

a. **Andantino**

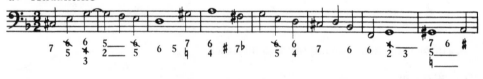

b.

2. Harmonize the following bass and soprano parts, introducing diminished seventh chords at the places marked by asterisks.

a. **Allegro**

b. **Tranquillo**

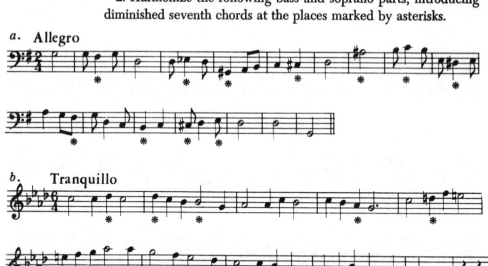

3. Harmonize the following bass and soprano parts, employing diminished seventh chords where appropriate.

a. **Moderato**

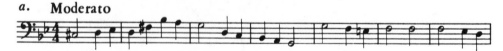

b. Con moto

Chapter 21: The Incomplete Major Ninth

1. Work out the following figured bass.

Moderato

2. Harmonize the following bass and soprano parts. Use incomplete major ninth chords at the places marked by the asterisks.

a. Adagio

b. **Andante**

CHAPTER 22: THE COMPLETE
DOMINANT NINTH

1. Work out the following figured bass.

2. Harmonize the following bass and soprano parts. Use complete dominant ninth chords at the places marked by the asterisks.

a.   **Allegretto**

b.   **Andante**

CHAPTER 23: NONDOMINANT HARMONY—
SEVENTH CHORDS

1. Work out the following figured basses.

a. **Allegretto**

b. **Moderato**

2. Harmonize the following bass and soprano parts. Use non-dominant seventh chords at the places marked by the asterisks.

a. **Andante**

b. **Lento**

3. Harmonize the following bass and soprano parts, introducing nondominant seventh chords where appropriate.

a. **Allegro**

b. **Larghetto**

CHAPTER 24: NINTH, ELEVENTH, AND THIRTEENTH CHORDS

1. Work out the following figured bass.

2. Harmonize the following bass and soprano parts. At the places marked by the asterisks, introduce an appropriate ninth, eleventh, or thirteenth chord effect.

a. **Andante**

3. Harmonize the following bass and soprano parts, using ninth, eleventh, and thirteenth chord effects where appropriate.

a.   **Andante**

b.   **Adagio**

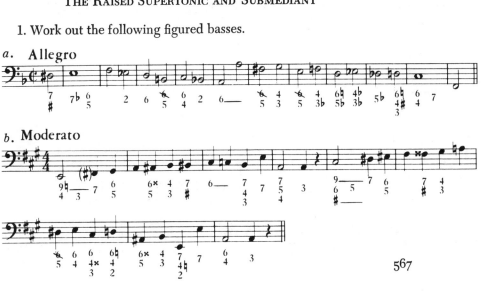

CHAPTER 25: CHROMATICALLY ALTERED CHORDS:
THE RAISED SUPERTONIC AND SUBMEDIANT

1. Work out the following figured basses.

a.   **Allegro**

b.   **Moderato**

2. Harmonize the following bass and soprano parts. Use suitable forms of raised II or VI at the places marked by the asterisks.

a. Allegretto

b. Adagio

CHAPTER 26: THE NEAPOLITAN SIXTH

1. Work out the following figured basses.

a. Allegretto

b. Moderato

2. Harmonize the following bass and soprano parts, introducing Neapolitan sixth chords where appropriate.

a. **Andante quasi agitato**

b. **Lento**

CHAPTER 27: AUGMENTED SIXTH CHORDS

1. Work out the following figured basses.

a. **Moderato**

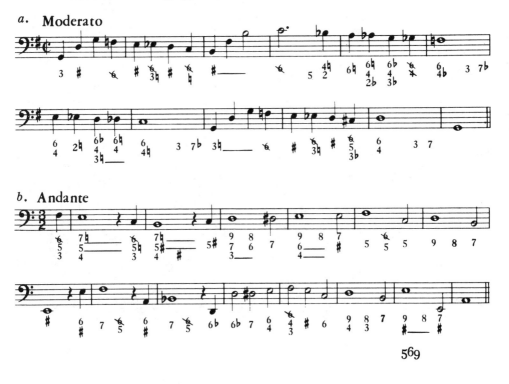

b. **Andante**

2. Harmonize the following bass and soprano parts. Use augmented sixth chords at the places marked by the asterisks.

a. **Moderato**

b. **Adagio**

CHAPTER 28: OTHER CHROMATIC CHORDS

1. Work out the following figured basses.

a. **Andantino**

b. **Maestoso**

2. Harmonize the following bass and soprano parts. Introduce chromatically altered chords of various types wherever practicable, insomuch as they can be explained by reference to the principles of common-practice harmony.

a. Lento

b. Moderato

Special Exercises
Based on Bach's
Chorale Harmonizations

The exercises that follow consist of phrases taken from Bach's
371 chorale harmonizations with most of the notes removed.
The object of each exercise is not specifically to restore the original
notes—though that might be a possible result—but rather to devise
a coherent and pleasing solution, applying deductive reasoning and
principles of harmony and voice leading, and exercising one's
musical intuition. After the student has completed each exercise, he
may compare his results with Bach's original and evaluate the differences between the two.

The following rules apply to these exercises:

1. All the phrases are in common time, a few with upbeats.
   All complete measures are printed here in equal width, so
   that there should be no difficulty in determining which beat
   a given note comes on.
2. All phrase endings are marked with a fermata, indicating
   that no motion should occur in any of the parts until the
   next phrase begins.
3. The chorale melodies themselves are mostly composed of
   quarter-note values; a few eighth notes, and some half notes
   at cadences, may be incorporated, but no values smaller
   than the eighth note.

4. All durations given here are like those in the originals. A quarter note, therefore, should not be interpreted as one of a pair of eighth notes which has suffered erasure of the other eighth note. No dotted or syncopated values are used except where actually indicated or clearly implied.

5. Sometimes a bass figure is included, with or without notes to fit it. The absence of such figures does not necessarily mean that root position is called for. On the other hand, where figures are given, the usual conventions in reading them apply; e.g., a 6 is understood to mean $\frac{6}{3}$, but not $\frac{6}{4}$ or $\frac{6}{5}$.

6. Slurs are employed to indicate melismas, that is, more than one note per syllable of text. They are omitted for melismas of two successive eighth notes, being understood. Rests are not to be used except where indicated, and then only in all parts.

Exercises of this type, further examples of which are not difficult to construct, are valuable for developing skills in chorale harmonization. They attempt to provide simultaneous emphasis on problems of harmony and counterpoint, in such a way that the ear perforce will search for melodic lines concurrently with specific harmonic points.

1. Chorale No. 152, *Meinen Jesum lass ich nicht, weil*

Use continuous ♩♩ in the bass, except as noted.

2. Chorale No. 256, *Freu dich sehr, o meine Seele*

3. Chorale No. 263, *Jesu, meine Freude*

4. Chorale No. 85, *O Gott, du frommer Gott*

5. Chorale No. 108, *Valet will ich dir geben*

6. Chorale No. 326, *Allein Gott in der Höh' sei Ehr*

7. Chorale No. 83, *Jesu Leiden, Pein und Tod*

6(♮)   6
        5♮

8. Chorale No. 131, *Liebster Jesu, wir sind hier*

Index of
Musical Examples

This index locates every musical example in this book cited from actual works; it also provides the birth and death dates of the composers. For Schubert's works, "D." numbers, referring to Otto Erich Deutsch's Thematic Catalogue, may be useful when the reader wishes to consult published scores or identify recordings; similarly, some of the "BWV" numbers of Bach's works are provided for pieces that might otherwise be difficult to identify in the collected editions. Haydn's Piano Sonatas are listed by the old numbering still used in several editions; the numbers of the chronological Landon edition, together with Hoboken's catalogue numbers, are given parenthetically. The "K." numbers, from Köchel's catalogue of Mozart's works, are so frequently employed that they are given in the main text as well as here. The student will find it helpful to become familiar with these bibliographical devices, since they are in wide use in libraries and scholarly works, and (except for Bach) are chronologically arranged. Opus numbers, whether provided by the composer or by the publisher, are often unreliable guides in this respect; Schubert's *Erlkönig*, Op. 1, for example, is D. 328, and his *Gretchen am Spinnrade*, Op. 2, is D. 118.

General Index

abrupt modulation, 220, 225–28, 454, 467–69, 523
see also remote relationships
accent, 199–201, 206
accented passing tone, 112
acciaccatura, 510–11
accidentals, accidental signs, 246, 387–88, 460–61, 491
in figured bass, 80–81
accompaniment, see melody; melody and accompaniment
acoustic principles of tuning, 535–43
acute accent sign ('), 42
added sixth, triad with, 359–65, 474–75, 477, 481, 520
Aeolian mode, 48, 462
alto clef, 291
ambiguity, tonal
of diminished seventh chord, 310, 319
of half-diminished seventh chord, 363
anacrusis, 90, 140, 201, 296
six-four chord as, 179
analysis
difficulties of, 105
of melody, 101–3, 104–5
see also harmonic analysis; melodic analysis
antecedent and consequent, 94, 142, 297
anticipation (ant.), 117–18, 123, 124
anticlassicism, 454, 465
appoggiatura, 112, 116, 118–22, 509–15
in augmented III, 121, 232
with delayed resolution, 121–22, 372–73
differentiated from suspension, 122–23
ninth, eleventh, and thirteenth, 370–83
old notation of, 120
preparation of, 118–19
simultaneous with resolution, 510

six-four chord, 169–75
unresolved, 373–75, 379–81, 466, 505–6, 509–10
see also appoggiatura chord; suspension
appoggiatura chord, 121, 269, 350, 375–78, 382–83, 388, 390, 442–45, 508–15
in cadences, 185–86, 188–89, 191
six-four, 169–75
arabic-numeral notation, 66–67, 309, 313, 340
in figured bass, 80
arpeggiating six-four chord, 178–80
arpeggiation of chord factors, 95, 97, 99, 110
artificial scales, 48, 477–78, 484–87, 518
ascending melodic minor
scale, 2, 41
triads, 43
atonality, 5, 455, 516–18, 520–21, 524–31
attendant chords, see secondary dominants
augmented fifth chords, 433–36
augmented fourth, resolution of, 233
augmented intervals, 4
augmented second, 310, 485
avoided, 40, 45
augmented six-five-three, 415, 417–18, 437–38, 440–42
augmented six-four-three, 415, 418–19, 436–37
related to whole-tone harmony, 483
augmented sixth (interval), 414–15, 422, 435
augmented sixth (plain chord), see Italian sixth
augmented sixth chords, 410, 414–16, 416–27, 435, 436–38, 439–42, 453, 483, 511
augmented triad, 13, 432, 433–36, 482–84, 521

585